## Philosophy

# TABLE OF CONTENTS & ACKNOWLEDGEMENTS

## Part Three: Personal Identity

## Part Four: Free Will

## Part Five: Morality

# Part One: Knowledge

# First Meditation:
# On what can be called into doubt

Some years ago I was struck by how many false things I had believed, and by how doubtful was the structure of beliefs that I had based on them. I realized that if I wanted to establish anything in the sciences that was stable and likely to last, I needed—just once in my life—to demolish everything completely and start again from the foundations. It looked like an enormous task, and I decided to wait until I was old enough to be sure that there was nothing to be gained from putting it off any longer. I have now delayed it for so long that I have no excuse for going on *planning* to do it rather than getting to work. So today I have set all my worries aside and arranged for myself a clear stretch of free time. I am here quite alone, and at last I will devote myself, sincerely and without holding back, to demolishing my opinions.

I can do this without showing that all my beliefs are false, which is probably more than I could ever manage. My reason tells me that as well as withholding assent from propositions that are obviously •false, I should also withhold it from ones that are •not completely certain and indubitable. So all I need, for the purpose of rejecting all my opinions, is to find in each of them at least *some* reason for doubt. I can do this without going through them one by one, which would take forever: once the foundations of a building have been undermined, the rest collapses of its own accord; so I will go straight for the basic principles on which all my former beliefs rested.

Whatever I have accepted until now as most true has come to me through my senses. But occasionally I have found that they have deceived me, and it is unwise to trust completely those who have deceived us even once.

[The next paragraph presents a series of considerations back and forth. It is set out here as a discussion between two people, but that isn't how Descartes presented it.]

**Hopeful**: Yet although the senses sometimes deceive us about objects that are very small or distant, that doesn't apply to my belief that I am here, sitting by the fire, wearing a winter dressing-gown, holding this piece of paper in my hands, and so on. It seems to be quite impossible to doubt beliefs like these, which come from the senses. Another example: how can I doubt that these hands or this whole body are mine? To doubt such things I would have to liken myself to brain-damaged madmen who are convinced they are kings when really they are paupers, or say they are dressed in purple when they are naked, or that they are pumpkins, or made of glass. Such people are insane, and I would be thought equally mad if I modelled myself on them.

**Doubtful** (sarcastically): What a brilliant piece of reasoning! As if I were not a man who sleeps at night and often has all the same experiences while asleep as madmen do when awake—indeed sometimes even more improbable ones. Often in my dreams I am convinced of just such familiar events—that I am sitting by the fire in my dressing-gown—when in fact I am lying undressed in bed!

**Hopeful**: Yet right now my eyes are certainly wide open when I look at this piece of paper; I shake my head and it isn't asleep; when I rub one hand against the other, I do it deliberately and know what I am doing. This wouldn't all happen with such clarity to someone asleep.

**Doubtful**: Indeed! As if I didn't remember other occasions when I have been tricked by exactly similar thoughts while asleep! As I think about this more carefully, I realize that there is never any reliable way of distinguishing being awake from being asleep. This discovery makes me feel dizzy, [joke:] which itself reinforces the notion that I may be asleep!

Suppose then that I am dreaming—it isn't true that I, with my eyes open, am moving my head and stretching out my hands. Suppose, indeed that I don't even *have* hands or any body at all. Still, it has to be admitted that the visions that come in sleep are like paintings: they must have been made as copies of real things; so at least these general *kinds* of things— eyes, head, hands and the body as a whole—must be real and not imaginary. For even when painters try to depict sirens and satyrs with the most extraordinary bodies, they simply jumble up the limbs of different kinds of real animals, rather than inventing natures that are entirely new. If they do succeed in thinking up something completely fictitious and unreal—not remotely like anything ever seen before—at least the colours used in the picture must be real. Similarly, although these general kinds of things— eyes, head, hands and so on—could be imaginary, there is no denying that certain even simpler and more universal kinds of things are real. These are the elements out of which we make all our mental images of things—the true and also the false ones.

These simpler and more universal kinds include *body*, and *extension*; the *shape* of extended things; their *quantity*, *size* and *number*; the *places* things can be in, the *time* through which they can last, and so on.

So it seems reasonable to conclude that physics, astronomy, medicine, and all other sciences dealing with things that have complex structures are doubtful; while arithmetic, geometry and other studies of the simplest and most general things—whether they really exist in nature or not—contain something certain and indubitable. For whether I am awake or asleep, two plus three makes five, and a square has only four sides. It seems impossible to suspect that such obvious truths might be false.

However, I have for many years been sure that there is an all-powerful God who made me to be the sort of creature that I am. How do I know that he hasn't brought it about that there is no earth, no sky, nothing that takes up space, no shape, no size, no place, while making sure that all these things appear to me to exist? Anyway, I sometimes think that others go wrong even when they think they have the most perfect knowledge; so how do I know that I myself don't go wrong every time I add two and three or count the sides of a square? Well, ·you might say·, God would not let me be deceived like that, because he is said to be supremely good. But, ·I reply·, if God's goodness would stop him from letting me be deceived •all the time, you would expect it to stop him from allowing me to be deceived even •occasionally; yet clearly I sometimes *am* deceived.

Some people would deny the existence of such a powerful God rather than believe that everything else is uncertain. Let us grant them—for purposes of argument—that there is no God, and theology is fiction. On their view, then, I am a product of fate or chance or a long chain of causes and effects. But the *less* powerful they make my original cause, the *more* likely it is that I am so imperfect as to be deceived all the time—because deception and error seem to be imperfections. Having no answer to these arguments, I am driven back to the position that doubts can properly be raised about any of my former beliefs. I don't reach this conclusion in a flippant or casual manner, but on the basis of powerful and well thought-out reasons. So in future, if I want to discover any certainty, I must withhold my assent from these former beliefs just as carefully as I withhold it from obvious falsehoods.

It isn't enough merely to have noticed this, though; I must make an effort to remember it. My old familiar opinions keep coming back, and against my will they capture my belief. It is as though they had a *right* to a place in my belief-system as a result of long occupation and the law of custom. These habitual opinions of mine are indeed highly probable; although they are in a sense doubtful, as I have shown, it is more reasonable to believe than to deny them. But if I go on viewing them in that light I shall never get out of the habit of confidently assenting to them. To conquer that habit, therefore, I had better switch right around and pretend (for a while) that these former opinions of mine are utterly false and imaginary. I shall do this until I have something to counter-balance the weight of old opinion, and the distorting influence of habit no longer prevents me from judging correctly. However far I go in my distrustful attitude, no actual harm will come of it, because my project won't affect how I •act, but only how I •go about acquiring knowledge.

So I shall suppose that some malicious, powerful, cunning demon has done all he can to deceive me—rather than this being done by God, who is supremely good and the source of truth. I shall think that the sky, the air, the earth, colours, shapes, sounds and all external things are merely dreams that the demon has contrived as traps for my judgment. I shall consider myself as having no hands or eyes, or flesh, or blood or senses, but as having falsely believed that I had all these things. I shall stubbornly persist in this train of thought; and even if I can't learn any truth, I shall at least do what I *can* do, which is to be on my guard against accepting any falsehoods, so that the deceiver—however powerful and cunning he may be—will be unable to affect me in the slightest. This will be hard work, though, and a kind of laziness pulls me back into my old ways. Like a prisoner who dreams that he is free, starts to suspect that it is merely a dream, and wants to go on dreaming rather than waking up, so I am content to slide back into my old opinions; I fear being shaken out of them because I am afraid that my peaceful sleep may be followed by hard labour when I wake, and that I shall have to struggle not in the light but in the imprisoning darkness of the problems I have raised.

## Second Meditation: The nature of the human mind, and how it is better known than the body

Yesterday's meditation raised doubts—ones that are too serious to be ignored—which I can see no way of resolving. I feel like someone who is suddenly dropped into a deep whirlpool that tumbles him around so that he can neither stand on the bottom nor swim to the top. However, I shall force my way up, and try once more to carry out the project that I started on yesterday. I will set aside anything that admits of the slightest doubt, treating it as though I had found it to be outright false; and I will carry on like that until I find something certain, or—at worst—until I become certain that there is no certainty. Archimedes said that if he had one firm and immovable point he could lift the world ·with a long enough lever·; so I too can hope for great things if I manage to find just one little thing that is solid and certain.

I will suppose, then, that everything I see is fictitious. I will believe that my memory tells me nothing but lies. I have no senses. Body, shape, extension, movement and place are illusions. So what remains true? Perhaps just the one fact that nothing is certain!

[This paragraph is presented as a further to-and-fro argument between two people. Remember that this isn't how Descartes wrote it.]

**Hopeful**: Still, how do I know that there isn't something—not on that list—about which there is no room for even the slightest doubt? Isn't there a God (call him what you will) who gives me the thoughts I am now having?

**Doubtful**: But why do I think this, since I might myself be the author of these thoughts?

**Hopeful**: But then doesn't it follow that I am, at least, *something*?

**Doubtful**: This is very confusing, because I have just said that I have no senses and no body, and I am so bound up with a body and with senses that one would think that I can't exist without them. Now that I have convinced myself that there is nothing in the world—no sky, no earth, no minds, no bodies—does it follow that I don't exist either?

**Hopeful**: No it does not follow; for if I *convinced myself of something* then I certainly *existed.*

**Doubtful**: But there is a supremely powerful and cunning deceiver who deliberately deceives me all the time!

**Hopeful**: Even then, if he is deceiving me I undoubtedly exist: let him deceive me all he can, he will never bring it about that *I am nothing* while *I think I am something.* So after thoroughly thinking the matter through I conclude that this proposition, *I am, I exist,* must be true whenever I assert it or think it.

But this 'I' that must exist—I still don't properly understand what it is; so I am at risk of confusing it with something else, thereby falling into error in the very item of knowledge that I maintain is the most certain and obvious of all. To get straight about what this 'I' is, I shall go back and think some more about what I believed myself to be before I started this meditation. I will eliminate from those beliefs anything that could be even slightly called into question by the arguments I have been using, which will leave me with only beliefs about myself that are certain and unshakable.

Well, then, what did I think I was? A man. But what is a man? Shall I say 'a rational animal'? No; for then I should have to ask what an animal is, and what rationality is—each question would lead me on to other still harder ones, and this would take more time than I can spare. Let me focus instead on the beliefs that spontaneously and naturally came to me whenever I thought about what I was. The first such belief was that I had a face, hands, arms and the whole structure of bodily parts that corpses also have—I call it *the body*. The next belief was that I ate and drank, that I moved about, and that I engaged in sense-perception and thinking; these things, I thought, were done by *the soul.* [In this work 'the soul' = 'the mind'; it has no religious implications.] If I gave any thought to what this soul was like, I imagined it to be something thin and filmy— like a wind or fire or ether—permeating my more solid parts. I was more sure about the body, though, thinking that I knew exactly what sort of thing it was. If I had tried to put my conception of the body into words, I would have said this:

> By a 'body' I understand whatever has a definite shape and position, and can occupy a ·region of· space in such a way as to keep every other body out of it; it can be perceived by touch, sight, hearing, taste or smell, and can be moved in various ways.

I would have added that a body can't start up movements by itself, and can move only through being moved by other things that bump into it. It seemed to me quite out of character for a body to be able to •initiate movements, or to able to •sense and think, and I was amazed that certain bodies—·namely, human ones·—*could* do those things.

But now that I am supposing there is a supremely powerful and malicious deceiver who has set out to trick me in every way he can—*now* what shall I say that I am? Can I *now* claim to have any of the features that I used to think belong to a body? When I think about them really carefully, I find that they are all open to doubt: I shan't waste time by showing this about each of them separately. Now, what about the features that I attributed to the soul? Nutrition or movement? Since now ·I am pretending that· I don't have a body, these are mere fictions. Sense-perception? One needs a body in order to perceive; and, besides, when dreaming I have seemed to perceive through the senses many things that I later realized I had not perceived in that way. Thinking? At last I have discovered it—thought! This is the one thing that can't be separated from me. I am, I exist—that is certain. But for how long? For as long as I am thinking. But perhaps no longer than that; for it *might* be that if I stopped thinking I would stop existing; and ·I have to treat that possibility as though it were actual, because· my present policy is to reject everything that isn't necessarily true. Strictly speaking, then, I am simply a thing that thinks—a mind, or soul, or intellect, or reason, these being words whose meaning I have only just come to know. Still, I am a real, existing thing. What kind of a thing? I have answered that: a thinking thing.

What else am I? I will use my imagination to see if I am anything more. I am not that structure of limbs and organs that is called a human body; nor am I a thin vapour that permeates the limbs—a wind, fire, air, breath, or whatever I imagine; for I have supposed all these things to be nothing ·because I have supposed all bodies to be nothing·. Even if I go on supposing *them* to be nothing, *I* am still something. But these things that I suppose to be nothing because they are unknown to me—might they not in fact be identical with the *I* of which I am aware? I don't know; and just now I shan't discuss the matter, because I can form opinions only about things that I know. I know that I exist, and I am asking: what is this *I* that I know? My knowledge of it can't depend on things of whose existence I am still unaware; so it can't depend on anything that I invent in my imagination. The word 'invent' points to what is wrong with relying on my imagination in this matter: if I used imagination to show that I was something or other, that would be mere invention, mere story-telling; for imagining is simply contemplating the shape or image of a bodily thing. [Descartes here relies on a theory of his about the psychology of imagination.] That makes imagination suspect, for while I know for sure that I exist, I know that everything relating to the nature of body ·including imagination· could be mere dreams; so it would be silly for me to say 'I will use my imagination to get a clearer understanding of what I am'—as silly, indeed, as to say 'I am now awake, and see some truth; but I shall deliberately fall asleep so as to see even more, and more truly, in my dreams'! If my mind is to get a clear understanding of its own nature, it had better not look to the imagination for it.

Well, then, what am I? A thing that thinks. What is that? A thing that doubts, understands, affirms, denies, wants, refuses, and also imagines and senses.

That is a long list of attributes for me to have—and it really is I who have them all. Why should it not be? Isn't it one and the same 'I' who now

doubts almost everything,
understands some things,
affirms this one thing—·namely, that I exist and think·,
denies everything else,
wants to know more,
refuses to be deceived,
imagines many things involuntarily, and
is aware of others that seem to come from the senses?

Isn't all this just as true as the fact that I exist, even if I am in a perpetual dream, and even if my creator is doing his best to deceive me? Which of all these activities is distinct from my thinking? Which of them can be said to be separate from myself? The fact that it is I who doubt and understand and want is so obvious that I can't see how to make it any clearer. But the 'I' who *imagines* is also this same 'I'. For even if (as I am pretending) none of the things that I imagine really exist, I *really do imagine them*, and this is part of my thinking. Lastly, it is also this same 'I' who senses, or is aware of bodily things seemingly through the senses. Because I may be dreaming, I can't say for sure that I now see the flames, hear the wood crackling, and feel the heat of the fire; but I certainly *seem* to see, to hear, and to be warmed. This cannot be false; what is called 'sensing' is strictly just this *seeming*, and when 'sensing' is understood in this restricted sense of the word it too is simply thinking.

All this is starting to give me a better understanding of what I am. But I still can't help thinking that bodies—of which I form mental images and which the senses investigate—are much more clearly known to me than is this puzzling 'I' that can't be pictured in the imagination. It would be surprising if this were right, though; for it would be surprising if I had a clearer grasp of things that I realize are doubtful, unknown and foreign to me—·namely, bodies·—than I have of what is true and known— namely my own self. But I see what the trouble is: I keep drifting towards that error because my mind likes to wander freely, refusing to respect the boundaries that truth lays down. Very well, then; I shall let it run free for a while, so that when the time comes to rein it in it won't be so resistant to being pulled back.

Let us consider the things that people ordinarily think they understand best of all, namely the bodies that we touch and see. I don't mean bodies in general—for our general thoughts are apt to be confused—but one particular body: this piece of wax, for example. It has just been taken from the honeycomb; it still tastes of honey and has the scent of the flowers from which the honey was gathered; its colour, shape and size are plain to see; it is hard, cold and can be handled easily; if you rap it with your knuckle it makes a sound. In short, it has everything that seems to be needed for a body to be known perfectly clearly. But as I speak these words I hold the wax near to the fire, and look! The taste and smell vanish, the colour changes, the shape is lost, the size increases; the wax becomes liquid and hot; you can hardly touch it, and it no longer makes a sound when you strike it. But is it still the same wax? Of course it is; no-one denies this. So what was it about the wax that I understood so clearly? Evidently it was not any of the features that the senses told me of; for all of them— brought to me through taste, smell, sight, touch or hearing—have now altered, yet it is still the same wax.

Perhaps what I now think about the wax indicates what its nature was all along. If that is right, then the wax was not the sweetness of the honey, the scent of the flowers, the whiteness, the shape, or the sound, but was rather *a body* that recently presented itself to me in those ways but now appears differently. But what exactly is this thing that I am now imagining? Well, if we take away whatever doesn't belong to the wax (·that is, everything that the wax *could* be without·), what is left is merely *something extended, flexible and changeable.* What do 'flexible' and 'changeable' mean here? I can imaginatively picture this piece of wax changing from round to square, from square to triangular, and so on. But that isn't what changeability is. In knowing that the wax is changeable I understand that it can go through *endlessly many* changes of that kind, far more than I can depict in my imagination; so it isn't my imagination that gives me my grasp of the wax as flexible and changeable. Also, what does 'extended' mean? Is the wax's extension also unknown? It increases if the wax melts, and increases again if it boils; the wax can be extended in many more ways (·that is, with many more shapes·) than I will ever bring before my imagination. I am forced to conclude that the nature of this piece of wax isn't revealed by my imagination, but is perceived by the mind alone. (I am speaking of •this particular piece of wax; the point is even clearer with regard to •wax in general.) This wax that is perceived by the mind alone is, of course, the same wax that I see, touch, and picture in my imagination—in short the same wax I thought it to be from the start. But although my perception of it *seemed* to be a case of vision and touch and imagination, it isn't so and it never was. Rather, it is purely a scrutiny by the mind alone— formerly an imperfect and confused one, but now vivid and clear because I am now concentrating carefully on what the wax consists in.

As I reach this conclusion I am amazed at how prone to error my mind is. For although I am thinking all this out within myself, silently, I do it with the help of words, and I am at risk of being led astray by them. When the wax is in front of us, we say that we *see* it, not that we *judge* it to be there from its colour or shape; and this might make me think that knowledge of the wax comes from what the eye sees rather than from the perception of the mind alone. But ·this is clearly wrong, as the following example shows·. If I look out of the window and see men crossing the square, as I have just done, I say that I *see* the men themselves, just as I say that I see the wax; yet do I see any more than hats and coats that could conceal robots? I *judge* that they are men. Something that I thought I saw with my eyes, therefore, was really grasped solely by my mind's faculty of judgment [= 'ability or capacity to make judgments'].

However, someone who wants to know more than the common crowd should be ashamed to base his doubts on ordinary ways of talking. Let us push ahead, then, and ask: *When* was my perception of the wax's nature more perfect and clear? Was it •when I first looked at the wax, and thought I knew it through my senses? Or is it •now, after I have enquired more carefully into the wax's nature and into how it is known? It would be absurd to hesitate in answering the question; for what clarity and sharpness was there in my earlier perception of the wax? Was there anything in it that •a lower animal couldn't have? But when I consider the wax apart from its outward forms—take its clothes off, so to speak, and consider it naked—then although my judgment may still contain errors, at least I am now having a perception of a sort that requires •a human mind.

But what am I to say about this mind, or about myself? (So far, remember, I don't admit that there is anything to me *except* a mind.) What, I ask, is this 'I' that seems to perceive the wax so clearly? Surely, I am aware of •my own self in a truer and more certain way than I am of •the wax, and also in a much more distinct and evident way. What leads me to think that •the wax exists—namely, that I see it— leads much more obviously to the conclusion that •I exist. What I see might not really be the wax; perhaps I don't even have eyes with which to see anything. But when I *see* or *think I see* (I am not here distinguishing the two), it is simply not possible that I who am now thinking am not *something.* Similarly, that •*I exist* follows from the other bases for judging that •*the wax exists* - that I touch it, that I imagine it, or any other basis—and similarly for my bases for judging that anything else exists outside me. As I came to perceive the wax more distinctly by applying not just sight and touch but other considerations, all this too contributed to my knowing myself even more distinctly, because whatever goes into my perception of •the wax or of any other body must do even more to establish the nature of •my own mind. What comes to my mind from bodies, therefore, helps me to know my mind distinctly; yet all of that pales into insignificance—it is hardly worth mentioning—when compared with what my mind contains *within itself* that enables me to know it distinctly.

See! With no effort I have reached the place where I wanted to be! I now know that even bodies are perceived not by the senses or by imagination but by the intellect alone, not through their being touched or seen but through their being understood; and this helps me to know plainly that I can perceive my own mind more easily and clearly than I can anything else. Since the grip of old opinions is hard to shake off, however, I want to pause and meditate for a while on this new knowledge of mine, fixing it more deeply in my memory.

# 2

# Proof of an External World

## G. E. Moore

It seems to me that, so far from its being true, as Kant declares to be his opinion, that there is only one possible proof of the existence of things outside of us, namely the one which he has given, I can now give a large number of different proofs, each of which is a perfectly rigorous proof; and that at many other times I have been in a position to give many others. I can prove now, for instance, that two human hands exist. How? By holding up my two hands, and saying, as I make a certain gesture with the right hand, 'Here is one hand', and adding, as I make a certain gesture with the left, 'and here is another'. And if, by doing this, I have proved *ipso facto* the existence of external things, you will all see that I can also do it now in numbers of other ways: there is no need to multiply examples.

But did I prove just now that two human hands were then in existence? I do want to insist that I did; that the proof which I gave was a perfectly rigorous one; and that it is perhaps impossible to give a better or more rigorous proof of anything whatever. Of course, it would not have been a proof unless three conditions were satisfied; namely (1) unless the premiss which I adduced as proof of the conclusion was different from the conclusion I adduced it to prove; (2) unless the premiss which I adduced was something which I *knew* to be the case, and not merely something which I believed but which was by no means certain, or something which, though in fact true, I did not know to be so; and (3) unless the conclusion did really follow from the premiss. But all these three conditions were in fact satisfied by my proof. (1) The premiss which I adduced in proof was quite certainly different from the conclusion, for the conclusion was merely 'Two human hands exist at this moment'; but the premiss was something far more specific than this – something which I expressed by showing you my hands, making certain gestures, and saying the words 'Here is one hand, and here is another'. It is quite obvious that the two were different, because it is quite obvious that the conclusion might have been true, even if the premiss had been false. In asserting the premiss I was asserting much more than I was asserting in asserting the conclusion. (2) I certainly did at the moment *know* that which I expressed by the combination of certain gestures with saying the words 'Here is one hand and here is another'. I *knew* that there was one hand in the place indicated by combining a certain gesture with my first utterance of 'here' and that there was another in the different place indicated by combining a certain gesture with my second utterance of 'here'. How absurd it would be to suggest that I did not know it, but only believed it, and that perhaps it was not the case! You might as well suggest that I do not know that I am now standing up and talking – that perhaps after all I'm not, and that it's not quite certain that I am! And finally (3) it is quite certain that the conclusion did follow from the premiss. This is as certain as it is that if there is one hand here and another here *now*, then it follows that there are two hands in existence *now*.

My proof, then, of the existence of things outside of us did satisfy three of the conditions necessary for a rigorous proof. Are there any other

From G. E. Moore, *Philosophical Papers* (New York: Collier Books, 1962), pp. 144–8.

conditions necessary for a rigorous proof, such that perhaps it did not satisfy one of them? Perhaps there may be; I do not know; but I do want to emphasise that, so far as I can see, we all of us do constantly take proofs of this sort as absolutely conclusive proofs of certain conclusions – as finally settling certain questions, as to which we were previously in doubt. Suppose, for instance, it were a question whether there were as many as three misprints on a certain page in a certain book. A says there are, B is inclined to doubt it. How could A prove that he is right? Surely he *could* prove it by taking the book, turning to the page, and pointing to three separate places on it, saying 'There's one misprint here, another here, and another here': surely that is a method by which it *might* be proved! Of course, A would not have proved, by doing this, that there were at least three misprints on the page in question, unless it was certain that there was a misprint in each of the places to which he pointed. But to say that he *might* prove it in this way, is to say that it *might* be certain that there was. And if such a thing as that could ever be certain, then assuredly it was certain just now that there was one hand in one of the two places I indicated and another in the other.

I did, then, just now, give a proof that there were *then* external objects; and obviously, if I did, I could *then* have given many other proofs of the same sort that there were external objects *then*, and could now give many proofs of the same sort that there are external objects *now*.

But, if what I am asked to do is to prove that external objects have existed *in the past*, then I can give many different proofs of this also, but proofs which are in important respects of a different *sort* from those just given. And I want to emphasise that, when Kant says it is a scandal not to be able to give a proof of the existence of external objects, a proof of their existence in the past would certainly *help* to remove the scandal of which he is speaking. He says that, if it occurs to anyone to question their existence, we ought to be able to confront him with a satisfactory proof. But by a person who questions their existence, he certainly means not merely a person who questions whether any exist at the moment of speaking, but a person who questions whether any have *ever* existed; and a proof that some have existed in the past would certainly therefore be relevant to *part* of what such a person is questioning. How then can I prove that there have been external objects in the past? Here is one proof. I can say: 'I held up two hands above this desk not very long ago; therefore two hands existed not very long ago; therefore at least two external objects have existed at some time in the past, QED'. This is a perfectly good proof, provided I *know* what is asserted in the premiss. But I *do* know that I held up two hands above this desk not very long ago. As a matter of fact, in this case you all know it too. There's no doubt whatever that I did. Therefore I have given a perfectly conclusive proof that external objects have existed in the past; and you will all see at once that, if this is a conclusive proof, I could have given many others of the same sort, and could now give many others. But it is also quite obvious that this sort of proof differs in important respects from the sort of proof I gave just now that there were two hands existing *then*.

I have, then, given two conclusive proofs of the existence of external objects. The first was a proof that two human hands existed at the time when I gave the proof; the second was a proof that two human hands had existed at a time previous to that at which I gave the proof. These proofs were of a different sort in important respects. And I pointed out that I could have given, then, many other conclusive proofs of both sorts. It is also obvious that I could give many others of both sorts now. So that, if these are the sort of proof that is wanted, nothing is easier than to prove the existence of external objects.

But now I am perfectly well aware that, in spite of all that I have said, many philosophers will still feel that I have not given any satisfactory proof of the point in question. And I want briefly, in conclusion, to say something as to why this dissatisfaction with my proofs should be felt.

One reason why, is, I think, this. Some people understand 'proof of an external world' as including a proof of things which I haven't attempted to prove and haven't proved. It is not quite easy to say *what* it is that they want proved – *what* it is that is such that unless they got a proof of it, they would not say that they had a proof of the existence of external things; but I can make an approach to explaining what they want by saying that if I had proved the propositions which I used as *premisses* in my two proofs, then they would perhaps admit that I had proved the existence of external things, but, in the absence of such a proof (which, of course, I have neither given nor attempted to give), they will say that I have not given what they mean by a proof of the existence of external things. In other words, they want a proof of what I assert *now* when I hold up my hands and say 'Here's one hand and here's another'; and, in the other case, they want a proof of what I assert *now* when I say 'I did hold up two hands above this desk just now'. Of course, what they really want is not merely a proof of these two propositions, but something like a general statement as to how *any* propositions of this sort may be proved. This, of course, I haven't given; and I do not believe it can be given: if this is what is meant by proof of the existence of external things, I do not believe that any proof of the existence of external things is possible. Of course, in some cases what might be called a proof of propositions which seem like these can be got. If one of you suspected that one of my hands was artificial he might be said to get a proof of my proposition 'Here's one hand, and here's another', by coming up and examining the suspected hand close up, perhaps touching and pressing it, and so establishing that it really was a human hand. But I do not believe that any proof is possible in nearly all cases. How am I to prove now that 'Here's one hand, and here's another'? I do not believe I can do it. In order to do it, I should need to prove for one thing, as Descartes pointed out, that I am not now dreaming. But how can I prove that I am not? I have, no doubt, conclusive reasons for asserting that I am not now dreaming; I have conclusive evidence that I am awake: but that is a very different thing from being able to prove it. I could not tell you what all my evidence is; and I should require to do this at least, in order to give you a proof.

But another reason why some people would feel dissatisfied with my proofs is, I think, not merely that they want a proof of something which I haven't proved, but that they think that, if I cannot give such extra proofs, then the proofs that I have given are not conclusive proofs at all. And this, I think, is a definite mistake. They would say: 'If you cannot prove your premiss that here is one hand and here is another, then you do not know it. But you yourself have admitted that, if you did not know it, then your proof was not conclusive. Therefore your proof was not, as you say it was, a conclusive proof.' This view that, if I cannot prove such things as these, I do not know them, is, I think, the view that Kant was expressing in the sentence which I quoted at the beginning of this lecture, when he implies that so long as we have no proof of the existence of external things, their existence must be accepted merely on *faith*. He means to say, I think, that if I cannot prove that there is a hand here, I must accept it merely as a matter of faith – I cannot know it. Such a view, though it has been very common among philosophers, can, I think, be shown to be wrong – though shown only by the use of premisses which are not known to be true, unless we do know of the existence of external things. I can know things, which I cannot prove; and among things which I certainly did know, even if (as I think) I could not prove them, were the premisses of my two proofs. I should say, therefore, that those, if any, who are dissatisfied with these proofs merely on the ground that I did not know their premisses, have no good reason for their dissatisfaction.

ANALYSIS 23.6 JUNE 1963

# IS JUSTIFIED TRUE BELIEF KNOWLEDGE?

*By* EDMUND L. GETTIER

VARIOUS attempts have been made in recent years to state necessary and sufficient conditions for someone's knowing a given proposition. The attempts have often been such that they can be stated in a form similar to the following:[1]

(a) S knows that P *IFF* (i) P is true,
(ii) S believes that P, and
(iii) S is justified in believing that P.

For example, Chisholm has held that the following gives the necessary and sufficient conditions for knowledge:[2]

(b) S knows that P *IFF* (i) S accepts P,
(ii) S has adequate evidence for P, and
(iii) P is true.

Ayer has stated the necessary and sufficient conditions for knowledge as follows:[3]

(c) S knows that P *IFF* (i) P is true,
(ii) S is sure that P is true, and
(iii) S has the right to be sure that P is true.

I shall argue that (a) is false in that the conditions stated therein do not constitute a *sufficient* condition for the truth of the proposition that S knows that P. The same argument will show that (b) and (c) fail if 'has adequate evidence for' or 'has the right to be sure that' is substituted for 'is justified in believing that' throughout.

I shall begin by noting two points. First, in that sense of 'justified' in which S's being justified in believing P is a necessary condition of S's knowing that P, it is possible for a person to be justified in believing a proposition that is in fact false. Secondly, for any proposition P, if S is justified in believing P, and P entails Q, and S deduces Q from P and accepts Q as a result of this deduction, then S is justified in believing Q. Keeping these two points in mind, I shall now present two cases

[1] Plato seems to be considering some such definition at *Theaetetus* 201, and perhaps accepting one at *Meno* 98.

[2] Roderick M. Chisholm, *Perceiving: a Philosophical Study*, Cornell University Press (Ithaca, New York, 1957), p. 16.

[3] A. J. Ayer, *The Problem of Knowledge*, Macmillan (London, 1956), p. 34.

in which the conditions stated in (a) are true for some proposition, though it is at the same time false that the person in question knows that proposition.

*Case I:*

Suppose that Smith and Jones have applied for a certain job. And suppose that Smith has strong evidence for the following conjunctive proposition:

(d) Jones is the man who will get the job, and Jones has ten coins in his pocket.

Smith's evidence for (d) might be that the president of the company assured him that Jones would in the end be selected, and that he, Smith, had counted the coins in Jones's pocket ten minutes ago. Proposition (d) entails:

(e) The man who will get the job has ten coins in his pocket.

Let us suppose that Smith sees the entailment from (d) to (e), and accepts (e) on the grounds of (d), for which he has strong evidence. In this case, Smith is clearly justified in believing that (e) is true.

But imagine, further, that unknown to Smith, he himself, not Jones, will get the job. And, also, unknown to Smith, he himself has ten coins in his pocket. Proposition (e) is then true, though proposition (d), from which Smith inferred (e), is false. In our example, then, all of the following are true: (*i*) (e) is true, (*ii*) Smith believes that (e) is true, and (*iii*) Smith is justified in believing that (e) is true. But it is equally clear that Smith does not *know* that (e) is true; for (e) is true in virtue of the number of coins in Smith's pocket, while Smith does not know how many coins are in Smith's pocket, and bases his belief in (e) on a count of the coins in Jones's pocket, whom he falsely believes to be the man who will get the job.

*Case II:*

Let us suppose that Smith has strong evidence for the following proposition:

(f) Jones owns a Ford.

Smith's evidence might be that Jones has at all times in the past within Smith's memory owned a car, and always a Ford, and that Jones has just offered Smith a ride while driving a Ford. Let us imagine, now, that Smith has another friend, Brown, of whose whereabouts he is totally ignorant. Smith selects three place-names quite at random, and constructs the following three propositions:

(g) Either Jones owns a Ford, or Brown is in Boston;

(h) Either Jones owns a Ford, or Brown is in Barcelona;
(i) Either Jones owns a Ford, or Brown is in Brest-Litovsk.

Each of these propositions is entailed by (f). Imagine that Smith realizes the entailment of each of these propositions he has constructed by (f), and proceeds to accept (g), (h), and (i) on the basis of (f). Smith has correctly inferred (g), (h), and (i) from a proposition for which he has strong evidence. Smith is therefore completely justified in believing each of these three propositions. Smith, of course, has no idea where Brown is.

But imagine now that two further conditions hold. First, Jones does *not* own a Ford, but is at present driving a rented car. And secondly, by the sheerest coincidence, and entirely unknown to Smith, the place mentioned in proposition (h) happens really to be the place where Brown is. If these two conditions hold then Smith does *not* know that (h) is true, even though (*i*) (h) *is* true, (*ii*) Smith does believe that (h) is true, and (*iii*) Smith is justified in believing that (h) is true.

These two examples show that definition (a) does not state a *sufficient* condition for someone's knowing a given proposition. The same cases, with appropriate changes, will suffice to show that neither definition (b) nor definition (c) do so either.

*Wayne State University*

# CIRCULARITY AND INDUCTION

*By* PETER ACHINSTEIN

1. RECENTLY[1] I suggested why an argument proposed by Max Black, which attempts to support an inductive rule by citing its past success, suffers from circularity. The inductive rule under discussion is this:

R: To argue from *Most instances of As examined under a wide variety of conditions have been B* to (probably) *The next A to be encountered will be B.*

The argument in favour of the rule is as follows:

(a): In most instances of the use of R in arguments with true premisses examined in a wide variety of conditions, R has been successful.
*Hence (probably)*:
In the next instance to be encountered of use of R in an argument with a true premiss, R will be successful.

[1] " The Circularity of a Self-Supporting Inductive Argument ", ANALYSIS, 22.6 (June 1962).

*The Philosophical Quarterly* Vol. 44, No. 174
ISSN 0031-8094

# THE INESCAPABILITY OF GETTIER PROBLEMS

BY LINDA ZAGZEBSKI

Gettier problems arise in the theory of knowledge when it is only by chance that a justified true belief is true. Since the belief might easily have been false in these cases, it is normally concluded that they are not instances of knowledge.[1] The moral drawn in the thirty years since Gettier published his famous paper is that either justified true belief (JTB) is not sufficient for knowledge, in which case knowledge must have an 'extra' component in addition to JTB, or else justification must be reconceived to *make it* sufficient for knowledge. I shall argue that given the common and reasonable assumption that the relation between justification and truth is close but not inviolable, it is not possible for either move to avoid Gettier counter-examples. What is more, it makes no difference if the component of knowledge in addition to true belief is identified as something other than justification, e.g., warrant or well-foundedness. I conclude that Gettier problems are inescapable for virtually every analysis of knowledge which at least maintains that knowledge is true belief plus something else.

Notice first that Gettier problems arise for both internalist and externalist notions of justification. On internalist theories the grounds for justification are accessible to the consciousness of the believer, and Gettier problems arise when there is nothing wrong with the internally accessible aspects of the cognitive situation, but there is a mishap in something inaccessible to the believer. Since justification does not guarantee truth, it is possible for there to be a break in the connection between justification and truth, but for that connection to be regained by chance.

The original 'Smith owns a Ford or Brown is in Barcelona' case is an example of this sort. Here we are to imagine that Smith comes to you bragging about his new Ford, shows you the car and the bill of sale, and generally gives you lots of evidence that he owns a Ford. Basing what you think on the evidence, you believe the proposition 'Smith owns a Ford', and from that you infer its disjunction with 'Brown is in Barcelona', where Brown is an acquaintance and you have no reason at all to think he is in Barcelona. It turns out that Smith is lying and owns no Ford, but Brown is

[1] 'Is Justified True Belief Knowledge?', *Analysis* 23 (1963), pp. 121–3.

by chance in Barcelona. Your belief 'Smith owns a Ford or Brown is in Barcelona' is true and justified, but it is hardly the case that you know it.

In this case the problem arises because in spite of the fact that you have done everything to reach the truth from your point of view and everything that anyone could expect of you, your efforts do not lead you to the truth. It is mere bad luck that you are the unwitting victim of Smith's lies, and only an accident that a procedure that usually leads you to the truth leads you to believe the falsehood 'Smith owns a Ford'. The fact that you end up with a true belief anyway is due to a second accidental feature of the situation – a feature that has nothing to do with your cognitive activity. What generates the problem for JTB, then, is that an accident of bad luck is cancelled out by an accident of good luck. The right goal is reached, but only by chance.

Internalist theories are not the only ones afflicted with Gettier problems, contrary to a recent claim made by Alvin Plantinga.[2] Consider how the problem arises for reliabilism. In this group of theories believers are justified when their beliefs are formed in a reliable, or truth-conducive, manner. On this account also there is no guarantee that justified beliefs are true, and a breakdown in the connection between a reliable belief-forming process and the truth is possible. When that happens, even if you manage to hit on the truth anyway, you do not have knowledge.

The well-known fake barn case can be described as an example of this sort. Here we are to imagine that you are driving through a region in which, unknown to you, the inhabitants have erected three barn façades for each real barn in an effort to make themselves look more prosperous. Your eyesight is normal and reliable enough in ordinary circumstances to spot a barn from the road. But in this case the fake barns are indistinguishable from the real barns at such a distance. As you look at a real barn you form the belief 'That's a fine barn'. The belief is true and justified, but is not knowledge.

As in the first case, the problem arises because of the combination of two accidental features of the cognitive situation. It is only an accident that visual faculties normally reliable in this sort of situation are not reliable in this particular situation; and it is another accident that you happened to be looking at a real barn and hit on the truth anyway. Again the problem arises because an accident of bad luck is cancelled out by an accident of good luck.

Gettier problems cannot be avoided by Alvin Plantinga's new theory either. Plantinga calls the property that in sufficient quantity converts true belief into knowledge 'warrant' rather than 'justification'. On his proposal warrant is the property a belief *B* has for believer *S* when *B* is produced in *S*

[2] Alvin Plantinga, *Warrant and Proper Function*, (Oxford UP, 1993), p. 48.

by *S*'s faculties working properly in the appropriate environment, according to a design plan successfully aimed at truth.[3] But Plantinga does not maintain that every warranted belief is true any more than reliabilists maintain that every reliably formed belief is true or internalists maintain that every internally justified belief is true. Let us see if we can form a Gettier case for Plantinga's theory parallel to the other two cases we have considered. To do so we need to look for a situation in which *S*'s faculties are working the way they were designed to in the appropriate environment, but *S* unluckily has a false belief. We can then add a second accident which makes the belief true after all.

Suppose that Mary has very good eyesight, but it is not perfect. It is good enough to allow her to identify her husband sitting in his usual chair in the living room from a distance of fifteen feet in somewhat dim light (the degree of dimness can easily be specified). She has made such an identification in these circumstances many times. Each time her faculties have been working properly and the environment has been appropriate for the faculties. There is nothing at all unusual about either her faculties or the environment in these cases. Her faculties may not be functioning perfectly, but they are functioning well enough, so that if she goes on to form the belief 'My husband is sitting in the living room', that belief has enough warrant to constitute knowledge when true and we can assume that it is almost always true.

The belief is *almost* always true, we say. That is because warrant in the degree necessary for knowledge does not guarantee truth, according to Plantinga. If it *did* guarantee truth, of course, the component of truth in the analysis of knowledge would be superfluous. Knowledge would simply be warranted belief. So it is possible for Mary to make a mistake even though her faculties are functioning properly enough for knowledge and the environment is normal for the faculties. Let us look at one such case.

Suppose Mary simply misidentifies the chair-sitter who is, let us suppose, her husband's brother. Her faculties may be working as well as they normally do when the belief is true and when we do not hesitate to say it is warranted in a degree sufficient for knowledge. It is not a question of their suddenly becoming defective, or at any rate, more defective than usual, nor is there a mismatch between her faculties and the environment. No one is dressing up as her husband to fool her, or anything like that, so the environment is not abnormal as the fake barn case is abnormal. Her degree of warrant is as high as it usually is when she correctly identifies her

[3] The wording I have used can be found in Plantinga's book *Warrant and Proper Function*. A very similar wording can be found in 'Positive Epistemic Status and Proper Function', in J.E. Tomberlin (ed.), *Philosophical Perspectives 2: Epistemology* (Atascadero: Ridgeview, 1988), pp. 1–50. In that paper he calls 'positive epistemic status' what he now calls 'warrant'.

husband since even in those cases it is true that she *might* have misidentified the chair-sitter if it had been her husband's brother instead. Of course, she usually has no reason to suspect that it *is* her husband's brother and we can imagine that she has no reason to suspect so in this case either. Maybe she knows that her husband's brother looks a lot like him, but she has no reason to believe that he is in the vicinity, and, in fact, has strong reason to believe he has gone to Australia. So in the case we are considering, when Mary forms the false belief, her belief is as warranted as her beliefs normally are in these circumstances. In spite of well-functioning faculties and a benign environment, she just makes a mistake.

Now, of course, *something* has gone wrong here, and that something is probably in Mary rather than in the environment. It may even be correct to say that there is a minor defect in her faculties; perhaps she is not perfectly attentive or she is a little too hasty in forming her belief. But she is no less attentive and no more hasty than she usually is in such cases and usually it does not matter. People do not have to be perfectly attentive and perfectly cautious and have perfect vision to have beliefs sufficiently warranted for knowledge on Plantinga's theory. And this is not a *mistake* in Plantinga's theory. It would surely be unreasonable of him to expect perfectly functioning faculties in a perfectly attuned environment as his criteria for the warrant needed for knowledge. So Mary's defect need not be sufficient to bring her degree of warrant down below that needed for knowledge on Plantinga's account.

We can now easily emend the case as a Gettier example. Mary's husband could be sitting on the other side of the room, unseen by her. In that case her belief 'My husband is sitting in the living room' is true and has sufficient warrant for knowledge on Plantinga's account, but she does not have knowledge.

In discussing Gettier problems Plantinga concludes: 'What is essential to Gettier situations is the production of a true belief despite a relatively minor failure of the cognitive situation to match its design'.[4] But this comment is problematic on his own account. As we have seen, Plantinga considers warrant a property that admits of degree, but it is clear that the degree of warrant sufficient for knowledge does not require faculties to be working perfectly in an environment perfectly matched to them. In Gettier-style cases such as the case of Mary, either the degree of warrant is sufficient for knowledge or it is not. If it is not, then a multitude of beliefs we normally think are warranted are not, and there is much less knowledge in the world than Plantinga's numerous examples suggest. On the other hand, if the degree of warrant *is* sufficient for knowledge, then Plantinga's theory faces Gettier problems structurally identical to those of the other

[4] 'Positive Epistemic Status and Proper Function', p. 43.

theories. Furthermore, even if some aspect of the Mary example makes it unpersuasive, there must still be cases of warranted false belief on Plantinga's theory if the component of truth in knowledge is not redundant. With such a case in hand a Gettier example can be constructed by adding a feature extraneous to the warrant of the believer which makes the belief true after all. In such a case the degree of warrant is unchanged, but it is not knowledge since it might just as well have been false.

It is not enough, then, to say that Gettier problems arise because of a minor mismatch between faculties and environment. What Plantinga should have said is that the problem is due to a relatively minor failure of the cognitive situation to connect to the truth. As long as the property that putatively converts true belief into knowledge is analysed in such a way that it is strongly linked with the truth, but does not guarantee it, it will always be possible to devise cases in which the link between such a property and the truth is broken but regained by accident. Such is the nature of Gettier cases.

The three examples we have considered suggest a general rule for the generation of Gettier cases. It really does not matter how the *particular* element of knowledge in addition to true belief is analysed. As long as there is a small degree of independence between this other element and the truth, we can construct Gettier cases by using the following procedure: start with a case of justified (or warranted) false belief. Make the element of justification (warrant) strong enough for knowledge, but make the belief false. The falsity of the belief will not be due to any systematically describable element in the situation, for if it were, such a feature could be used in the analysis of the components of knowledge other than true belief, and then truth would be entailed by the other components of knowledge, contrary to the hypothesis. The falsity of the belief is therefore due to some element of luck. Now emend the case by adding another element of luck, only this time an element which makes the belief true after all. The second element must be independent of the element of warrant so that the degree of warrant is unchanged. The situation might be described as one element of luck counteracting another. We now have a case in which the belief is justified (warranted) in a sense strong enough for knowledge, the belief is true, but it is not knowledge. The conclusion is that as long as the concept of knowledge closely connects the justification component and the truth component, but permits *some* degree of independence between them, justified true belief will never be sufficient for knowledge.

It is often observed that in typical Gettier cases the justified belief depends upon or otherwise 'goes through' a false belief, so a way to handle these cases is to add what are commonly called 'defeasibility conditions' to the analysis of knowledge. This move was especially popular during the sixties and seventies. It adds to the requirement that knowledge be justified true belief the restriction that the belief in question must also be justified in certain counterfactual situations. One way to define these conditions is in terms of the psychological effect on the subject, as in Steven Levy's definition of a defeasibility condition as 'a requirement to the effect that for *S* to know that *p* there must be no other evidence against *p* strong enough to undermine *S*'s belief that *p*, should this evidence come to *S*'s attention'.[5]

The three cases I have just described do have the feature that there is a false belief in the neighbourhood of the belief in question which is such that, should the subject discover its falsehood, that would undermine the belief in the proposition in question. So your belief that either Smith owns a Ford or Brown is in Barcelona is undermined if you discover that Smith does not own a Ford. Your belief that this is a barn is undermined if you discover that most objects that look like barns in this vicinity are not real barns. Mary's belief that her husband is sitting in the living room is undermined if she discovers that that man sitting over *there* in a particular chair in the living room is not her husband. In each case were *S* to be advised of the falsity of the underlying belief, *S* would retract the belief under discussion. The belief would be defeated by such new information.

This move puts a strain on the independence of the justification/defeasibility condition and the truth condition. If *S*'s belief that *p* is false, there will obviously be many other propositions which are logically or evidentially connected to *p* which are false also. Should *S* become aware of any of these propositions, that may easily undermine *S*'s belief that *p*, assuming *S* is rational. This means that the falsehood of *p* is incompatible with a strong defeasibility condition, contrary to the hypothesis that the justification and defeasibility components of knowledge do not entail the truth condition. This problem is even more apparent in statements of the defeasibility condition in terms of evidential support rather than a psychological requirement, as in Pappas and Swain's definition: 'the evidence *e* must be sufficiently complete that no further additions to *e* would result in a loss of justification and hence a loss of knowledge'.[6] Obviously, if the belief is *false*, further additions to *e* will result in a loss of justification, and hence a loss of knowledge.

Strong defeasibility conditions, then, threaten the assumption of independence between the justification (warrant) condition and the truth

[5] Steven Levy, 'Defeasibility Theories of Knowledge', *Canadian Journal of Philosophy* 7 (1977), p. 115.

[6] George Pappas and Marshall Swain (eds), *Essays on Knowledge and Justification* (Ithaca and London: Cornell UP, 1978), p. 27.

condition for knowledge. But weaker defeasibility conditions are subject to Gettier-style counter-examples following the pattern described above. In each case we find an example of a false belief which satisfies the justification and defeasibility conditions, and then make the belief true anyway due to features of the situation independent of the satisfaction of those conditions.

Suppose Dr Jones, a physician, has very good inductive evidence that her patient, Smith, is suffering from virus *X*. Smith exhibits all of the symptoms of this virus, and a blood test has shown that his antibody levels against virus *X* are extremely high. In addition, let us suppose that the symptoms are not compatible with any other known virus, all of the evidence upon which Jones bases her diagnosis is true, and there is no evidence accessible to her which counts significantly against the conclusion. The proposition that Smith is suffering from virus *X* really is extremely probable on the evidence.

In this case there is nothing defective in the justification of Dr Jones' belief that Smith has virus *X* and no false belief figures causally or evidentially in her justification, nor is there any false belief in the neighbourhood. Furthermore, she would have believed that Smith has virus *X* in a wide range of counterfactual situations. None the less, let us suppose that the belief is false. Smith's symptoms are due to a distinct and unknown virus *Y* and the fact that he exhibits high antibody levels to virus *X* is due to idiosyncratic features of his biochemistry which cause him to maintain unusually high antibody levels long after a past infection. In this case Dr Jones' belief that Smith is presently suffering from virus *X* is false, but it is both justified and undefeated. Of course, given that the belief is false, there must be *some* evidence against it accessible to her in some counterfactual circumstances, so if defeasibility conditions are strong enough, no false empirical belief passes the test. But as said above, that is to impose an unreasonably strong defeasibility condition, one that makes the justification/defeasibility condition entail truth. The most reasonable conclusion to draw in this case, then, is that Jones' belief is justified and undefeated, but false.

Now to construct a Gettier-style example we simply add the feature that Smith has very recently contracted virus *X*, but so recently that he does not yet exhibit symptoms caused by *X*, nor has there been time for a change in the antibody levels due to this recent infection. So while the evidence upon which Dr Jones bases her diagnosis does make it highly probable that Smith has *X*, the fact that Smith has *X* has nothing to do with that evidence. In this case, then, Dr Jones' belief that Smith has virus *X* is true, justified and undefeated, but it is not knowledge.

It appears, then, that no account of knowledge as true belief plus something else can withstand Gettier objections as long as there is a small degree of independence between truth and the other conditions of knowledge. What are our alternatives? We have already seen that one way to solve the problem is to give up the independence between the justification condition and the truth condition. Justification would be defined in such a way that no false belief can satisfy it. Since Gettier cases are based on situations in which the belief is true, but it might just as well have been false, all such cases would be excluded from the class of justified (warranted) beliefs. On this approach the element of truth in the account of knowledge is superfluous and knowledge is simply justified (warranted) belief. '*S* is justified in believing *p*' entails *p*. Few philosophers have supported this view.[7]

So Gettier problems can be avoided if there is no degree of independence at all between truth and justification. A second way to avoid them is to go to the opposite extreme and to make the justification condition and the truth condition almost completely independent. It could still be the case that justification puts the subject in the best position available for getting the truth, but if the best position is not very good, most justified beliefs will be false. Perhaps most justified scientific hypotheses since the world began have been false. Perhaps Plato, Spinoza, Kant and Hegel were justified in believing their metaphysical theories, but most of their theories (at least) were false. Still, if one of them is true, some theorists might be willing to call it knowledge. On this approach the element of luck permitted in the state of knowledge is so great that alleged counter-examples based on luck do not count against it. From this viewpoint, Gettier cases would simply be accepted as cases of knowledge. After all, if knowledge is mostly luck anyway, there will be nothing bothersome about a case in which the truth is acquired by luck.

Perhaps neither of these alternatives will appeal to most philosophers, who find the idea that there is a small but real degree of independence between justification and the acquisition of truth just too attractive to give up. A third reaction to the problem, then, is to accept the fact that no 'true belief + x' account of knowledge will be sufficient, but that it will always be necessary to add the element of luck to the analysis. So knowledge is true belief + x + luck. This approach recognizes the fact that the concept

[7] An exception is Robert Almeder, 'Truth and Evidence', *The Philosophical Quarterly*, 24 (1974), pp. 365–8. Almeder's reason for maintaining that '*S* is justified in believing *p*' entails *p* is that the *determination* of the fact that a belief *p* is justified entails the determination of the fact that *p* is true. I find this implausible, since (1) there are many ways to determine the truth-value of a proposition *p* independently of the justification of a particular believer in believing *p*; and (2) even if the act of determining that a belief is justified included the determination of its truth, it does not follow that the fact that a belief is justified entails its truth.

we substitute for 'x' ought to be one that has a strong general connection with the acquisition of truth, but that an inviolable connection would be unreasonable. On the other hand, it also recognizes the fact that we are much less forgiving with the concept of knowledge itself. The connection between justification or whatever it is we substitute for 'x' and truth must exist in each and every particular case of knowledge. The notion of knowledge requires success, both in reaching the goal of truth, and in reaching it via the right cognitive path. The notion of justification or warrant is less stringent, requiring only that the right path is one that is *usually* successful at getting the truth. It is this difference between the notion of knowledge and the notion of justification that is responsible for Gettier problems.

Almost every contemporary theory of justification or warrant aims only to give the conditions for putting the believer in the best position for getting the truth. The best position is assumed to be very good, but imperfect, for such is life. Properly functioning faculties need not be working perfectly, but only well enough; reliable belief-producing mechanisms need not be perfectly reliable, only reliable enough; evidence for a belief need not support it conclusively, but only well enough; and so on. As long as the truth is never assured by the conditions which make the state justified, there will be situations in which a false belief is justified. I have argued that with this common, in fact, almost universal assumption, Gettier cases will never go away.

*Loyola Marymount University*

# Part Two:
# Mind and Body

personal identity intersect. A dying professor, her old friend (a clergyman), and her student discuss quite spontaneously the famous philosophical theories of John Locke, Joseph Butler, and Anthony Collins—seminal thinkers of the seventeenth and eighteenth centuries—about personal identity. At issue is the question of what sense, if any, can be made of the very idea of personal survival.

# In Defense of Mind–Body Dualism

BRIE GERTLER

Brie Gertler works primarily on philosophical problems in the philosophy of mind. She teaches at the University of Virginia.

> How quaint, the idea that our minds somehow float free of the cold, hard, physical world. Surely dualism is the stuff of fantasy, an indulgence of poets and daydreamers, an echo of antiquated worldviews long ago demolished by the relentless progress of science. Though we may occasionally find comfort in imagining that our minds are special, in our more sober moments we must face the facts: our thoughts and feelings, and those of our loved ones, are just as much a part of the brute material order as sticks and stones.

This sentiment expresses a common attitude. The prevalence of this attitude may explain why physicalism, the view that sensations and other mental states are entirely physical, is generally the default position about the mind. On first approaching the mind–body problem, most scientifically minded people assume that physicalism simply has to be true.

However, the sentiment above seriously misrepresents present-day versions of dualism, the belief that some mental states are nonphysical. Many contemporary dualists are fully *naturalistic*. That is, they hold that mental states are just as much a part of the natural order as sticks and stones; and they favor a scientific approach to the mind, one that is independent of religious considerations. In essence, the contemporary dispute between physicalists and naturalistic dualists is a disagreement about what kinds of *data* there are about the nature of mind, and what sort of *theory*—dualist or physicalist—best explains the data.

In this essay, I defend naturalistic dualism. I take, as my starting point, an argument made by René Descartes in his *Meditations*. I expand and defend this argument, drawing on some ideas developed by contemporary philosophers.[1] The expanded argument is, I think, much more powerful than most physicalists recognize. After making my case for dualism, I offer some criticisms of physicalism. The paper will close by defending dualism from the charge that the picture of reality it provides is unacceptably *spooky*.

But first, I must explain in more detail the point at issue between physicalists and dualists. What is it, precisely, that physicalists assert, and dualists deny? Our answer to this question will reveal the type of reasoning that a defense of dualism must employ.

## 1. PHYSICALISM, DUALISM, AND THE NEED FOR THOUGHT EXPERIMENTS

Physicalism comes in various forms. I will focus on the most straightforward version, the *identity thesis*, which has been defended by numerous

---

This article was commissioned by the editor expressly for the thirteenth edition of this anthology.

philosophers. According to the identity thesis, every type of mental state is identical to some type of physical state. Here is an example of a particular identity claim, relating pain to C-fibers, a group of nerve cells that fire when pain is experienced.

**(P)** Pain = C-fiber stimulation[2]

In this statement, "pain" refers to a type of sensation, the type of sensation you have when you stub your toe or bite your lip. This type of sensation is usually caused by tissue damage (in the toe or the lip), but it needn't be. For instance, a person who has had both feet amputated could nonetheless experience the "stubbed toe" sensation. So damage to the toe is merely the ordinary cause of that sort of sensation; the sensation itself is not spatially located *in* the toe. And it is the sensation itself, not its cause, which is most obviously a *mental* state. Throughout this essay, "pain" will refer to the sensation itself, and not its usual or real cause.

Actually, identity theorists are not committed to any particular identity thesis, such as (P). Their key claim is that every type of mental state is identical to some type of physical state, but they needn't claim that science has yet uncovered any particular identities. Still, (P) illustrates the *kind* of identity the physicalist has in mind. I will continue to use it in this way.

The first thing to notice about (P) is that it is extremely strong. It does not say merely that pain is perfectly correlated with C-fiber stimulation. Nor does it say that pain will always accompany, and be accompanied by, C-fiber stimulation. Rather, it says that pain just *is*—is nothing over and above—C-fiber stimulation. This means that pain *couldn't possibly* be present in the absence of C-fiber stimulation, or vice versa, any more than Superman could be present in the absence of Clark Kent, or water could be present in the absence of $H_2O$. So an identity statement goes beyond a claim about what is *actually* the case, to a claim about what is *possible*—or, really, what is *impossible.*

Because identity statements (statements about what is identical to what) entail that certain scenarios are impossible, they cannot be confirmed by empirical methods alone. To see why this is, imagine that we are in the best-case situation for empirical investigation: We are somehow able to monitor all of the creatures in the universe, and to determine which creatures have C-fibers that are undergoing stimulation, and which creatures are experiencing pain. (To determine whether people are experiencing pain, we might simply ask them; to determine this for infants and animals, we might observe their behavior.) Suppose that we learn that these are perfectly correlated: C-fiber stimulation is present in all and only those creatures that are currently experiencing pain. Even this very tidy result does not establish the identity thesis, for we still do not know whether it is *possible* that one of these be present in the absence of the other. The perfect correlation might be an odd coincidence. Or, more plausibly, it might be that one of these causes the other. (A prominent dualist position holds that physical events, like the firing of C-fibers, *cause* mental events like pain. This allows us to explain how aspirin can block pain by affecting the brain.) Or it might be that pain and C-fiber stimulation are products of a common cause: Perhaps stubbing one's toe simultaneously causes both the pain sensation and C-fiber stimulation. These explanations of the correlation are alternatives to saying that pain is *identical to* C-fiber stimulation (e.g., if C-fiber stimulation causes pain then these cannot be identical, for nothing causes itself).

The upshot is that even a perfect correlation does not establish the identity thesis. It shows only that one of these factors *is not,* in fact, present in the absence of the other. But it does not show that one of these factors *could not possibly* be present in the absence of the other. And the identity thesis requires this latter, stronger claim.

If the identity thesis is true, then physicalism is true. Dualists deny the identity thesis, and believe that mental states are distinct from (that is, they are not identical to) physical states. Dualism thus implies that it is *possible* that pain is present in the absence of C-fiber stimulation. Dualists can accept that these are perfectly correlated; but, they claim, these are two distinct states, and so it is not *impossible* that one is present while the other is absent. (Again, perhaps their perfect correlation is due to some causal connection.)

I will defend dualism by arguing that it is possible that you experience pain even if you are in *no* physical state, that is, even if you have no body whatsoever. If pain can occur in the absence of *any* physical state, then physicalism is false.[3]

Because the dispute between physicalism and dualism concerns whether a particular scenario is *possible,* empirical evidence will not resolve it. We must therefore turn to another sort of evidence, gained from thought experiments. Thought experiments can help us to determine whether situations that don't actually occur—such as the presence of pain in the absence of C-fiber stimulation—are nonetheless possible.

Unlike scientific experiments, which are ordinarily conducted in a laboratory, thought experiments are conducted from the comfort of the armchair. One performs a thought experiment by attempting to imagine a given scenario, and then carefully reflecting on the outcome of this exercise. It may seem odd to think that such armchair reflection can yield genuine progress on a thorny issue like the mind–body problem. But because the dispute between physicalists and dualists concerns the sheer *possibility* of a given scenario, neither of these positions can be established without thought experiments.[4]

Here are some examples of thought experiments designed to reveal whether a given scenario is possible.

(A) You have never seen a book that is 100 feet tall. (According to *Guinness World Records,* the world's largest book—a photographic tour of the Asian country of Bhutan—is 5 feet tall by 7 feet wide.) Still, a moment's reflection reveals that you can imagine a 100-foot-tall book. While the high costs of production and the dim sales prospects mean that no one is likely ever to create such a book, these impediments don't absolutely *rule out* its creation. For instance, it is easy to imagine the production being financed by an eccentric millionaire.

We have just resolved the question, "Is it possible that a book be 100 feet tall?" by use of a thought experiment. On reflection, there seemed to be only practical obstacles to the creation of a 100-foot-tall book, and we could imagine overcoming those obstacles. Short of building the giant book ourselves, it is hard to see how this question could be resolved without the use of thought experiments.

(B) You have never seen an object that is blue all over and (simultaneously) orange all over. Can you imagine such an object? It seems clear that you cannot. This exercise of imagination leads you to believe that nothing could possibly be blue all over and orange all over.

(C) You have never encountered a married bachelor. I expect that you will find yourself unable to conceive of a married bachelor, since you will be unable to conceive of a married person who meets the requirements for being a bachelor (which include, of course, being unmarried). Because nothing can be simultaneously married and unmarried, it is impossible that there be any married bachelors.

In the first two cases, you drew on your *concepts* (**book, blue object,** etc.) in trying to *imagine* the described scenario. But in this third case your concepts are more directly involved, because the thought experiment involves *conceiving* rather than *imagining.* To imagine something is to form a sensory (perhaps visual) picture of it. Because no picture of a man will fully express his marital status, mere imagination will not do the trick here. Rather, you exercise the concepts directly, and find that you cannot conceive of a married bachelor because your concept **bachelor** includes the concept **unmarried,** and nothing that satisfies that concept can simultaneously satisfy the concept **married.** (It is no surprise that *conceive* and *concept* have the same Latin root.)

Of course, the results of a thought experiment are not guaranteed to be accurate. Like experiments done in the laboratory, thought experiments can go astray in any number of ways: Your imagination may be limited in a way that makes you unable to imagine a 100-foot-tall book; you may mistakenly think that 'bachelor' refers to any man who lives alone; etc. But as with other types of experiment, these mistakes can be minimized if we take care in designing and performing the experiment. Most importantly, engaging in thought experiments is our only way of determining whether scenarios that haven't actually occurred, and will never actually occur, are nonetheless possible.

In these thought experiments, we try to imagine or conceive a particular scenario, to determine whether it is possible. This exercise is known as a *conceivability test*. There are other types of thought experiments as well, but conceivability tests lie at the heart of most of the leading arguments for dualism, including the one that I will now present.

## 2. THE DISEMBODIMENT ARGUMENT

The argument that I will use is a descendant of an argument given by Descartes. I will call it the Disembodiment Argument. Its basic structure is disarmingly simple, but of course the devil—or, as Descartes might say, the malicious demon—is in the details.

The argument centers on the possibility that pain is present in the absence of any physical state.[5] Arguments for dualism usually focus on pain or other sensations, because the experience of sensations seems to present the greatest challenge to physicalism. Descartes himself believed that thoughts, such as "my senses sometimes mislead me," posed an equal challenge to physicalism, but contemporary philosophers are divided on that claim. We needn't concern ourselves with that issue. If our argument succeeds in showing that pain can be present in the absence of any physical state, we will have established dualism, for we will have shown that pain is not identical to anything physical, and thus that at least *some* mental states (viz., pains) are not physical. And that is precisely what the dualist maintains, and the physicalist denies.

As with other thought experiments, this one requires that you actively engage in the exercise of imagining or conceiving. This will unfortunately require a tiny bit of pain. So pinch yourself—lightly!—and, while doing so, put yourself into the position of the "I" in the following line of reasoning.

1. Even though I firmly believe that I have physical features, I can conceive of experiencing *this very pain* while possessing no physical features. In other words, I can conceive of experiencing *this very pain* while disembodied.
2. If I can conceive of a particular scenario occurring, then that scenario is possible.

So,

3. It is possible that *this very pain* occurs in a disembodied being.
4. If *this very pain* was identical to some physical state, then it could not possibly occur in a disembodied being.

So,

5. *This very pain* is not identical to any physical state.

So,

(Conclusion) The identity thesis, which says that every mental state is identical to some physical state, is false.

The major premises in this argument are (1) and (2). Premise (3) follows from these; premise (4) expresses an accepted fact about the nature of identity; and premise (5) follows from (3) and (4).

The best way to target this argument, then, is to deny either (1) or (2). This is precisely what physicalists have done. I will first discuss premise (2), and then take up premise (1).

### Premise (2)

The chief criticism of premise (2) is that it involves a kind of intellectual hubris. In conceiving of something, we are simply exercising our *concepts*. And why should we think that our concepts accurately reflect the way the world is? Perhaps we are out of touch with reality, and our concepts don't correspond to real objects or properties. In that case, the fact that we can conceive of a particular scenario occurring provides no reason to think that that scenario is genuinely possible.

In reply to this criticism, it is crucial to note that *all* of our reasoning—in philosophy and elsewhere—must use some concepts, to define the topic we are investigating. In biology, we begin with some concept of reproduction, which empirical investigation may lead us to refine. In ethics, we begin with some concept of the good, which philosophical reasoning helps us to clarify and develop. And of course physicalists also rely on concepts—including concepts of the physical—in defending their view.

Occasionally, we may find that nothing satisfies a given concept, and so we may abandon investigations relating to it. This is what happened in the case of witchcraft: Most people came to deny that anything in reality corresponded to the concept **witchcraft,** and the study of witchcraft was replaced by research into superstitions and mental pathologies, phenomena that led to the mistaken belief in witchcraft. But while we must allow for the possibility that we'll refine or even abandon our concepts, concepts are indispensable at the outset of an investigation. For there is no way to proceed with an inquiry unless we have *some* concept of the subject matter we are investigating. The blanket objection that conceivability arguments are illegitimate because they use *our concepts* is, then, misguided.

However, there is a more nuanced version of the worry that premise (2) oversteps our intellectual bounds. Unlike the previous objection, this one acknowledges that we must employ concepts in order to reason at all. And it concedes that thought experiments using simple, straightforward concepts such as **bachelor** can help us to determine what is possible. But it rejects premise (2) on the grounds that it is too general: Not *everything* we can conceive is possible. For some of our concepts are clouded or obscure, and so cannot play the proper role in conceivability tests. In particular, this objection says that our concepts **pain** and **physical** are limited or unclear. Using such faulty concepts, what we can or cannot conceive does not reveal what is or is not possible.

This type of objection was advanced against Descartes' original argument by his contemporary Antoine Arnauld. Arnauld pointed out that a geometry student who hadn't yet encountered the proof of the Pythagorean Theorem could argue as follows:

> I can conceive of a right triangle with the following property: the square of its hypotenuse is unequal to the sum of the squares of its other two sides. Therefore, it is possible for a right triangle to have this property.

Clearly, this argument is invalid: The fact that the student could conceive this scenario does not mean that the scenario is possible.

Descartes anticipated Arnauld's objection, and had a ready response. He acknowledged that his argument will fail unless the relevant concepts are "complete and adequate." The student was able to conceive of a right triangle that violated the Pythagorean Theorem only because his concept **right triangle** was limited. But our concepts of mentality and of the physical are not limited in this way, or so Descartes claimed. That's why he thought that our ability to conceive disembodied pains was genuine evidence that disembodied pains were possible.[6]

In effect, Descartes' reply deflects attention away from premise (2), and makes premise (1) the focus of the argument. For everyone can agree that, if we have a comprehensive understanding of something, then conceivability tests provide a reliable guide to what is possible, involving that thing. It is because you fully understand what it means to be a bachelor that, when you find yourself unable to conceive of a married bachelor, you can justifiedly conclude that it's impossible that anything be a married bachelor. And if the geometry student gained a comprehensive grasp of right triangles, then he could similarly rely on conceivability tests. For a comprehensive grasp of right triangles would prevent him from conceiving of a right triangle that violated the Pythagorean Theorem.

Let us agree, then, that conceivability tests can reveal what is possible or impossible, *so long as the concepts involved are sufficiently comprehensive.* This amounts to qualifying premise (2), to read as follows:

2.* If, *using concepts that are sufficiently comprehensive,* I can conceive of a particular scenario occurring, then that scenario is possible.

Our new premise (2*) is unobjectionable, for it is trivially true. To say that a concept is "sufficiently comprehensive," in this sense, is just to say that it is suitable for use in conceivability tests. If follows, then, that conceivability tests *using sufficiently comprehensive concepts* reveal what is (and what is not) possible.

Because (2*) is trivially true, the burden of the argument now falls on the first premise. Let us consider premise (1) in more detail.

### Premise (1)

We must modify premise (1) to fit our new second premise. It now becomes (1*).

1.* *Using concepts that are sufficiently comprehensive,* I can conceive of experiencing *this very pain* while disembodied.

Together, (1*) and (2*) yield (3), so the rest of the argument proceeds as before.

Again because (2*) is trivially true, the entire weight of the argument now rests on (1*). To evaluate (1*), we must determine whether the concepts at work in the "pinch" test are sufficiently comprehensive. That is, when you conceive of experiencing *this very pain* (the pinch) while disembodied, are your concepts **pain** and **physical** sufficiently clear and complete, like your concept **bachelor?** Or might they be confused or incomplete, like the geometry student's concept **right triangle?**

*This is the core issue on which the Disembodiment Argument rests.* The argument will succeed only if your concepts of pain and of the physical are sufficiently comprehensive to allow you to conclude, from the fact that you can conceive of experiencing pain while disembodied, that this is possible. Physicalists generally deny this. They believe that, in conceiving of disembodied pain, we are like Arnauld's geometry student, who conceives of a right triangle that violates the Pythagorean Theorem.

I now turn to discuss our concepts of the physical and of pain. We will see that **pain** plays a much more important role in the Disembodiment Argument.

## 3. OUR CONCEPT OF THE PHYSICAL

Consider what "physical" means. What conditions must something meet in order to qualify as *physical?*

Descartes thought that the essence of the physical was to be extended in space. But modern physics posits entities—such as fields and waves—that sit uncomfortably with the notion of spatial extension. And because modern physics is still evolving, we should not define the physical in terms of a currently favored theory. For further advances in physics might eventually lead us to reject whatever theory we currently favor.

In response to these worries, many philosophers now conceptualize the physical, for purposes of the mind–body problem, as "the inanimate" or "the nonmental." [7] In this way, the concept **physical** is defined by contrast with the concepts **animate** or **mental.** This suggestion nicely captures the issue at hand. On this reading of "physical," the central point of contention between physicalists and dualists is as follows:

> Are mental states ultimately, fundamentally nonmental? Are mental states, states of mental things like you and me, ultimately identical (or reducible) to states that are *also* had by inanimate, nonmental things, like sticks and stones?

The dualist will answer "no," claiming that mental states are part of the basic fabric of the universe. The physicalist will answer "yes," claiming that mental states are simply patterns of basic physical (that is, nonmental) phenomena. I propose that we adopt this way of conceptualizing the physical. States that are physical, in this sense, are ultimately constituted by phenomena that are nonmental.

As regards the Disembodiment Argument, this understanding of **physical** will affect how you perform the conceivability test described in (1*). To be disembodied is to have *no* physical—ultimately nonmental—features. So you are to attempt to conceive of experiencing *this very pain* while being a *purely* mental entity, an entity that, at least for a moment, has no features in common with sticks and stones.[8]

I now turn to the more significant concept for our purposes, the concept **pain.**

## 4. OUR CONCEPT OF PAIN

Recall that the Disembodiment Argument will succeed only if our concept of pain is sufficiently comprehensive, in the sense explained above. Is it?

Someone with the concept **pain** might be ignorant of non-essential features of pain: for instance, whether aspirin or ibuprofen more quickly relieves pain. But such features are not relevant to the possibility of disembodied pain. The Disembodiment Argument requires only that we grasp the *essential* features of pain, those that are relevant to the possibility of disembodied pain.[9]

Still, establishing that our concept **pain** is sufficiently comprehensive, in this sense, is a difficult task. The standard expressed by "sufficiently comprehensive" is very high, and as physicalists are quick to point out, most of our concepts do not meet this standard. The classic example concerns water. Before learning chemistry, each of us could presumably conceive that water was present in the absence of $H_2O$. And arguably, we can still conceive this. (For we can imagine that chemists develop a new technique for analyzing substances and that, using this technique, they discover that all of the stuff we call "water" contains an additional element, one undetectable by previous methods.) But while we can conceive that water is present in the absence of $H_2O$, this scenario is of course impossible, because water simply *is* $H_2O$. Clearly, then, our concept **water** is not sufficiently comprehensive to be used in this type of conceivability test.

Physicalists who cite the water example predict that, once neuroscience has developed more fully, we will come to regard our ability to conceive of disembodied pain in a similar way. That is, we will see that it involves the use of inadequate concepts, and therefore provides no real evidence for the possibility of disembodied pain, just as our ability to conceive of water that is not $H_2O$ provides no evidence for the possibility of non-$H_2O$ water.

To defend the Disembodiment Argument, we need to block the analogy between **water** and **pain.** This requires showing that our concept **pain** is importantly different from concepts such as **water,** to justify the claim that **pain** (unlike **water**) is sufficiently comprehensive. And this is precisely what I will now attempt to do.

First, we must understand *why* our concept **water** is not sufficiently comprehensive. It fails to meet this standard for a simple reason. Namely, we conceptualize water as something that has a *hidden essence,* an essence that can be discovered only by careful scientific investigation. (The hidden essence of water is in fact $H_2O$.) This is why armchair reflection will not reveal whether non-$H_2O$ water is really possible.

But we don't conceptualize pain this way. *We conceptualize pain as something that has no hidden essence.* Pain wears its essential nature on its sleeve, as it were.

Here we have reached the fundamental, driving idea behind the Disembodiment Argument. As we conceptualize pain, pain has no hidden essence. If you *feel* that you are in pain, then you are in pain; determining whether you are in pain does not require scientific investigation. For the appearance (feeling) of pain just is pain itself. As one contemporary commentator has put it, "there is no appearance/reality distinction in the case of sensations" such as pain.[10]

How does this observation—that the appearance of pain is pain itself—help us to defend (1*)? The challenge, in defending (1*), is to show that our concept **pain** is sufficiently comprehensive for use in conceivability tests. The observation that the *feeling* of pain *is* pain accomplishes this. To determine whether you are really in pain, you need not investigate beyond the feeling of pain. For instance, you need not examine your brain to see whether your C-fibers are undergoing stimulation. (By contrast, investigation *is* required to determine whether something that seems like water—that looks and tastes like water—really is water.) This implies that pain has no hidden essence. So even if pain is perfectly correlated with C-fiber stimulation, C-fiber stimulation is not *essential* to pain; for if it were, then C-fiber stimulation would be the hidden essence of pain, and you couldn't be sure that you were in pain unless you determined that your C-fibers were firing. And if C-fiber stimulation is not essential to pain, then it is not *impossible* that pain be present in the absence of C-fiber stimulation. Hence, pain is not identical to C-fiber stimulation.

Let me be clear about my case here. I am not suggesting that we can't be mistaken about pain.[11] My point is just that there is *some* evidence for pain that is absolutely conclusive, for it is, simultaneously, evidence for pain and pain itself. This is evidence of the standard sort: that *hurting* sensation. That sensation is both the appearance of pain and the reality of pain.

Nor am I suggesting that the conceivability test at the heart of the Disembodiment Argument is easy to perform. You must pay close attention to your current "pinching" sensation, making sure that you are not reading more (or less) into it than what it presents. And you must carefully engage in the exercise of conceiving. This is why Descartes advised that, before engaging in the *Meditations,* we should find a quiet place and free our minds from distractions.

But as long as you exercise care, you should be able—through keeping your attention on the pinching feeling, while simultaneously trying to conceive that you are disembodied—to confirm, or disconfirm, (1*) for yourself. For my part, I find that this exercise confirms (1*). And because I assume that we are basically similar, as regards our sensations and concepts, I expect that you will find this as well.

This is, then, the basic argument for dualism. As modified, the key premise of the argument is (1*). That premise is supported by the simple but powerful thought that, according to our concept **pain,** the feeling of pain *is* pain; pain has no essential features that are hidden. So in attending to the pinching sensation, we have access to the essential feature of pain, namely, how it feels. This means that our concept **pain** is sufficiently comprehensive for use in conceivability tests. Your ability to conceive of disembodied pain therefore establishes that disembodied pain is possible, even if (in fact) everyone who experiences pain also has a body. This possibility refutes the identity thesis and establishes dualism.

## 5. A PHYSICALIST OBJECTION

Physicalists have put forth the following objection to this kind of argument:

> The argument shows only that, *according to our concept **pain,*** pain may be present in the absence of C-fiber stimulation. Still, we must bear in mind the example of water. *According to our concept **water,*** water may be present in the absence of $H_2O$. Just as the latter case does not lead us to doubt that water = $H_2O$, the former case should not lead us to doubt that pain = C-fiber stimulation.

As I explained in Section 2, our concepts define the subject matter that we are investigating. And our concepts also determine how we interpret evidence. It is because we conceptualize water as something that has a hidden essence that our discovery that water is correlated with $H_2O$ leads us to believe that water = $H_2O$. If we conceptualized water differently—e.g., as *any clear liquid*—then we wouldn't accept "water = $H_2O$."

By the same token, our concept of pain defines what it is that we are investigating when we try to understand the nature of pain. According to this concept, we are investigating that *hurting* sensation. And because pain has no hidden essence, according to our concept, the discovery that pain is correlated with C-fiber stimulation will not justify "pain = C-fiber stimulation."

Above, I said that empirical investigation could not establish that a certain scenario is *impossible.* This is why even a perfect correlation between pain and C-fiber stimulation could not establish that it is impossible that pain be present without C-fiber stimulation, and hence could not establish that these were identical. How, then, did empirical investigation establish that water = $H_2O$? The answer is simple: Empirical investigation did *not* single-handedly establish this. Empirical investigation established only a correlation between water and $H_2O$. What justified the identity claim was an additional fact, a fact about our *concept* of water, namely, that we conceptualize water as having a hidden essence. But we don't take the fact that a substance has a particular appearance (it is clear, drinkable, etc.) to be *conclusive evidence* that it is water; Rather, we think that, to conclusively determine whether something is water, we must discover its microstructure. The fact that water has a hidden essence was already implicit in our concept **water;** and this is why the discovery that water was perfectly correlated with $H_2O$ led us to believe that $H_2O$ was the hidden essence of water, and hence that water = $H_2O$.

By contrast, we don't think of pain as having a hidden essence. This is why you treat the *appearance* of pain—that *hurting* sensation—as conclusive evidence that you are in pain. And it is why we don't need scientific investigation to discover the *essence* of pain, though of course such investigation can discover interesting and important facts about pain.

Above, I said that concepts are crucially important because they define the topic that we are investigating. Anyone who interprets the correlation between pain and C-fiber stimulation as evidence that pain = C-fiber stimulation is straying from our concept, and hence simply changing the topic. The topic we're investigating, pain, is defined by our concept **pain;** and according to that concept, pain has no hidden essence.

But why not simply change the topic, and claim that nothing corresponds to our original concept **pain,** because every mental state has a hidden physical essence? The problem with this move is that we can still ask why we should accept the claim that pain = C-fiber stimulation. In the case of other identities, such as water = $H_2O$, there is a simple answer: You conceptualize water as having a hidden essence, and empirical investigation has discovered that $H_2O$ is that hidden essence. Because there is no parallel justification for "pain = C-fiber stimulation," we have no reason to accept that identity claim.

Arguably, this distinctive feature of our pain concept—that, as we conceptualize pain, the appearance of pain *is* its reality—is possessed only by mental concepts. For our concepts of nonmental things do attribute a gap between whether the thing appears to satisfy the concept and whether it actually does so. If this is correct, our argument for dualism cannot be applied to anything that is not mental.

## 6. BUT WHAT ABOUT MENTAL CAUSATION?

The previous section discussed a physicalist objection to the method used in the Disembodiment Argument. However, a physicalist might instead criticize the *conclusion* of that argument, as follows:

> The Disembodiment Argument does provide *some* reason to think that disembodied pain is possible. But we should not embrace this conclusion until we carefully examine its consequences. And in fact the conclusion has one consequence that is utterly unacceptable: if dualism is true, then our mental states do not truly cause our bodily movements. That is, dualism leads to *epiphenomenalism,* the claim that the mental has no physical effects. But epiphenomenalism is repugnant.[12] So even if we are not sure quite where the argument goes wrong, it must go wrong somewhere.

Leading arguments for physicalism rest on the idea that accepting the identity thesis is the only way to preserve mental causation. But only a very strong version of the identity thesis will salvage mental causation as intended; and that version of the thesis faces problems that are as serious as the worry about epiphenomenalism. Or so I will argue.

The identity thesis is usually motivated by the following idea. If we want to explain why I leaped out of my chair (a physical event), we need not invoke anything other than previous physical events: I sat on a thumb tack, and this caused (via a train of other physical events) C-fiber stimulation, which then caused my leap out of the chair. To say that such an explanation requires us to invoke a mental state like pain *in addition* to C-fiber stimulation would be to deny that physics is complete. But all of our evidence is that physics *is* complete: We have never encountered a case where we were *forced* to go beyond the realm of the physical to explain a physical event. Now if physics is complete, then citing physical events will suffice to explain my leaping out of the chair. We need not mention pain in this explanation. So *if* pain causally contributes to my leaping from the chair, then pain must be physical—that is, it must be *identical to* a physical state such as C-fiber stimulation.

There are various objections that could be made to this argument. To my mind, the most promising is this: The nature of causation, and what it means to say that one event caused another, is far from clear. For example, David Hume argued that the best we can expect, in attempting to explain why an event occurred, is to identify a regularity: *This type of event is regularly preceded by that type of event.* But then why not say that *suddenly leaping out of one's chair* is regularly preceded by *feeling pain*? The physicalist will claim that there is also a physical event that regularly precedes such leaping, and so the mental event is superfluous. However, this response assumes that, in a competition between mental and physical causes, the physical cause will always win out. (Why not say that it is the physical event that is superfluous?) This assumption would be justified if we had some *deeper* account of how physical causation occurs, one that favored physical-to-physical causation over mental-to-physical causation. But there is no accepted understanding of how causation occurs; and contemporary Humeans believe that there is no deeper *fact* about how causation occurs, because causal statements merely report regularities. The bottom line is this: Physical causation is largely a mystery, and so we should be hesitant to use our limited understanding of physical causation to rule out the possibility of nonphysical causation. The argument that dualism commits us to epiphenomenalism is far from conclusive.

But even if you think that the identity thesis better accommodates mental causation, it faces another problem, sometimes called the *problem of chauvinism*. If pain = C-fiber stimulation, then creatures whose physical structure differs significantly from ours cannot feel pain. In other words, the identity thesis is chauvinistic, because it identifies pain with a physical state that may be specific to creatures on Earth.

To see the problem, suppose that we encounter an alien civilization that seems very similar to ours. In this civilization, legislative debate is often reduced to partisan squabbles. Its members spend their leisure time in a range of activities, from hiking to watching reality TV. It seems easy to imagine that aliens whose activities were so similar to ours could nonetheless differ physiologically from humans. Perhaps their planet does not have the abundance of $H_2O$ and oxygen that Earth has, and so their physical and neural constitution is very different from ours. Even so, it seems entirely conceivable that such creatures feel pain. (We can suppose that some of these aliens are in hospitals, recovering from surgery.) But if pain *is just* C-fiber stimulation, then no creature who lacked C-fibers *could possibly* feel pain. The identity thesis does seem to be objectionably chauvinistic.

To my mind, it is highly implausible that the capacity for pain requires a physical constitution like ours. Remember, what is at issue here is not the *likelihood* that there are alien creatures who feel pain; it is the sheer *possibility* of this scenario. And it seems incredible that pain *couldn't possibly* be experienced by creatures who lacked C-fibers.

I have argued that, while the concern about whether dualism can do justice to mental causation is legitimate, the reasoning to show that dualism commits us to epiphenomenalism is open to question. Accepting the identity thesis obviously commits us to chauvinism, but it is not entirely clear that accepting dualism commits us to epiphenomenalism. And chauvinism is at least as repugnant as epiphenomenalism.

Some physicalists have responded to the chauvinism problem by retreating from the simple version of the identity thesis. In its simple version, the identity thesis claims that each type of mental state is identical to some type of physical state. The retreat from this simple version claims that pain *in humans* is identical to C-fiber stimulation; pain *in aliens* may be identical to some other physical state.[13] This move does avoid the chauvinism problem. But the retreat from the simple identity thesis means that we cannot explain such seemingly obvious causal generalizations about pain as "being in pain causes one to urgently try to change one's situation." For there is no single property that answers to "being in pain"; there is *pain-in-humans,* and *pain-in-aliens,* but on the proposal being considered, these are completely different properties. Because this modification of the identity thesis prevents us from allowing for familiar causal generalizations, it limits the alleged causal benefits of physicalism.

Until this point, I have been concerned solely with "identity" versions of physicalism. But in the face of the difficulties I have described, some physicalists adopt a weaker position, claiming that the relations between physical and mental states fall short of identity. Unfortunately, this weaker, "nonreductive" brand of physicalism faces precisely the same worries about epiphenomenalism that dualism allegedly faces. For the epiphenomenalism worry stems from the claim that pain ≠ C-fiber stimulation. So long as my pain isn't identical to the firing of my C-fibers, then we can always ask *which* of these factors caused me to leap out of the chair. Was it the pain, or was it the C-fiber stimulation? The danger is that the physical factor will fully explain my leap, and thus the mental factor will be superfluous.[14] The benefit of the identity thesis is that it blocks such questions. (Compare: Because Superman is identical to Clark Kent, it makes no sense to ask whether it was Superman *or* Clark Kent who stepped out of the phone booth.) Because avoiding epiphenomenalism is the chief consideration in favor of physicalism, these weaker physicalist positions seem unmotivated. Finally, it's worth noting that these weaker brands of physicalism are just as vulnerable to the Disembodiment Argument, for even the weakest brand of physicalism must hold that you could not feel the pinch you're feeling right now if you were disembodied.

Let me sum up the results of this section. According to physicalists, dualism implies that mental events, such as thoughts and sensations, never have physical effects. Many physicalists claim that the only way to avoid this "repugnant" epiphenomenalism is to accept the identity thesis. In response, I have outlined an objectionable consequence of the identity thesis: that those with different physical constitutions could not possibly experience pain or any other sensation that we experience. This chauvinistic result is at least as worrisome as epiphenomenalism. And the simple identity thesis is patently chauvinistic, while it is less clear that dualism leads to epiphenomenalism. Chauvinism can be avoided by modifying the identity thesis, but this modification sacrifices much of the alleged causal benefits of the identity thesis.

## 7. BUT ISN'T DUALISM *SPOOKY?*

Despite all this, there may be a lingering sense that dualism is just plain weird, or *spooky.*

But is dualism any spookier than physicalism? Bertrand Russell observed that those who accept the findings of modern science are hardly in a position to accuse dualists of spookiness.

> The plain man thinks that material objects must certainly exist, since they are evident to the senses. Whatever else may be doubted, it is certain that anything you can bump into must be real; this is the plain man's metaphysic. This is all very well, but the physicist comes along and shows that you never bump into anything: even when you run your hand along a stone wall, you do not really touch it. When you think you touch a thing, there are certain electrons and protons, forming part of your body, which are attracted and repelled by certain electrons and protons in the thing you think you are touching, but there is no actual contact. . . . The electrons and protons themselves, however, are only crude first approximations, a way of collecting into a bundle either trains of waves or the statistical probabilities of various different kinds of events. Thus matter has become altogether too ghostly to be used as an adequate stick with which to beat the mind.[15]

Russell's point is that commitments of physical science, which is unquestionably naturalistic, are just as spooky or "ghostly" as dualism. And Russell was writing in 1935; subsequent advances in physics have made the physical realm appear all the more exotic. Contemporary physicists do not agree on the basic structure of the world, but the entities posited by relatively mainstream physical theories—vibrating strings, basic particles subject to quantum indeterminacy—seem spooky enough.

Surely, dualism does not *spookify* our overall picture of the world. That picture was already plenty spooky, due to the progress of physics itself. So there is no reason to hold that dualism is spooky, or that it conflicts with a broadly scientific, naturalistic picture of reality.

## Conclusion

Most contemporary thinkers believe that minds are part of the natural order, and that scientific research can yield important information about how the mind works. Naturalistic dualists agree. And dualism is not undermined by empirical evidence, because empirical evidence reveals only correlations. Moreover, dualists can accept causal explanations of these correlations (e.g., the correlation between taking aspirin and pain reduction is explained by the fact that aspirin suppresses the biochemicals responsible for activating C-fibers).

At the outset of this essay, I noted that the dispute between physicalists and dualists can be interpreted as a disagreement as to what kinds of data there are about the nature of mind, and what kind of theory will best explain those data. The thought experiment at the center of the Disembodiment Argument provides data that favor dualism: We seem able to conceive of disembodied pain. Given that our concept of pain appears to be sufficiently comprehensive for use in a conceivability test, the proper conclusion is that pain could be present in a being that lacked physical features. This means that dualism is true.

Physicalists will discount the importance of data generated by conceivability tests. But these data are essential to defining the topic at hand, whether that topic is bachelors, water, or pain. So any claim that clashes with these data diverges from our original topic, and should therefore be rejected. The claim that "pain = C-fiber stimulation" clashes with the data generated by our conceivability test. It thus diverges from our original topic—pain, as defined by our concept **pain**—and hence we should reject it.

Any naturalist worth her salt will follow the evidence where it leads. And in this case, the evidence leads to dualism.

## NOTES

1. My development of this argument most closely parallels Saul Kripke's argument in Lecture III of his book *Naming and Necessity* (Cambridge, MA: Harvard University Press, 1980). The other leading contemporary arguments for dualism are also naturalistic: Frank Jackson's Knowledge Argument, given in "The Qualia Problem," in this volume; and David Chalmers' Zombie Argument, given in Chapter 4 of his book *The Conscious Mind* (Oxford: Oxford University Press, 1996). Some of the ideas in this essay borrow from these other arguments as well.
2. This is a *type-identity* thesis: it identifies a *type* of mental state with a *type* of physical state. For simplicity, I will focus on type-identities. But my argument also challenges the thesis that every *particular* (or "token") mental state, such as the pain I'm feeling right now, is identical to some *particular* ("token") physical state. This latter claim is known as a *token-identity* thesis. Unlike the type-identity thesis, it allows that two instances of a single mental type (such as pain) can belong to different physical types. This distinction will surface briefly in Section 6.
3. Some philosophers believe that conceivability arguments in this direction don't succeed in undermining physicalism, since my ability to conceive of disembodied pain shows only that such a pain *could* be disembodied, not that my pain is actually distinct from my body. But we can sidestep this objection by focusing, in the thought experiment, on the idea that *this very pain* could be disembodied.
4. Of course, empirical evidence can tell us that a certain scenario is *possible*. If we observed that pain occurred in the absence of C-fiber stimulation, we would of course conclude that this was possible. So it might seem that this type of empirical observation could support dualism. However, even this observation would not settle the issue. For the physicalist will simply take this as evidence that we must look elsewhere to find the physical state identical to pain. Unless we have empirical evidence of a pain that is unaccompanied by *any* physical state—which seems highly unlikely—the physicalist can always hold out for the discovery of a physical state that does perfectly correlate with pain. I will assume, for the sake of argument, that there is a physical state that perfectly correlates with pain, and I will follow standard practice in speaking as if C-fiber stimulation is this state.
5. This means that it applies both to identities like "pain = C-fiber stimulation" and to the claim that every particular pain is identical to *some* physical state or other. That is, it applies to both type-identity and token-identity versions of physicalism. (These versions were distinguished in note 3.)
6. In his version of the argument, Descartes doesn't distinguish pains from thoughts more generally.
7. David Papineau proposes that we understand the physical as "the inanimate." See Papineau, "*Thinking about Consciousness.* Oxford University Press, 2002. Barbara Montero proposes that we understand it as "the nonmental." See "The Body Problem," *Noûs* 33 (1999), pp. 183–200.
8. This should be qualified a bit, for purely mental entities may share temporal features with sticks and stones, e.g., existing on a Tuesday. And of course they may share necessary features like "being such that $2+2=4$." So the issue is whether you can conceive of experiencing *this very pain* while sharing no contingent, nontemporal features with inanimate, nonmental objects.
9. Strictly speaking, our concept **pain** is sufficiently comprehensive only if we grasp both the essential features of pain and any features entailed by those essential features. The geometry student erred because he didn't grasp a property (the property expressed by the Pythagorean Theorem) entailed

by the essential feature of a right triangle *being a three-sided polygon with one angle equal to 90°*.

10. Christopher Hill, *Sensations: A Defense of Type Materialism* (Cambridge: Cambridge University Press, 1991), p. 127.
11. You might mistakenly believe that you're in pain if a trusted friend tells you that you are, at a time when you are steadfastly refusing to introspect your own feelings. (This is certainly an odd case, however, and seems more plausible for emotional pain than for the kind of pinch we are concerned with.) Or you might be tricked into believing that you're in pain: In a (cruel) fraternity hazing ritual, blindfolded recruits are told that they will be burnt with a cigarette in a certain spot. Ice is then applied to the spot, yielding shock rather than pain. Still, for a moment the victims react as if they were in pain, and they seem to believe that they are undergoing pain. (An alternative interpretation is that the recruits *are* in pain, but the pain has a curious origin: It is produced by the expectation of pain.)
12. The charge that epiphenomenalism is "repugnant" was made by David Lewis in "What Experience Teaches." This article appeared in W. Lycan, ed., *Mind and Cognition* (Oxford: Blackwell Publishing, 1990), pp. 499–519.
13. Lewis, "Mad Pain and Martian Pain," in N. Block, ed., *Readings in the Philosophy of Psychology, Vol. I.* (Harvard University Press, 1980), pp. 216–222.
14. The idea that non-reductive physicalism faces the problem of epiphenomenalism was made by Jaegwon Kim. See "The Nonreductivist's Troubles with Mental Causation," reprinted as Chapter 17 of Kim's book *Supervenience and Mind* (Cambridge: Cambridge University Press, 1993).
15. Russell, "What Is the Soul?" from his book *In Praise of Idleness and Other Essays* (NY: W. W. Norton, 1935).

# The Mind Is the Brain

PETER CARRUTHERS

Peter Carruthers works mainly in the areas of epistemology and the philosophy of mind and language. He teaches at the University of Maryland.

## I. MIND/BRAIN IDENTITY

...Even if descriptions of conscious experiences are logically independent of all descriptions of physical states (as the cartesian conception implies) it may in fact be the case that those descriptions are descriptions of the very same things. This is just what the thesis of mind/brain identity affirms. It holds that just as a particular cloud is, as a matter of fact, a great many water droplets suspended close together in the atmosphere; and just as a particular flash of lightning is, as a matter of fact, a certain sort of discharge of electrical energy; so a pain or a thought is (is identical with) some state of the brain or central nervous system.

The identity-thesis is a version of strong materialism: it holds that all mental states and events are in fact physical states and events. But it is not, like behaviourism and functionalism, a thesis about meaning: it does not claim that words such as 'pain' and 'after-image' may be analysed or defined in terms of descriptions of brain-processes. (This would be manifestly absurd.) Rather, it is a contingent thesis about the things in the world which our words refer to: it holds that the ways of thinking represented by our terms for conscious states, and the ways of thinking represented by some of our terms for brain-states, are in fact different ways of thinking of the very same (physical) states and events. So 'pain' does not mean 'such-and-such a stimulation of the neural fibres' (just as 'lightning' does not mean 'such-and-such a discharge of electricity'); yet for all that, the two terms in fact refer to the very same thing....

### (A) An Argument for the Identity-Thesis

...We believe very firmly that some mental states and events are causally necessary for the occurrence of some physical ones. For example, I believe that if I had not been conscious of a pain in my foot (mental event), I should not have gone to the doctor (physical event). My awareness of the pain was, I believe, a causally-necessary condition of my later visit to the doctor. But as we also noted, it seems most unlikely that we shall ever need to advert to anything other than physical-physical causality when we investigate the detailed causal nexus behind any given physical event. On the contrary, it seems likely that there will always be physical events providing us with a sufficient causal explanation of any particular bodily movement. For example, as we trace the causes of my legs moving me in the direction of the doctor's surgery, through events in the muscles of my legs and feet, through events in the nerves of my spinal column, into events in the cells of my brain, it seems most unlikely that the chain of physical causation will eventually run out. So it is unlikely that we shall be forced to appeal to any non-physical event in order to provide a satisfactory explanation of my visit to the surgery.

Now the only way in which we can hold on to both beliefs—the belief that some mental events are causally necessary for the occurrence of some physical ones, and the belief that it is unnecessary to appeal to anything other than physical events in providing causal explanations of other physical events—is by believing that some mental events *are* physical ones. Then

From Peter Carruthers, *Introducing Persons: An Introduction to the Philosophy of the Mind* (London: Croom Helm, 1986), Ch. 5 (ISBN 0203005732). Reprinted by permission of Taylor & Francis Books Ltd.

somewhere in the chain of physical causes of my visit to the doctor there will be a brain event which is (is identical with) my awareness of a sensation of pain.

This argument for the general truth of the mind/brain identity-thesis may be summarised as follows.

(1) Some conscious states and events are causally necessary for the occurrence of some physical ones.

(2) In a completed neuro-physiological science there will be no need to advert to anything other than physical-physical causality.

(C) So some conscious states and events are (are identical with) physical (brain) states and events.

The argument is valid. And although its conclusion only claims that some conscious states are physical, it can easily be developed in such a way as to entail the stronger conclusion, that all are. For almost every kind of conscious state can sometimes be causally necessary for a physical one. Sometimes a particular bodily movement would not have taken place if: I had not made a particular decision; I had not thought a particular thought; I had not been aware of a particular sensation; I had not had a particular after-image; and so on. Then since it seems extremely unlikely that some conscious states are physical while some are not, it follows that all are.

Premiss (1) forms an important part of our common-sense view of ourselves and the world. We believe that conscious processes can make a difference to the world. Indeed as we saw in section 2.iv, we also believe the stronger thesis that conscious events form part of the true causal explanations of many physical events. Then the only way in which we can hold on to this belief, while denying the identity-thesis, is by denying premiss (2). We would have to deny that all physical events have purely physical causes.

Yet premiss (2) forms an important part of our scientific worldview. The more science progresses, the more likely it seems that all physical events will ultimately be explicable in purely physical terms. On the basis of what we know already, it would be quite extraordinary if it were to turn out that a physical event, such as one particular brain-cell firing off an electro-chemical impulse to another, sometimes has no physical cause. It would be even more extraordinary if this event were to prove to be, not random, but caused by something nonphysical. The existence of nonphysical causes of physical events would require us to recognise whole new species of causal relations and causal laws.

Given its validity and the strength of its premises, the argument above could reasonably be taken as a proof of the identity-thesis, were it not for the myriad objections which can be raised against that thesis. In later sections we shall consider a number of them, many of which involve apparent breaches of Leibniz's Law ('identical things share identical properties'). Despite the strength of the argument in its support, the identity-thesis will only be rationally acceptable if we can reply adequately to each of the objections....

## II. PRELIMINARY DIFFICULTIES

In the last section we presented an argument in support of the identity-thesis which would have been convincing if considered purely on its own terms. Over the next three sections we shall reply to all the main objections which have been raised against that thesis, beginning with some of the less serious ones. They will get more serious as we go along.

### (A) Certainty

Our first objection derives from Descartes, who deployed a similar argument in support of strong dualism. It runs as follows:

(1) I may be absolutely certain of my own experiences, when I have them.

(2) I cannot have the same degree of certainty about the existence of any physical state, including my own brain-states.

(C) So (by Leibniz's Law) my conscious experiences are not in fact identical with brain-states.

Although both the premises in this argument are true, the argument itself commits a fallacy (is invalid). For... Leibniz's Law only operates in contexts which are not intentional. And it is obvious that the context created by the phrase 'X is certain that...' is an intentional one.

For example, the police may be certain that Mr. Hyde is the murderer, while they have no inkling that Dr Jekyll is the murderer, despite the fact that Jekyll and Hyde are one and the same man. And Oedipus may be certain that Jocasta loves him without believing that his mother loves him, despite the fact that Jocasta is his mother. So from the fact that I have complete certainty about my own conscious states without having certainty about my own brain-states, it does not follow that my conscious states are not brain-states. For just as one and the same woman may be presented to Oedipus in two different guises—as Jocasta, and as his mother—so perhaps one and the same brain-state may be presented to me under two different aspects: in a third-person way (as a brain-state), and via the qualitative feel of what it is like to be in that state.

## (B) Privacy

This second argument is a variation on the first. It runs as follows:

(1) Conscious states are private to the person who has them.

(2) Brain-states are not private: like any other physical state, they form part of the public realm.

(C) So (by Leibniz's Law) conscious states are not in fact identical with brain-states.

However, the term 'private' is ambiguous: something can be private in respect of knowledge (only I can know of it), or it can be private in respect of ownership (only I can possess it). Taken in the first way, the argument is the same as that above, and commits the same fallacy. But taken in the second way, premiss (2) is false.

It is true that only I can 'own' my conscious states: no one else can feel my pain, or think my thought. But it is equally true in this sense that only I can own my brain-states. For no one else can possess my brain-state either. Any brain-state which they have will be, necessarily, their own brain-state, not mine. Conscious states are certainly not unique in respect of privacy of ownership. The same is true of blushes and sneezes as well as brain-states: no one else can blush my blush or sneeze my sneeze. Indeed it seems that in general the identity-conditions for states and events are tied to the identities of the subjects who possess them.

## (C) Value

A thought can be wicked. A desire can be admirable. But no brain-state can be either wicked or admirable. We may therefore argue as follows:

(1) Conscious states are subject to norms: they can be good or bad, wicked or admirable.

(2) No purely physical states are subject to norms: no brain-state can be either wicked or admirable.

(C) So (by Leibniz's Law) conscious states are not identical with brain-states.

We might immediately be inclined to quarrel with premiss (2). For can a particular stabbing not be wicked? And what is a stabbing if not a physical event? But it may be replied that it is not the stabbing itself—considered merely as a physical event—which is wicked, but rather the intention behind it. And in general, physical states and events are only subject to norms if they are intentional (or at least foreseen).

This reply is sufficient to save the truth of premiss (2), but at the cost of revealing the same fallacy in the argument as was involved in the argument from certainty. For if it is only things which are intended (or foreseen) which can be wicked, then the context created by '...is wicked' will be an intentional one. For example, if the fact that it is wicked of Mary to have a particular desire implies that she either intentionally adopted that desire, or at least foresaw that she would continue to possess it if she took no steps to eradicate it, then it is no objection to the identity-thesis that it is, on the other hand, not wicked of her to be in such-and-such a brain-state. For you can foresee E (that you will marry Jocasta) without foreseeing F (that you will marry your mother), even though E is identical with F. And certainly she neither intended nor foresaw that she should be in that particular brain-state.

## (D) Colour

An after-image can be green, a pain can be sharp and piercing. But it is hardly likely that any brain-state will be either green or sharp and piercing. There will then be many arguments which take the following sort of form:

(1) I am experiencing a fading green after-image.

(2) No brain-states are green.

(C) So (by Leibniz's Law) my after-image is not identical with any brain-state.

One mistake in this argument is that it treats my after-image as though it were a particular individual thing, having greenness as a property. Now it is true that the sentence 'I experience a green after-image' has the same grammatical form as the sentence 'I pick up a green book', which creates the impression that greenness is a property of the after-image in just the same way that it is a property of the book. But this impression is misleading. For the book in question might have had some other colour, while remaining the numerically-same book. But can we make any sense of the idea that the very same after-image which I have now, might have been red?

Of course what is true, is that I might now have been experiencing a red after-image rather than a green one. But can we make sense of the idea that it might have been this very same after-image (which happens to be green) which would then have been red? I suggest not. Rather, the greenness is essential to the identity of that particular after-image. The reason being that it is a mistake to treat the fading after-image as if it were a kind of object or individual thing. It is rather an event, or happening. And the greenness is in fact part of the event of experiencing-a-fading-green-after-image, as opposed to being a property *of* it.

This reply on its own is not sufficient to rebut the argument. For it seems certain that greenness is not part of the event of undergoing-such-and-such-a-change-in-brain-state. So how can that event be identical with the event of experiencing-a-fading-green-after-image, if greenness really is part of the latter event? For must not identical events have identical parts? For example, if the battle of Waterloo is (is identical with) the battle which lost Napoleon the war, then if a particular cavalry charge is part of the battle of Waterloo, it must also be part of the battle which lost Napoleon the war. For they are the very same battle (the very same event).

The second mistake in the argument is to think that an experience can be green, or a conscious event have greenness as one of its parts, in anything like the same sense that a physical object can be green, or a physical event have greenness as one of its parts. Experiences are not literally green in the way that grass is literally green. Rather, the 'greenness' of my green after-image consists in my having an experience which is like the experience of seeing a green patch (and it is the patch which is green, not the experience). Then if to have a green after-image is to be in state like the state one is in when one sees a green patch, and if the possession of that after-image is identical with some brain-state, it will indeed follow that the brain-state too is like the state one is in when one sees a green patch. But there is no difficulty about this. For the latter state too will be identical with some brain-state. And it seems entirely plausible that there should be some resemblance between the two brain-states.

The point can be put like this: green after-images are experiences *of* green, rather than things (or events) which *are* (or which contain) green. A green after-image is, as it were, an event of being under-the-impression-that-one-is-seeing-a-green-patch. If this is so, then the after-image can be identical with a brain-state without breaching Leibniz's Law, so long as the brain-state too can in this sense be 'of' green. If green after-images represent green, rather than literally being green, then there will be no difficulty here so long as it is possible for brain-states to represent. This question will be pursued below.

## (E) Felt Quality

This objection arises out of the last one. Even if after-images are not literally coloured, still they do literally have phenomenal (felt) characteristics, which we describe by means of the colour-terms ('sensation of red', 'sensation of green', etc.). For example there is the qualitative 'feel' which is common to the experiences of having a green after-image and seeing green grass. Indeed all experiences have distinctive qualitative feels, which we are each of us aware of in our own case. But can any brain-state have a distinctive feel? For example, think of a particular brain-state—say one group of brain cells firing off impulses to another group—and ask yourself 'What is the distinctive feel of this event?' It is hard even to get a grip on the question. How can any brain-event feel like a sensation of red, for example? Surely only another sensation can, in the required sense, *feel like* a sensation of red.

The argument sketched above may be summarised as follows:

(1) All experiences have distinctive felt qualities.

(2) Brain-states do not have distinctive felt qualities.

(C) So (by Leibniz's Law) experiences are not in fact identical with brain-states.

Once again we have been misled by grammatical form, this time into thinking of the qualitative feel of an experience as being genuinely a property of it. (Thus we say 'The pain has a distinctive feel' just as we say 'The car has a distinctive colour'.) It would be more accurate to say that the experience itself *is* (is identical with) a distinctive qualitative feel. The experience of pain is not different from the feel of pain. Rather they are one and the same. So it is entirely irrelevant whether or not a brain-state can possess (have as a property) a particular qualitative feel. Since the experience itself is identical with its qualitative feel, the real question is whether or not a brain-state, too, can be identical with a qualitative feel. And we have as yet been given no reason for thinking that this cannot be so.

## (F) Complete Knowledge

Someone could know all physical facts about the brain without knowing what the different experiences feel like. Thus no amount of information about brain-processes will ever allow a congenitally blind person to know what a sensation of red feels like. But if there is information about feelings which would not be conveyed by any amount of information about the brain, then feelings cannot themselves be brain-states. The argument is as follows:

(1) Complete knowledge of physical states would not imply knowledge of what experiences feel like.

(2) If experiences were physical states, then complete knowledge of the physical would imply complete knowledge of experiences.

(C) So experiences are not physical states.

Although this argument, like the argument from certainty, involves an intentional term (the context created by the phrase 'X knows that...' being an intentional one) it does not commit the same fallacy. This is because the premises speak of complete knowledge, knowledge from all points of view. Oedipus certainly could not have complete knowledge of Jocasta without knowing that she is his mother. (So if he does know everything about her, but does not know that she is his mother, then she is *not* his mother.)

Both of the premises in the above argument are true. But the argument is invalid, because of a shift in the meaning of the term 'knowledge'. Knowing what an experience feels like is not propositional (factual) knowledge, but rather practical (recognitional) knowledge. It is a matter of knowing how to do something rather than knowing that something is the case. Knowing what a sensation of red feels like is a matter of being able to recognise it when you have one: it is a practical skill. Now of course no amount of factual information will necessarily give you a practical skill. As the name suggests, this will generally require practice. So the sense in which premiss (1) is true is this: no amount of factual knowledge about the brain will necessarily enable you to recognise your experiences when you have them.

Premiss (2), on the other hand, is only true if restricted to factual knowledge (practical knowledge being excluded). If Jocasta is Oedipus's mother, then if he has complete knowledge of (all facts about) Jocasta, he must have complete knowledge of his mother. But it does not follow that he must be capable of recognising her when he sees her. He may have been told every fact that there is to know about his mother (the exact length of her nose, the colour of her eyes, the number and colour of hairs on her head, and so on) and yet still not be able to recognise her. This will depend upon how good he is at translating factual information into visual imagery. If he is particularly bad at it, he may have to identify his mother by ticking-off all the facts piece-meal ('length of nose . . . yes; colour of eyes . . . yes;' and so on).

It is thus entirely consistent with the identity-thesis that you cannot teach a blind person what sensations of red are like by telling them facts about the brain. Although sensations are brain-states, knowing what they are like is a matter of being able to recognise them ('straight off') when you have them. And it is hardly surprising that people cannot acquire such a recognitional skill by being given the bare facts; they will of course need practise in having those states.

## III. FURTHER DIFFICULTIES

In this section we shall consider two of the arguments we originally presented in support of weak dualism (and hence, by implication, against the thesis of mind/brain identity). These are the arguments from intentionality, and from spatial position.

### (A) Intentionality

Recall the claim that conscious states are unique in being intentional. Our argument was as follows:

(1) Conscious states are intentional, or representational, states.

(2) No merely physical state (e.g. of the brain) can be intentional in its own right.

(C) So (by Leibniz's Law) conscious states are not identical with brain-states.

This argument is valid, and premiss (1) is obviously true. So everything turns on the acceptability of premiss (2).

There is a general philosophical problem about representation. Much of the philosophy of language is concerned with the question: how is it possible for anything to represent—or be *about*—anything else? So it may be that the difficulty we experience in trying to understand how an arrangement of cellular connections could represent anything, is merely a specific instance of the general difficulty of understanding how anything at all can represent anything. In any case the problem of representation is not made any *less* of a problem by supposing that the states which do the representing are non-physical ones.

Perhaps the claim that physical states can be representations-in-their-own-right cannot be made entirely convincing in the absence of a solution to the general problem of representation. Nevertheless we can at least get an inkling of how intentionality can be embodied in a physical system, in advance of a solution to that problem. For by looking at systems which are, manifestly, purely physical—e.g. computers and computer-controlled machines—we can begin to see how they can display some of the distinctive features of intentional states. If we can see the beginnings of intentionality embodied in a physical system such as a computer, then there is no reason in principle why full-blown intentionality (beliefs, desires and the rest) should not be embodied in the biological computer which is the human brain.

One distinctive feature of intentional states is that they represent things in one way rather than another. For a crude analogue of this, imagine a computer linked to a video-camera and mechanical arm. The computer is programmed to scan the input from the camera, and to grab with its arm any yellow object. In order for the grabbing-operation to be successful it must also be able to interpret from the input the shapes, sizes and spatial positions of those objects. But the computer does not select objects on the basis of their shape or size, but only on the basis of their colour.

Now suppose that the only yellow objects which are ever presented to the machine are in fact lemons, its purpose being to select lemons from a passing array of fruit. Of course lemons do also have a characteristic shape, but the computer is indifferent with respect to shape. It initiates a grabbing motion only in response to the yellow colour. Then there is almost a sense in which the machine might be said to desire the yellow objects which it grabs, but not the lemon-shaped objects, even though the yellow objects are all lemon-shaped.

Of course I do not want to say that such a machine would literally have a desire for yellow objects. Though quite what is missing here, which would be present in the case of a genuine desire, is not easy to see. Perhaps we can only make sense of something having a particular desire against a wider background, a network of other desires and beliefs. Or perhaps only a being which is alive, which has needs (and which may consequently be said to have 'a good') can have desires. The important point for our purposes here is that we have found an analogue for the intentionality of desire in the concept of 'differential response'. Just as Oedipus will respond differently to one and the same woman presented to him now as Jocasta, now as his mother; so the machine will respond differently to one and the same bit of fruit presented to it now as a yellow thing (its shape being obscured), now as a lemon-shaped thing (its colour being obscured).

The other distinctive feature of intentional states, is that they can be directed at non-existent objects. And it is apt to seem unintelligible how any physical system could do this. Here again my strategy is to construct, by way of reply, a crude physical analogue for this aspect of the intentionality of desire. Thus consider the sort of behaviour which might be displayed by a Cruise missile. It is programmed to take photographs of the terrain beneath it at various points along its route, to scan those photographs for landmarks in order to check its position, and adjust its direction accordingly. Now suppose that as a result of an error, it is programmed to find a distinctively-shaped lake at a particular point on its route, but that no such lake exists. As a result, the missile circles round and around the area, until finally it runs out of fuel and crashes. Here we might almost say 'The missile was searching for a lake which did not exist'.

Note that the intentionality displayed in the Cruise missile's 'desire' is not merely derivative from the thoughts and intentions of the computer programer. True enough, that 'desire' was caused to exist by the programer. But its intentionality—its directedness on a non-existent object—is actually displayed in the behaviour of the missile itself. For it has entered a cycle of behaviour which we know will only be terminated if it succeeds in photographing a lake with a particular distinctive shape; but we also know that no such lake exists.

I conclude that there is no reason in principle why a merely-physical system should not display the various features characteristic of intentional states. So we have been given no reason for supposing that beliefs and desires are not themselves physical (brain) states.

## (B) Spatial Position

Recall from [an earlier] section the following argument:

(1) All brain-states must occupy some particular position in space.

(2) It is nonsense (meaningless) to attribute any particular spatial position to a state of consciousness.

(C) So (by Leibniz's Law) conscious states cannot be identical with brain-states.

This argument is valid. Premiss (1) is obviously true. So everything depends upon the truth of premiss (2). I shall not waste time quibbling that some conscious states (e.g. pains) are apparently attributed spatial positions. For the identity-thesis extends to all conscious states without exception. And in any case it is unlikely that some conscious states are identical with brain-states and some not. I shall focus on the hardest case for the identity-theorist; namely, thoughts.

An identity-theorist might be tempted to respond to the above argument by conceding that our ordinary concept of thought makes attributions of spatial position to them nonsensical, but by rejecting that ordinary conception as mistaken. They may insist that every thought (properly conceived of) does in fact have a place, namely the place of its identical brain-state. But for them to take this line would be a mistake. For then the thesis of mind/brain identity would no longer represent a contingent discovery, but would be something which we have stipulated as true through a change of meaning.

In fact we should be entitled to reply to the identity-theorist as follows. 'If you mean the word "thought" as we usually do, then your thesis is false; indeed necessarily false. But if, on the other hand, you wish to give the word a different meaning for your own special purposes, then you are perfectly entitled to do so. But don't pretend that you have made a momentous discovery, or that you are saying anything which conflicts with what the weak dualist believes. All you have done is given a new definition.' (It is rather as if someone were to give new definitions of the words 'red' and 'green', in such a way that it then makes sense to ascribe those words to numbers; and were then to announce, as if they had discovered something terribly important, 'Contrary to what has always been believed, every even number is red and every odd one green.')

A more promising strategy for the identity-theorist would be to suggest that we have again been misled by the grammatical form of phrases like 'my thought of my mother' into conceiving of a thought as if it were a special kind of individual thing or object. For obviously, if a thought were really a physical object like a grain of sand or a brain-cell, then it would have to occupy some precise position in space. So perhaps we need to be reminded that a thought is an action, and an action is a species of event (a 'happening'). And then the general question becomes: what are the criteria for attributing spatial positions to events?

Often the place of an event can be pinned down no more precisely than the place of the subject of that event. And in such cases requests for more precise specifications will seem nonsensical. Thus the place of the event of Mary-growing-older is wherever Mary is. And the question 'Is the event of Mary-growing-older taking place two inches behind her right eye?' seems just as nonsensical as the parallel question about the event of Mary-thinking-of-her-mother. Yet for all that the process of ageing is a purely physical one.

Now we only need to be reminded of these facts to realise that we do in fact attribute spatial positions to thoughts; namely: whenever we say where the thinker of that thought is. And the fact that requests for more detailed specifications of the spatial positions of thoughts sound nonsensical, need not show that thoughts themselves are nonphysical. Thinking, like ageing, may be a physical process whose subject is the whole human being.

However, the position of an event is not always simply the position of its subject. An event can also take place in part of its subject. Thus the position of Mary's-left-big-toe-turning-blue is not simply wherever Mary is. It is, more precisely, wherever her left foot is. For if Mary is lying on a river-bank with her left foot in the water, then the event takes place in the water; whereas Mary herself is not in the water.

It seems likely that the physical event which is, according to the identity-theorist, the event of Mary-thinking-of-her-mother, takes place in some particular region of her brain. So we still have a problem, if the closest we can get to the spatial position of Mary's thought is the spatial position of Mary. If the brain-event can be two inches behind her right eye, whilst it is nonsensical to describe the thought of her mother as occurring two inches behind her right eye, then the thought and the brain-event cannot be identical.

The correct way for an identity-theorist to respond, is by denying that it is nonsensical to ascribe precise spatial positions to thoughts. The only real evidence which the objector has for this claim, is that most of us would be left gaping, our minds completely blank, if asked whether Mary's thought is two inches behind her right eye. But this does not show that the question is literally meaningless. It only shows firstly, that it is not the sort of question which itself points you in the direction in which you have to look for an answer. (Contrast: 'Where is the dam cracking?' It is part of the ordinary notion of a crack, that in order to find them you have to search in specific locations.) And secondly, that we can have no idea where to look for an answer until we have acquired some further information.

Suppose you were asked 'In what specific region of her body is the event of Mary-catching-a-cold taking place?' This too would have a tendency to make your mind go blank, partly because it is no part of the ordinary concept of a cold that in order to establish whether someone has a cold you have to search in specific locations within the body. But on reflection you may realise that what you are really being asked is: 'In virtue of changes in what parts of Mary's body is it becoming true that she has a cold?' This at least is a question you can understand. But if you know nothing of viruses, or medicine generally, you may not even know what sorts of things would be relevant to the discovery of the answer. Yet when you are told that colds are viruses, and that viruses enter the body at specific locations, then you know what would constitute an answer. Note, moreover, that it would be hardly very plausible to say that the term 'a cold' had changed its meaning for you when you acquired this information.

The question about the specific location of Mary's act of thinking about her mother is essentially similar. The first step in dispelling the puzzlement which it causes is to realise that what we are in fact being asked is: 'In virtue of changes in what specific region of Mary is it becoming true that she is thinking of her mother?' The next step is to learn that each conscious event is identical with some brain-event. Then we know that in order to answer the question, we should first need to discover which brain-event is identical with Mary's thought, and then discover where that brain-event is occurring. Yet we do not need to regard our acceptance of the identity-thesis as altering the meaning of the term 'thought', any more than our acceptance that colds are viruses alters the meaning of the term 'a cold.' We may thus deny the claim made in premiss (2) of the argument above....

## Conclusion

In [the first] section we presented an argument for thinking it likely that all conscious states are identical with brain-states. Then in the sections following we have replied to all the various possible objections to this idea. Since there is good reason to believe the identity-thesis to be true, and no good reason to believe it false, the case for that thesis is rationally convincing. We should therefore embrace the thesis of mind/brain identity, and declare ourselves to be strong materialists.

Chapter 12

# The mind–body problem

## Jerry Fodor

MODERN philosophy of science has been devoted largely to the formal and systematic description of the successful practices of working scientists. The philosopher does not try to dictate how scientific inquiry and argument ought to be conducted. Instead he tries to enumerate the principles and practices that have contributed to good science. The philosopher has devoted the most attention to analyzing the methodological peculiarities of the physical sciences. The analysis has helped to clarify the nature of confirmation, the logical structure of scientific theories, the formal properties of statements that express laws and the question of whether theoretical entities actually exist.

It is only rather recently that philosophers have become seriously interested in the methodological tenets of psychology. Psychological explanations of behavior refer liberally to the mind and to states, operations and processes of the mind. The philosophical difficulty comes in stating in unambiguous language what such references imply.

Traditional philosophies of mind can be divided into two broad categories: dualist theories and materialist theories. In the dualist approach the mind is a nonphysical substance. In materialist theories the mental is not distinct from the physical; indeed, all mental states, properties, processes and operations are in principle identical with physical states, properties, processes and operations. Some materialists, known as behaviorists, maintain that all talk of mental causes can be eliminated from the language of psychology in favor of talk of environmental stimuli and behavioral responses. Other materialists, the identity theorists, contend that there are mental causes and that they are identical with neurophysiological events in the brain.

In the past 15 years a philosophy of mind called functionalism that is neither dualist nor materialist has emerged from philosophical reflection on developments in artificial intelligence, computational theory, linguistics, cybernetics and psychology. All these fields, which are collectively known as the cognitive sciences, have in common a certain level of abstraction and a concern with systems that process information. Functionalism, which seeks to provide a philosophical account of this level of abstraction, recognizes the possibility that systems as diverse as human beings, calculating machines and disembodied spirits could all have mental states.

Jerry Fodor, 'The Mind–Body Problem', *Scientific American* 244 (January 1981).

In the functionalist view the psychology of a system depends not on the stuff it is made of (living cells, metal or spiritual energy) but on how the stuff is put together. Functionalism is a difficult concept, and one way of coming to grips with it is to review the deficiencies of the dualist and materialist philosophies of mind it aims to displace.

The chief drawback of dualism is its failure to account adequately for mental causation. If the mind is nonphysical, it has no position in physical space. How, then, can a mental cause give rise to a behavioral effect that has a position in space? To put it another way, how can the nonphysical give rise to the physical without violating the laws of the conservation of mass, of energy and of momentum?

The dualist might respond that the problem of how an immaterial substance can cause physical events is not much obscurer than the problem of how one physical event can cause another. Yet there is an important difference: there are many clear cases of physical causation but not one clear case of nonphysical causation. Physical interaction is something philosophers, like all other people, have to live with. Nonphysical interaction, however, may be no more than an artifact of the immaterialist construal of the mental. Most philosophers now agree that no argument has successfully demonstrated why mindbody causation should not be regarded as a species of physical causation.

Dualism is also incompatible with the practices of working psychologists. The psychologist frequently applies the experimental methods of the physical sciences to the study of the mind. If mental processes were different in kind from physical processes, there would be no reason to expect these methods to work in the realm of the mental. In order to justify their experimental methods many psychologists urgently sought an alternative to dualism.

In the 1920's John B. Watson of Johns Hopkins University made the radical suggestion that behavior does not have mental causes. He regarded the behavior of an organism as its observable responses to stimuli, which he took to be the causes of its behavior. Over the next 30 years psychologists such as B. F. Skinner of Harvard University developed Watson's ideas into an elaborate world view in which the role of psychology was to catalogue the laws that determine causal relations between stimuli and responses. In this 'radical behaviorist' view the problem of explaining the nature of the mind-body interaction vanishes; there is no such interaction.

Radical behaviorism has always worn an air of paradox. For better or worse, the idea of mental causation is deeply ingrained in our everyday language and in our ways of understanding our fellow men and ourselves. For example, people commonly attribute behavior to beliefs, to knowledge and to expectations. Brown puts gas in his tank because he believes the car will not run without it. Jones writes not 'acheive' but 'achieve' because he knows the rule about putting *i* before *e*. Even when a behavioral response is closely tied to an environmental stimulus, mental processes often intervene. Smith carries an umbrella because the sky is cloudy, but the weather is only part of the story. There are apparently also mental links in the causal chain: observation and expectation. The clouds affect Smith's behavior only because he observes them and because they induce in him an expectation of rain.

The radical behaviorist is unmoved by appeals to such cases. He is prepared to dismiss references to mental causes, however plausible they may seem, as the residue of outworn creeds. The radical behaviorist predicts that as psychologists come to understand more about the relations between stimuli and responses they will find it increasingly possible to explain behavior without postulating mental causes.

The strongest argument against behaviorism is that psychology has not turned out this way; the opposite has happened. As psychology has matured, the framework of mental states and processes that is apparently needed to account for experimental observations has grown all the more elaborate. Particularly in the case of human behavior psychological theories satisfying the methodological tenets of radical behaviorism have proved largely sterile, as would be expected if the postulated mental processes are real and causally effective.

Nevertheless, many philosophers were initially drawn to radical behaviorism because, paradoxes and all, it seemed better than dualism. Since a psychology committed to immaterial substances was unacceptable, philosophers turned to radical behaviorism because it seemed to be the only alternative materialist philosophy of mind. The choice, as they saw it, was between radical behaviorism and ghosts.

By the early 1960's philosophers began to have doubts that dualism and radical behaviorism exhausted the possible approaches to the philosophy of mind. Since the two theories seemed unattractive, the right strategy might be to develop a materialist philosophy of mind that nonetheless allowed for mental causes. Two such philosophies emerged, one called logical behaviorism and the other called the central-state identity theory.

Logical behaviorism is a semantic theory about what mental terms mean. The basic idea is that attributing a mental state (say thirst) to an organism is the same as saying that the organism is disposed to behave in a particular way (for example to drink if there is water available). On this view every mental ascription is equivalent in meaning to an if-then statement (called a behavioral hypothetical) that expresses a behavioral disposition. For example, 'Smith is thirsty' might be taken to be equivalent to the dispositional statement. 'If there were water available, then Smith would drink some.' By definition a behavioral hypothetical includes no mental terms. The if-clause of the hypothetical speaks only of stimuli and the then-clause speaks only of behavioral responses. Since stimuli and responses are physical events, logical behaviorism is a species of materialism.

The strength of logical behaviorism is that by translating mental language into the language of stimuli and responses it provides an interpretation of psychological explanations in which behavioral effects are attributed to mental causes. Mental causation is simply the manifestation of a behavioral disposition. More precisely, mental causation is what happens when an organism has a behavioral disposition and the if-clause of the behavioral hypothetical expressing the disposition happens to be true. For example, the causal statement 'Smith drank some water because he was thirsty' might be taken to mean 'If there were water available, then Smith would drink some, and there was water available.'

I have somewhat oversimplified logical behaviorism by assuming that each mental ascription can be translated by a unique behavioral hypothetical. Actually the logical behaviorist often maintains that it takes an open-ended set (perhaps an infinite set) of behavioral hypotheticals to spell out the behavioral disposition expressed by a mental term. The mental ascription 'Smith is thirsty' might also be satisfied by the hypothetical 'If there were orange juice available, then Smith would drink some' and by a host of other hypotheticals. In any event the logical behaviorist does not usually maintain he can actually enumerate all the hypotheticals that correspond to a behavioral disposition expressing a given mental term. He only insists that in principle the meaning of any mental term can be conveyed by behavioral hypotheticals.

The way the logical behaviorist has interpreted a mental term such as thirsty is modeled after the way many philosophers have interpreted a physical disposition such as fragility. The physical disposition 'The glass is fragile' is often taken to mean something like 'If the glass were struck, then it would break.' By the same token the logical behaviorist's analysis of mental causation is similar to the received analysis of one kind of physical causation. The causal statement 'The glass broke because it was fragile' is taken to mean something like 'If the glass were struck, then it would break, and the glass was struck.'

By equating mental terms with behavioral dispositions the logical behaviorist has put mental terms on a par with the nonbehavioral dispositions of the physical sciences. That is a promising move, because the analysis of nonbehavioral dispositions is on relatively solid philosophical ground. An explanation attributing the breaking of a glass to its fragility is surely something even the staunchest materialist can accept. By arguing that mental terms are synonymous with dispositional terms, the logical behaviorist has provided something the radical behaviorist could not: a materialist account of mental causation.

Nevertheless, the analogy between mental causation as construed by the logical behaviorist and physical causation goes only so far. The logical behaviorist treats the manifestation of a disposition as the sole form of mental causation, whereas the physical sciences recognize additional kinds of causation. There is the kind of causation where one physical event causes another, as when the breaking of a glass is attributed to its having been struck. In fact, explanations that involve event-event causation are presumably more basic than dispositional explanations, because the manifestation of a disposition (the breaking of a fragile glass) always involves event-event causation and not vice versa. In the realm of the mental many examples of event-event causation involve one mental state's causing another, and for this kind of causation logical behaviorism provides no analysis. As a result the logical behaviorist is committed to the tacit and implausible assumption that psychology requires a less robust notion of causation than the physical sciences require.

Event-event causation actually seems to be quite common in the realm of the mental. Mental causes typically give rise to behavioral effects by virtue of their interaction with other mental causes. For example, having a headache causes a disposition to take aspirin only if one also has the desire to get rid of the headache, the belief that aspirin exists, the belief that taking aspirin reduces headaches and so on. Since mental states interact in generating behavior, it will be necessary to find a construal of psychological explanations that posits mental processes: causal sequences of mental events. It is this construal that logical behaviorism fails to provide.

Such considerations bring out a fundamental way in which logical behaviorism is quite similar to radical behaviorism. It is true that the logical behaviorist, unlike the radical behaviorist, acknowledges the existence of mental states. Yet since the underlying tenet of logical behaviorism is that references to mental states can be translated out of psychological explanations by employing behavioral hypotheticals, all talk of mental states and processes is in a sense heuristic. The only facts to which the behaviorist is actually committed are facts about relations between stimuli and responses. In this respect logical behaviorism is just radical behaviorism in a semantic form. Although the former theory offers a construal of mental causation, the construal is Pick-wickian. What does not really exist cannot cause anything, and the logical behaviorist, like the radical behaviorist, believes deep down that mental causes do not exist.

An alternative materialist theory of the mind to logical behaviorism is the central-state identity theory. According to this theory, mental events, states and processes are identical with neurophysiological events in the brain, and the property of being in a certain mental state (such as having a headache or believing it will rain) is identical with the property of being in a certain neurophysiological state. On this basis it is easy to make sense of the idea that a behavioral effect might sometimes have a chain of mental causes; that will be the case whenever a behavioral effect is contingent on the appropriate sequence of neurophysiological events.

The central-state identity theory acknowledges that it is possible for mental causes to interact causally without ever giving rise to any behavioral effect, as when a person thinks for a while about what he ought to do and then decides to do nothing. If mental processes are neurophysiological, they must have the causal properties of neurophysiological processes. Since neurophysiological processes are presumably physical processes, the central-state identity theory ensures that the concept of mental causation is as rich as the concept of physical causation.

The central-state identity theory provides a satisfactory account of what the mental terms in psychological explanations refer to, and so it is favored by psychologists who are dissatisfied with behaviorism. The behaviorist maintains that mental terms refer to nothing or that they refer to the parameters of stimulus-response relations. Either way the existence of mental entities is only illusory. The identity theorist, on the other hand, argues that mental terms refer to neurophysiological states. Thus he can take seriously the project of explaining behavior by appealing to its mental causes.

The chief advantage of the identity theory is that it takes the explanatory constructs of psychology at face value, which is surely something a philosophy of mind ought to do if it can. The identity theory shows how the mentalistic explanations of psychology could be not mere heuristics but literal accounts of the causal history of behavior. Moreover, since the identity theory is not a semantic thesis, it is immune to many arguments that cast in doubt logical behaviorism. A drawback of logical behaviorism is that the observation 'John has a headache' does not seem to mean the same thing as a statement of the form 'John is disposed to behave in such and such a way.' The identity theorist, however, can live with the fact that 'John has a headache' and 'John is in such and such a brain state' are not synonymous. The assertion of the identity theorist is not that these sentences mean the same thing but only that they are rendered true (or false) by the same neurophysiological phenomena.

The identity theory can be held either as a doctrine about mental particulars (John's current pain or Bill's fear of animals) or as a doctrine about mental universals, or properties (having a pain or being afraid of animals). The two doctrines, called respectively token physicalism and type physicalism, differ in strength and plausibility. Token physicalism maintains only that all the mental particulars that happen to exist are neurophysiological, whereas type physicalism makes the more sweeping assertion that all the mental particulars there could possibly be are neurophysiological. Token physicalism does not rule out the logical possibility of machines and disembodied spirits having mental properties. Type physicalism dismisses this possibility because neither machines nor disembodied spirits have neurons.

Type physicalism is not a plausible doctrine about mental properties even if token physicalism is right about mental particulars. The problem with type physicalism is that the psychological constitution of a system seems to depend not on its hardware, or physical composition, but on its software, or program. Why should the philosopher dismiss the possibility that silicon-based Martians have pains, assuming that the silicon is properly organized? And why should the philosopher rule out the possibility of machines having beliefs, assuming that the machines are correctly programmed? If it is logically possible that Martians and machines could have mental properties, then mental properties and neurophysiological processes cannot be identical, however much they may prove to be coextensive.

What it all comes down to is that there seems to be a level of abstraction at which the generalizations of psychology are most naturally pitched. This level of abstraction cuts across differences in the physical composition of the systems to which psychological generalizations apply. In the cognitive sciences, at least, the natural domain for psychological theorizing seems to be all systems that process information. The problem with type physicalism is that there are possible information-processing systems with the same psychological constitution as human beings but not the same physical organization. In principle all kinds of physically different things could have human software.

This situation calls for a relational account of mental properties that abstracts them from the physical structure of their bearers. In spite of the objections to logical behaviorism that I presented above, logical behaviorism was at least on the right track in offering a relational interpretation of mental properties: to have a headache is to be disposed to exhibit a certain pattern of relations between the stimuli one encounters and the responses one exhibits. If that is what having a headache is, however, there is no reason in principle why only heads that are physically similar to ours can ache. Indeed, according to logical behaviorism, it is a necessary truth that any system that has our stimulus-response contingencies also has our headaches.

All of this emerged 10 or 15 years ago as a nasty dilemma for the materialist program in the philosophy of mind. On the one hand the identity theorist (and not the logical behaviorist) had got right the causal character of the interactions of mind and body. On the other the logical behaviorist (and not the identity theorist) had got right the relational character of mental properties. Functionalism has apparently been able to resolve the dilemma. By stressing the distinction computer science draws between hardware and software the functionalist can make sense of both the causal and the relational character of the mental.

The intuition underlying functionalism is that what determines the psychological type to which a mental particular belongs is the causal role of the particular in the mental life of the organism. Functional individuation is differentiation with respect to causal role. A headache, for example; is identified with the type of mental state that among other things causes a disposition for taking aspirin in people who believe aspirin relieves a headache, causes a desire to rid oneself of the pain one is feeling, often causes someone who speaks English to say such things as 'I have a headache' and is brought on by overwork, eyestrain and tension. This list is presumably not complete. More will be known about the nature of a headache as psychological and physiological research discovers more about its causal role.

Functionalism construes the concept of causal role in such a way that a mental state can be defined by its causal relations to other mental states. In this respect functionalism is completely different from logical behaviorism. Another major difference is that functionalism is not a reductionist thesis. It does not foresee, even in principle, the elimination of mentalistic concepts from the explanatory apparatus of psychological theories.

The difference between functionalism and logical behaviorism is brought out by the fact that functionalism is fully compatible with token physicalism. The functionalist would not be disturbed if brain events turn out to be the only things with the functional properties that define mental states. Indeed, most functionalists fully expect it will turn out that way.

Since functionalism recognizes that mental particulars may be physical, it is compatible with the idea that mental causation is a species of physical causation. In other words, functionalism tolerates the materialist solution to the mind-body problem provided by the central-state identity theory. It is possible for the functionalist to assert both that mental properties are typically defined in terms of their relations and that interactions of mind and body are typically causal in however robust a notion of causality is required by psychological explanations. The logical behaviorist can endorse only the first assertion and the type physicalist only the second. As a result functionalism seems to capture the best features of the materialist alternatives to dualism. It is no wonder that functionalism has become increasingly popular.

Machines provide good examples of two concepts that are central to functionalism: the concept that mental states are interdefined and the concept that they can be realized by many systems. The illustration on the next page contrasts a behavioristic Coke machine with a mentalistic one. Both machines dispense a Coke for 10 cents. (The price has not been affected by inflation.) The states of the machines are defined by reference to their causal roles, but only the machine on the left would satisfy the behaviorist. Its single state (*So*) is completely specified in terms of stimuli and responses. *So* is the state a machine is in if, and only if, given a dime as the input, it dispenses a Coke as the output.

The machine on the right in the illustration has interdefined states (*S1* and *S2*), which are characteristic of functionalism. *S1* is the state a machine is in if, and only if, (1) given a nickel, it dispenses nothing and proceeds to *S2*, and (2) given a dime, it dispenses a Coke and stays in *S1*. *S2* is the state a machine is in if, and only if, (1) given a nickel, it dispenses a Coke and proceeds to *S1*, and (2) given a dime, it dispenses a Coke and a nickel and proceeds to *S1*. What *S1* and *S2* jointly amount to is the machine's dispensing a Coke if it is given a dime, dispensing a Coke and a nickel if it is given a dime and a nickel and waiting to be given a second nickel if it has been given a first one.

Since *S1* and *S2* are each defined by hypothetical statements, they can be viewed as dispositions. Nevertheless, they are not behavioral dispositions because the consequences an input has for a machine in *S1* or *S2* are not specified solely in terms of the output of the machine. Rather, the consequences also involve the machine's internal states.

Nothing about the way I have described the behavioristic and mentalistic Coke machines puts constraints on what they could be made of. Any system whose states bore the proper relations to inputs, outputs and other states could be one of these machines. No doubt it is reasonable to expect such a system to be constructed out of such things as wheels, levers and diodes (token physicalism for Coke machines).

Similarly, it is reasonable to expect that our minds may prove to be neurophysiological (token physicalism for human beings).

Nevertheless, the software description of a Coke machine does not logically require wheels, levers and diodes for its concrete realization. By the same token, the software description of the mind does not logically require neurons. As far as functionalism is concerned a Coke machine with states *S1* and *S2* could be made of ectoplasm, if there is such stuff and if its states have the right causal properties. Functionalism allows for the possibility of disembodied Coke machines in exactly the same way and to the same extent that it allows for the possibility of disembodied minds.

To say that *S1* and *S2* are interdefined and realizable by different kinds of hardware is not, of course, to say that a Coke machine has a mind. Although interdefinition and functional specification are typical features of mental states, they are clearly not sufficient for mentality. What more is required is a question to which I shall return below.

Some philosophers are suspicious of functionalism because it seems too easy. Since functionalism licenses the individuation of states by reference to their causal role, it appears to allow a trivial explanation of any observed event *E*, that is, it appears to postulate an *E*-causer. For example, what makes the valves in a machine open? Why, the operation of a valve opener. And what is a valve opener? Why, anything that has the functionally defined property of causing valves to open.

In psychology this kind of question-begging often takes the form of theories that in effect postulate homunculi with the selfsame intellectual capacities the theorist set out to explain. Such is the case when visual perception is explained by simply postulating psychological mechanisms that process visual information. The behaviorist has often charged the mentalist, sometimes justifiably, of mongering this kind of question-begging pseudo explanation. The charge will have to be met if functionally defined mental states are to have a serious role in psychological theories.

The burden of the accusation is not untruth but triviality. There can be no doubt that it is a valve opener that opens valves, and it is likely that visual perception is mediated by the processing of visual information. The charge is that such putative functional explanations are mere platitudes. The functionalist can meet this objection by allowing functionally defined theoretical constructs only where mechanisms exist that can carry out the function and only where he has some notion of what such mechanisms might be like. One way of imposing this requirement is to identify the mental processes that psychology postulates with the operations of the restricted class of possible computers called Turing machines.

A Turing machine can be informally characterized as a mechanism with a finite number of program states. The inputs and outputs of the machine are written on a tape that is divided into squares each of which includes a symbol from a finite alphabet. The machine scans the tape one square at a time. It can erase the symbol on a scanned square and print a new one in its place. The machine can execute only the elementary mechanical operations of scanning, erasing, printing, moving the tape and changing state.

The program states of the Turing machine are defined solely in terms of the input symbols on the tape, the output symbols on the tape, the elementary operations and the other states of the program. Each program state is therefore functionally defined by the part it plays in the overall operation of the machine. Since the functional role of a state depends on the relation of the state to other states as well as to inputs and outputs, the relational character of the mental is captured by the Turing-machine version of functionalism. Since the definition of a program state never refers to the physical structure of the system running the program, the Turing-machine version of functionalism also captures the idea that the character of a mental state is independent of its physical realization. A human being, a roomful of people, a computer and a disembodied spirit would all be a Turing machine if they operated according to a Turing-machine program.

The proposal is to restrict the functional definition of psychological states to those that can be expressed in terms of the program states of Turing machines. If this restriction can be enforced, it provides a guarantee that psychological theories will be compatible with the demands of mechanisms. Since Turing machines are very simple devices, they are in principle quite easy to build. Consequently by formulating a psychological explanation as a Turing-machine program the psychologist ensures that the explanation is mechanistic, even though the hardware realizing the mechanism is left open.

There are many kinds of computational mechanisms other than Turing machines, and so the formulation of a functionalist psychological theory in Turing-machine notation provides only a sufficient condition for the theory's being mechanically realizable. What makes the condition interesting, however, is that the simple Turing machine can perform many complex tasks. Although the elementary operations of the Turing machine are restricted, iterations of the operations enable the machine to carry out any well-defined computation on discrete symbols.

An important tendency in the cognitive sciences is to treat the mind chiefly as a device that manipulates symbols. If a mental process can be functionally defined as an operation on symbols, there is a Turing machine capable of carrying out the computation and a variety of mechanisms for realizing the Turing machine. Where the manipulation of symbols is important the Turing machine provides a connection between functional explanation and mechanistic explanation.

The reduction of a psychological theory to a program for a Turing machine is a way of exorcising the homunculi. The reduction ensures that no operations have been postulated except those that could be performed by a familiar mechanism. Of course, the working psychologist usually cannot specify the reduction for each functionally individuated process in every theory he is prepared to take seriously. In practice the argument usually goes in the opposite direction; if the postulation of a mental operation is essential to some cherished psychological explanation, the theorist tends to assume that there must be a program for a Turing machine that will carry out that operation.

The 'black boxes' that are common in flow charts drawn by psychologists often serve to indicate postulated mental processes for which Turing reductions are wanting. Even so, the possibility in principle of such reductions serves as a methodological constraint on psychological theorizing by determining what functional definitions are to be allowed and what it would be like to know that everything has been explained that could possibly need explanation.

Such is the origin, the provenance and the promise of contemporary functionalism. How much has it actually paid off? This question is not easy to answer because much of what is now happening in the philosophy of mind and the cognitive sciences is directed at exploring the scope and limits of the functionalist explanations of behavior. I shall, however, give a brief overview.

An obvious objection to functionalism as a theory of the mind is that the functionalist definition is not limited to mental states and processes. Catalysts, Coke machines, valve openers, pencil sharpeners, mousetraps and ministers of finance are all in one way or another concepts that are functionally defined, but none is a mental concept such as pain, belief and desire. What, then, characterizes the mental? And can it be captured in a functionalist framework?

The traditional view in the philosophy of mind has it that mental states are distinguished by their having what are called either qualitative content or intentional content. I shall discuss qualitative content first.

It is not easy to say what qualitative content is; indeed, according to some theories, it is not even possible to say what it is because it can be known not by description but only by direct experience. I shall nonetheless attempt to describe it. Try to imagine looking at a blank wall through a red filter. Now change the filter to a green one and leave everything else exactly the way it was. Something about the character of your experience changes when the filter does, and it is this kind of thing that philosophers call qualitative content. I am not entirely comfortable about introducing qualitative content in this way, but it is a subject with which many philosophers are not comfortable.

The reason qualitative content is a problem for functionalism is straight-forward. Functionalism is committed to defining mental states in terms of their causes and effects. It seems, however, as if two mental states could have all the same causal relations and yet could differ in their qualitative content. Let me illustrate this with the classic puzzle of the inverted spectrum.

It seems possible to imagine two observers who are alike in all relevant psychological respects except that experiences having the qualitative content of red for one observer would have the qualitative content of green for the other. Nothing about their behavior need reveal the difference because both of them see ripe tomatoes and flaming sunsets as being similar in color and both of them call that color 'red.'

Moreover, the causal connection between their (qualitatively distinct) experiences and their other mental states could also be identical. Perhaps they both think of Little Red Riding Hood when they see ripe tomatoes, feel depressed when they see the color green and so on. It seems as if anything that could be packed into the notion of the causal role of their experiences could be shared by them, and yet the qualitative content of the experiences could be as different as you like. If this is possible, then the functionalist account does not work for mental states that have qualitative content. If one person is having a green experience while another person is having a red one, then surely they must be in different mental states.

The example of the inverted spectrum is more than a verbal puzzle. Having qualitative content is supposed to be a chief factor in what makes a mental state conscious. Many psychologists who are inclined to accept the functionalist framework are nonetheless worried about the failure of functionalism to reveal much about the nature of consciousness. Functionalists have made a few ingenious attempts to talk themselves and their colleagues out of this worry, but they have not, in my view, done so with much success. (For example, perhaps one is wrong in thinking one can imagine what an inverted spectrum would be like.) As matters stand, the problem of qualitative content poses a serious threat to the assertion that functionalism can provide a general theory of the mental.

Functionalism has fared much better with the intentional content of mental states. Indeed, it is here that the major achievements of recent cognitive science are found. To say that a mental state has intentional content is to say that it has certain semantic properties. For example, for Enrico to believe Galileo was Italian apparently involves a three-way relation between Enrico, a belief and a proposition that is the content of the belief (namely the proposition that Galileo was Italian). In particular it is an essential property of Enrico's belief that it is about Galileo (and not about, say, Newton) and that it is true if, and only if, Galileo was indeed Italian. Philosophers are divided on how these considerations fit together, but it is widely agreed that beliefs involve semantic properties such as expressing a proposition, being true or false and being about one thing rather than another.

It is important to understand the semantic properties of beliefs because theories in the cognitive sciences are largely about the beliefs organisms have. Theories of learning and perception, for example, are chiefly accounts of how the host of beliefs an organism has are determined by the character of its experiences and its genetic endowment. The functionalist account of mental states does not by itself provide the required insights. Mousetraps are functionally defined, yet mousetraps do not express propositions and they are not true or false.

There is at least one kind of thing other than a mental state that has intentional content: a symbol. Like thoughts, symbols seem to be about things. If someone says 'Galileo was Italian,' his utterance, like Enrico's belief, expresses a proposition about Galileo that is true or false depending on Galileo's homeland. This parallel between the symbolic and the mental underlies the traditional quest for a unified treatment of language and mind. Cognitive science is now trying to provide such a treatment.

The basic concept is simple but striking. Assume that there are such things as mental symbols (mental representations) and that mental symbols have semantic properties. On this view having a belief involves being related to a mental symbol, and the belief inherits its semantic properties from the mental symbol that figures in the relation. Mental processes (thinking, perceiving, learning and so on) involve causal interactions among relational states such as having a belief. The semantic properties of the words and sentences we utter are in turn inherited from the semantic properties of the mental states that language expresses.

Associating the semantic properties of mental states with those of mental symbols is fully compatible with the computer metaphor, because it is natural to think of the computer as a mechanism that manipulates symbols. A computation is a causal chain of computer states and the links in the chain are operations on semantically interpreted formulas in a machine code. To think of a system (such as the nervous system) as a computer is to raise questions about the nature of the code in which it computes and the semantic properties of the symbols in the code. In fact, the analogy between minds and computers actually implies the postulation of mental symbols. There is no computation without representation.

The representational account of the mind, however, predates considerably the invention of the computing machine. It is a throwback to classical epistemology, which is a tradition that includes philosophers as diverse as John Locke, David Hume, George Berkeley, René Descartes, Immanuel Kant, John Stuart Mill and William James.

Hume, for one, developed a representational theory of the mind that included five points. First, there exist 'Ideas,' which are a species of mental symbol. Second, having a belief involves entertaining an Idea. Third, mental processes are causal associations of Ideas. Fourth, Ideas are like pictures. And fifth, Ideas have their semantic properties by virtue of what they resemble: the Idea of John is about John because it looks like him.

Contemporary cognitive psychologists do not accept the details of Hume's theory, although they endorse much of its spirit. Theories of computation provide a far richer account of mental processes than the mere association of Ideas. And only a few psychologists still think that imagery is the chief vehicle of mental representation. Nevertheless, the most significant break with Hume's theory lies in the abandoning of resemblance as an explanation of the semantic properties of mental representations.

Many philosophers, starting with Berkeley, have argued that there is something seriously wrong with the suggestion that the semantic relation between a thought and what the thought is about could be one of resemblance. Consider the thought that John is tall. Clearly the thought is true only of the state of affairs consisting of John's being tall. A theory of the semantic properties of a thought should therefore explain how this particular thought is related to this particular state of affairs.

According to the resemblance theory, entertaining the thought involves having a mental image that shows John to be tall. To put it another way, the relation between the thought that John is tall and his being tall is like the relation between a tall man and his portrait.

The difficulty with the resemblance theory is that any portrait showing John to be tall must also show him to be many other things: clothed or naked, lying, standing or sitting, having a head or not having one, and so on. A portrait of a tall man who is sitting down resembles a man's being seated as much as it resembles a man's being tall. On the resemblance theory it is not clear what distinguishes thoughts about John's height from thoughts about his posture.

The resemblance theory turns out to encounter paradoxes at every turn. The possibility of construing beliefs as involving relations to semantically interpreted mental representations clearly depends on having an acceptable account of where the semantic properties of the mental representations come from. If resemblance will not provide this account, what will?

The current idea is that the semantic properties of a mental representation are determined by aspects of its functional role. In other words, a sufficient condition for having semantic properties can be specified in causal terms. This is the connection between functionalism and the representational theory of the mind. Modern cognitive psychology rests largely on the hope that these two doctrines can be made to support each other.

No philosopher is now prepared to say exactly how the functional role of a mental representation determines its semantic properties. Nevertheless, the functionalist recognizes three types of causal relation among psychological states involving mental representations, and they might serve to fix the semantic properties of mental representations. The three types are causal relations among mental states and stimuli, mental states and responses and some mental states and other ones.

Consider the belief that John is tall. presumably the following facts, which correspond respectively to the three types of causal relation, are relevant to determining the semantic properties of the mental representation involved in the belief. First, the belief is a normal effect of certain stimulations, such as seeing John in circumstances that reveal his height. Second, the belief is the normal cause of certain behavioral effects, such as uttering 'John is tall.' Third, the belief is a normal cause of certain other beliefs and a normal effect of certain other beliefs. For example, anyone who believes John is tall is very likely also to believe someone is tall. Having the first belief is normally causally sufficient for having the second belief. And anyone who believes everyone in the room is tall and also believes John is in the room will very likely believe John is tall. The third belief is a normal effect of the first two. In short, the functionalist maintains that the proposition expressed by a given mental representation depends on the causal properties of the mental states in which that mental representation figures.

The concept that the semantic properties of mental representations are determined by aspects of their functional role is at the center of current work in the cognitive sciences. Nevertheless, the concept may not be true. Many philosophers who are unsympathetic to the cognitive turn in modern psychology doubt its truth, and many psychologists would probably reject it in the bald and unelaborated way that I have sketched it. Yet even in its skeletal form, there is this much to be said in its favor: It legitimizes the notion of mental representation, which has become increasingly important to theorizing in every branch of the cognitive sciences. Recent advances in formulating and testing hypotheses about the character of mental representations in fields ranging from phonetics to computer vision suggest that the concept of mental representation is fundamental to empirical theories of the mind.

The behaviorist has rejected the appeal to mental representation because it runs counter to his view of the explanatory mechanisms that can figure in psychological theories. Nevertheless, the science of mental representation is now flourishing. The history of science reveals that when a successful theory comes into conflict with a methodological scruple, it is generally the scruple that gives way. Accordingly the functionalist has relaxed the behaviorist constraints on psychological explanations. There is probably no better way to decide what is methodologically permissible in science than by investigating what successful science requires.

**Matter and Consciousness**

A Contemporary Introduction to the Philosophy of Mind

Revised Edition

Paul M. Churchland

**A Bradford Book**
The MIT Press
Cambridge, Massachusetts
London, England

*4. Functionalism*

According to *functionalism*, the essential or defining feature of any type of mental state is the set of causal relations it bears to (1) environmental effects on the body, (2) other types of mental states, and (3) bodily behavior. Pain, for example, characteristically results from some bodily damage or trauma; it causes distress, annoyance, and practical reasoning aimed at relief; and it causes wincing, blanching, and nursing of the traumatized area. Any state that plays exactly that functional role is a pain, according to functionalism. Similarly, other types of mental states (sensations, fears, beliefs, and so on) are also defined by their unique causal roles in a complex economy of internal states mediating sensory inputs and behavioral outputs.

This view may remind the reader of behaviorism, and indeed it is the heir to behaviorism, but there is one fundamental difference between the two theories. Where the behaviorist hoped to define each type of mental state solely in terms of environmental input and behavioral output, the functionalist denies that this is possible. As he sees it, the adequate characterization of almost any mental state involves an ineliminable reference to a variety of other mental states with which it is causally connected, and so a reductive definition solely in terms of publicly observable inputs and outputs is quite impossible. Functionalism is therefore immune to one of the main objections against behaviorism.

Thus the difference between functionalism and behaviorism. The difference between functionalism and the identity theory will emerge from the following argument raised against the identity theory.

Imagine a being from another planet, says the functionalist, a being with an alien physiological constitution, a constitution based on the chemical element silicon, for example, instead of on the element carbon, as ours is. The chemistry and even the physical structure of the alien's brain would have to be systematically different from ours. But even so, that alien brain could well sustain a functional economy of internal states whose mutual *relations* parallel perfectly the mutual relations that define our own mental states. The alien may have an internal state that meets all the conditions for being a pain state, as outlined earlier. That state, considered from a purely physical point of view, would have a very different makeup from a human pain state, but it could nevertheless be identical to a human pain state from a purely functional point of view. And so for all of his functional states.

If the alien's functional economy of internal states were indeed *functionally isomorphic* with our own internal economy—if those states were causally connected to inputs, to one another, and to behavior in ways that parallel our own internal connections—then the alien would have pains, and desires, and hopes, and fears just as fully as we, despite the differences in the physical system that sustains or realizes those functional states. What is important for mentality is not the matter of which the creature is made, but the structure of the internal activities which that matter sustains.

If we can think of one alien constitution, we can think of many, and the point just made can also be made with an artificial system. Were we to create an electronic system—a computer of some kind—whose internal economy were functionally isomorphic with our own in all the relevant ways, then it too would be the subject of mental states.

What this illustrates is that there are almost certainly many more ways than one for nature, and perhaps even for man, to put together a thinking, feeling, perceiving creature. And this raises a problem for the identity theory, for it seems that there is no single type of physical state to which a given type of mental state must always correspond. Ironically, there are *too many* different kinds of physical systems that can realize the functional economy characteristic of conscious intelligence. If we consider the universe at large, therefore, and the future as well as the present, it seems quite unlikely that the identity theorist is going to find the one-to-one match-ups between the concepts of our common-sense mental taxonomy and the concepts of an overarching theory that encompasses all of the relevant physical systems. But that is what intertheoretic reduction is standardly said to require. The prospects for universal identities, between types of mental states and types of brain states, are therefore slim.

If the functionalists reject the traditional 'mental-type = physical type' identity theory, virtually all of them remain committed to a weaker 'mental token = physical token' identity theory, for they still maintain that each *instance* of a given type of mental state is numerically identical with some specific physical state in some physical system or other. It is only universal (type/type) identities that are rejected. Even so, this rejection is typically taken to support the claim that the science of psychology is or should be *methodologically autonomous* from the various physical sciences such as physics, biology, and even neurophysiology. Psychology, it is claimed, has its own irreducible laws and its own abstract subject matter.

As this book is written, functionalism is probably the most widely held theory of mind among philosophers, cognitive psychologists, and artificial intelligence researchers. Some of the reasons are apparent from the preceding discussion, and there are further reasons as well. In characterizing mental states as essentially functional states, functionalism places the concerns of psychology at a level that abstracts from the teeming detail of a brain's neurophysiological (or crystallographic, or microelectronic) structure. The science of psychology, it is occasionally said, is methodologically autonomous from those other sciences (biology, neuroscience, circuit theory) whose concerns are with what amount to engineering details. This provides a rationale for a great deal of work in cognitive psychology and artificial intelligence, where researchers postulate a system of abstract functional states and then test the postulated system, often by way of its computer simulation, against human behavior in similar circumstances. The aim of such work is to discover in detail the functional organization that makes us what we are. (Partly in order to evaluate the prospects for a functionalist philosophy of mind, we shall examine some of the recent research in artificial intelligence in chapter 6.)

**Arguments against Functionalism**

Current popularity aside, functionalism also faces difficulties. The most commonly posed objection cites an old friend: sensory qualia. Functionalism may escape one of behaviorism's fatal flaws, it is said, but it still falls prey to the other. By attempting to make its *relational* properties the definitive feature of any mental state, functionalism ignores the 'inner' or qualitative nature of our mental states. But their qualitative nature is the essential feature of a great many types of mental state (pain, sensations of color, of temperature, of pitch, and so on), runs the objection, and functionalism is therefore false.

The standard illustration of this apparent failing is called "the inverted spectrum thought-experiment". It is entirely conceivable, runs the story, that the range of color sensations that I enjoy upon viewing standard objects is simply inverted relative to the color sensations that you enjoy. When viewing a tomato, I may have what is really a sensation-of-green where you have the normal sensation-of-red; when viewing a banana, I may have what is really sensation-of-blue where you have the normal sensation-of-yellow; and so forth. But since we have no way of comparing our inner qualia, and since I shall make all the same observational discriminations among objects that you will, there is no way to tell whether my spectrum is inverted relative to yours.

The problem for functionalism arises as follows. Even if my spectrum is inverted relative to yours, we remain functionally isomorphic with one another. My visual sensation upon viewing a tomato is *functionally* identical with your visual sensation upon viewing a tomato. According to functionalism, therefore, they are the very same type of state, and it does not even make sense to suppose that my sensation is 'really' a sensation-of-green. If it meets the functional conditions for being a sensation-of-red, then by definition it is a sensation-of-red. According to functionalism, apparently, a spectrum inversion of the kind described is ruled out by definition. But such inversions are entirely conceivable, concludes the objection, and if functionalism entails that they are not conceivable, then functionalism is false.

Another qualia-related worry for functionalism is the so-called "absent qualia problem". The functional organization characteristic of conscious intelligence can be instantiated ( = realized or instanced) in a considerable variety of physical systems, some of them radically different from a normal human. For example, a giant electronic computer might instantiate it, and there are more radical possibilities still. One writer asks us to imagine the people of China—all $10^9$ of them—organized into an intricate game of mutual interactions so that collectively they constitute a giant brain which exchanges inputs and outputs with a single robot body. That system of the robot-plus-$10^9$-unit-brain could presumably instantiate the relevant functional organization (though no doubt it would be much slower in its activities than a human or a computer), and would therefore be the subject of mental states, according to functionalism. But surely, it is urged, the complex states that there play the functional roles of pain, pleasure, and sensations-of-color would not have intrinsic qualia as ours do, and would therefore fail to be genuine mental states. Again, functionalism seems at best an incomplete account of the nature of mental states.

It has recently been argued that both the inverted-qualia and the absent-qualia objections can be met, without violence to functionalism and without significant violence to our common-sense intuitions about qualia. Consider the inversion problem first. I think the functionalist is right to insist that the type-identity of our visual sensations be reckoned according to their functional role. But the objector is also right in insisting that a relative inversion of two people's qualia, without functional inversion, is entirely conceivable. The apparent inconsistency between these positions can be dissolved by insisting that (1) our functional states (or rather, their physical realizations) do indeed have an intrinsic nature on which our introspective identification of those states depends; while also insisting that (2) such intrinsic natures are nevertheless not essential to the type-identity of a given mental state, and may indeed *vary* from instance to instance of the same type of mental state.

What this means is that the qualitative character of your sensation-of-red might be different from the qualitative character of my sensation-of-red, slightly or substantially, and a third person's sensation-of-red might be different again. But so long as all three states are standardly caused by red objects and standardly cause all three of us to believe that something is red, then all three states are sensations-of-red, whatever their intrinsic qualitative character. Such intrinsic qualia merely serve as salient features that permit the quick introspective identification of sensations, as black-on-orange stripes serve as a salient feature for the quick visual identification of tigers. But specific qualia are not essential to the type-identity of mental states, any more than black-on-orange stripes are essential to the type-identity of tigers.

Plainly, this solution requires the functionalist to admit the *reality* of qualia, and we may wonder how there can be room for qualia in his materialist world-picture. Perhaps they can be fit in as follows: *identify* them with physical properties of whatever physical states instantiate the mental (functional) states that display them. For example, identify the qualitative nature of your sensations-of-red with that physical feature (of the brain state that instantiates it) to which your mechanisms of introspective discrimination are in fact responding when you judge that you have a sensation-of-red. If materialism is true, then there must *be* some internal physical feature or other to which your discrimination of sensations-of-red is keyed: *that* is the quale of your sensations-of-red. If the pitch of a sound can turn out to be the frequency of an oscillation in air pressure, there is no reason why the quale of a sensation cannot turn out to be, say, a spiking frequency in a certain neural pathway. (More likely, it will be a peculiar group or *set* of spiking frequencies, as claimed by the *vectorial* or *across-fiber pattern* theory of sensory coding. 'Spikes' are the tiny electrochemical pulses by which our brain cells communicate with each other along the thin fibers that connect them. For more on all of this, see Chapter 7.)

This entails that creatures with a physical constitution different from ours may have qualia different from ours, despite being psychologically isomorphic with us. It does not entail that they *must* have different qualia, however. If the qualitative character of my sensation-of-red is really a spiking frequency of 90 hertz in a certain neural pathway, it is possible that an electromechanical robot might enjoy the very same qualitative character if, in reporting sensations-of-red, the robot were responding to a spiking frequency of 90 hertz in a corresponding *copper* pathway. It might be the spiking frequency that matters to our respective mechanisms of discrimination, not the nature of the medium that carries it.

This proposal also suggests a solution to the absent qualia problem. So long as the physical system at issue is functionally isomorphic with us, to the last detail, then it will be equally capable of subtle introspective discriminations among its sensations. Those discriminations must be made on some systematic physical basis, that is, on some characteristic physical features of the states being discriminated. Those features at the objective focus of the system's discriminatory mechanisms, *those* are its sensory qualia—though the alien system is no more likely to appreciate their true physical nature than we appreciate the true physical nature of our own qualia. Sensory qualia are therefore an inevitable concomitant of any system with the kind of functional organization at issue. It may be difficult or impossible to 'see' the qualia in an alien system, but it is equally difficult to 'see' them even when looking into a human brain.

I leave it to the reader to judge the adequacy of these responses. If they are adequate, then, given its other virtues, functionalism must be conceded a very strong position among the competing contemporary theories of mind. It is interesting, however, that the defense offered in the last paragraph found it necessary to take a leaf from the identity theorist's book (types of quale are reduced to or identified with types of physical state), since the final objection we shall consider also tends to blur the distinction between functionalism and reductive materialism.

Consider the property of *temperature*, runs the objection. Here we have a paradigm of a physical property, one that has also been cited as the paradigm of a successfully *reduced* property, as expressed in the intertheoretic identity

"temperature = mean kinetic energy of constituent molecules".

Strictly speaking, however, this identity is true only for the temperature of a gas, where simple particles are free to move in ballistic fashion. In a *solid*, temperature is realized differently, since the interconnected molecules are confined to a variety of vibrational motions. In a *plasma*, temperature is something else again, since a plasma has no constituent molecules; they, and their constituent atoms, have been ripped to pieces. And even a *vacuum* has a so-called 'blackbody' temperature—in the distribution of electromagnetic waves coursing through it. Here temperature has nothing to do with the kinetic energy of particles.

It is plain that the physical property of temperature enjoys 'multiple instantiations' no less than do psychological properties. Does this mean that thermodynamics (the theory of heat and temperature) is an 'autonomous science', separable from the rest of physics, with its own irreducible laws and its own abstract nonphysical subject matter?

Presumably not. What it means, concludes the objection, is that *reductions are domain-specific*:

temperature-in-a-gas = the mean kinetic energy of the gas's molecules,

whereas

temperature-in-a-vacuum = the blackbody distribution of the vacuum's transient radiation.

Similarly, perhaps

joy-in-a-human = resonances in the lateral hypothalamus,

whereas

joy-in-a-Martian = something else entirely.

This means that we may expect some type/type reductions of mental states to physical states after all, though they will be much narrower than was first suggested. Furthermore, it means that functionalist claims concerning the radical autonomy of psychology cannot be sustained. And last, it suggests that functionalism is not so profoundly different from the identity theory as was first made out.

As with the defense of functionalism outlined earlier, I leave the evaluation of this criticism to the reader. We shall have occasion for further discussion of functionalism in later chapters. At this point, let us turn to the final materialist theory of mind, for functionalism is not the only major reaction against the identity theory.

## *Suggested Readings*


Putnam, Hilary, "Minds and Machines," in *Dimensions of Mind*, ed. Sidney Hook (New York: New York University Press, 1960).

Putnam, Hilary, "Robots: Machines or Artificially Created Life?" *Journal of Philosophy*, vol. LXI, no. 21 (1964).

Putnam, Hilary, "The Nature of Mental States," in *Materialism and the Mind-Body Problem*, ed. David Rosenthal (Englewood Cliffs, NJ: Prentice-Hall, 1971).

Fodor, Jerry, *Psychological Explanation* (New York: Random House, 1968).

Dennett, Daniel, *Brainstorms* (Montgomery, Vermont: Bradford, 1978; Cambridge, MA: MIT Press).


## *Concerning Difficulties with Functionalism*


Block, Ned, "Troubles with Functionalism," in *Minnesota Studies in the Philosophy of Science*, vol. IX ed. C. W. Savage (Minneapolis: University of Minnesota Press, 1978). Reprinted in *Readings in Philosophy of Psychology*, ed. N. Block (Cambridge, MA: Harvard University Press, 1980).

Churchland, Paul and Patricia, "Functionalism, Qualia, and Intentionality," *Philosophical Topics*, vol. 12, no. 1 (1981). Reprinted in *Mind, Brain, and Function*, eds. J. Biro and R. Shahan (Norman, OK: University of Oklahoma Press, 1982).

Churchland, Paul, "Eliminative Materialism and the Propositional Attitudes," *Journal of Philosophy*, vol. LXXVIII, no. 2 (1981).

Shoemaker, Sidney, "The Inverted Spectrum," *Journal of Philosophy*, vol. LXXIX, no. 7 (1982).

Enc, Berent, "In Defense of the Identity Theory," *Journal of Philosophy*, vol. LXXX, no. 5 (1983).

*5. Eliminative Materialism*

The identity theory was called into doubt not because the prospects for a materialist account of our mental capacities were thought to be poor, but because it seemed unlikely that the arrival of an adequate materialist theory would bring with it the nice one-to-one match-ups, between the concepts of folk psychology and the concepts of theoretical neuroscience, that intertheoretic reduction requires. The reason for that doubt was the great variety of quite different physical systems that could instantiate the required functional organization. *Eliminative materialism* also doubts that the correct neuroscientific account of human capacities will produce a neat reduction of our common-sense framework, but here the doubts arise from a quite different source.

As the eliminative materialists see it, the one-to-one match-ups will not be found, and our common-sense psychological framework will not enjoy an intertheoretic reduction, *because our common-sense psychological framework is a false and radically misleading conception of the causes of human behavior and the nature of cognitive activity.* On this view, folk psychology is not just an incomplete representation of our inner natures; it is an outright *mis*representation of our internal states and activities. Consequently, we cannot expect a truly adequate neuroscientific account of our inner lives to provide theoretical categories that match up nicely with the categories of our common-sense framework. Accordingly, we must expect that the older framework will simply be eliminated, rather than be reduced, by a matured neuroscience.

**Historical Parallels**

As the identity theorist can point to historical cases of successful intertheoretic reduction, so the eliminative materialist can point to historical cases of the outright elimination of the ontology of an older theory in favor of the ontology of a new and superior theory. For most of the eighteenth and nineteenth centuries, learned people believed that heat was a subtle *fluid* held in bodies, much in the way water is held in a sponge. A fair body of moderately successful theory described the way this fluid substance—called "caloric"—flowed within a body, or from one body to another, and how it produced thermal expansion, melting, boiling, and so forth. But by the end of the last century it had become abundantly clear that heat was not a substance at all, but just the energy of motion of the trillions of jostling molecules that make up the heated body itself. The new theory—the "corpuscular/kinetic theory of matter and heat"—was much more successful than the old in explaining and predicting the thermal behavior of bodies. And since we were unable to *identify* caloric fluid with kinetic energy (according to the old theory, caloric is a material *substance;* according to the new theory, kinetic energy is a form of *motion*), it was finally agreed that there is *no such thing* as caloric. Caloric was simply eliminated from our accepted ontology.

A second example. It used to be thought that when a piece of wood burns, or a piece of metal rusts, a spiritlike substance called "phlogiston" was being released: briskly, in the former case, slowly in the latter. Once gone, that 'noble' substance left only a base pile of ash or rust. It later came to be appreciated that both processes involve, not the loss of something, but the *gaining* of a substance taken from the atmosphere: oxygen. Phlogiston emerged, not as an incomplete description of what was going on, but as a radical misdescription. Phlogiston was therefore not suitable for reduction to or identification with some notion from within the new oxygen chemistry, and it was simply eliminated from science.

Admittedly, both of these examples concern the elimination of something nonobservable, but our history also includes the elimination of certain widely accepted 'observables'. Before Copernicus' views became available, almost any human who ventured out at night could look up at *the starry sphere of the heavens,* and if he stayed for more than a few minutes he could also see that it *turned,* around an axis through Polaris. What the sphere was made of (crystal?) and what made it turn (the gods?) were theoretical questions that exercised us for over two millennia. But hardly anyone doubted the existence of what everyone could observe with their own eyes. In the end, however, we learned to reinterpret our visual experience of the night sky within a very different conceptual framework, and the turning sphere evaporated.

Witches provide another example. Psychosis is a fairly common affliction among humans, and in earlier centuries its victims were standardly seen as cases of demonic possession, as instances of Satan's spirit itself, glaring malevolently out at us from behind the victims' eyes. That witches exist was not a matter of any controversy. One would occasionally see them, in any city or hamlet, engaged in incoherent, paranoid, or even murderous behavior. But observable or not, we eventually decided that witches simply do not exist. We concluded that the concept of a witch is an element in a conceptual framework that misrepresents so badly the phenomena to which it was standardly applied that literal application of the notion should be permanently withdrawn. Modern theories of mental dysfunction led to the elimination of witches from our serious ontology.

The concepts of folk psychology—belief, desire, fear, sensation, pain, joy, and so on—await a similar fate, according to the view at issue. And when neuroscience has matured to the point where the poverty of our current conceptions is apparent to everyone, and the superiority of the new framework is established, we shall then be able to set about *re*conceiving our internal states and activities, within a truly adequate conceptual framework at last. Our explanations of one another's behavior will appeal to such things as our neuropharmacological states, the neural activity in specialized anatomical areas, and whatever other states are deemed relevant by the new theory. Our private introspection will also be transformed, and may be profoundly enhanced by reason of the more accurate and penetrating framework it will have to work with—just as the astronomer's perception of the night sky is much enhanced by the detailed knowledge of modern astronomical theory that he or she possesses.

The magnitude of the conceptual revolution here suggested should not be minimized: it would be enormous. And the benefits to humanity might be equally great. If each of us possessed an accurate neuroscientific understanding of (what we now conceive dimly as) the varieties and causes of mental illness, the factors involved in learning, the neural basis of emotions, intelligence, and socialization, then the sum total of human misery might be much reduced. The simple increase in mutual understanding that the new framework made possible could contribute substantially toward a more peaceful and humane society. Of course, there would be dangers as well: increased knowledge means increased power, and power can always be misused.

## Arguments for Eliminative Materialism

The arguments for eliminative materialism are diffuse and less than decisive, but they are stronger than is widely supposed. The distinguishing feature of this position is its denial that a smooth intertheoretic reduction is to be expected—even a species-specific reduction—of the framework of folk psychology to the framework of a matured neuroscience. The reason for this denial is the eliminative materialist's conviction that folk psychology is a hopelessly primitive and deeply confused conception of our internal activities. But why this low opinion of our common-sense conceptions?

There are at least three reasons. First, the eliminative materialist will point to the widespread explanatory, predictive, and manipulative failures of folk psychology. So much of what is central and familiar to us remains a complete mystery from within folk psychology. We do not know what *sleep* is, or why we have to have it, despite spending a full third of our lives in that condition. (The answer, "For rest," is mistaken. Even if people are allowed to rest continuously, their need for sleep is undiminished. Apparently, sleep serves some deeper functions, but we do not yet know what they are.) We do not understand how *learning* transforms each of us from a gaping infant to a cunning adult, or how differences in *intelligence* are grounded. We have not the slightest idea how *memory* works, or how we manage to retrieve relevant bits of information instantly from the awesome mass we have stored. We do not know what *mental illness* is, nor how to cure it.

In sum, the most central things about us remain almost entirely mysterious from within folk psychology. And the defects noted cannot be blamed on inadequate time allowed for their correction, for folk psychology has enjoyed no significant changes or advances in well over 2,000 years, despite its manifest failures. Truly successful theories may be expected to reduce, but significantly unsuccessful theories merit no such expectation.

This argument from explanatory poverty has a further aspect. So long as one sticks to normal brains, the poverty of folk psychology is perhaps not strikingly evident. But as soon as one examines the many perplexing behavioral and cognitive deficits suffered by people with *damaged* brains, one's descriptive and explanatory resources start to claw the air (see, for example chapter 7.3, p. 143). As with other humble theories asked to operate successfully in unexplored extensions of their old domain (for example, Newtonian mechanics in the domain of velocities close to the velocity of light, and the classical gas law in the domain of high pressures or temperatures), the descriptive and explanatory inadequacies of folk psychology become starkly evident.

The second argument tries to draw an inductive lesson from our conceptual history. Our early folk theories of motion were profoundly confused, and were eventually displaced entirely by more sophisticated theories. Our early folk theories of the structure and activity of the heavens were wildly off the mark, and survive only as historical lessons in how wrong we can be. Our folk theories of the nature of fire, and the nature of life, were similarly cockeyed. And one could go on, since the vast majority of our past folk conceptions have been similarly exploded. All except folk psychology, which survives to this day and has only recently begun to feel pressure. But the phenomenon of conscious intelligence is surely a more complex and difficult phenomenon than any of those just listed. So far as accurate understanding is concerned, it would be a *miracle* if we had got *that* one right the very first time, when we fell down so badly on all the others. Folk psychology has survived for so very long, presumably, not because it is basically correct in its representations, but because the phenomena addressed are so surpassingly difficult that any useful handle on them, no matter how feeble, is unlikely to be displaced in a hurry.

A third argument attempts to find an a priori advantage for eliminative materialism over the identity theory and functionalism. It attempts to counter the common intuition that eliminative materialism is distantly possible, perhaps, but is much less probable than either the identity theory or functionalism. The focus again is on whether the concepts of folk psychology will find vindicating match-ups in a matured neuroscience. The eliminativist bets no; the other two bet yes. (Even the functionalist bets yes, but expects the match-ups to be only species-specific, or only person-specific. Functionalism, recall, denies the existence only of *universal* type/type identities.)

The eliminativist will point out that the requirements on a reduction are rather demanding. The new theory must entail a set of principles and embedded concepts that mirrors very closely the specific conceptual structure to be reduced. And the fact is, there are vastly many more ways of being an explanatorily successful neuroscience while *not* mirroring the structure of folk psychology, than there are ways of being an explanatorily successful neuroscience while also *mirroring* the very specific structure of folk psychology. Accordingly, the a priori probability of eliminative materialism is not lower, but substantially *higher* than that of either of its competitors. One's initial intuitions here are simply mistaken.

Granted, this initial a priori advantage could be reduced if there were a very strong presumption in favor of the truth of folk psychology—true theories are better bets to win reduction. But according to the first two arguments, the presumptions on this point should run in precisely the opposite direction.

### Arguments against Eliminative Materialism

The initial plausibility of this rather radical view is low for almost everyone, since it denies deeply entrenched assumptions. That is at best a question-begging complaint, of course, since those assumptions are precisely what is at issue. But the following line of thought does attempt to mount a real argument.

Eliminative materialism is false, runs the argument, because one's introspection reveals directly the existence of pains, beliefs, desires, fears, and so forth. Their existence is as obvious as anything could be.

The eliminative materialist will reply that this argument makes the same mistake that an ancient or medieval person would be making if he insisted that he could just see with his own eyes that the heavens form a turning sphere, or that witches exist. The fact is, all observation occurs within some system of concepts, and our observation judgments are only as good as the conceptual framework in which they are expressed. In all three cases—the starry sphere, witches, and the familiar mental states—precisely what is challenged is the integrity of the background conceptual frameworks in which the observation judgments are expressed. To insist on the validity of one's experiences, *traditionally interpreted*, is therefore to beg the very question at issue. For in all three cases, the question is whether we should *re*conceive the nature of some familiar observational domain.

A second criticism attempts to find an incoherence in the eliminative materialist's position. The bald statement of eliminative materialism is that the familiar mental states do not really exist. But that statement is meaningful, runs the argument, only if it is the expression of a certain *belief*, and an *intention* to communicate, and a *knowledge* of the language, and so forth. But if the statement is true, then no such mental states exist, and the statement is therefore a meaningless string of marks or noises, and cannot be true. Evidently, the assumption that eliminative materialism is true entails that it cannot be true.

The hole in this argument is the premise concerning the conditions necessary for a statement to be meaningful. It begs the question. If eliminative materialism is true, then meaningfulness must have some different source. To insist on the 'old' source is to insist on the validity of the very framework at issue. Again, an historical parallel may be helpful here. Consider the medieval theory that being biologically *alive* is a matter of being ensouled by an immaterial *vital spirit*. And consider the following response to someone who has expressed disbelief in that theory.

> My learned friend has stated that there is no such thing as vital spirit. But this statement is incoherent. For if it is true, then my friend does not have vital spirit, and must therefore be *dead*. But if he is dead, then his statement is just a string of noises, devoid of meaning or truth. Evidently, the assumption that antivitalism is true entails that it cannot be true! Q.E.D.

This second argument is now a joke, but the first argument begs the question in exactly the same way.

A final criticism draws a much weaker conclusion, but makes a rather stronger case. Eliminative materialism, it has been said, is making mountains out of molehills. It exaggerates the defects in folk psychology, and underplays its real successes. Perhaps the arrival of a matured neuroscience will require the elimination of the occasional folk-psychological concept, continues the criticism, and a minor adjustment in certain folk-psychological principles may have to be endured. But the large-scale elimination forecast by the eliminative materialist is just an alarmist worry or a romantic enthusiasm.

Perhaps this complaint is correct. And perhaps it is merely complacent. Whichever, it does bring out the important point that we do not confront two simple and mutually exclusive possibilities here: pure reduction versus pure elimination. Rather, these are the end points of a smooth spectrum of possible outcomes, between which there are mixed cases of partial elimination and partial reduction. Only empirical research (see chapter 7) can tell us where on that spectrum our own case will fall. Perhaps we should speak here, more liberally, of "revisionary materialism", instead of concentrating on the more radical possibility of an across-the-board elimination. Perhaps we should. But it has been my aim in this section to make it at least intelligible to you that our collective conceptual destiny lies substantially toward the revolutionary end of the spectrum.

## *Suggested Readings*


Feyerabend, Paul, "Comment: 'Mental Events and the Brain,'" *Journal of Philosophy*, vol. LX (1963). Reprinted in *The Mind/Brain Identity Theory*, ed. C. V. Borst (London: Macmillan, 1970).

Feyerabend, Paul, "Materialism and the Mind-Body Problem," *Review of Metaphysics*, vol. XVII (1963). Reprinted in *The Mind/Brain Identity Theory*, ed. C. V. Borst (London: Macmillan, 1970).

Rorty, Richard, "Mind-Body Identity, Privacy, and Categories," *Review of Metaphysics*, vol. XIX (1965). Reprinted in *Materialism and the Mind-Body Problem*, ed. D. M. Rosenthal (Englewood Cliffs, NJ: Prentice-Hall, 1971).

Rorty, Richard, "In Defense of Eliminative Materialism," *Review of Metaphysics*, vol. XXIV (1970). Reprinted in *Materialism and the Mind-Body Problem*, ed. D. M. Rosenthal (Englewood Cliffs, NJ: Prentice-Hall, 1971).

Churchland, Paul, "Eliminative Materialism and the Propositional Attitudes," *Journal of Philosophy*, vol. LXXVIII, no. 2 (1981).

Dennett, Daniel, "Why You Can't Make a Computer that Feels Pain," in *Brainstorms* (Montgomery, VT: Bradford, 1978; Cambridge, MA: MIT Press).

Churchland, Paul, "Some Reductive Strategies in Cognitive Neurobiology," *Mind*, vol. 95, no. 379 (1986).

## from "Epiphenomenal Qualia"[3]

It is undeniable that the physical, chemical and biological sciences have provided a great deal of information about the world we live in and about ourselves. I will use the label 'physical information' for this kind of information, and also for information that automatically comes along with it. For example, if a medical scientist tells me enough about the processes that go on in my nervous system, and about how they relate to happenings in the world around me, to what has happened in the past and is likely to happen in the future, to what happens to other similar and dissimilar organisms, and the like, he or she tells me—if I am clever enough to fit it together appropriately—about what is often called the functional role of those states in me (and in organisms in general in similar cases). This information, and its kin, I also label 'physical'.

I do not mean these sketchy remarks to constitute a definition of 'physical information', and of the correlative notions of physical property, process, and so on, but to indicate what I have in mind here. It is well known that there are problems with giving a precise definition of these notions, and so of the thesis of Physicalism that all (correct) information is physical information. But—unlike some—I take the question of definition to cut across the central problems I want to discuss in this paper.

I am what is sometimes known as a "qualia freak".[4] I think that there are certain features of the bodily sensations especially, but also of certain perceptual experiences, which no amount of purely physical information includes. Tell me everything physical there is to tell about what is going on in a living brain, the kind of states, their functional role, their relation to what goes on at other times and in other brains, and so on and so forth, and be I as clever as can be in fitting it all together, you won't have told me about the hurtfulness of pains, the itchiness of itches, the pangs of jealousy, or about the characteristic experience of tasting a lemon, smelling a rose, hearing a loud noise or seeing the sky.

There are many qualia freaks, and some of them say that their rejection of Physicalism is an unargued intuition. I think that they are being unfair to themselves. They have the following argument. Nothing you could tell of a physical sort captures the smell of a rose, for instance. Therefore, Physicalism is false. By our lights this is a perfectly good argument. It is obviously not to the point to question its validity, and the premise is intuitively obviously true both to them and to me.

I must, however, admit that it is weak from a polemical point of view. There are, unfortunately for us, many who do not find the premise intuitively obvious. The task then is to present an argument whose premises are obvious to all, or at least to as many as possible. This I try to do in §I with what I will call "the Knowledge argument". In §II I contrast the Knowledge argument with the Modal argument and in §III with the "What is it like to be" argument. In §IV I tackle the question of the causal role of qualia. The major factor in stopping people from admitting qualia is the belief that they would have to be given a causal role with respect to the physical world and especially the brain; and it is hard to do this without sounding like someone who believes in fairies. I seek in §IV to turn this objection by arguing that the view that qualia are epiphenomenal[5] is a perfectly possible one.

### I. The Knowledge Argument for Qualia

People vary considerably in their ability to discriminate colours. Suppose that in an experiment to catalogue this variation Fred is discovered. Fred has better colour vision than anyone else on record; he makes

3 From *The Philosophical Quarterly* Volume 32, Number 127, April 1982; pp. 127–130 and pp. 133–136. Reproduced by permission of Wiley-Blackwell Inc.

4 Qualia (pronounced KWAH-lee-a; singular *quale* [KWAH-lay]) are subjective qualities of conscious experience, for example, pains, tastes, the visual experience of colors.

5 An epiphenomenon (plural *epiphenomena*) is something caused by some system of events, but having no effects in that system. An example is the sound made by a running car: it's caused by vibrations at various places in the car, but it has no effect on the car. An epiphenomenalist about mind holds that mental events are epiphenomena—physically caused, but having no mental or physical effect.

every discrimination that anyone has ever made, and moreover he makes one that we cannot even begin to make. Show him a batch of ripe tomatoes and he sorts them into two roughly equal groups and does so with complete consistency. That is, if you blindfold him, shuffle the tomatoes up, and then remove the blindfold and ask him to sort them out again, he sorts them into exactly the same two groups.

We ask Fred how he does it. He explains that all ripe tomatoes do not look the same colour to him, and in fact that this is true of a great many objects that we classify together as red. He sees two colours where we see one, and he has in consequence developed for his own use two words '$red_1$' and '$red_2$' to mark the difference. Perhaps he tells us that he has often tried to teach the difference between $red_1$ and $red_2$ to his friends but has got nowhere and has concluded that the rest of the world is $red_1$- $red_2$ colourblind—or perhaps he has had partial success with his children, it doesn't matter. In any case he explains to us that it would be quite wrong to think that because 'red' appears in both '$red_1$' and '$red_2$' that the two colours are shades of the one colour. He only uses the common term 'red' to fit more easily into our restricted usage. To him $red_1$ and $red_2$ are as different from each other and all the other colours as yellow is from blue. And his discriminatory behaviour bears this out: he sorts $red_1$ from $red_2$ tomatoes with the greatest of ease in a wide variety of viewing circumstances. Moreover, an investigation of the physiological basis of Fred's exceptional ability reveals that Fred's optical system is able to separate out two groups of wave-lengths in the red spectrum as sharply as we are able to sort out yellow from blue.

I think that we should admit that Fred can see, really see, at least one more colour than we can; $red_1$ is a different colour from $red_2$. We are to Fred as a totally red-green colour-blind person is to us. H.G. Wells' story "The Country of the Blind" is about a sighted person in a totally blind community.[6] This person never manages to convince them that he can see, that he has an extra sense. They ridicule this sense as quite inconceivable, and treat his capacity to avoid falling into ditches, to win fights and so on as precisely that capacity and nothing more. We would be making their mistake if we refused to allow that Fred can see one more colour than we can.

What kind of experience does Fred have when he sees $red_1$ and $red_2$? What is the new colour or colours like? We would dearly like to know but do not; and it seems that no amount of physical information about Fred's brain and optical system tells us. We find out perhaps that Fred's cones respond differentially to certain light waves in the red section of the spectrum that make no difference to ours (or perhaps he has an extra cone) and that this leads in Fred to a wider range of those brain states responsible for visual discriminatory behaviour. But none of this tells us what we really want to know about his colour experience. There is something about it we don't know. But we know, we may suppose, everything about Fred's body, his behaviour and dispositions to behaviour and about his internal physiology, and everything about his history and relation to others that can be given in physical accounts of persons. We have all the physical information. Therefore, knowing all this is *not* knowing everything about Fred. It follows that Physicalism leaves something out.

To reinforce this conclusion, imagine that as a result of our investigations into the internal workings of Fred we find out how to make everyone's physiology like Fred's in the relevant respects; or perhaps Fred donates his body to science and on his death we are able to transplant his optical system into someone else—again the fine detail doesn't matter. The important point is that such a happening would create enormous interest. People would say, "At last we will know what it is like to see the extra colour, at last we will know how Fred has differed from us in the way he has struggled to tell us about for so long". Then it cannot be that we knew all along all about Fred. But *ex hypothesi* we did know all along everything about Fred that features in the physicalist scheme; hence the physicalist scheme leaves something out.

Put it this way. *After* the operation, we will know *more* about Fred and especially about his colour experiences. But beforehand we had all the physical information we could desire about his body and brain, and indeed everything that has ever featured

6 [Author's note] H.G. Wells, *The Country of the Blind and Other Stories* (London, n.d.).

in physicalist accounts of mind and consciousness. Hence there is more to know than all that. Hence Physicalism is incomplete.

Fred and the new colour(s) are of course essentially rhetorical devices. The same point can be made with normal people and familiar colours. Mary is a brilliant scientist who is, for whatever reason, forced to investigate the world from a black and white room *via* a black and white television monitor. She specialises in the neurophysiology of vision and acquires, let us suppose, all the physical information there is to obtain about what goes on when we see ripe tomatoes, or the sky, and use terms like 'red', 'blue', and so on. She discovers, for example, just which wave-length combinations from the sky stimulate the retina, and exactly how this produces *via* the central nervous system the contraction of the vocal chords and expulsion of air from the lungs that results in the uttering of the sentence 'The sky is blue'. (It can hardly be denied that it is in principle possible to obtain all this physical information from black and white television, otherwise the Open University[7] would *of necessity* need to use colour television.)

What will happen when Mary is released from her black and white room or is given a colour television monitor? Will she *learn* anything or not? It seems just obvious that she will learn something about the world and our visual experience of it. But then it is inescapable that her previous knowledge was incomplete. But she had *all* the physical information. *Ergo* there is more to have than that, and Physicalism is false.

Clearly the same style of Knowledge argument could be deployed for taste, hearing, the bodily sensations and generally speaking for the various mental states which are said to have (as it is variously put) raw feels, phenomenal features or qualia. The conclusion in each case is that the qualia are left out of the physicalist story. And the polemical strength of the Knowledge argument is that it is so hard to deny the central claim that one can have all the physical information without having all the information there is to have.

...

7 A British university offering distance education, partly through broadcast lectures.

## IV. The Bogey of Epiphenomenalism

Is there any really *good* reason for refusing to countenance the idea that qualia are causally impotent with respect to the physical world? I will argue for the answer no, but in doing this I will say nothing about two views associated with the classical epiphenomenalist position. The first is that mental *states* are inefficacious with respect to the physical world. All I will be concerned to defend is that it is possible to hold that certain *properties* of certain mental states, namely those I've called qualia, are such that their possession or absence makes no difference to the physical world. The second is that the mental is *totally* causally inefficacious. For all I will say it may be that you have to hold that the instantiation of *qualia* makes a difference to *other mental states* though not to anything physical. Indeed general considerations to do with how you could come to be aware of the instantiation of qualia suggest such a position.

Three reasons are standardly given for holding that a quale like the hurtfulness of a pain must be causally efficacious in the physical world, and so, for instance, that its instantiation must sometimes make a difference to what happens in the brain. None, I will argue, has any real force....

(i) It is supposed to be just obvious that the hurtfulness of pain is partly responsible for the subject seeking to avoid pain, saying 'It hurts' and so on. But, to reverse Hume, anything can fail to cause anything. No matter how often B follows A, and no matter how initially obvious the causality of the connection seems, the hypothesis that A causes B can be overturned by an over-arching theory which shows the two as distinct effects of a common underlying causal process.

To the untutored the image on the screen of Lee Marvin's fist moving from left to right immediately followed by the image of John Wayne's head moving in the same general direction looks as causal as anything. And of course throughout countless Westerns images similar to the first are followed by images similar to the second. All this counts for precisely nothing when we know the over-arching theory concerning how the relevant images are both effects of an underlying causal process involving the projector and the film. The epiphenomenalist can say exactly the same about the connection between, for example, hurtfulness and behaviour. It is simply a consequence of the fact that certain happenings in the brain cause both.

(ii) The second objection relates to Darwin's Theory of Evolution. According to natural selection the traits that evolve over time are those conducive to physical survival. We may assume that qualia evolved over time—we have them, the earliest forms of life do not—and so we should expect qualia to be conducive to survival. The objection is that they could hardly help us to survive if they do nothing to the physical world.

The appeal of this argument is undeniable, but there is a good reply to it. Polar bears have particularly thick, warm coats. The Theory of Evolution explains this (we suppose) by pointing out that having a thick, warm coat is conducive to survival in the Arctic. But having a thick coat goes along with having a heavy coat, and having a heavy coat is *not* conducive to survival. It slows the animal down.

Does this mean that we have refuted Darwin because we have found an evolved trait—having a heavy coat—which is not conducive to survival? Clearly not. Having a heavy coat is an unavoidable concomitant of having a warm coat (in the context, modern insulation was not available), and the advantages for survival of having a warm coat outweighed the disadvantages of having a heavy one. The point is that all we can extract from Darwin's theory is that we should expect any evolved characteristic to be either conducive to survival *or* a by-product of one that is so conducive. The epiphenomenalist holds that qualia fall into the latter category. They are a by-product of certain brain processes that are highly conducive to survival.

(iii) The third objection is based on a point about how we come to know about other minds. We know about other minds by knowing about other behaviour, at least in part. The nature of the inference is a matter of some controversy, but it is not a matter of controversy that it proceeds from behaviour. That is why we think that stones do not feel and dogs do feel. But, runs the objection, how can a person's behaviour provide any reason for believing he has qualia like mine, or indeed any qualia at all, unless this behaviour can be regarded as the *outcome* of the qualia. Man Friday's footprint was evidence of Man Friday because footprints are causal outcomes of feet attached to people. And an epiphenomenalist cannot regard behaviour, or indeed anything physical, as an outcome of qualia.

But consider my reading in *The Times* that Spurs[8] won. This provides excellent evidence that *The Telegraph* has also reported that Spurs won, despite the fact that (I trust) *The Telegraph* does not get the results from *The Times*. They each send their own reporters to the game. *The Telegraph*'s report is in no sense an outcome of *The Times'*, but the latter provides good evidence for the former nevertheless.

The reasoning involved can be reconstructed thus. I read in *The Times* that Spurs won. This gives me reason to think that Spurs won because I know that Spurs' winning is the most likely candidate to be what caused the report in *The Times*. But I also know that Spurs' winning would have had many effects, including almost certainly a report in *The Telegraph*.

I am arguing from one effect back to its cause and out again to another effect. The fact that neither effect causes the other is irrelevant. Now the epiphenomenalist allows that qualia are effects of what goes on in the brain. Qualia cause nothing physical but are caused by something physical. Hence the epiphenomenalist can argue from the behaviour of others to the qualia of others by arguing from the behaviour of others back to its causes in the brains of others and out again to their qualia.

You may well feel for one reason or another that this is a more dubious chain of reasoning than its model in the case of newspaper reports. You are right. The problem of other minds is a major philosophical problem, the problem of other newspaper reports is not. But there is no special problem of Epiphenomenalism as opposed to, say, Interactionism here.

There is a very understandable response to the three replies I have just made. "All right, there is no knockdown refutation of the existence of epiphenomenal qualia. But the fact remains that they are an excrescence. They *do* nothing, they *explain* nothing, they serve merely to soothe the intuitions of dualists, and it is left a total mystery how they fit into the

8 The London soccer team Tottenham Hotspur.

world view of science. In short we do not and cannot understand the how and why of them."

This is perfectly true; but is no objection to qualia, for it rests on an overly optimistic view of the human animal, and its powers. We are the products of Evolution. We understand and sense what we need to understand and sense in order to survive. Epiphenomenal qualia are totally irrelevant to survival. At no stage of our evolution did natural selection favour those who could make sense of how they are caused and the laws governing them, or in fact why they exist at all. And that is why we can't.

It is not sufficiently appreciated that Physicalism is an extremely optimistic view of our powers. If it is true, we have, in very broad outline admittedly, a grasp of our place in the scheme of things. Certain matters of sheer complexity defeat us—there are an awful lot of neurons—but in principle we have it all. But consider the antecedent probability that everything in the Universe be of a kind that is relevant in some way or other to the survival of *homo sapiens*. It is very low surely. But then one must admit that it is very likely that there is a part of the whole scheme of things, maybe a big part, which no amount of evolution will ever bring us near to knowledge about or understanding. For the simple reason that such knowledge and understanding is irrelevant to survival.

Physicalists typically emphasise that we are a part of nature on their view, which is fair enough. But if we are a part of nature, we are as nature has left us after however many years of evolution it is, and each step in that evolutionary progression has been a matter of chance constrained just by the need to preserve or increase survival value. The wonder is that we understand as much as we do, and there is no wonder that there should be matters which fall quite outside our comprehension. Perhaps exactly how epiphenomenal qualia fit into the scheme of things is one such.

This may seem an unduly pessimistic view of our capacity to articulate a truly comprehensive picture of our world and our place in it. But suppose we discovered living on the bottom of the deepest oceans a sort of sea slug which manifested intelligence. Perhaps survival in the conditions required rational powers. Despite their intelligence, these sea slugs have only a very restricted conception of the world by comparison with ours, the explanation for this being the nature of their immediate environment. Nevertheless they have developed sciences which work surprisingly well in these restricted terms. They also have philosophers, called slugists. Some call themselves tough-minded slugists, others confess to being soft-minded slugists.

The tough-minded slugists hold that the restricted terms (or ones pretty like them which may be introduced as their sciences progress) suffice in principle to describe everything without remainder. These tough-minded slugists admit in moments of weakness to a feeling that their theory leaves something out. They resist this feeling and their opponents, the soft-minded slugists, by pointing out—absolutely correctly—that no slugist has ever succeeded in spelling out how this mysterious residue fits into the highly successful view that their sciences have and are developing of how their world works.

Our sea slugs don't exist, but they might. And there might also exist super beings which stand to us as we stand to the sea slugs. We cannot adopt the perspective of these super beings, because we are not them, but the possibility of such a perspective is, I think, an antidote to excessive optimism.

## from "What Mary Didn't Know"[9]

...

### I. Three Clarifications

The knowledge argument does not rest on the dubious claim that logically you cannot imagine what sensing red is like unless you have sensed red. Powers of imagination are not to the point. The contention about Mary is not that, despite her fantastic grasp of neurophysiology and everything else physical, she *could not imagine* what it is like to sense red; it is that, as a matter of fact, she *would not know*. But if physicalism is true, she would know; and no great powers of imagination would be called for. Imagination is a faculty that those who *lack* knowledge need to fall back on.

9 From *The Journal of Philosophy* 83 (May 1986), pp. 291–295 (excerpt).

Secondly, the intensionality of knowledge[10] is not to the point. The argument does not rest on assuming falsely that, if $S$ knows that $a$ is $F$ and if $a = b$, then $S$ knows that $b$ is $F$. It is concerned with the nature of Mary's total body of knowledge before she is released: is it complete, or do some facts escape it? What is to the point is that $S$ may know that $a$ is $F$ and *know* that $a = b$, yet arguably not know that $b$ is $F$, by virtue of not being sufficiently logically alert to follow the consequences through. If Mary's lack of knowledge were at all like this, there would be no threat to physicalism in it. But it is very hard to believe that her lack of knowledge could be remedied merely by her explicitly following through enough logical consequences of her vast physical knowledge. Endowing her with great logical acumen and persistence is not in itself enough to fill in the gaps in her knowledge. On being let out, she will not say "I could have worked all this out before by making some more purely logical inferences."

Thirdly, the knowledge Mary lacked which is of particular point for the knowledge argument against physicalism is *knowledge about the experiences of others*, not about her own. When she is let out, she has new experiences, color experiences she has never had before. It is not, therefore, an objection to physicalism that she learns *something* on being let out. Before she was let out, she could not have known facts about her experience of red, for there were no such facts to know. That physicalist and nonphysicalist alike can agree on. After she is let out, things change; and physicalism can happily admit that she learns this; after all, some physical things will change, for instance, her brain states and their functional roles. The trouble for physicalism is that, after Mary sees her first ripe tomato, she will realize how impoverished her conception of the mental life of *others* has been *all along*. She will realize that there was, all the time she was carrying out her laborious investigations into the neurophysiologies of others and into the functional roles of their internal states, something about these people she was quite unaware of. All along their experiences (or many of them, those got from tomatoes, the sky, ...) had a feature conspicuous to them but until now hidden from her (in fact, not in logic). But she knew all the physical facts about them all along; hence, what she did not know until her release is not a physical fact about their experiences. But it is a fact about them. That is the trouble for physicalism....

10 To say that knowledge is intensional is to say that one might know something when it is expressed in one way but not know *the same thing* when it is expressed another way. For example, I might know that Snoop Dogg is a rap musician but deny any knowledge of Calvin Cordozar Broadus, Jr. Yet they're the same person.

# Can Computers Think?

JOHN SEARLE

American philosopher John Searle (1932– ) has taught for many decades at the University of California at Berkeley. He is well known for his contributions to the philosophy of language and the philosophy of mind. Searle was a student of J. L. Austin and P. F. Strawson, selections from whose works appear in this volume.

The selection included here, which was originally presented in 1984 as a public lecture, includes Searle's famous example of the Chinese Room. Through this example, one of the most widely discussed in philosophy of mind and cognitive science, Searle seeks to defend the view that thinking does not consist in computation alone. In his discussion, Searle makes reference to the works of a number of scientists and computer scientists who were active in the mid-1980s, including Herbert Simon, Alan Newell, Freeman Dyson, Marvin Minsky, and John McCarthy.

Though we do not know in detail how the brain functions, we do know enough to have an idea of the general relationships between brain processes and mental processes. Mental processes are caused by the behaviour of elements of the brain. At the same time, they are realised in the structure that is made up of those elements. I think this answer is consistent with the standard biological approaches to biological phenomena. Indeed, it is a kind of commonsense answer to the question, given what we know about how the world works. However, it is very much a minority point of view. The prevailing view in philosophy, psychology, and artificial intelligence is one which emphasises the analogies between the functioning of the human brain and the functioning of digital computers. According to the most extreme version of this view, the brain is just a digital computer and the mind is just a computer program. One could summarise this view—I call it "strong artificial intelligence," or "strong AI"—by saying that the mind is to the brain, as the program is to the computer hardware.

This view has the consequence that there is nothing essentially biological about the human mind. The brain just happens to be one of an indefinitely large number of different kinds of hardware computers that could sustain the programs which make up human intelligence. On this view, any physical system whatever that had the right program with the right inputs and outputs would have a mind in exactly the same sense that you and I have minds. So, for example, if you made a computer out of old beer cans powered by windmills; if it had the right program, it would have to have a mind. And the point is not that for all we know it

Reprinted by permission of the publisher from *Minds, Brains, and Science* by John R. Searle, pp. 28–41, Cambridge, Mass.: Harvard University Press. 

might have thoughts and feelings, but rather that it must have thoughts and feelings, because that is all there is to having thoughts and feelings: implementing the right program.

Most people who hold this view think we have not yet designed programs which are minds. But there is pretty much general agreement among them that it's only a matter of time until computer scientists and workers in artificial intelligence design the appropriate hardware and programs which will be the equivalent of human brains and minds. These will be artificial brains and minds which are in every way the equivalent of human brains and minds.

Many people outside of the field of artificial intelligence are quite amazed to discover that anybody could believe such a view as this. So, before criticising it, let me give you a few examples of the things that people in this field have actually said. Herbert Simon of Carnegie-Mellon University says that we already have machines that can literally think. There is no question of waiting for some future machine, because existing digital computers already have thoughts in exactly the same sense that you and I do. Well, fancy that! Philosophers have been worried for centuries about whether or not a machine could think, and now we discover that they already have such machines at Carnegie-Mellon. Simon's colleague Alan Newell claims that we have now discovered (and notice that Newell says "discovered" and not "hypothesised" or "considered the possibility," but we have *discovered*) that intelligence is just a matter of physical symbol manipulation; it has no essential connection with any specific kind of biological or physical wetware or hardware. Rather, any system whatever that is capable of manipulating physical symbols in the right way is capable of intelligence in the same literal sense as human intelligence of human beings. Both Simon and Newell, to their credit, emphasise that there is nothing metaphorical about these claims; they mean them quite literally. Freeman Dyson is quoted as having said that computers have an advantage over the rest of us when it comes to evolution. Since consciousness is just a matter of formal processes, in computers these formal processes can go on in substances that are much better able to survive in a universe that is cooling off than beings like ourselves made of our wet and messy materials. Marvin Minsky of MIT says that the next generation of computers will be so intelligent that we will "be lucky if they are willing to keep us around the house as household pets." My all-time favourite in the literature of exaggerated claims on behalf of the digital computer is from John McCarthy, the inventor of the term "artificial intelligence." McCarthy says even "machines as simple as thermostats can be said to have beliefs." And indeed, according to him, almost any machine capable of problem-solving can be said to have beliefs. I admire McCarthy's courage. I once asked him: "What beliefs does your thermostat have?" And he said: "My thermostat has three beliefs—it's too hot in here, it's too cold in here, and it's just right in here." As a philosopher, I like all these claims for a simple reason. Unlike most philosophical theses, they are reasonably clear, and they admit of a simple and decisive refutation. It is this refutation that I am going to undertake in this chapter.

The nature of the refutation has nothing whatever to do with any particular stage of computer technology. It is important to emphasise this point because the temptation is always to think that the solution to our problems must wait on some as yet uncreated technological wonder. But in fact, the nature of the refutation is completely independent of any state of technology. It has to do with the very definition of a digital computer, with what a digital computer is.

It is essential to our conception of a digital computer that its operations can be specified purely formally; that is, we specify the steps in the operation of the computer in terms of abstract symbols—sequences of zeroes and ones printed on a tape, for example. A typical computer "rule" will determine that when a machine is in a certain state and it has a certain symbol on its tape, then it will perform a certain operation such as erasing the symbol or printing another symbol and then enter another state such as moving the tape one square to the left. But the symbols have no meaning; they have no semantic content; they are not about anything. They have to be specified purely in terms of their formal or syntactical structure. The zeroes and ones, for example, are just numerals; they don't even stand for numbers. Indeed, it is this feature of digital computers that makes them so powerful. One and the same type of hardware, if it is appropriately designed, can be used to run an indefinite range of different programs. And one and the same program can be run on an indefinite range of different types of hardwares.

But this feature of programs, that they are defined purely formally or syntactically, is fatal to the view that mental processes and program processes are identical. And the reason can be stated quite simply. There is more to having a mind than having formal or syntactical processes. Our internal mental states, by definition, have certain sorts of contents. If I am thinking about Kansas City or wishing that I had a cold beer to drink or wondering if there will be a fall in interest rates, in each case my mental state has a certain mental content in addition to whatever formal features it might have. That is, even if my thoughts occur to me in strings of symbols, there must be more to the thought than the abstract strings, because strings by themselves can't have any meaning. If my thoughts are to be *about* anything, then the strings must have a *meaning* which makes the thoughts about those things. In a word, the mind has more than a syntax, it has a semantics. The reason that no computer program can ever be a mind is simply that a computer program is only syntactical, and minds are more than syntactical. Minds are semantical, in the sense that they have more than a formal structure, they have a content.

To illustrate this point I have designed a certain thought-experiment. Imagine that a bunch of computer programmers have written a program that will enable a computer to simulate the understanding of Chinese. So, for example, if the computer is given a question in Chinese, it will match the question against its memory, or data base, and produce appropriate answers to the questions in Chinese. Suppose for the sake of argument that the computer's answers are as good as those of a native Chinese speaker. Now then, does the computer, on the basis of this, understand Chinese, does it literally understand Chinese, in the way that Chinese speakers understand Chinese? Well, imagine that you are locked in a room, and in this room are several baskets full of Chinese symbols. Imagine that you (like me) do not understand a word of Chinese, but that you are given a rule book in English for manipulating these Chinese symbols. The rules specify the manipulations of the symbols purely formally, in terms of their syntax, not their semantics. So the rule might say: "Take a squiggle-squiggle sign out of basket number one and put it next to a squoggle-squoggle sign from basket number two." Now suppose that some other Chinese symbols are passed into the room, and that you are given further rules for passing back Chinese symbols out of the room. Suppose that unknown to you the symbols passed into the room are called "questions" by the people outside the room, and the symbols you pass back out of the room are called "answers to the questions." Suppose, furthermore, that the programmers are so good at designing the programs and that you are so good at manipulating the symbols, that very soon your answers are indistinguishable from those of a native Chinese speaker. There you are locked in your room shuffling your Chinese symbols and passing out Chinese symbols in response to incoming Chinese symbols. On the basis of the situation as I have described it, there is no way you could learn any Chinese simply by manipulating these formal symbols.

Now the point of the story is simply this: by virtue of implementing a formal computer program from the point of view of an outside observer, you behave exactly as if you understood Chinese, but all the same you don't understand a word of Chinese. But if going through the appropriate computer program for understanding Chinese is not enough to give *you* an understanding of Chinese, then it is not enough to give *any other digital computer* an understanding of Chinese. And again, the reason for this can be stated quite simply. If you don't understand Chinese, then no other computer could understand Chinese because no digital computer, just by virtue of running a program, has anything that you don't have. All that the computer has, as you have, is a formal program for manipulating uninterpreted Chinese symbols. To repeat, a computer has a syntax, but no semantics. The whole point of the parable of the Chinese room is to remind us of a fact that we knew all along. Understanding a language, or indeed, having mental states at all, involves more than just having a bunch of formal symbols. It involves having an interpretation, or a meaning attached to those symbols. And a digital computer, as defined, cannot have more than just formal symbols because the operation of the computer, as I said earlier, is defined in terms of its ability to implement programs. And these programs are purely formally specifiable—that is, they have no semantic content.

We can see the force of this argument if we contrast what it is like to be asked and to answer questions in English, and to be asked and to answer questions in some language where we have no knowledge of any of the meanings of the words. Imagine that in the Chinese room you are also given questions in English about such things as your age or your life history, and that you answer these questions. What is the difference between the Chinese case and the English case? Well again, if like me you understand no Chinese and you do understand English, then the difference is obvious. You understand the questions in English because they are expressed in symbols whose meanings are known to you. Similarly, when you give the answers in English you are producing symbols which are meaningful to you. But in the case of the Chinese, you have none of that. In the case of the Chinese, you simply manipulate formal symbols according to a computer program, and you attach no meaning to any of the elements.

Various replies have been suggested to this argument by workers in artificial intelligence and in psychology, as well as philosophy. They all have something in common; they are all inadequate. And there is an obvious reason why they have to be inadequate, since the argument rests on a very simple logical truth, namely, syntax alone is not sufficient for semantics, and digital computers insofar as they are computers have, by definition, a syntax alone.

I want to make this clear by considering a couple of the arguments that are often presented against me.

Some people attempt to answer the Chinese room example by saying that the whole system understands Chinese. The idea here is that though I, the person in the room manipulating the symbols do not understand Chinese, I am just the central processing unit of the computer system. They argue that it is the whole system, including the room, the baskets full of symbols and the ledgers containing the programs and perhaps other items as well, taken as a totality, that understands Chinese. But this is subject to exactly the same objection I made before. There is no way that the system can get from the syntax to the semantics. I, as the central processing unit have no way of figuring out what any of these symbols means; but then neither does the whole system.

Another common response is to imagine that we put the Chinese understanding program inside a robot. If the robot moved around and interacted causally with the world, wouldn't that be enough to guarantee that it understood Chinese? Once again the inexorability of the semantics-syntax distinction overcomes this manoeuvre. As long as we suppose that the robot has only a computer for a brain then, even though it might behave exactly as if it understood Chinese, it would still have no way of getting from the syntax to the semantics of Chinese. You can see this if you imagine that I am the computer. Inside a room in the robot's skull I shuffle symbols without knowing that some of them come in to me from television cameras attached to the robot's head and others go out to move the robot's arms and legs. As long as all I have is a formal computer program, I have no way of attaching any meaning to any of the symbols. And the fact that the robot is engaged in causal interactions with the outside world won't help me to attach any meaning to the symbols unless I have some way of finding out about that fact. Suppose the robot picks up a hamburger and this triggers the symbol for hamburger to come into the room. As long as all I have is the symbol with no knowledge of its causes or how it got there, I have no way of knowing what it means. The causal interactions between the robot and the rest of the world are irrelevant unless those causal interactions are represented in some mind or other. But there is no way they can be if all that the so-called mind consists of is a set of purely formal, syntactical operations.

It is important to see exactly what is claimed and what is not claimed by my argument. Suppose we ask the question that I mentioned at the beginning: "Could a machine think?" Well, in one sense, of course, we are all machines. We can construe the stuff inside our heads as a meat machine. And of course, we can all think. So, in one sense of "machine," namely that sense in which a machine is just a physical system which is capable of performing certain kinds of operations, in that sense, we are all machines, and we can think. So, trivially, there are machines that can think. But that wasn't the question that bothered us. So let's try a different formulation of it. Could an artefact think? Could a man-made machine think? Well, once again, it depends on the kind of artefact. Suppose we designed a machine that was molecule-for-molecule indistinguishable from a human being. Well then, if you can duplicate the causes, you can presumably duplicate the effects. So once again, the answer to that question is, in principle at least, trivially yes. If you could build a machine that had the same structure as a human being, then presumably that machine would be able to think. Indeed, it would be a surrogate human being. Well, let's try again.

The question isn't: "Can a machine think?" or: "Can an artefact think?" The question is: "Can a digital computer think?" But once again we have to be very careful in how we interpret the question. From a mathematical point of view, anything whatever can be described *as if* it were a digital computer. And that's because it can be described as instantiating or implementing a computer program. In an utterly trivial sense, the pen that is on the desk in front of me can be described as a digital computer. It just happens to have a very boring computer program. The program says: "Stay there." Now since in this sense, anything whatever is a digital computer, because anything whatever can be described as implementing a computer program, then once again, our question gets a trivial answer. Of course our brains are digital computers, since they implement any number of computer programs. And of course our brains can think. So once again, there is a trivial answer to the question. But that wasn't really the question we were trying to ask. The question we wanted to ask is this: "Can a digital computer, as defined, think?" That is to say: "Is instantiating or implementing the right computer program with the right inputs and outputs, sufficient for, or constitutive of, thinking?" And to this question, unlike its predecessors, the answer is clearly "no." And it is "no" for the reason that we have spelled out, namely, the computer program is defined purely syntactically. But thinking is more than just a matter of manipulating meaningless symbols, it involves meaningful semantic contents. These semantic contents are what we mean by "meaning."

It is important to emphasise again that we are not talking about a particular stage of computer technology. The argument has nothing to do with the forthcoming, amazing advances in computer science. It has nothing to do with the distinction between serial and parallel processes, or with the size of programs, or the speed of computer operations, or with computers that can interact causally with their environment, or even with the invention of robots. Technological progress is always grossly exaggerated, but even subtracting the exaggeration, the development of computers has been quite remarkable, and we can reasonably expect that even more remarkable progress will be made in the future. No doubt we will be much better able to simulate human behaviour on computers than we can at present, and certainly much better than we have been able to in the past. The point I am making is that if we are talking about having mental states, having a mind, all of these simulations are simply irrelevant. It doesn't matter how good the technology is, or how rapid the calculations made by the computer are. If it really is a computer, its operations have to be defined syntactically, whereas consciousness, thoughts, feelings, emotions, and all the rest of it involve more than a syntax. Those features, by definition, the computer is unable to *duplicate* however powerful may be its ability to *simulate*. The key distinction here is between duplication and simulation. And no simulation by itself ever constitutes duplication.

What I have done so far is give a basis to the sense that those citations I began this talk with are really as preposterous as they seem. There is a puzzling question in this discussion though, and that is: "Why would anybody ever have thought that computers could think or have feelings and emotions and all the rest of it?" After all, we can do computer simulations of any process whatever that can be given a formal description. So, we can do a computer simulation of the flow of money in the British economy, or the pattern of power distribution in the Labour party. We can do computer simulation of rain storms in the home counties, or warehouse fires in East London. Now, in each of these cases, nobody supposes that the computer simulation is actually the real thing; no one supposes that a computer simulation of a storm will leave us all wet, or a computer simulation of a fire is likely to burn the house down. Why on earth would anyone in his right mind suppose a computer simulation of mental processes actually had mental processes? I don't really know the answer to that, since the idea seems to me, to put it frankly, quite crazy from the start. But I can make a couple of speculations.

First of all, where the mind is concerned, a lot of people are still tempted to some sort of behaviourism. They think if a system behaves as if it understood Chinese, then it really must understand Chinese. But we have already refuted this form of behaviourism with the Chinese room argument. Another assumption made by many people is that the mind is not a part of the biological world, it is not a part of the world of nature. The strong artificial intelligence view relies on that in its conception that the mind is purely formal; that somehow or other, it cannot be treated as a concrete product of biological processes like any other biological product. There is in these discussions, in short, a kind of residual dualism. AI partisans believe that the mind is more than a part of the natural biological world; they believe that the mind is purely formally specifiable. The paradox of this is that the AI literature is filled with fulminations against some view called "dualism," but in fact, the whole thesis of strong AI rests on a kind of dualism. It rests on a rejection of the idea that the mind is just a natural biological phenomenon in the world like any other.

I want to conclude this chapter by putting together the thesis of the last chapter and the thesis of this one. Both of these theses can be stated very simply. And indeed, I am going to state them with perhaps excessive crudeness. But if we put them together I think we get a quite powerful conception of the relations of minds, brains and computers. And the argument has a very simple logical structure, so you can see whether it is valid or invalid. The first premise is:

1. *Brains cause minds.*

Now, of course, that is really too crude. What we mean by that is that mental processes that we consider to constitute a mind are caused, entirely caused, by processes going on inside the brain. But let's be crude, let's just abbreviate that as three words—brains cause minds. And that is just a fact about how the world works. Now let's write proposition number two:

2. *Syntax is not sufficient for semantics.*

That proposition is a conceptual truth. It just articulates our distinction between the notion of what is purely formal and what has content. Now, to these two propositions—that brains cause minds and that syntax is not sufficient for semantics—let's add a third and a fourth:

3. *Computer programs are entirely defined by their formal, or syntactical, structure.*

That proposition, I take it, is true by definition; it is part of what we mean by the notion of a computer program.

4. *Minds have mental contents; specifically, they have semantic contents.*

And that, I take it, is just an obvious fact about how our minds work. My thoughts, and beliefs, and desires are about something, or they refer to something, or they concern states of affairs in the world; and they do that because their content directs them at these states of affairs in the world. Now, from these four premises, we can draw our first conclusion; and it follows obviously from premises 2, 3 and 4:

CONCLUSION 1. *No computer program by itself is sufficient to give a system a mind. Programs, in short, are not minds, and they are not by themselves sufficient for having minds.*

Now, that is a very powerful conclusion, because it means that the project of trying to create minds solely by designing programs is doomed from the start. And it is important to re-emphasise that this has nothing to do with any particular state of technology or any particular state of the complexity of the program. This is a purely formal, or logical, result from a set of axioms which are agreed to by all (or nearly all) of the disputants concerned. That is, even most of the hardcore enthusiasts for artificial intelligence agree that in fact, as a matter of biology, brain processes cause mental states, and they agree that programs are defined purely formally. But if you put these conclusions together with certain other things that we know, then it follows immediately that the project of strong AI is incapable of fulfilment.

However, once we have got these axioms, let's see what else we can derive. Here is a second conclusion:

CONCLUSION 2. *The way that brain functions cause minds cannot be solely in virtue of running a computer program.*

And this second conclusion follows from conjoining the first premise together with our first conclusion. That is, from the fact that brains cause minds and that programs are not enough to do the job, it follows that the way that brains cause minds can't be solely by running a computer program. Now that also I think is an important result, because it has the consequence that the brain is not, or at least is not just, a digital computer. We saw earlier that anything can trivially be described as if it were a digital computer, and brains are no exception. But the importance of this conclusion is that the computational properties of the brain are simply not enough to explain its functioning to produce mental states. And indeed, that ought to seem a commonsense scientific conclusion to us anyway because all it does is remind us of the fact that brains are biological engines; their biology matters. It is not, as several people in artificial intelligence have claimed, just an irrelevant fact about the mind that it happens to be realised in human brains.

Now, from our first premise, we can also derive a third conclusion:

CONCLUSION 3. *Anything else that caused minds would have to have causal powers at least equivalent to those of the brain.*

And this third conclusion is a trivial consequence of our first premise. It is a bit like saying that if my petrol engine drives my car at seventy-five miles an hour, then any diesel engine that was capable of doing that would have to have a power output at least equivalent to that of my petrol engine. Of course, some other system might cause mental processes using entirely different chemical or biochemical features from those the brain in fact uses. It might turn out that there are beings on other planets, or in other solar systems, that have mental states and use an entirely different biochemistry from ours. Suppose that Martians arrived on earth and we concluded that they had mental states. But suppose that when their heads were opened up, it was discovered that all they had inside was green slime. Well still, the green slime, if it functioned to produce consciousness and all the rest of their mental life, would have to have causal powers equal to those of the human brain. But now, from our first conclusion, that programs are not enough, and our third conclusion, that any other system would have to have causal powers equal to the brain, conclusion four follows immediately:

CONCLUSION 4. *For any artefact that we might build which had mental states equivalent to human mental states, the implementation of a computer program would not by itself be sufficient. Rather the artefact would have to have powers equivalent to the powers of the human brain.*

The upshot of this discussion I believe is to remind us of something that we have known all along: namely, mental states are biological phenomena. Consciousness, intentionality, subjectivity and mental causation are all a part of our biological life history, along with growth, reproduction, the secretion of bile, and digestion.

# Part Three:
# Personal Identity

# Chapter xxvii: Identity and diversity

**1.** Another context in which the mind compares things [= 'considers things together'] is their *very being*: when we consider something as existing at a given time and place and compare it with itself existing at another time, we are led to form the ideas of *identity* and *diversity.* [In this context 'diversity' means 'non-identity'. To say that *x is diverse from y* is to say only that *x is not y*.] When we see a thing—any thing, of whatever sort—to be in a certain place at a certain time, we are sure that it is *that very thing* and not *another thing existing at that time in some other place*, however alike the two may be in all other respects. And in this consists *identity*, when the ideas to which it is attributed don't vary from what they were at the moment of their former existence that we are comparing with the present. We never find—and can't even conceive of—two things of the same kind existing in the same place at the same time, so we rightly conclude that whatever exists in a certain place at a certain time excludes all ·others· of the same kind, and is there itself alone. So when we ask whether a thing is 'the same' or not, we are always referring to something that existed at a given time in a given place, a thing that at that instant was certainly the same as itself and not the same as anything else. From this it follows that •one thing can't have two beginnings of existence because it is impossible for one thing to be in different places ·at the same time·, and •two things can't have one beginning, because it is impossible for two things of the same kind to exist in the same instant at the very same place. Thus, what had one beginning is the same thing; and what had a different beginning in time and place from that is not the same but diverse. The difficulties philosophers have had with this relation ·of identity· have arisen from their not attending carefully to the precise notions of the things to which it is attributed.

**2.** We have ideas of only three sorts of substances: *God, finite intelligences*, and *bodies.* **1** God is without beginning, eternal, unalterable, and everywhere; and so there can be no doubt concerning his identity. **2** Each finite spirit had its determinate time and place of beginning to exist, so its relation to that time and place will always determine its identity for as long as it exists. **3** The same holds for every particle of matter, which continues as the same as long as no matter is added to or removed from it. . . . These three sorts of 'substances' (as we call them) don't exclude *one another* out of the same place, but we can't conceive any of them allowing another *of the same kind* into its place. If that were to happen, the notions and names of identity and diversity would be useless, and there would be no way of distinguishing substances or anything else from one another. For example: if two bodies could be in the same place at the same time, then those two portions of matter would be one and the same, whatever their size. Indeed, *all* bodies would be one and the same, because allowing two bodies to be in one place ·at one time· allows for all bodies to do so. To suppose this ·to be possible· is to obliterate the distinction between identity and diversity, the difference between *one* and *more*. . . .

·That all concerned the identity of *substances*·. There remain *modes* and *relations*, but because they ultimately depend on substances [Locke says they are 'ultimately terminated in substances'], the identity and diversity of each particular one of them will be determined in the same way as the identity of particular substances.

Questions of identity and diversity don't arise for things whose existence consists in a sequence ·of events·, such as the actions of finite beings, e.g. motion and thought. Because each of these ·events· perishes the moment it begins, they can't exist at different times or in different places, as enduring things can; and therefore no motion or thought can be the same as any earlier motion or thought.

**3.** There has been much enquiry after the *principle of individuation*; but what I have said enables us easily to discover what that is: it is *existence itself*, which ties a being of a given sort to a particular time and place that can't be shared by any other being of the same kind. This seems easier to conceive in *simple* substances or modes, but if we are careful we can just as easily apply it to *compound* ones. Consider an atom, i.e. a continued body under one unchanging surface, existing at a particular time and place: it is evident that at that instant it is the same as itself. For being at that instant what it is and nothing else, it is the same and so must continue as long as its existence is continued; for so long it will be the same and no other. [That sentence is Locke's.] Similarly, if two or more atoms are joined together into a single mass, every one of those atoms will be the same by the foregoing rule. And while they exist united together, the mass whose parts they are must be the same mass, or the same body, however much the parts have been re-arranged. But if one atom is removed from the mass, or one new one added, it is no longer the same mass, or the same body. The identity of living creatures depends not on a mass of the same particles but on something else. For in them the variation of large amounts of matter doesn't alter the identity. An oak growing from a sapling to a great tree, and then lopped, is still the same oak; and a colt grown up to be a horse, sometimes fat, sometimes lean, is the same horse throughout all this. In neither case is there the same mass of matter, though there truly is the same oak, or horse. That is because in these two cases, a mass of matter and a living body, identity isn't applied to the same thing.

**4.** How, then, does an oak differ from a mass of matter? The answer seems to me to be this: the *mass* is merely the cohesion of particles of matter anyhow united, whereas the *oak* is such a disposition of particles as constitutes the parts of an oak, and an organization of those parts that enables the whole to receive and distribute nourishment so as to continue and form the wood, bark, and leaves, etc. of an oak, in which consists the vegetable life. Thus, something is *one plant* if it has an organization of parts in one cohering body partaking of one common life, and it continues to be *the same plant* as long as it partakes of the same life, even if that life is passed along to new particles of matter vitally united to the living plant, in a similar continued organization suitable for that sort of plants. This organization is at any one instant in some one *collection of matter*, which distinguishes it from all others at that instant; and what has the identity that makes the same *plant* is

> that *individual life*, existing constantly from that moment forwards and backwards, in the same continuity of imperceptibly succeeding parts united to the living body of the plant.

It also makes all the parts of it be parts of the same plant, for as long as they exist united in that continued organization that is fit to convey that common life to all the parts so united.

**5.** The identity of lower animals is sufficiently like that for anyone to be able to see, from what I have said, what makes one animal and continues it the same. It can be illustrated by something similar, namely the identity of machines. *What is a watch?* Clearly it is nothing but a construction of parts organized to a certain end—an end that it can attain when sufficient force is applied to it. If we suppose this machine to be one continued body whose parts were repaired, added to, or subtracted from, by a constant addition or separation of imperceptible parts, with one common life, it would be very much like the body of an animal; with the difference that in an animal the fitness of the organization and the motion wherein life consists begin together, because the motion comes from within; but in a machine the force can be seen to come from outside, and is often lacking even when the machine is in order and well fitted to receive it—·for example, when a clock isn't wound up·.

**6.** This also shows what the identity of the *same man* consists in, namely: a participation in the same continued life by constantly fleeting particles of matter that are successively vitally united to the same organized body. If you place the identity of man in anything but this, you'll find it hard to make an embryo and an adult the same man, or a well man and a madman the same man. ·Your only chance of doing this is by tying 'same man' to 'same soul', but by that standard you will· make it possible for Seth, Ismael, Socrates, Pilate, St. Augustine, and Cesare Borgia to be the same man. If identity of soul alone makes the same man, and nothing in the nature of matter rules out an individual spirit's being united to different bodies, it will be possible that those men with their different characters and living at widely different times, may have been the same man! That strange way of using the word 'man' is what one is led to by giving it a meaning from which body and shape are excluded. . . .

**7.** So unity of substance does not constitute all sorts of identity. To conceive and judge correctly about identity, we must consider what idea the word it is applied to stands for: it is one thing to be the same *substance*, another the same *man*, and a third the same *person*, if 'person', 'man', and 'substance' are names for three different ideas; for such as is the idea belonging to that name, such must be the identity. If this had been more carefully attended to, it might have prevented a great deal of that confusion that often occurs regarding identity, and especially personal identity, to which

I now turn ·after one more section on 'same man'·.

**8.** An animal is a living organized body; and consequently the same animal, as I have said, is the same continued life communicated to different particles of matter, as they are successively united to that organized living body. And whatever other definitions are propounded, there should be no doubt that the word 'man' as we use it stands for the idea of an animal of a certain form. ·The time-hallowed definition of 'man' as 'rational animal' is wrong·. If we should see •a creature of our own shape and ·physical· constitution, though it had no more reason all its life than a cat or a parrot, we would still call him a man; and anyone who heard •a cat or a parrot talk, reason, and philosophize would still think it to be a cat or a parrot and would describe it as such. One of these two is •a dull, irrational man, the other •a very intelligent rational parrot. [Locke then quotes a tediously long traveller's tale about encountering a rational parrot. His point is that someone who believes this account will go thinking of this rational animal as a parrot, not as a man.]

**9.** With 'same man' in hand, let us turn to 'same person'. To find what *personal* identity consists in, we must consider what 'person' stands for. I think it is *a thinking intelligent being, that has reason and reflection, and can consider itself as itself, the same thinking thing at different times and places.* What enables it to think of itself is its *consciousness*, which is inseparable from thinking and (it seems to me) essential to it. It is impossible for anyone to perceive, without perceiving that he perceives. When we see, hear, smell, taste, feel, meditate, or will anything, we know that we do so. It is always like that with our present sensations and perceptions. And it is through this that everyone is to himself that which he calls 'self', not raising the question of whether the same self is continued in the same substance. Consciousness always accompanies thinking, and makes everyone to be what he calls 'self' and thereby distinguishes himself from all other thinking things; in this alone consists personal identity, i.e. the sameness of a rational being; and as far as this consciousness can be extended backwards to any past action or thought, so far reaches the identity of that person; it is the same self now that it was then; and this present self that now reflects on it is the one by which that action was performed.

**10.** Given that it is the same *person*, is it the same identical *substance*? Most people would think that it *is* the same substance if these perceptions with their consciousness always remained present in the mind, making the same thinking thing always consciously present and (most people would think) evidently the same to itself. What seems to make the difficulty—·that is, to make it at least questionable whether the same person must be the same substance·—is the following fact. •Consciousness is often interrupted by forgetfulness, and at no moment of our lives do we have the whole sequence of all our past actions before our eyes in one view; even the best memories lose the sight of one part while they are viewing another. Furthermore, •for the greatest part of our lives we don't reflect on our past selves at all, because we are intent on our present thoughts or (in sound sleep) have no thoughts at all, or at least none with the consciousness that characterizes our waking thoughts. In all these cases our consciousness is interrupted, and we lose the sight of our past selves, and so doubts are raised as to whether or not we are the same thinking thing, i.e. the same substance.

That may be a reasonable question, but it has nothing to do with personal identity. For the latter, the question is about what makes the same *person*, and not whether the same identical *substance* always thinks in the same person. Different substances might all partake in a single consciousness and thereby be united into one person, just as different bodies can enter into the same life and thereby be united into one animal, whose identity is preserved throughout that change of substances by the unity of the single continued life. What makes a man be himself *to himself* is sameness of consciousness, so personal identity depends entirely on that—whether the consciousness is tied to one substance throughout or rather is continued in a series of different substances. For as far as any thinking being can repeat the idea of any past action with the same consciousness that he had of it at first, and with the same consciousness he has of his present actions, so far is he the same personal self. For it is by the consciousness he has of his present thoughts and actions that he is *self to himself* now, and so will be the same self as far as the same consciousness can extend to actions past or to come. Distance of time doesn't make him two or more persons, and nor does change of substance; any more than a man is made to be two men by having a long or short sleep or by changing his clothes.

**11.** Our own bodies give us some kind of evidence for this. All the particles of your body, while they are vitally united to a single thinking conscious self—so that you feel when they are touched, and are affected by and conscious of good or harm that happens to them—are a part of yourself, i.e. of your thinking conscious self. Thus the limbs of his body are to everyone a part of himself; he feels for them and is concerned for them. Cut off a hand and thereby separate it from that consciousness the person had of its heat, cold, and other states, and it is then no longer a part of himself, any more than is the remotest material thing. Thus we see the substance of which the personal self consisted at one time may be varied at another without change of personal identity; for there is no doubt that it is the same person, even though one of its limbs has been cut off.

**12.** But it is asked: *Can it be the same person if the substance changes?* and *Can it be different persons if the same substance does the thinking throughout?*

·Before I address these questions in sections 13 and 14, there's a preliminary point I want to make. It is that· neither question is alive for those who hold that thought is a property of a purely material animal constitution, with no immaterial substance being involved. Whether or not they are right about that, they obviously conceive personal identity as being preserved in something other than identity of substance; just as animal identity is preserved in identity of life, not of substance. ·This pair of questions does present a challenge to· •those who hold that only immaterial substances can think, ·and that sameness of person requires sameness of immaterial substance. Before •they can confront their materialist opponents, they· have to show why personal identity can't be preserved through a change of immaterial substances, just as animal identity is preserved through a change of material substances. Unless they say that what makes the same life ·and thus the animal identity· in lower animals is one immaterial spirit, just as (according to them) one immaterial spirit makes the same person in men—and Cartesians at least won't take that way out, for fear of making the lower animals thinking things too.

**13.** As to the first question, *If the thinking substance is changed, can it be the same person?*, I answer that this can be settled only by those who know •what kind of substances they are that think, and •whether the consciousness of past actions can be transferred from one such substance to another. Admittedly, if the same consciousness were •the same individual action, it couldn't be transferred ·because in that case bringing a past headache (say) into one's consciousness would be bringing back *that very headache*, and *that* is tied to the substance to which it occurred. But a present consciousness of a past event isn't like that. Rather·, it is •a present *representation of* a past action, and we have still to be shown why something can't be represented to the mind as having happened though really it did not. How far the consciousness of past actions is tied to one individual agent, so that another can't possibly have it, will be hard for us to determine until we know

- •what kind of action it is that can't be done without a reflex act of perception accompanying it, and
- •how such an action is done by thinking substances who can't think without being conscious of it.

In our present state of knowledge it is hard to see how it can be impossible, in the nature of things, for an intellectual substance to have represented to it as done by itself something that it never did, and was perhaps done by some other agent. . . . Until we have a clearer view of the nature of thinking substances, we had better assume that such changes of substance within a single person never do *in fact* happen, basing this on the goodness of God. Having a concern for the happiness or misery of his creatures, he won't transfer from one ·substance· to another the consciousness that draws reward or punishment with it. . . .

**14.** The second question, *Can it be different persons if the same substance does the thinking throughout?*, seems to me to arise out of the question of whether the following is possible:

> An immaterial being that has been conscious of the events in its past is wholly stripped of all that consciousness, losing it beyond the power of ever retrieving it again; so that now it (as it were) opens a new account, with a new starting date, having a consciousness that can't reach ·back· beyond this new state.

·Really, the question is whether if this happened it could be the same *person* who had first one consciousness and then another, with no possibility of communication between them·. [Locke says that this must be regarded as possible by 'those who hold pre-existence', that is, who believe in reincarnation. He attacks them, thereby attacking the separation of 'same person' from 'same consciousness', and proposes a thought-experiment:] Reflect on yourself, and conclude that you have in yourself an immaterial spirit that is what thinks in you, keeps you the same throughout the constant change of your body, and is what you call 'myself'. Now try to suppose also that it is the same soul that was in Nestor or Thersites at the siege of Troy. This isn't obviously absurd; for souls, as far as we know anything of their nature, can go with any portion of matter as well as with any other; so the •soul ·or thinking substance· that is now *yourself* may once really have been the •soul of someone else, such as Thersites or Nestor. But you don't now have any consciousness of any of the actions either of those two; so can you conceive yourself as being the same •*person* with either of them? Can their actions have anything to do with you? Can you attribute those actions to yourself, or think of them as yours more than the actions of any other men that ever existed? ·Of course you can't·. . . .

**15.** So we can easily conceive of being the same person at the resurrection, though in a body with partly different parts or structure from what one has now, as long as the same consciousness stays with the soul that inhabits the body. But the soul alone, in the change of bodies, would not be accounted enough to make the same man—except by someone who identifies the soul with the man. If the soul of a prince, carrying with it the consciousness of the prince's past life, were to enter and inform the body of a cobbler who has been deserted by his own soul, everyone sees that he would be the same person as the prince, accountable only for the prince's actions; but who would say it was the same man? The body contributes to making the man, and in this case I should think everyone would let the body settle the 'same man' question, not dissuaded from this by the soul, with all its princely thoughts. To everyone but himself he would be the same cobbler, the same man. I know that in common parlance 'same person' and 'same man' stand for the same thing; and of course everyone will always be free to speak as he pleases, giving words what meanings he thinks fit, and changing them as often as he likes. Still, when we want to explore what makes the same spirit, man, or person, we must fix the ideas of spirit, man, or person in our minds; and when we have become clear about what we mean by them, we shan't find it hard to settle, for each of them, when it is 'the same' and when not.

**16.** But although the same •immaterial substance or soul does not by itself, in all circumstances, make the same man, it is clear that •consciousness unites actions—whether from long ago or from the immediately preceding moment—into the same person. Whatever has the consciousness of present and past actions is the same person to whom they both belong. If my present consciousness that I am now writing were also a consciousness that •I saw an overflowing of the Thames last winter and that •I saw Noah's ark and the flood, I couldn't doubt that I who write this now am the same self that saw the Thames overflowed last winter and viewed the flood at the general deluge—place that self in what substance you please. I could no more doubt this than I can doubt that I who write this am the same *myself* now while I write as I was yesterday, whether or not I consist of all the same substance, material or immaterial. For sameness of substance is irrelevant to sameness of self: I am as much involved in—and as justly accountable for—•an action that was done a thousand years ago and is appropriated to me now by this self-consciousness as I am for •what I did a moment ago.

**17.** *Self* is that conscious thinking thing that feels or is conscious of pleasure and pain and capable of happiness or misery, and so is concerned for itself as far as that consciousness extends. (This holds true whatever substance the thinking thing is made up of; it doesn't matter whether it is spiritual or material, simple or compounded.) You must find that while your little finger is brought under your consciousness it is as much a part of yourself as is your head or your heart. If the finger were amputated and this consciousness went along with it, deserting the rest of the body, it is evident that the little finger would then be the person, the same person; and ·this· self would then would have nothing to do with the rest of the body. As with spatial separation so also with temporal: something with which the consciousness of this present thinking thing can join itself makes the same person, and is one self with it, as everyone who reflects will perceive.

**18.** Personal identity is the basis for all the right and justice of reward and punishment. What everyone is concerned for, for himself, is happiness and misery—with no concern for what becomes of any substance that isn't connected with that consciousness. [Locke goes on to apply that to his 'finger' example, supposing that the finger takes the original consciousness with it, and that the rest of the body acquires a new consciousness.]

**19.** This illustrates my thesis that personal identity consists not in the identity of substance but in the identity of consciousness. If Socrates and the present mayor of Queenborough agree in *that*, they are the same person; if Socrates awake doesn't partake of the same consciousness as Socrates sleeping, they aren't the same person. And to punish Socrates awake for something done by sleeping Socrates without Socrates awake ever being conscious of it would be as unjust as to punish someone for an action of his twin brother's merely because their outsides were so alike that they couldn't be distinguished.

**20.** It may be objected: 'Suppose I wholly lose the memory of some parts of my life beyond any possibility of retrieving them, so that I shall never be conscious of them again; aren't I still the same person who did those actions, had those thoughts that I once was conscious of, even though I have now forgotten them?' To this I answer that we must be careful about what the word 'I' is applied to. This objector is thinking of sameness of the *man*, and calls it 'I' because he assumes that the same man is the same *person*. But ·the assumption isn't necessarily correct·. If one man could have distinct disconnected consciousnesses at different times, that *same man* would certainly make different *persons* at different times. That this is what people in general think can be seen in the most solemn declaration of their opinions: human laws don't punish the madman for the sane man's actions, or the sane man for what the madman did, because they treat them as two persons. This is reflected in common speech when we say that someone is 'not himself' or is 'beside himself'.Those phrases insinuate that the speaker thinks—or that those who coined the phrases thought—that the self was changed, the self-same person was no longer in that man.

**21.** 'It is still hard to conceive that Socrates, the same individual man, might be two persons.' To help us with this we must consider what is meant by 'Socrates', or 'the same individual man'. ·There are three options·. The same man might be any of these:

**1** the same individual, immaterial, thinking substance; in short, the numerically-same soul and nothing else,

**2** the same animal, without any regard to an immaterial soul,

**3** the same immaterial spirit united to the same animal.

Help yourself! On any of these accounts of 'same man', it is impossible for personal identity to consist in anything but consciousness, or reach any further than that does.

According to **1**, a man born of different women, and in distant times, might still be the same man. Anyone who allows *this* must also allow that the same man could be two distinct persons. . . .

According to **2** and **3**, •Socrates in this life cannot be the same man as •anyone in the after-life. The only way to do this—·allowing for the possibility that •Socrates in Athens and •Socrates in Limbo are the same man·—is through an appeal to sameness of consciousness; and that amounts to equating human identity—·'same man'·—with personal identity. But ·that equation is problematic, because· it makes it hard to see how the •infant Socrates can be the same man as •Socrates after the resurrection. There seems to be little agreement about what makes a man, and thus about what makes the same individual man; but whatever we think about that, if we are not to fall into great absurdities we must agree that sameness of person resides in consciousness.

**22.** You may want to object: 'But isn't a man drunk and sober the same person? Why else is he punished for what he does when drunk, even if he is never afterwards conscious of it? He is just as much a single person as a man who walks in his sleep and is answerable, while awake, for any harm he did in his sleep.' ·Here is my reply to that·. Human laws punish both, with a justice suitable to the state of knowledge of those who administer the law: in these cases they can't distinguish for sure what is real from what is counterfeit; and so they don't allow the ignorance in drunkenness or sleep as a plea. Granted: punishment is tied to personhood, which is tied to consciousness, and the drunkard may not be conscious of what he did; but the courts justly punish him, because •his bad actions are proved *against* him, and •his lack of consciousness of them can't be proved *for* him. It may be reasonable to think that on the great day when the secrets of all hearts are laid open, nobody will be held accountable for actions of which he knows nothing; everybody will receive his sentence with his conscience ·agreeing with God's judgment by· accusing or excusing him.

**23.** Nothing but consciousness can unite remote existences into the same person. The identity of substance won't do it. For whatever substance there is, and whatever it is like, without consciousness there is no person. A substance without consciousness can no more be a person that a carcass can. [In the remainder of this section, and in section **24**, Locke discusses possible cases: two persons who take turns in animating one animal body ('the night man and the day man'); and one person who alternately animates two different animal bodies. The central emphasis throughout is on the uselessness in these questions of the concept of the same immaterial substance.]

**25.** I agree ·that on the question of contingent fact· the more probable opinion is that this consciousness is tied to, and is a state of, a single immaterial substance. Please yourself about that. However, every thinking being that can experience happiness or misery must grant that

> there is something, *himself*, that he is concerned for and wants to be happy; and that this self has existed continuously for a period of time and therefore may exist for months and years to come, with no set limit to its duration, and thus may be the same self carried by consciousness into the future.

It is through this consciousness that he finds himself to be the same self that acted thus and so some years ago and through which he is happy or miserable now. In all these thoughts we place sameness of *self* in sameness not of *substance* but of *consciousness*. Substances might come and go through the duration of such a consciousness; and *for as long as a substance is in a vital union with the thing containing this consciousness* it is a part of that same self. Thus, any part of my body, while vitally united to that which is conscious in me, is a part of myself (·for example my little finger, while it relates to me in such a way that if it is damaged I feel pain·); but when the vital union is broken, what was a part of myself a moment ago is now not so, any more than a part of another man's self is a part of me. [The rest of the section illustrates and repeats this line of thought.]

**26.** 'Person', I take it, is the name for this *self*. Wherever you find what you call 'myself', anyone else may say there is 'the same person'. 'Person' is a forensic term [= 'a term designed for use in legal proceedings'], having to do with actions and their merit; and so it applies only to active thinking beings that are capable of a law, and of happiness and misery. It is only through consciousness that this personality [Locke's word] extends itself beyond present existence to what is past, becoming concerned and accountable; the person owns and attributes *past* actions to itself for the same reason that it does the *present*. All this is founded in a concern for happiness, which unavoidably accompanies consciousness—something that is conscious of pleasure and pain desires that the self that is conscious should be happy. As for past actions that the self cannot through consciousness square with or join to the present self—it can no more be concerned with them than if they had never been done. To •receive pleasure or pain, i.e. reward or punishment, on account of any such action is all of a piece with •being born happy or miserable, without any ·merit or· demerit at all. Suppose a man were punished now for what he had done in another life of which he cannot have any consciousness, how does that ·so-called· punishment differ from simply being created miserable?. . . .

**27.** In treating this subject I have considered as perhaps-possible some states of affairs—·e.g. the one about the prince and the cobbler·—that will look strange to some readers, and perhaps *are* strange. But I think they are permissible, given our ignorance about the nature of the thinking thing in us which we look on as our*selves*. If we knew with regard to this thinking thing

- •what it is, or
- •how it is tied to a certain system of fleeting animal spirits [see note in viii.12], or
- •whether or not it can perform its operations of thinking and memory outside of a body organized as ours is, and
- •whether God has decided that every such spirit ·or thinking thing· shall be united to only one such body, with its memory depending on the health of that body's organs,

we might see the absurdity of some of the cases I considered. But as we are in the dark about these matters, we ordinarily think of the ·thinking thing or· soul of a man as an immaterial substance, owing nothing to matter and compatible with any kind of matter; and on that basis there cannot from the nature of things be any absurdity in supposing that the same soul might at different times be united to different bodies, making *one man* with each of them for as long as they were united. . . .

**28.** To conclude: •any substance that begins to exist must during its existence necessarily be the same; •any complex of substances that begins to exist must during the existence of its component parts be the same; •any mode that begins to exist is throughout its existence the same. . . . It appears from this that the difficulty or obscurity that people have found in this matter has arisen from the poor use of words rather than from any obscurity in things themselves. For whatever makes the specific idea to which the name is applied, if we steadily keep to that idea it will be easy for us to distinguish same and different, with no doubts arising. ·I defend this in the next, final section·.

**29.** •Suppose we take a man to be *a rational spirit*, then it is easy to know what is the same man, namely the same spirit—whether or not it is embodied. •Suppose our idea of a man is *a rational spirit vitally united to a body with a certain structure*; then such a rational spirit will be the same man as long as it is united to such a body, though it needn't be the same body throughout. •If anyone's idea of a man is that of the vital union of parts in a certain shape [here = 'structure'], as long as that vital union and shape remain in a compound body, remaining the same except for a turnover in its constituent particles, it will be the same man. For the complex idea we use when classifying a thing as being of a certain kind also determines what it is for a thing of that kind to continue in existence.

# The Self

## DAVID HUME

There are some philosophers, who imagine we are every moment intimately conscious of what we call our Self; that we feel its existence and its continuance in existence; and are certain, beyond the evidence of a demonstration, both of its perfect identity and simplicity....

Unluckily all these positive assertions are contrary to that very experience, which is pleaded for them, nor have we any idea of *self,* after the manner it is here explained. For from what impression could this idea be derived? This question 'tis impossible to answer without a manifest contradiction and absurdity; and yet 'tis a question, which must necessarily be answered, if we would have the idea of self pass for clear and intelligible. It must be some one impression, that gives rise to every real idea. But self or person is not any one impression, but that to which our several impressions and ideas are supposed to have a reference. If any impression gives rise to the idea of self, that impression must continue invariably the same, through the whole course or our lives; since self is supposed to exist after that manner. But there is no impression constant and invariable. Pain and pleasure, grief and joy, passions and sensations succeed each other, and never all exist at the same time. It cannot, therefore, be from any of these impressions, or from any other, that the idea of self is derived; and consequently there is no such idea.

But farther, what must become of all our particular perceptions upon this hypothesis? All these are different, and distinguishable, and separable from each other, and may be separately considered, and may exist separately, and have no need of any thing to support their existence. After what manner, therefore, do they belong to self; and how are they connected with it? For my part, when I enter most intimately into what I call *myself,* I always stumble on some particular perception or other, of heat or cold, light or shade, love or hatred, pain or pleasure. I never can catch *myself* at any time without a perception, and never can observe any thing but the perception. When my perceptions are removed for any time, as by sound sleep; so long am I insensible of *myself,* and may truly be said not to exist. And were all my perceptions removed by death, and could I neither think, nor feel, nor see, nor love, nor hate after the dissolution of my body, I should be entirely annihilated, nor do I conceive what is farther requisite to make me a perfect nonentity. If any one upon serious and unprejudiced reflection, thinks he has a different notion of *himself,* I must confess I can reason no longer with him. All I can allow him is, that he may be in the right as well as I, and that we are essentially different in this particular. He may, perhaps, perceive something simple and continued, which he calls *himself;* though I am certain there is no such principle in me.

But setting aside some metaphysicians of this kind, I may venture to affirm of the rest of mankind, that they are nothing but a bundle or collection of different perceptions, which succeed each other with an inconceivable rapidity, and are in a perpetual flux and movement. Our eyes cannot turn in their sockets without varying our perceptions. Our thought is still more variable than our sight; and all our other senses and faculties contribute to this change; nor is there any single power of the soul, which remains unalterably the same, perhaps for one moment. The mind is a kind of theatre, where several perceptions successively make their appearance; pass, re-pass, glide away, and mingle in an infinite variety of postures and situations. There is properly no *simplicity* in it at one time, nor *identity* in

---

From David Hume, *A Treatise of Human Nature.* First published in England in 1738.

different; whatever natural propension we may have to imagine that simplicity and identity. The comparison of the theatre must not mislead us. They are the successive perceptions only, that constitute the mind; nor have we the most distant notion of the place, where these scenes are represented, or of the materials, of which it is composed.

What then gives us so great a propension to ascribe an identity to these successive perceptions, and to suppose ourselves possessed of an invariable and uninterrupted existence through the whole course of our lives?...

We have a distinct idea of an object, that remains invariable and uninterrupted through a supposed variation of time; and this idea we call that of *identity* or *sameness*. We have also a distinct idea of several different objects existing in succession, and connected together by a close relation; and this to an accurate view affords as perfect a notion of *diversity*, as if there was no manner of relation among the objects. But though these two ideas of identity, and a succession of related objects be in themselves perfectly distinct, and even contrary, yet 'tis certain, that in our common way of thinking they are generally confounded with each other. That action of the imagination, by which we consider the uninterrupted and invariable object, and that by which we reflect on the succession of related objects, are almost the same to the feeling, nor is there much more effort of thought required in the latter case than in the former. The relation facilitates the transition of the mind from one object to another, and renders its passage as smooth as if it contemplated one continued object. This resemblance is the cause of the confusion and mistake, and makes us substitute the notion of identity, instead of that of related objects....

Thus we feign the continued existence of the perceptions of our senses, to remove the interruption; and run into the notion of a *soul*, and *self*, and *substance*, to disguise the variation. But we may farther observe, that where we do not give rise to such a fiction, our propension to confound identity with relation is so great, that we are apt to imagine something unknown and mysterious, connecting the parts, beside their relation; and this I take to be the case with regard to the identity we ascribe to plants and vegetables. And even when this does not take place, we still feel a propensity to confound these ideas, though we are not able fully to satisfy ourselves in that particular, nor find any thing invariable and uninterrupted to justify our notion of identity.

Thus the controversy concerning identity is not merely a dispute of words. For when we attribute identity, in an improper sense, to variable or interrupted objects, our mistake is not confined to the expression, but is commonly attended with a fiction, either of something invariable and uninterrupted, or of something mysterious and inexplicable, or at least with a propensity to such fictions. What will suffice to prove this hypothesis to the satisfaction of every fair enquirer, is to show from daily experience and observation, that the objects, which are variable or interrupted, and yet are supposed to continue the same, are such only as consist of a succession of parts, connected together by resemblance, contiguity, or causation....

A ship, of which a considerable part has been changed by frequent reparations, is still considered as the same: nor does the difference of the materials hinder us from ascribing an identity to it. The common end, in which the parts conspire, is the same under all their variations, and affords an easy transition of the imagination from one situation of the body to another....

Though every one must allow, that in a very few years both vegetables and animals endure a *total* change, yet we still attribute identity to them, while their form, size, and substance are entirely altered. An oak, that grows from a small plant to a large tree, is still the same oak; though there be not one particle of matter, or figure of its parts the same. An infant becomes a man, and is sometimes fat, sometimes lean, without any change in his identity....A man, who hears a noise, that is frequently interrupted and renewed, says, it is still the same noise; though 'tis evident the sounds have only a specific identity or resemblance, and there is nothing numerically the same, but the cause, which produced them. In like manner it may be said without breach of the propriety of language, that such a church, which was formerly of brick, fell to ruin, and that the parish rebuilt the same church of free-stone, and according to modern architecture. Here neither the form nor materials are the same, nor is there any thing common to the two objects, but their relation to the inhabitants of the parish; and yet this alone is sufficient to make us denominate them the same....

From thence it evidently follows, that identity is nothing really belonging to these different perceptions, and uniting them together; but is merely a quality, which we attribute to them, because of the union of their ideas in the imagination, when we reflect upon them....

The only question, therefore, which remains, is, by what relations this uninterrupted progress of our thought is produced, when we consider the successive existence of a mind or thinking person. And here 'tis evident we must confine ourselves to resemblance and causation.... Also, as memory alone acquaints us with the continuance and extent of this succession of perceptions, 'tis to be considered, upon that account chiefly, as the source of personal identity. Had we no memory, we never should have any notion of causation, nor consequently of that chain of causes and effects, which constitute our self or person.

# Divided Minds and the Nature of Persons

DEREK PARFIT

Derek Parfit is a fellow of All Souls College, Oxford.

It was the split-brain cases which drew me into philosophy. Our knowledge of these cases depends on the results of various psychological tests, as described by Donald MacKey.[1] These tests made use of two facts. We control each of our arms, and see what is in each half of our visual fields, with only one of our hemispheres. When someone's hemispheres have been disconnected, psychologists can thus present to this person two different written questions in the two halves of his visual field, and can receive two different answers written by this person's two hands.

Here is a simplified imaginary version of the kind of evidence that such tests provide. One of these people looks fixedly at the centre of a wide screen, whose left half is red and right half is blue. On each half in a darker shade are the words, "How many colours can you see?" With both hands the person writes, "Only one". The words are now changed to read, "Which is the only colour that you can see?" With one of his hands the person writes "Red", with the other he writes "Blue".

If this is how such a person responds, I would conclude that he is having two visual sensations—that he does, as he claims, see both red and blue. But in seeing each colour he is not aware of seeing the other. He has two streams of consciousness, in each of which he can see only one colour. In one stream he sees red, and at the same time, in his other stream, he sees blue. More generally, he could be having at the same time two series of thoughts and sensations, in having each of which he is unaware of having the other.

This conclusion has been questioned. It has been claimed by some that there are not *two* streams of consciousness, on the ground that the sub-dominant hemisphere is a part of the brain whose functioning involves no consciousness. If this were true, these cases would lose most of their interest. I believe that it is not true, chiefly because, if a person's dominant hemisphere is

From *Mindwaves*, ed. Colin Blakemore & Susan Greenfield (Oxford: Basil Blackwell, 1987), pp. 19–25.
Reprinted by permission of Blackwell Publishing.

destroyed, this person is able to react in the way in which, in the split-brain cases, the sub-dominant hemisphere reacts, and we do not believe that such a person is just an automaton, without consciousness. The sub-dominant hemisphere is, of course, much less developed in certain ways, typically having the linguistic abilities of a three-year-old. But three-year-olds are conscious. This supports the view that, in split-brain cases, there *are* two streams of consciousness.

Another view is that, in these cases, there are two persons involved, sharing the same body. Like Professor MacKay, I believe that we should reject this view. My reason for believing this is, however, different. Professor MacKay denies that there are two persons involved because he believes that there is only one person involved. I believe that, in a sense, the number of persons involved is none.

## THE EGO THEORY AND THE BUNDLE THEORY

To explain this sense I must, for a while, turn away from the split-brain cases. There are two theories about what persons are, and what is involved in a person's continued existence over time. On the *Ego Theory,* a person's continued existence cannot be explained except as the continued existence of a particular *Ego,* or *subject of experiences.* An Ego Theorist claims that, if we ask what unifies someone's consciousness at any time—what makes it true, for example, that I can now both see what I am typing and hear the wind outside my window—the answer is that these are both experiences which are being had by me, this person, at this time. Similarly, what explains the unity of a person's whole life is the fact that all of the experiences in this life are had by the same person, or subject of experiences. In its best-known form, the *Cartesian view,* each person is a persisting purely mental thing—a soul, or spiritual substance.

The rival view is the *Bundle Theory.* Like most styles in art—Gothic, baroque, rococo, etc.—this theory owes its name to its critics. But the name is good enough. According to the Bundle Theory, we can't explain either the unity of consciousness at any time, or the unity of a whole life, by referring to a person. Instead we must claim that there are long series of different mental states and events—thoughts, sensations, and the like—each series being what we call one life. Each series is unified by various kinds of causal relation, such as the relations that hold between experiences and later memories of them. Each series is thus like a bundle tied up with string.

In a sense, a Bundle Theorist denies the existence of persons. An outright denial is of course absurd. As Reid protested in the eighteenth century, 'I am not thought, I am not action, I am not feeling; I am something which thinks an acts and feels.' I am not a series of events but a person. A Bundle Theorist admits this fact, but claims it to be only a fact about our grammar, or our language. There are persons or subjects in this language-dependent way. If, however, persons are believed to be more than this—to be separately existing things, distinct from our brains and bodies, and the various kinds of mental states and events—the Bundle Theorist denies that there are such things.

The first Bundle Theorist was Buddha, who taught "anatta", or the *No Self view.* Buddhists concede that selves or persons have "nominal existence", by which they mean that persons are merely combinations of other elements. Only what exists by itself, as a separate element, has instead what Buddhists call "actual existence". Here are some quotations from Buddhist texts:

> At the beginning of their conversation the king politely asks the monk his name, and receives the following reply: 'Sir, I am known as "Nagasena"; my fellows in the religious life address me as "Nagasena". Although my parents gave me the name . . . it is just an appellation, a form of speech, a description, a conventional usage. "Nagasena" is only a name, for no person is found here.'
>
> A sentient being does exist, you think, O Mara? You are misled by a false conception. This bundle of elements is void of Self, In it there is no sentient being. Just as a set of wooden parts Receives the name of carriage, So do we give to elements. The name of fancied being.
>
> Buddha has spoken thus: 'O Brethren, actions do exist, and also their consequences, but the person that acts does not. There is no one to cast away this set of elements, and no one to assume a new set of them. There exists no Individual, it

is only a conventional name given to a set of elements'[2]

Buddha's claims are strikingly similar to the claims advanced by several Western writers. Since these writers knew nothing of Buddha, the similarity of these claims suggests that they are not merely part of one cultural tradition, in one period. They may be, as I believe they are, true.

## WHAT WE BELIEVE OURSELVES TO BE

Given the advances in psychology and neurophysiology, the Bundle Theory may now seem to be obviously true. It may seem uninteresting to deny that there are separately existing Egos, which are distinct from brains and bodies and the various kinds of mental states and events. But this is not the only issue. We may be convinced that the Ego Theory is false, or even senseless. Most of us, however, even if we are not aware of this, also have certain beliefs about what is involved in our continued existence over time. And these beliefs would only be justified if something like the Ego Theory was true. Most of us therefore have false beliefs about what persons are, and about ourselves.

These beliefs are best revealed when we consider certain imaginary cases, often drawn from science fiction. One such case is *teletransportation*. Suppose that you enter a cubicle in which, when you press a button, a scanner records the states of all of the cells in your brain and body, destroying both while doing so. This information is then transmitted at the speed of light to some other planet, where a replicator produces a perfect organic copy of you. Since the brain of your Replica is exactly like yours, it will seem to remember living your life up to the moment when you pressed the button, its character will be just like yours, and it will be in every other way psychologically continuous with you. This psychological continuity will not have its normal cause, the continued existence of your brain, since the causal chain will run through the transmission by radio of your "blueprint".

Several writers claim that, if you chose to be teletransported, believing this to be the fastest way of travelling, you would be making a terrible mistake. This would not be a way of travelling, but a way of dying. It may not, they concede, be quite as bad as ordinary death. It might be some consolation to you that, after your death, you will have this Replica, which can finish the book that you are writing, act as parent to your children, and so on. But, they insist, this Replica won't be you. It will merely be someone else, who is exactly like you. This is why this prospect is nearly as bad as ordinary death.

Imagine next a whole range of cases, in each of which, in a single operation, a different proportion of the cells in your brain and body would be replaced with exact duplicates. At the near end of this range, only 1 or 2 per cent would be replaced; in the middle, 40 or 60 per cent; near the far end, 98 or 99 per cent. At the far end of this range is pure teletransportation, the case in which all of your cells would be "replaced".

When you imagine that some proportion of your cells will be replaced with exact duplicates, it is natural to have the following beliefs. First, if you ask, "Will I survive? Will the resulting person be me?", there must be an answer to this question. Either you will survive, or you are about to die. Second, the answer to this question must be either a simple "Yes" or a simple "No". The person who wakes up either will or will not be you. There cannot be a third answer, such as that the person waking up will be half you. You can imagine yourself later being half-conscious. But if the resulting person will be fully conscious, he cannot be half you. To state these beliefs together: to the question, "Will the resulting person be me?", there must always *be* an answer, which must be all-or-nothing.

There seem good grounds for believing that, in the case of teletransportation, your Replica would not be you. In a slight variant of this case, your Replica might be created while you were still alive, so that you could talk to one another. This seems to show that, if 100 per cent of your cells were replaced, the result would merely be a Replica of you. At the other end of my range of cases, where only 1 per cent would be replaced, the resulting person clearly *would* be you. It therefore seems that, in the cases in between, the resulting person must be either you, or merely a Replica. It seems that one of these must be true, and that it makes a great difference which is true.

## HOW WE ARE NOT WHAT WE BELIEVE

If these beliefs were correct, there must be some critical percentage, somewhere in this range of cases, up to which the resulting person would be you, and beyond which he would merely be your Replica. Perhaps, for example, it would be you who would wake up if the proportion of cells replaced were 49 per cent, but if just a few more cells were also replaced, this would make all the difference, causing it to be someone else who would wake up.

That there must be some such critical percentage follows from our natural beliefs. But this conclusion is most implausible. How could a few cells make such a difference? Moreover, if there is such a critical percentage, no one could ever discover where it came. Since in all these cases the resulting person would believe that he was you, there could never be any evidence about where, in this range of cases, he would suddenly cease to be you.

On the Bundle Theory, we should reject these natural beliefs. Since you, the person, are not a separately existing entity, we can know exactly what would happen without answering the question of what will happen to you. Moreover, in the case in the middle of my range, it is an empty question whether the resulting person would be you, or would merely be someone else who is exactly like you. These are not here two different possibilities, one of which must be true. These are merely two different descriptions of the very same course of events. If 50 per cent of your cells were replaced with exact duplicates, we could call the resulting person you, or we could call him merely your Replica. But since these are not here different possibilities, this is a mere choice of words.

As Buddha claimed, the Bundle Theory is hard to believe. It is hard to accept that it could be an empty question whether one is about to die, or will instead live for many years.

What we are being asked to accept may be made clearer with this analogy. Suppose that a certain club exists for some time, holding regular meetings. The meetings then cease. Some years later, several people form a club with the same name, and the same rules. We can ask, "Did these people revive the very same club? Or did they merely start up another club which is exactly similar?" Given certain further details, this would be another empty question. We could know just what happened without answering this question. Suppose that some one said: "But there must be an answer. The club meeting later must either be, or not be, the very same club." This would show that this person didn't understand the nature of clubs.

In the same way, if we have any worries about my imagined cases, we don't understand the nature of persons. In each of my cases, you would know that the resulting person would be both psychologically and physically exactly like you, and that he would have some particular proportion of the cells in your brain and body—90 per cent, or 10 per cent, or, in the case of teletransportation, 0 per cent. Knowing this, you know everything. How could it be a real question what would happen to you, unless you are a separately existing Ego, distinct from a brain and body, and the various kinds of mental state and event? If there are no such Egos, there is nothing else to ask a real question about.

Accepting the Bundle Theory is not only hard; it may also affect our emotions. As Buddha claimed, it may undermine our concern about our own futures. This effect can be suggested by redescribing this change of view. Suppose that you are about to be destroyed, but will later have a Replica on Mars. You would naturally believe that this prospect is about as bad as ordinary death, since your Replica won't be you. On the Bundle Theory, the fact that your Replica won't be you just consists in the fact that, though it will be fully psychologically continuous with you, this continuity won't have its normal cause. But when you object to teletransportation you are not objecting merely to the abnormality of this cause. You are objecting that this cause won't get *you* to Mars. You fear that the abnormal cause will fail to produce a further and all-important fact, which is different from the fact that your Replica will be psychologically continuous with you. You do not merely want there to be psychological continuity between you and some future person. You want to *be* this future person. On the Bundle Theory, there is no such special further fact. What you fear will not happen, in this imagined case, *never* happens. You want the person on Mars to be you in a specially intimate way in which no future person will ever be you. This means that, judged from the standpoint of your natural beliefs, even ordinary survival is about as bad as teletransportation. *Ordinary survival is about as bad as being destroyed and having a Replica.*

## HOW THE SPLIT-BRAIN CASES SUPPORT THE BUNDLE THEORY

The truth of the Bundle Theory seems to me, in the widest sense, as much a scientific as a philosophical conclusion. I can imagine kinds of evidence which would have justified believing in the existence of separately existing Egos, and believing that the continued existence of these Egos is what explains the continuity of each mental life. But there is in fact very little evidence in favour of this Ego Theory, and much for the alternative Bundle Theory.

Some of this evidence is provided by the split-brain cases. On the Ego Theory, to explain what unifies our experiences at any one time, we should simply claim that these are all experiences which are being had by the same person. Bundle Theorists reject this explanation. This disagreement is hard to resolve in ordinary cases. But consider the simplified split-brain case that I described. We show to my imagined patient a placard whose left half is blue and right half is red. In one of this person's two streams of consciousness, he is aware of seeing only blue, while at the same time, in his other stream, he is aware of seeing only red. Each of these two visual experiences is combined with other experiences, like that of being aware of moving one of his hands. What unifies the experiences, at any time, in each of this person's two streams of consciousness? What unifies his awareness of seeing only red with his awareness of moving one hand? The answer cannot be that these experiences are being had by the same person. The answer cannot explain the unity of each of this person's two streams of consciousness, since it ignores the disunity between these streams. This person is now having all of the experiences in both of his two streams. If this fact was what unified these experiences, this would make the two streams one.

These cases do not, I have claimed, involve two people sharing a single body. Since there is only one person involved, who has two streams of consciousness, the Ego Theorist's explanation would have to take the following form. He would have to distinguish between persons and subjects of experiences, and claim that, in split-brain cases, there are *two* of the latter. What unifies the experiences in one of the person's two streams would have to be the fact these experiences are all being had by the same subject of experiences. What unifies the experiences in this person's other stream would have to be the fact that they are being had by another subject of experiences. When this explanation takes this form, it becomes much less plausible. While we could assume that "subject of experiences", or "Ego", simply meant "person", it was easy to believe that there are subjects of experiences. But if there can be subjects of experiences that are not persons, and if in the life of a split-brain patient there are at any time two different subjects of experiences—two different Egos—why should we believe that there really are such things? This does not amount to a refutation. But it seems to me a strong argument against the Ego Theory.

As a Bundle Theorist, I believe that these two Egos are idle cogs. There is another explanation of the unity of consciousness, both in ordinary cases and in split-brain cases. It is simply a fact that ordinary people are, at any time, aware of having several different experiences. This awareness of several different experiences can be helpfully compared with one's awareness, in short-term memory, of several different experiences. Just as there can be a single memory of just having had several experiences, such as hearing a bell strike three times, there can be a single state of awareness both of hearing the fourth striking of this bell, and of seeing, at the same time, ravens flying past the bell-tower.

Unlike the Ego Theorist's explanation, this explanation can easily be extended to cover split-brain cases. In such cases there is, at any time, not one state of awareness of several different experiences, but two such states. In the case I described, there is one state of awareness of both seeing only red and of moving one hand, and there is another state of awareness of both seeing only blue and moving the other hand. In claiming that there are two such states of awareness, we are not postulating the existence of unfamiliar entities, two separately existing Egos which are not the same as the single person whom the case involves. This explanation appeals to a pair of mental states which would have to be described anyway in a full description of this case.

I have suggested how the split-brain cases provide one argument for one view about the nature of persons. I should mention another such argument, provided by an imagined extension of these cases, first discussed at length by David Wiggins.[3]

In this imagined case a person's brain is divided, and the two halves are transplanted into a pair of different bodies. The two resulting people live quite separate lives. This imagined case shows that personal identity is not what matters. If I was about to divide, I should conclude that neither of the resulting people will be me. I will have ceased to exist. But this way of ceasing to exist is about as good—or as bad—as ordinary survival.

Some of the features of Wiggins's imagined case are likely to remain technically impossible. But the case cannot be dismissed, since its most striking feature, the division of one stream of consciousness into separate streams, has already happened. This is a second way in which the actual split-brain cases have great theoretical importance. They challenge some of our deepest assumptions about ourselves.[4]

## NOTES

1. See MacKay's contribution, chapter 1 of *Mindwaves,* ed. Colin Blakemore and Susan Greenfield (Oxford: Basil Blackwell, 1987), pp. 5–16.
2. For the sources of these and similar quotations, see my *Reasons and Persons* pp. 502–3, 532. (Oxford: Oxford University Press, 1984).
3. At the end of his *Identity and Spatio-temporal Continuity* (Oxford: Blackwell, 1967).
4. I discuss these assumptions further in part 3 of my *Reasons and Persons.*

# 37 An Argument for Animalism

*Eric T. Olson*

It is a truism that you and I are human beings. It is also a truism that a human being is a kind of animal: roughly a member of the primate species *Homo sapiens.* It would seem to follow that we are animals. Yet that claim is deeply controversial. Plato, Augustine, Descartes, Spinoza, Leibniz, Locke, Berkeley, Hume, Kant, and Hegel all denied it. With the notable exception of Aristotle and his followers, it is hard to find a major figure in the history of Western philosophy who thought that we are animals. The view is no more popular in non-Western traditions. And probably nine out of ten philosophers writing about personal identity today either deny outright that we are animals or say things that are clearly incompatible with it.

This is surprising. Isn't it obvious that we are animals? I will try to show that it isn't obvious, and that Plato and the others have their reasons for thinking otherwise. Before doing that I will explain how I understand the claim that we are animals. My main purpose, though, is to make a case for this unpopular view. I won't rely on the brief argument I began with. My strategy is to ask what it would mean if we weren't animals. Denying that we are animals is harder than you might think.

## 1. What Animalism Says

When I say that we are animals, I mean that each of us is numerically identical with an animal. There is a certain human organism, and that organism is you. You and it are one and the same. This view has been called animalism (not a very nice name, but I haven't got a better one). Simple though it may appear, this is easily misunderstood. Many claims that sound like animalism are in fact different.

First, some say that we are animals and yet reject animalism.[1] How is that possible? How can you be an animal, and yet not be one? The idea is that there is a sense of the verb *to be* in which something can "be" an animal without being identical with any animal. Each of us "is" an animal in the sense of being "constituted" by one. That means roughly that you are in the same place and made of the same matter as an animal. But you and that animal could come apart (more on this later). And since a thing can't come apart from itself, you and the animal are not identical.

I wish people wouldn't say things like this. If you are not identical with a certain animal, that animal is something other than you. And I doubt whether there is any interesting sense in which you can be something other than yourself. Even if there is, expressing a view on which no one is identical with an animal by saying that we *are* animals is badly misleading. It discourages us from asking important questions: what we *are* identical with if not animals, for instance. Put plainly and honestly, these philosophers are saying that each of us is a non-animal that relates in some intimate way to an animal. They put it by saying that we *are* animals because that sounds more plausible. This is salesman's hype, and we shouldn't be fooled. In any case, the "constitutionalists" do not say that we are animals in the straightforward sense in which I mean it. They are not animalists.

The existence of the constitution view shows that animalism is not the same as *materialism*. Materialism is the view that we are material things; and we might be material things but not animals. Animalism implies materialism (animals are material things), but not vice versa. It may seem perverse for a materialist to reject animalism. If we are material things of any sort, surely we are animals? Perverse or not, though, the view that we are material non-organisms is widely held.

Animalism says that *we* are animals. That is compatible with the existence of non-animal people (or persons, if you prefer). It is often said that to be a person is to have certain mental qualities: to be rational, intelligent, and self-conscious, say. Perhaps a person must also be morally responsible, and have free will. If something like that is right, then gods or angels might be people but not animals.

Nor does our being animals imply that all animals, or even all human animals, are people. Human beings in a persistent vegetative state are biologically alive, but their mental capacities are permanently destroyed. They are certainly human animals. But we might not want to call them people. The same goes for human embryos.

So the view that we are animals does not imply that to be a person is nothing other than to be an animal of a certain sort – that being an animal is part of what it is to be a person. Inconveniently enough, this view has also been called animalism. It isn't the animalism that I want to defend. In fact it looks rather implausible. I don't know whether there could be inorganic people, as for instance traditional theism asserts. But mere reflection on what it is to be a person doesn't seem to rule it out. Of course, if people are animals by definition, it follows that we are animals, since we are obviously people. But the reverse entailment doesn't hold: we might be animals even if something could be a person without being an animal.

If I don't say that all people are animals, which people do I mean? Is animalism the mere tautology that all animal people are animals? No. I say that you and I and the other people who walk the earth are animals. If you like, all *human* people are animals, where a human person is roughly someone who relates to a human animal in the way that you and I do, whatever way that is. (Even idealists can agree that we are in some sense human, and not, say, feline or angelic.) Many philosophers deny that *any* people are animals. So there is nothing trivial about this claim.

"Animalism" is sometimes stated as the view that we are *essentially or most fundamentally* animals. We are essentially animals if we couldn't possibly exist without being animals. It is less clear what it is for us to be most fundamentally animals, but this is usually taken to imply at least that our identity conditions derive from our being animals, rather than from our being, say, people or philosophers or material objects – even though we *are* people and philosophers and material objects.

Whether our being animals implies that we are essentially or most fundamentally animals depends on whether human animals are essentially or most fundamentally animals. If the animal that you are is essentially an animal, then so are you. If it is only contingently an animal, then you are only contingently an animal. Likewise, you are most fundamentally an animal if and only if the animal that you are is most fundamentally an animal. The claim that each of us is identical with an animal is neutral on these questions. Most philosophers think that every animal is essentially and most fundamentally an animal, and I am inclined to agree. But you could be an animalist in my sense without accepting this.

Is animalism the view that we are identical with our bodies? That depends on what it is for something to be someone's body. If a person's body is by definition a sort of animal, then I suppose being an animal amounts to being one's body.

It is often said, though, that someone could have a partly or wholly inorganic body. One's body might include plastic or metal limbs. Someone might even have an entirely robotic body. I take it that no animal could be partly or wholly inorganic. If you cut off an animal's limb and replace it with an inorganic prosthesis, the animal just gets smaller and has something inorganic attached to it. So perhaps after having some or all of your parts replaced by inorganic gadgets of the right sort you would be identical with your body, but would not be an animal. Animalism may imply that you are your body, but you could be your body without being an animal. Some philosophers even say that being an animal rules out being identical with one's body. If you replaced enough of an animal's parts with new ones, they say, it would end up with a different body from the one it began with.

Whether these claims about bodies are true depends on what it is for something to be someone's body. What does it *mean* to say that your body is an animal, or that someone might have a robotic body? I have never seen a good answer to this question (see van Inwagen 1980 and Olson 2006). So I will talk about people and animals, and leave bodies out of it.

Finally, does animalism say that we are *merely* animals? That we are nothing more than biological organisms? This is a delicate point. The issue is whether being "more than just" or "not merely" an animal is compatible with being an animal – that is, with being identical with an animal.

If someone complains that the committee is more than just the chairman, she means that it is not the chairman: it has other members too. If we are more than just animals in something like this sense, then we are not animals. We have parts that are not parts of any animal: immaterial souls, perhaps.

On the other hand, we say that Descartes was more than just a philosopher: he was also a mathematician, a Frenchman, a Roman Catholic, and many other things. That is of course compatible with his being a philosopher. We can certainly be more than "mere" animals in this sense, and yet still be animals. An animal can have properties other than being an animal, and which don't follow from its being an animal. Our being animals does not rule out our being mathematicians, Frenchmen, or Roman Catholics – or our being people, socialists, mountaineers, and many other things. At least there is no evident reason why it should. Animalism does not imply that we have a fixed, "animal" nature, or that we have only biological or naturalistic properties, or that we are no different, in any important way, from other animals. There may be a vast psychological and moral gulf between human animals and organisms of other species. We may be very special animals. But for all that we may be animals.

## 2. Alternatives

One reason why it may seem obvious that we are animals is that it is unclear what else we could be. If we're not animals, what are we? What are the alternatives to animalism? This is a question that philosophers ought to ask more often. Many views about personal identity clearly rule out our being animals, but leave it a mystery what sort of things we might be instead. Locke's account is a notorious example. His detailed account of personal identity doesn't even tell us whether we are material or immaterial.

Well, there is the traditional idea that we are simple immaterial substances, or, alternatively, compound things made up of an immaterial substance and a biological organism.

There is the view, mentioned earlier, that we are material objects "constituted by" human animals. You and a certain animal are physically indistinguishable. Nonetheless you and it are two different things.

Some say that we are temporal parts of animals. Animals and other persisting objects exist at different times by having different temporal parts or "stages" located at those times. You are made up of those stages of a human animal (or, in science fiction, of several animals) that are "psychologically interconnected" (Lewis 1976). Since your animal's embryonic stages have no mental properties at all, they aren't psychologically connected with anything, and so they aren't parts of you. Hence, you began later than the animal did.

Hume famously proposed that each of us is "a bundle or collection of different perceptions, which succeed each other with an inconceivable rapidity, and are in a perpetual flux and movement" (1888: 252). Strictly speaking you are not made of bones and sinews, or of atoms, or of matter. You are literally composed of thoughts. Whether Hume actually believed this is uncertain; but some do (e.g. Quinton 1962).

Every teacher of philosophy has heard it said that we are something like computer programs. You are a certain complex of information "realized" in your brain. (How else could you survive Star-Trek teletransportation?) That would mean that you are not a concrete object at all. You are a universal. There could literally be more than one of you, just as there is more than one concrete instance of the web browser *Netscape 6.2*.

There is even the paradoxical view that we don't really exist at all. There are many thoughts and experiences, but no beings that *have* those thoughts or experiences. The existence of human people is an illusion – though of course no one is deluded about it. Philosophers who have denied or at least doubted their own existence include Parmenides, Spinoza, Hume, Hegel (as I read them, anyway), Russell (1985: 50), and Unger (1979). We also find the view in Indian Buddhism.

There are other views about what we might be, but I take these to be animalism's main rivals. One of these claims, or another one that I haven't mentioned, must be true. There must be *some* sort of thing that we are. If there is anything sitting in your chair and reading these words, it must have some basic properties or other.

For those who enjoy metaphysics, these are all fascinating proposals. Whatever their merits, though, they certainly are strange. No one but a philosopher could have thought of them. And it would take quite a bit of philosophy to get anyone to believe one of them. Compared with these claims, the idea that we are animals looks downright sensible. That makes its enduring unpopularity all the more surprising.

## 3. Why Animalism is Unpopular

Why is animalism so unpopular? Historically, the main reason (though by no means the only one) is hostility to materialism. Philosophers have always found it hard to believe that a material object, no matter how physically complex, could produce thought or experience. And an animal is a material object (I assume that vitalism is false). Since it is plain enough that *we* can think, it is easy to conclude that we couldn't be animals.

But why do modern-day materialists reject animalism, or at least say things that rule it out? The main reason, I believe, is that when they think about personal identity they don't ask what sort of things we are. They don't ask whether we are animals, or what we might be if we aren't animals, or how we relate to the human animals that are so intimately connected with us. Or at least they don't ask that first. No one who *began* by asking what we are would hit on the idea that we must be computer programs or bundles of thoughts or non-animals made of the same matter as animals.

The traditional problem of personal identity is not what we are, but what it takes for us to persist. It asks what is necessary, and what is sufficient, for a person existing at one time to be identical with something present at another time: what sorts of adventures we could survive, and what would inevitably bring our existence to an end. Many philosophers seem to think that an answer to this question would tell us all there is to know about the metaphysics of personal identity. This is not so. Claims about what it takes for us to persist do not by themselves tell us what other fundamental properties we have: whether we are material or immaterial, simple or composite, abstract or concrete, and so on. At any rate, the single-minded focus on our identity over time has tended to put other metaphysical questions about ourselves out of philosophers' minds.

What is more, the most popular solution to this traditional problem rules out our being animals. It is that we persist by virtue of some sort of psychological continuity. You are, necessarily, that future being that in some sense inherits its mental features – personality, beliefs, memories, values, and so on – from you. And you are that past being whose mental features you have inherited. Philosophers disagree about what sort of inheritance this has to be: whether those mental features must be continuously physically realized, for instance. But most accept the general idea. The persistence of a human animal, on the other hand, does not consist in mental continuity.

The fact that each human animal starts out as an unthinking embryo and may end up as an unthinking vegetable shows that no sort of mental continuity is necessary for a human animal to persist. No human animal is mentally continuous with an embryo or vegetable.

To see that no sort of mental continuity is sufficient for a human animal to persist, imagine that your cerebrum is put into another head. The being who gets that organ, and he alone, will be mentally continuous with you on any account of what mental continuity is. So if mental continuity of any sort suffices for you to persist, you would go along with your transplanted cerebrum. You wouldn't stay behind with an empty head.

What would happen to the human animal associated with you? Would *it* go along with its cerebrum? Would the surgeons pare that animal down to a small chunk of yellowish-pink tissue, move it across the room, and then supply it with a new head, trunk, and other parts? Surely not. A detached cerebrum is no more an organism than a detached liver is an organism. The empty-headed thing left behind, by contrast, *is* an animal. It may even remain alive, if the surgeons are careful to leave the lower brain intact. The empty-headed being into which your cerebrum is implanted is also an animal. It looks for all the world like there are two human animals in the story. One of them loses its cerebrum and gets an empty head. The other has its empty head filled with that organ. No animal moves from one head to another. The surgeons merely move an organ from one animal to another. If this is right, then no sort of psychological continuity suffices for the identity of a human animal over time. One human animal could be mentally continuous with another one (supposing that they can have mental properties at all).

If we tell the right kind of story, it is easy enough to get most people, or at any rate most Western-educated philosophy students, to say that *you* would go along with your transplanted cerebrum. After all, the one who got that organ would act like you and think she was you. Why deny that she would be who she thinks she is? But "your" animal – the one you would be if you were any animal – would stay behind. That means that you and that animal could go your separate ways. And a thing and itself can never go their separate ways.

It follows that you are not that animal, or indeed any other animal. Not only are you not essentially an animal. You are not an animal at all, even contingently. Nothing that is even contingently an animal would move to a different head if its cerebrum were transplanted. The human animals in the story stay where they are and merely lose or gain organs.[2]

So the thought that leads many contemporary philosophers to reject animalism – or that would lead them to reject it if they accepted the consequences of what they believe – is something like this: You would go along with your transplanted cerebrum; but no human animal would go along with its transplanted cerebrum. More generally, some sort of mental continuity suffices for us to persist, yet no sort of mental continuity suffices for an animal to persist. It follows that we are not animals. If we were animals, we should have the identity conditions of animals. Those conditions would have nothing to do with psychological facts. Psychology would be irrelevant to our identity over time. That goes against 300 years of thinking about personal identity.

This also shows that animalism is a substantive metaphysical thesis with important consequences. There is nothing harmless about it.

## 4. The Thinking-Animal Argument

I turn now to my case for animalism.

It seems evident that there *is* a human animal intimately related to you. It is the one located where you are, the one we point to when we point to you, the one sitting in your chair. It seems equally evident that human animals can think.

They can act. They can be aware of themselves and the world. Those with mature nervous systems in good working order can, anyway. So there is a thinking, acting human animal sitting where you are now. But you think and act. *You* are the thinking being sitting in your chair.

It follows from these apparently trite observations that you are an animal. In a nutshell, the argument is this: (1) There is a human animal sitting in your chair. (2) The human animal sitting in your chair is thinking. (If you like, every human animal sitting there is thinking.) (3) You are the thinking being sitting in your chair. The one and only thinking being sitting in your chair is none other than you. Hence, you are that animal. That animal is you. And there is nothing special about you: we are all animals. If anyone suspects a trick, here is the argument's logical form:

1. $(x)(x$ is a human animal & $x$ is sitting in your chair)
2. $(x)((x$ is a human animal & $x$ is sitting in your chair) $\supset x$ is thinking)
3. $(x)((x$ is thinking & $x$ is sitting in your chair) $\supset x =$ you)
4. $(x)(x$ is a human animal & $x =$ you)

The reader can verify that it is formally valid. (Compare: A man entered the bank vault. The man who entered the vault – any man who did – stole the money. Snodgrass, and no one else, entered the vault and stole the money. Doesn't it follow that Snodgrass is a man?)

Let us be clear about what the thinking-animal argument purports to show. Its conclusion is that we are human animals. That is, one of the things true of you is that you are (identical with) an animal. That of course leaves many metaphysical questions about ourselves unanswered. It doesn't by itself tell us whether we are essentially or most fundamentally animals, for instance, or what our identity conditions are. That depends on the metaphysical nature of human animals: on whether human animals are essentially animals, and what their identity conditions are. These are further questions. I argued in the previous section that no sort of mental continuity is either necessary or sufficient for a human animal to persist. If that is right, then our being animals has important and highly contentious metaphysical implications. But it might be disputed, even by those who agree that we are animals. The claim that we are animals is not the end of the story about personal identity. It is only the beginning. Still, it is important to begin in the right place.

The thinking-animal argument is deceptively simple. I suspect that its very simplicity has prevented many philosophers from seeing its point. But there is nothing sophistical about it. It has no obvious and devastating flaw that we teach our students. It deserves to be better known.[3]

In any case, the argument has three premises, and so there are three ways of resisting it. One could deny that there is any human animal sitting in your chair. One could deny that any such animal thinks. Or one could deny that you are the thinking being sitting there. Anyone who denies that we are animals is committed to accepting one of these claims. They are not very plausible. But let us consider them.

## 5. Alternative One: There Are No Human Animals

Why suppose that there is no human animal sitting in your chair? Presumably because there are no human animals anywhere. If there are any human animals at all, there is one sitting there. (I assume that you aren't a Martian foundling.) And if there are no human animals, it is hard to see how there could be any organisms of other sorts. So denying the argument's first premise amounts to denying that there are, strictly speaking, any organisms. There appear to be, of course. But that is at best a well-founded illusion.

There are venerable philosophical views that rule out the existence of organisms. Idealism, for instance, denies that there are any material objects at all (so I should describe it, anyway). And there is the view that nothing can have different parts at different times (Chisholm 1976: 145–158). Whenever something appears to lose or gain a part, the truth of the matter is that one object, made of the first set of parts, ceases to exist (or becomes scattered) and is instantly replaced by a numerically different object made of the second set of parts. Organisms, if there were such things, would constantly assimilate new particles and expel others. If nothing can survive a change of any of its parts, organisms are metaphysically impossible. What we think of as an organism is in reality only a succession of different "masses of matter" that each take on organic form for a brief moment – until a single particle is gained or lost – and then pass that form on to a numerically different mass.

But few opponents of animalism deny the existence of animals. They have good reason not to, quite apart from the fact that this is more or less incredible. Anything that would rule out the existence of animals would also rule out most of the things we might be if we are not animals. If there are no animals, there are no beings constituted by animals, and no temporal parts of animals. And whatever rules out animals may tell against Humean bundles of perceptions as well. If there are no animals, it is not easy to see what we *could* be.

## 6. Alternative Two: Human Animals Can't Think

The second alternative is that there is an animal sitting in your chair, but it isn't thinking. (Let any occurrence of a propositional attitude, such as the belief that it's raining or the hope that it won't, count as "thinking".) *You* think, but the animal doesn't. The reason for this can only be that the animal can't think. If it were able to think, it would be thinking now. And if *that* animal can't think – despite its healthy, mature human brain, lengthy education, surrounding community of thinkers, and appropriate evolutionary history – then no human animal can. And if no human animal can think, no animal of any sort could. (We can't very well say that dogs can think but human animals can't.) Finally, if no animal could ever think – not even a normal adult human animal – it is hard to see how any organism could have any mental property whatever. So if your animal isn't thinking, that is apparently because it is impossible for any organism to have mental properties.

The claim, then, is that animals, including human animals, are no more intelligent or sentient than trees. We could of course say that they are "intelligent" in the sense of being the bodies of intelligent people who are not themselves animals. And we could call organisms like dogs "sentient" in the sense of being the bodies of sentient non-animals that stand to those animals as you and I stand to human animals. But that is loose talk. The strict and sober truth would be that only non-organisms could ever think.

This is rather hard to believe. Anyone who denies that animals can think (or that they can think in the way that we think) needs to explain why they can't. What stops a typical human animal from using its brain to think? Isn't that what that organ is *for*?

Traditionally, those who deny that animals can think deny that any material object could do so. That seems natural enough: if *any* material thing could think, it would be an animal. Thinking things must be immaterial, and so must we. Of course, simply denying that any material thing could think does nothing to explain why it couldn't. But again, few contemporary opponents of animalism believe that we are immaterial.

Someone might argue like this: "The human animal sitting in your chair is just your body. It is absurd to suppose that your body reads or thinks about philosophy. The thinking thing there – you – must therefore be something other than the animal. But that doesn't mean that you are immaterial. You might be a material thing other than your body."

It may be false to say that your body is reading. There is certainly *something* wrong with that statement. What is less clear is whether it is wrong because the phrase 'your body' denotes something that you in some sense have – a certain human organism – that is unable to read. Compare the word 'body' with a closely related one: *mind*. It is just as absurd to say that Alice's mind weighs 120 pounds, or indeed any other amount, as it is to say that Alice's body is reading. (If that seems less than obvious, consider the claim that Alice's mind is sunburned.) Must we conclude that Alice has something – a clever thing, for Alice has a clever mind – that weighs nothing? Does this show that thinking beings have no mass? Surely not. I think we should be equally wary of drawing metaphysical conclusions from the fact that the phrase 'Alice's body' cannot always be substituted for the name 'Alice'. In any case, the "body" argument does nothing to explain why a human animal should be unable to think.

Anyone who claims that some material objects can think but animals cannot has his work cut out for him. Shoemaker (1984: 92–97, 1999) has argued that animals cannot think because they have the wrong identity conditions. Mental properties have characteristic causal roles, and these, he argues, imply that psychological continuity must suffice for the bearers of those properties to persist. Since this is not true of any organism, no organism could have mental properties. But material things with the right identity conditions *can* think, and organisms can "constitute" such things. I have discussed this argument in another place (Olson 2002a). It is a long story, though, and I won't try to repeat it here.

## 7. Alternative Three: You Are Not Alone

Suppose, then, that there is a human animal sitting in your chair, and suppose that it thinks. Is there any way to resist the conclusion that you are that thinking animal? We can hardly say that the animal thinks but you don't. (If anything thinks, you do.) Nor can we deny that you exist, when there is a rational animal thinking your thoughts. How, then, could you fail to be that thinking animal? Only if you are not the only thinker there. If you are not *the* thinking thing sitting there, you must be one of at least two such thinkers. You exist. You think. There is also a thinking human animal there. Presumably it has the same psychological qualities as you have. But it isn't you. There are two thinking beings wherever we thought there was just one. There are two philosophers, you and an animal, sitting there and reading this. You are never truly alone: wherever you go, a watchful human animal goes with you.

This is not an attractive picture. Its adherents may try to comfort us by proposing linguistic hypotheses. Whenever two beings are as intimately related as you and your animal are, they will say, we "count them as one" for ordinary purposes (Lewis 1976). When I write on the copyright form that I am the sole author of this essay, I don't mean that every author of this essay is numerically identical with me. I mean only that every author of this essay bears some relation to me that does not imply identity: that every such author is co-located with me, perhaps. My wife is not a bigamist, even though she is, I suppose, married both to me and to the animal. At any rate it would be seriously misleading to describe our relationship as a *ménage à quatre.*

This is supposed to show that the current proposal needn't contradict anything that we say or believe when engaged in the ordinary business of life. Unless we are doing metaphysics, we don't distinguish strict numerical identity from the intimate relation that each of us bears to a certain human animal. Ordinary people have no opinion about how many numerically different thinking beings there are. Why should they? What matters in real life is not how many thinkers there are strictly speaking, but how many *non-overlapping* thinkers.

Perhaps so. Still, it hardly makes the current proposal easy to believe. Is it not strange to suppose that there are two numerically different thinkers wherever we thought there was just one?

In any event, the troubles go beyond mere overcrowding. If there really are two beings, a person and an animal, now thinking your thoughts and performing your actions, you ought to wonder which one you are. You may think you're the person (the one that isn't an animal). But doesn't the animal think that *it* is a person too? It has all the same reasons for thinking so as you have. Yet it is mistaken. If you *were* the animal and not the person, you'd still think you were the person. So for all you know, you're the one making the mistake. Even if you are a person and not an animal, you could never have any reason to believe that you are.[4]

For that matter, if your animal can think, that ought to make *it* a person. It has the same mental features as you have. (Otherwise we should expect an explanation for the difference, just as we should if the animal can't think at all.) It is, in Locke's words, "a thinking intelligent being, that has reason and reflection, and can consider itself as itself, the same thinking thing, in different times and places" (1975: 335). It satisfies every ordinary definition of 'person'. But it would be mad to suppose that the animal sitting in your chair is a *person* numerically different from you – that each human person shares her location and her thoughts with *another* person. If nothing else, this would contradict the claim that people – all people – have psychological identity conditions, thus sweeping away the main reason for denying that we are animals in the first place.

On the other hand, if ordinary human animals are not people, familiar accounts of what it is to be a person are all far too permissive. Having the psychological and moral features that you and I have would not be enough to make something a person. There could be rational, intelligent, self-conscious *non*-people. In fact there would be at least one such rational non-person for every genuine person. That would deprive personhood of any psychological or moral significance.

## 8. Hard Choices

That concludes my argument for animalism. We could put the same point in another way. There are about six billion human animals walking the earth. Those animals are just like ourselves. They sit in our chairs and sleep in our beds. They work, and talk, and take holidays. Some of them do philosophy. They have just the mental and physical attributes that we take ourselves to have. So it seems, anyway. This makes it hard to deny that *we* are those animals. The apparent existence of rational human animals is an inconvenient fact for the opponents of animalism. We might call it the *problem of the thinking animal.*

But what of the case against animalism? It seems that you would go along with your cerebrum if that organ were transplanted. More generally, some sort of mental continuity appears to suffice for us to persist.[5] And that is not true of any animal. Generations of philosophers have found this argument compelling. How can they have gone so badly wrong?

One reason, as I have said, is that they haven't asked the right questions. They have thought about what it takes for us to persist through time, but not about what we are.

Here is another. If someone is mentally just like you, that is strong evidence for his being you. Even stronger if there is continuously physically realized mental continuity between him and you. In fact it is conclusive evidence, given that brain transplants belong to science fiction. Moreover, most of us find mental continuity more interesting and important than brute physical continuity. When we hear a story, we don't much care which person at the end of the tale is the same animal as a given person at the beginning. We care far more who is psychologically continuous with that person. If mental and animal continuity often came apart, we might think differently. But they don't.

These facts can easily lead us to suppose that the one who remembers your life in the transplant story is you. Easier still if we don't know how problematic that claim is – if we don't realize that it would rule out our being animals. To those who haven't reflected on the problem of the thinking animal – and that includes most philosophers – it can seem dead obvious that we persist by virtue of mental continuity. But if we are animals, this is a mistake, though an understandable one.

Of course, opponents of animalism can play this game too. They can attempt to explain why it is natural to suppose that there are human animals, or that human animals can think, or that you are the thinking thing sitting in your chair, in a way that does not imply that those claims are true. (That is the point of the linguistic hypotheses I mentioned earlier.) What to do? Well, I invite you to compare the thinking-animal argument with the transplant argument. Which is more likely: That there are no animals? That no animal could ever think? That you are one of at least two intelligent beings sitting in your chair? Or that you would not, after all, go along with your transplanted cerebrum?

## 9. What it Would Mean if We Were Animals

What would it mean if we were animals? The literature on personal identity gives the impression that this is a highly counterintuitive, "tough-minded" idea, radically at odds with our deepest convictions. It is certainly at odds with most of that literature. But I doubt whether it conflicts with anything that we all firmly believe.

If animalism conflicts with any popular beliefs, they will have to do with the conditions of our identity over time. As we have seen, the way we react (or imagine ourselves reacting) to certain fantastic stories suggests that we take ourselves to persist by virtue of mental continuity. Our beliefs about *actual* cases, though, suggest no such thing. In every actual case, the number of people we think there are is just the number of human animals. Every actual case in which we take someone to survive or perish is a case where a human animal survives or perishes.

If anything, the way we regard actual cases suggests a conviction that our identity does not consist in mental continuity, or at any rate that mental continuity is unnecessary for us to persist. When someone lapses into a persistent vegetative state, his friends and relatives may conclude that his life no longer has any value. They may even conclude that he has ceased to exist *as a person*. But they don't ordinarily suppose that their loved one no longer exists at all, and that the living organism on the hospital bed is something numerically different from him – even when they come to believe that there is no mental continuity between the vegetable and the person. *That* would be a tough-minded view.

And most of us believe that we were once foetuses. When we see an ultrasound picture of a 12-week-old foetus, it is easy to believe we are seeing something that will, if all goes well, be born, learn to talk, go to school, and eventually become an adult human person. Yet none of us is in any way mentally continuous with a 12-week-old foetus.

Animalism may conflict with religious beliefs: with the belief in reincarnation or resurrection, for instance (though whether there is any real conflict is less obvious than it may seem: see van Inwagen 1978). But few accounts of personal identity are any more compatible with those beliefs. If resurrection and reincarnation rule out our being animals, they probably rule out our being anything except immaterial substances, or perhaps computer programs. On this score animalism is no worse off than its main rivals.

And don't we have a strong conviction that we are animals? We all think that we are human beings. And until the philosophers got hold of us, we took human beings to be animals. Of course that doesn't show that we *are* animals. But it shows that we seem to be. It is the opponents of animalism who insist that this appearance is deceptive: that the animal you see in the mirror is not really you. That we are animals ought to be the default position. If anything is hard to believe, it's the alternatives.[6]

## Notes

1 E.g. Shoemaker 1984: 113f. For what it's worth, my opinion of "constitutionalism" can be found in Olson 2001.

2 For more on this crucial point see Olson 1997: 114–119.

3 The argument is not entirely new. As I see it, it only makes explicit what is implicit in Carter 1989, Ayers 1990: 283f., Snowdon 1990, and Olson 1997: 100–109.

4 Some say that revisionary linguistics can solve this problem too (Noonan 1998). The idea is roughly this. First, not just any rational, self-conscious being is a person, but only those that have psychological identity conditions. Human animals, despite their mental properties, are not people because they lack psychological identity conditions. Second, the word 'I' and other personal pronouns refer only to people. Thus, when the animal associated with you says 'I', it doesn't refer to itself. Rather, it refers to you, the person associated with it. When it says, "I am a person," it does not say falsely that *it* is a person, but truly that *you* are. So the animal is not mistaken about which thing it is, and neither are you. You can infer that you are a person from the linguistic facts that you are whatever you refer to when you say 'I', and that 'I' refers only to people. I discuss this ingenious proposal in Olson 2002b.

5 In fact this is not so. Let the surgeons transplant each of your cerebral hemispheres into a different head. Both offshoots will be mentally continuous with you. But they can't both *be* you, for the simple reason that one thing (you) cannot be identical with two things. We cannot say in general that anyone who is mentally continuous with you must be you. Exceptions are possible. So it ought to come as no great surprise if the original cerebrum transplant is another exception.

6 I thank Trenton Merricks and Gonzalo Rodriguez-Pereyra for comments on an earlier version.

## References

Ayers, M. 1990. *Locke*, vol. 2. London: Routledge.

Carter, W. R. 1989. How to change your mind. *Canadian Journal of Philosophy* 19: 1–14.

Chisholm, R. 1976. *Person and Object.* La Salle, IL: Open Court.

Hume, D. 1888. *Treatise of Human Nature*, ed. by L. A. Selby-Bigge. Oxford: Clarendon Press. (Original work 1739. Partly reprinted in Perry 1975.)

Lewis, D. 1976. Survival and identity. In A. Rorty, ed., *The Identities of Persons*. Berkeley: California. (Repr. in his *Philosophical Papers* vol. I. New York: Oxford University Press. 1983.)

Locke, J. 1975. *An Essay Concerning Human Understanding*, ed. P. Nidditch. Oxford: Clarendon Press, (Original work, 2nd ed., originally published 1694. Partly reprinted in Perry 1975.)

Noonan, Harold. 1998. Animalism versus Lockeanism: a current controversy. *Philosophical Quarterly* 48: 302–318.

Olson, E. 1997. *The Human Animal: Personal Identity Without Psychology*. New York: Oxford University Press.

—. 2001. Material coincidence and the indiscernibility problem. *Philosophical Ouarterly* 51: 337–355.

—. 2002a. What does functionalism tell us about personal identity? *Noûs* 36: 682–698.

—. 2002b. Thinking animals and the reference of 'I'. *Philosophical Topics* 30: 189–208.

—. 2006. There is no bodily criterion of personal identity. In F. MacBride, ed., *Identity and Modality*. Oxford: Oxford University Press.

Perry, J., ed. 1975. *Personal Identity*. Berkeley: University of California Press.

Quinton, A. 1962. The soul. *Journal of Philosophy* 59: 393–403. (Reprinted in Perry 1975.)

Russell, B. 1985. *The Philosophy of Logical Atomism*. La Salle, IL: Open Court. Original work 1918.

Shoemaker, S. 1984. Personal identity: a materialist's account. In S. Shoemaker and R. Swinburne, *Personal Identity*. Oxford: Blackwell.

—. 1999. Self, body, and coincidence. *Proceedings of the Aristotelian Society, Supplementary Volume* 73: 287–306.

Snowdon, Paul. 1990. Persons, animals, and ourselves. In C. Gill, ed., *The Person and the Human Mind*. Oxford: Clarendon Press.

Unger, P. 1979. I do not exist. In G. F. MacDonald, ed., *Perception and Identity*. London: Macmillan. (Reprinted in M. Rea, ed., *Material Constitution*. Lanham, MD: Rowman and Littlefield. 1997.)

van Inwagen, P. 1978. The possibility of resurrection. *International Journal for the Philosophy of Religion* 9: 114–121. (Reprinted in his "*The Possibility of Resurrection" and Other Essays in Christian Apologetics*. Boulder: Westview. 1997.)

—. 1980. Philosophers and the words 'human body'. In van Inwagen, ed., *Time and Cause*. Dordrecht: Reidel.

# Personal Identity and the Past

Marya Schechtman

Philosophy, Psychiatry, & Psychology, Volume 12, Number 1, March 2005, pp. 9-22 (Article)

Published by The Johns Hopkins University Press
*DOI: 10.1353/ppp.2005.0032*

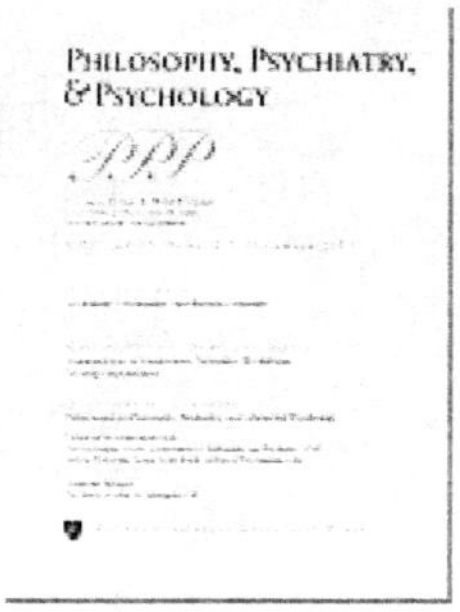

# Personal Identity and the Past

Marya Schechtman

Abstract: In the second edition of the *Essay Concerning Human Understanding,* John Locke argues that personal identity over time consists in sameness of consciousness rather than the persistence of any substance, material or immaterial. Something about this view is very compelling, but as it stands it is too vague and problematic to provide a viable account of personal identity. Contemporary "psychological continuity theorists" have tried to amend Locke's view to capture his insights and avoid his difficulties. This paper argues that the standard approach fails because it takes Locke to be a memory theorist, and does not focus enough on his claim that we need continuity of consciousness for personal persistence. An alternative reading of Locke is offered, emphasizing the role of self-understanding in producing continuity of consciousness. This alternative overcomes the difficulties with the standard approach, and shows how it is possible to attribute unconscious psychological elements to a person, even when personal persistence is defined in terms of consciousness.

Keywords: personal identity, consciousness, memory, unconscious, self understanding.

In the second edition of the *Essay Concerning Human Understanding,* John Locke takes up the question of what makes someone the same person throughout her entire life. His response to this question has served as the starting point for many of the views of personal identity represented in the philosophical literature today. Locke's important contribution is to argue that the continuation of a person is independent of the continuation of any substance—either physical (the body) or nonphysical (the soul). I am the same person as someone who existed in the past, says Locke, if and only if I can extend my current consciousness back to that person's actions. This assertion is usually interpreted as a "memory theory" of personal identity—the view that whatever actions and experiences a person can remember are, for that reason, her actions and experiences.

In some respects, Locke's view is extremely compelling, but at the same time a simple memory theory is totally implausible. Although Locke's arguments that continuation of substance cannot serve as a viable account of personal identity are powerful, a view that implies that a person can have no experiences that he does not (or cannot easily) remember consciously seems far too strong. Locke might or might not be willing to bite the bullet and accept that no forgotten experiences can be ours, but most philosophers are not. The contemporary theorists who base their views on Locke's insight ("psychological continuity theorists") have thus altered his original account, trying to keep the basic insight while avoiding the counterintuitive implications. This has met with mixed success. Psychological continuity theories do fix some of the obvious difficulties with Locke's original view, but they do so at a cost. These amended views lose much of the appeal of Locke's original picture and undermine much of the original argument for a psychological account of identity.

In what follows, I argue that this cost is incurred because psychological continuity theories take a wrong turn in developing Locke's view. They concentrate too much on the notion of memory, and not enough on the notion of consciousness. As a result, they end up with views that neither fully capture Locke's original insight nor fully avoid the implausibilities of his view. I propose an alternative development of Locke's insight that emphasizes the importance of self-understanding. This view captures most of what Locke says about why consciousness is so central to personhood and personal identity without being committed to the implausible view that only experiences of which we are conscious can be ours. I begin with a brief review of Locke's view, the objections to it, and the development of psychological continuity theories to answer those objections. Next, I describe some of the deficiencies of psychological continuity theories, and outline my proposed alternative.

## Locke's Argument

Locke's central contribution to work on personal identity is his insistence that identity must be defined in terms of sameness of consciousness rather than sameness of substance. It is not the continuation of either an immaterial soul or a body that constitutes the continuation of the person, he says, but rather the continued flow of consciousness. There are two basic elements of his argument for this claim. To make the claim intuitively plausible, he uses a number of hypothetical cases in which continuation of consciousness is separated from continuation of substance, showing that our judgment in such cases would be that the person goes with the consciousness. He also provides a more theoretical discussion about what it is to be a person, arguing that once we understand this clearly we see that identity must be defined in terms of consciousness rather than substance. It is helpful to review briefly each aspect of his discussion.

Locke gets us to see the force of his view through the use of a series of imagined cases. He asks us to imagine, for instance, the mental life of a prince "entering and informing" the body of a cobbler, and argues that everyone would see that the resulting person is the same person as the prince rather than the cobbler (Locke 1979, 340). He suggests that we imagine someone who has the same soul as Nestor or Thersites at the siege of Troy, but without consciousness of any of their actions, and tells us that it is obvious that this person is no more the same person as Nestor or Thersites than he would be if his body happened to share some of the same matter that had once composed theirs (Locke 1979, 339). He asks us also to imagine a man who has two distinct consciousnesses sharing his body—one by day and one by night—with no communication between them, and says that it is clear that there are two distinct persons sharing one body in such a case (Locke 1979, 344–345).

This view of personal continuation is not, of course, uncontroversial. It is, however, widely accepted, and whether or not this is the final word on what it is to be a person, it undoubtedly captures one important strand of our thought about ourselves. The same basic intuition is expressed, for instance, by William James in *The Principles of Psychology* when he says,

> The Soul, however, when closely scrutinized, guarantees no immortality of a sort *we care for.* The enjoyment of the atom-like simplicity of their substance *in sécular séculorum* would not to most people seem a consummation devoutly to be wished. The substance must give rise to a stream of consciousness continuous with the present stream, in order to arouse our hope, but of this the mere persistence of the substance *per se* offers no guarantee. (James 1950, 348)

This idea can also be seen when we recognize that there is a real sense in which we would view total, irreversible amnesia as a form of death. Faced with the prospect of such amnesia we might well distribute remembrances, write letters to loved ones, and in other ways act as if we were anticipating death.

The Lockean insight is also seen in the impulse to view Multiple Personality Disorder as a circumstance in which more than one person share a body. Of course, describing this disorder in this way is by no means uncontroversial, and later I examine some of the reasons we might want to say that there is only one person per body, even in cases such as this. The point here, however, is to get clearer on the intuition behind the Lockean view, not to argue that there is a monolithic problem of personal identity to which it provides the unique solution. It is, I think, at least uncontroversial to claim that in Multiple Personality Disorder we are not presented unproblematically with a single person. The fact that these cases seem to present, at least sometimes, genuinely independent streams of consciousness, which may have no awareness of one another, seems reason enough to say that there is some very important sense in which distinct persons co-occupy a body just as Locke took his revolving day and night consciousness to do.

This, then, is the basic intuition behind Locke's view, and it is in many respects a familiar and compelling one. Locke further supports his account of identity by giving a more general definition of the concept of the person revealed in these cases. He tells us that *person* stands for "a thinking, intelligent Being, that has reason and reflection, and can consider it self as it self, the same thinking thing in different times and places" (Locke 1979, 335). To be a person is to have self-consciousness, viewing oneself as a persisting subject. This means that a person becomes the same person who has past experiences or undertook past actions when her consciousness includes them. "As far as any Intelligent Being can repeat the *Idea* of any past action with the same consciousness it had of it at first, and with the same consciousness it has of any present Action;" says Locke, "so far it is the same *personal self*" (Locke 1979, 336). His view in a nutshell, then, is that "*Personal Identity* consists, not in the Identity of Substance, but, as I have said, in the Identity of *consciousness*" (Locke 1979, 342).

Locke expands on this concept of person by telling us that *person* is a "Forensick Term appropriating Actions and their Merit; and so belongs only to intelligent Agents capable of a Law, and Happiness and Misery" (Locke 1979, 346). This characterization sets out two features that Locke takes to be unique to personhood, and that he uses to support his definition of personal identity in terms of sameness of consciousness. First, persons are capable of a special sort of self-interested concern and second, they are moral agents, capable of taking actions for which they can be held responsible. Both of these capacities, he argues, are linked to consciousness. To care about the unfolding of our lives, we need to have a conscious conception of ourselves as having a future to care about. Moreover, it is through consciousness that we experience pleasure and pain, and so the extent of our concern is the extent of our conscious experience. He puts it this way: "*Self* is that conscious thinking thing, (whatever Substance, made up of whether Spiritual, or Material, Simple or Compounded, it matters not) which is sensible, or conscious of Pleasure and Pain, capable of Happiness or Misery, and so is concern'd for it *self* as far as that consciousness extends" (Locke 1979, 341). He also argues that moral responsibility requires consciousness. To be moral agents, we must be able to plan and to recognize that actions we take now have consequences in the future. Here he taps the intuitions unearthed by the kinds of hypothetical cases described above. He says, for instance, "for suppose a Man punish'd now, for what he had done in another Life, whereof he could be made to have no consciousness at all, what difference is there between that Punishment, and being created miserable?" (Locke 1979, 347). Again the case of Multiple Personality Disorder gives us a real-life example of what Locke has in mind here. Such cases have raised tricky questions in legal contexts about how to assign culpability when the consciousness of the personality who allegedly committed a crime is unavailable to other personalities in the same body.

Locke thus taps into a widely held concept of the person according to which a person is a self-conscious subject. On this picture, personal identity or continuation through time depends on the continuation of consciousness. In particular, if one is conscious of oneself as the same self who existed at some past time, this consciousness actually makes one the same person as that past self. The failure of such self-consciousness, on the other hand, signals the end of the person. Attempting to capture this conception of the person, Locke thus tells us that we become the same person as some past person by extending our consciousness back to her experiences because in doing so we become aware not only of those experiences themselves, but of the fact that we are the ones who had them. This awareness gives us consciousness of ourselves as persisting beings, and so constitutes the fact of our identity with the past person—a fact that would not hold were we not conscious of her experiences.

Although there is undoubtedly something very compelling about Locke's view of personal identity, it is problematic as it stands. It is not entirely obvious just what the details of the view are, but it is generally read as a "memory theory"—the view that whatever experiences a person remembers are, for that reason, her experiences. Locke tells us that a person makes past experiences hers by extending her consciousness back in time to them, but as Thomas Reid suggests, "Mr. Locke attributes to consciousness the conviction we have of our past actions, as if a man may now be conscious of what he did twenty years ago. It is impossible to understand the meaning of this, unless by consciousness be meant memory, the only faculty by which we have an immediate knowledge of our past actions" (Reid 1976, 115). Although I have argued elsewhere that this is an oversimplified reading of Locke (Schechtman 1996, 105–112), it seems obvious that memory must be a large part of the picture.

A simple memory theory, however, is not plausible on its own. It is at the same time too weak and too strong. This theory is too weak because it seems that it takes more than simply remembering an experience to make me the person who did it. As many objectors have pointed out, memory is good evidence that a past experience is ours, but on its own it does not seem quite enough to make it ours. To use a variation on a science fiction case that appears often in the literature, the fact that a neurosurgeon may develop a technique whereby she could implant in my brain the recollection of an experience had by her grandmother does not now make me the person who had that experience (i.e., her grandmother). The memory theory is too strong because even when we are thinking of ourselves as conscious subjects rather than substances, it seems obvious that we can and do forget experiences that are nonetheless ours. If the mind of the prince were, for example, to enter the body of the cobbler but along the way lose the memory of what the prince ate for breakfast or repress the memory of a rather unfortunate interaction with the vice chancellor, we would not want to deny that these were, nonetheless, experiences of the prince and so of the person inhabiting the cobbler's body. To provide a plausible account of identity, then, the simple memory theory needs some development.[1] This is the task undertaken by psychological continuity theorists.

## Psychological Continuity Theories

Psychological continuity theorists take on the goal of providing an account of personal identity over time that captures what seems so right in Locke's observations but is more plausible in the details. There have been several strategies for dealing with the implausible aspects of the simple memory theory; I review some of the most fundamental. First, consider the objection that merely remembering some past experience does not seem enough to make me the person who had it. One response to this difficulty is to require that there be more than one memory connection between a present and past person if we are to judge that they are the same person. In the example where a neurosurgeon implants one memory from her grandmother's life in someone's brain, a large part of the reason we are unwilling to make a judgment of identity is that there is only a single, out-of-context connection between the post-operative person and the presurgery grandmother. Psychological continuity theorists thus generally require that there be "enough" connections between people at two times if we are to say they are the same person. There is, of course, a great deal of difficulty in individuating connections, let alone in finding a nonarbitrary number of connections to determine identity. The general idea, however, is that there must be some threshold level of memory connection between a present person and a past one that is required to make them the same person.

Even if a person remembers a great many experiences of a past person, however, it may seem that the relation of memory is too weak to support identity—at least if *memory* is taken to mean no more than having an experience of recollection. For this reason, it has been very common for psychological continuity theorists to require that for a past experience to be attributed to a person, he must not only recall the experience, but the recollection must be properly caused by the original experience. The idea of proper cause is generally spelled out in terms of the continued functioning of a single brain in which a memory trace is laid down at the time of the original experience.

To address the sense that memory theories are too strong, a different but related set of changes is made to the simple memory theory. A first step in overcoming this difficulty is recognizing that there is a fundamental difference between the types of cases Locke amasses to make the case that memory is crucial to personal identity and the kinds of cases marshaled to show that the memory theory seems so implausible. The cases Locke describes all involve a person experiencing wholesale memory loss, and so having her conscious connection to the past severed entirely. The cases where it seemed obvious that a lapse of memory does not result in a change of person were cases in which only a few memories were lost, but others stayed in place, providing a connection to the past time, if not to those particular past events. Once again, then, the issue is how many memory connections to a past time are present. In this context, however, the significance of the number of connections suggests that there are really two distinct questions at issue here: one is the question of whether a person in the present is the same person as some person in the past (or whether a particular person survives into the future). The second is the question of whether some particular past action or experience is attributable to a person in the present. What our discussion seems to show is that the intuition that memory is crucial to issues of identity applies most clearly to the first question. Locke's general claim seems plausible when we take him to be saying that, for a person to continue into the future, there must be someone in the future who remembers some (enough) of her experiences, and therefore takes herself to be that person. It seems less plausible when we take it to say that, for a person to be the person who had some particular experience or undertook some particular action, she must remember having that experience or taking that action.

One natural way of responding to this implausible feature of a simple memory theory is thus to separate the questions of what makes a person at one time the same person as a person at another time from the question of what makes a particular action or experience the action or experience of a given person.[2] It is then possible to offer a view according to which a person at the present time is the same as some person in the past if the present person has enough memories of the past to allow for a conception of herself as a continuing subject, without being committed to the idea that it is memory that makes a particular action or experience attributable to a person. It will then be necessary, of course, to offer some account of attribution as well.

Psychological continuity theorists follow this strategy either implicitly or explicitly, separating these questions, and taking the question of identifying persons at two different times with one another as prior. To answer this question they take as their basic starting point a reading of Locke, which says that a person at time $t_2$ is the same person as a person at an earlier time $t_1$ just in case the person at $t_2$ remembers some of the experiences of the person at time $t_1$. They then amend this view to try and overcome any residual implausibility. First they allow that a person need not remember even one experience from every part of his life. There may be some phases of the past—perhaps those very remote in time—that one does not directly remember at all, but that nonetheless seem to be part of one's life. Psychological continuity theorists account for this fact by requiring not direct memory, but overlapping chains of direct memory to make a person at one time the same as a person at another. If I currently have some memories of my 30th birthday, and if the person whose experiences I remember on that day had some memories of my 20th birthday, and the person whose experiences are remembered on that day had memories of my 10th birthday, and that person had memories of my 6th birthday, then I now am the same person as that person celebrating my 6th birthday, even if I have no direct memories of that day whatsoever. These theorists also suggest that memory is not the only psychological connection that can contribute to identity, but that the persistence of beliefs, values, desires, or the connections between intentions and the later actions that carry them out can also serve as identity-constituting connections between persons at different times.

The final form of the psychological continuity theory's answer to the question of what makes a person at time $t_2$ the same person as a person at time $t_1$ is that it is an overlapping chain of psychological connections including memory and other connections between the person at $t_2$ and the person at $t_1$. The answer to the second question—the question of what makes a particular action or experience that of a particular person—is often implicit in psychological continuity theories and rests on the answer to the first. The idea is simple and natural: the criterion outlined tells us whether a person at $t_2$ is the same as a person at $t_1$. If they are the same, then whatever experiences are attributable to the earlier person at $t_1$ are also attributable to the person at $t_2$. If, that is, the cobbler body before us is determined to be the same person who was previously in the prince body, then he is the person who ate breakfast in the prince's body or had that bad interaction with the vice chancellor, whether he remembers it or not.

This strategy, of course, requires that we have some way of attributing experiences to persons at a time. This sort of attribution is usually taken for granted, but the underlying idea is pretty clear. It is assumed that there is a primitive notion of unity of consciousness at a time. At any particular moment, there is some set of experiences experienced as co-conscious, and all of these belong to a single person. If a later person remembers some but not all of the experiences that were co-conscious earlier, she thereby connects himself to the entire earlier person, and makes all of the experiences that were co-conscious at that time hers. This position is in the background in most psychological continuity theories, but is made explicit in an early version of this view put forth by H. P. Grice. Grice defines what he calls a "total temporary state" or "t.t.s." To give an idea of what he means by this, he says that a t.t.s. is "composed of all the experiences any one person is having at any given time. Thus, if I am now thinking of Hitler and feeling a pain, and having no other experiences, there will be occurring now a total temporary state containing as elements a thought of Hitler and a feeling of pain" (Grice 1976, 86). He then defines personal identity over time in terms of overlapping chains of memory connections between t.t.s.'s. The same strategy can also be found in versions of the psychological continuity theory offered by Sydney Shoemaker (1984), John Perry (1976), David Lewis (1983), and Derek Parfit (1984).[3]

Psychological continuity theories thus start with the basic Lockean insight that persons are essentially self-conscious entities, and that their identity over time should be defined in terms of the extension of consciousness. They read this as the claim that personal identity should be defined in terms of memory connection, and alter this view to avoid some of the more obvious objections. They end by offering a view according to which a person at one time is the same person as a person at an earlier time if the present person is connected to the earlier one by overlapping chains of sufficient numbers of psychological connections. When people at two different times have been determined to be the same person, any experiences or actions that are attributable to the one person are also attributable to the other.

## Problems With Psychological Continuity Theories

Psychological continuity theories present a rather tidy solution to the difficulties described, but in the end they are not that much more satisfying than a straight memory theory. These theories, too, seem both too weak and too strong, if in a different way from the memory theory itself. They seem too weak because it is not obvious that the relation in terms of which they define identity really does any better than Locke's original view at quieting the sense that memory alone is not enough to constitute identity, and may even do worse. In the finished psychological continuity theory, what we have are a collection of independent "persons-at-times" that are cobbled together through memory and other connections with the requirement that there be some critical mass of memory connections and some (usually physical) causal connection between present memory experiences and past experiences of which they are memories. Although the requirements added to the simple memory theory do in some sense make a stronger connection between the different temporal parts of a person's life and between a person and the experiences that are attributed to her, it is not clear that it is stronger in the right way—that is, that is stronger in a way that will answer the original worries.

First, consider the requirement that there be some critical number of memory connections in place before we make a judgment of personal identity. This amounts to a difference in degree rather than kind from the simple memory theory. What we have here is just a collection of memories, and it is not clear that that is enough where one memory was not. It is not obvious how the addition of connections besides memory could help here either, because these give us even less conscious access to the past. This, of course, is why the requirement of causal connection is added, but it is not evident that that does the work psychological continuity theorists want it to, either. What this amounts to, really, is a requirement of sameness of substance. In addition to having the experience of remembering some set of experiences in the past, it requires that there be a causal pathway, through a continuing body, from the experiences to the recollections. There is no indication that this changes the phenomenological character of the experience at all, only that it guarantees that a single body (or at least brain) is present for both the experience and the recollection.

This requirement does make us feel better about the worry that memory alone is not enough to constitute identity, but how does it do so? Essentially by appealing to the intuitions supporting a sameness of substance view—the very intuitions that Locke's arguments were meant to overcome. For this reason, Locke's original arguments can be brought into play against this means of developing his insight. Why should it matter to us that the memory experiences in question be in one substance rather than another if it does not change the character of consciousness? If the memory experiences alone are not sufficiently strong to constitute identity, why should their being placed in a substance continuous with the one that had the experiences be a "consummation devoutly to be desired"? Or, put another way, why on this view should the fact that this lump of stuff here will have memories of these experiences in the future be more comforting than the fact that those who come after me will remember me when I am gone? I do not deny that it may feel more comforting. There is no doubt that one strand of our thought on personal identity places that identity in the continuation of substance, and there is much to be said for sameness of substance views. Locke, however, has identified another strand of thought according to which what matters is the character of our experience. To solve difficulties with that view by adding a requirement of sameness of substance is not to develop the basic insight, but to reject it. If the simple memory theory provides too weak a relation to constitute identity, then the psychological continuity theory does as well.

Indeed, the psychological continuity theory may be even worse off in this regard because of the method by which it attributes particular actions and experiences to persons. On the simple memory theory, one needed to be directly conscious of an action or experience for it to be hers. Although, as we have discussed, this seems like too strong a requirement in the end, at least we had some explanation for why this relation was supposed to be important. Those experiences of which we are directly conscious are experiences that must necessarily affect our well-being. Their nature matters to us because we experience them.

They are also, at least according to Locke, tied to responsibility in this way, because we can know them to be our actions or experiences, we have a responsibility to and for them that we could not otherwise have. The Lockean insight thus seems to rest on the special relation we have to experiences while we are conscious of them. According to the psychological continuity theory, however, there are many experiences—and even whole life phases—that are counted as mine even though I no longer have any consciousness of them at all. They are no more connected to my present consciousness than they would be by a sameness of substance view. The original appeal of Locke's theory is thus lost on this view.

None of this is to deny that memory—at least conceived as a simple recollection (even appropriately caused)—is too weak a relation to seem intuitively plausible as the relation which constitutes personal identity. It is just to say that psychological continuity theories do not remedy the deficits of the simple memory theory in a way which counts as a development of Locke's insight. One response to the recognition of the weakness of the memory theory, of course, is simply to reject the Lockean insight in favor of a sameness of substance view, and many have done just that. If, however, we think that there is still something valuable in the original arguments against sameness of substance views, the way to speak to the weakness of the memory theory would be to develop an account of psychological continuity defined in terms of conscious connections richer and deeper than memory, or to deepen our account of memory itself. Simply adding more of the same or continuity of substance will not do the trick.

A seemingly contradictory set of intuitions also suggests that the psychological continuity theory is too strong, particularly in its account of attribution. Even though this theory allows that experiences and life phases of which we are no longer conscious can be ours, attribution still depends on an initial act of consciousness. It is because we are connected through overlapping chains to some past time at which we were conscious of an action or experience that the life phase and its experiences become ours. This is problematic because it leaves no room in the view for the impact and attribution of unconscious (or nonconscious)[4] experiences to a person. If the person was not conscious of an experience at the time to which she is currently connected by overlapping chains, then the experience cannot be hers. It seems clear, however, that experiences of which we are not conscious can be part of our psychological lives. To name just two species, dispositional states and repressed states seem as if they can contribute to identity every bit as much as consciously entertained states, but they are ruled out as attributable to the person on this view.

It might be protested that psychological continuity theories are in fact perfectly plausible on this matter. All they require is that an experience have been conscious at some time. Then, if the time at which the experience was conscious is linked via other conscious connections to the present, the unconscious state is made part of the present person through its attribution at the past time. This will probably capture many of the states we wish to attribute to a person despite the fact that she is not conscious of them, but it will not entirely solve the psychological continuity theorists' problem. First of all, this view does not give us a way to distinguish between psychic elements that are at one time a part of consciousness and then lost forever and those which remain as unconscious states. Because the state's connection to the present is only a courtesy via the connection of the past person to the present person through other states, there is no difference on this view between an experience that was part of consciousness and then faded entirely and, for example, a repressed state that is still actively at work in a person's psychological life, although no longer part of consciousness. There is an important difference between an experience that is mine because I experienced it in the past but have now forgotten it entirely, and one that is mine because I have repressed it and am still suffering the symptoms of that repression, and there is no clear way to capture this difference in the psychological continuity theory.

Moreover, it seems likely that some experiences or features of our psychological lives may be ours even if we are never explicitly conscious of them. We can be affected by a great deal that does not make its way into the realm of consciously entertained experience. Although this claim is itself plausible enough, it may seem that to make it I have to revert to the perspective behind sameness of substance views as I earlier accused psychological continuity theorists of doing. Things are a bit more complicated in this instance, however. The idea that unconscious states can be part of who we are arises in the context where we are thinking of ourselves as psychological subjects, and not just as substances, and this is, among other reasons, because many states of which we are not conscious are implicated in the relations of concern and responsibility that Locke identifies. There is a vast difference between the case where an experience was had by a particular substance (soul or body) that is currently cut off from it—as in Locke's hypothetical cases—and a case where we say that a person has an (again, in a general, nontechnical sense) unconscious memory, or belief, or desire. In the latter case, there is an assumption that the state is not simply wiped out of the psychological economy, but is still playing a role. It will impact a person's well-being and the nature of her consciousness even if she is not directly aware of the state itself and cannot become so. It can, moreover, inspire the feelings of guilt or shame or pride associated with moral agency even if the source of these feelings remains obscure. The relation we have to our unconscious states is thus generally far more intimate and far more relevant to our present consciousness than states that we would consider "not ours" on the Lockean view—states that befell this substance but have no impact on current experience at all. It thus seems both necessary and possible to find a way to make unconscious states attributable to a person within a broad Lockean perspective. The psychological continuity theory, however, does not seem to have a means of doing so.

What this discussion of the failing of the psychological continuity theory reveals is that what originally looked like a clash of intuitions about whether an experience a person does not remember can be his experience is really about consciousness rather than memory itself. Memory became important in the discussion as the medium through which consciousness is continued over time. The real conflict of intuitions, which makes development of the Lockean insight so difficult, is the conflict between our sense that the person (understood as psychological subject) should be identified with conscious mental activity only and the sense that the psychological subject is more extensive and includes non-conscious mental activity as well. Both ideas have their appeal. Freud has pointed out many *motives* for identifying ourselves with our consciousness—in doing so we can avoid acknowledging characteristics, fantasies, desires, and experiences that are, for one reason or another, unpalatable. Locke, on the other hand, tries to present *reasons* for identifying the person with conscious psychological life. The reasons involve first the fact that it is the continuation of conscious experience that seems both necessary and sufficient for our own continuation, and second the ways in which our consciousness of experiences underlies the special kind of self-interested concern and moral agency that distinguish persons from other kinds of creatures.

Our discussion of how psychological continuity theories grow out of Locke's view, and how they fall short of their goals, has given us the tools we need to develop Locke's insight in a more satisfying way. From Locke we have the reasons, outlined in the previous paragraph, for identifying the person with the conscious self. To develop his insight, we thus need a view that incorporates the role of self-conscious awareness in the constitution of identity, and also recognizes the link between identity and issues of self-interested concern and moral responsibility. From psychological continuity theories, we get the strategy of separating these two elements, offering distinct but interrelated accounts of personal continuation and the attribution of particular actions and of experiences—the first depending on conscious connections between the different parts of a person's life, and the second allowing for the attribution of experiences a person does not remember. Their theory of attribution does not, however, seem to do the work it needs to. Ultimately, it loses the relation to concern and responsibility that is so important in the Lockean view, and it does not say enough about the difference between experiences that are really dead to us and those which, though not part of consciousness, are an active part of our psychological lives. To give a more satisfying development of the Lockean insight, then, we need to give a better account of how and when states of which a person is not conscious can be attributed to her. I offer such an alternative in the next section.

## An Alternative Account

The task of developing the Lockean insight is now twofold. First, it is necessary to give an account of the kind of connection to the past that a person must have to develop the type of self-conception that constitutes personal identity. Second, it is necessary to give an account of the attribution of particular actions and experiences that allows for the attribution of unconscious elements as well as conscious ones. It is easiest to begin with the first task. Locke tells us that we make ourselves selves, and so determine our identity, by forming a self-conscious conception of ourselves as persisting subjects. The exact nature of this self-conception is never really spelled out, however. In the hands of psychological continuity theorists, it becomes the requirement that we have a sufficient number of memories of past experiences to connect us to a past time. Undoubtedly, this is a very important part of how we come to have our self-conceptions, but as a full account, it is rather thin. All that is required to have the appropriate sort of self-conception—the kind that determines personal identity and continuation into the future—is to have knowledge of what some collection of experiences is like from the inside. It is enough, on this view, just to have access to a certain number of memories. There is no further requirement on how these memories are to cohere or to be associated with present states.

The alternative development of the Lockean view I suggest adds to the recognition of the importance of memory and brute self-consciousness a recognition of the importance of being intelligible to ourselves. To have the kind of self-conception that constitutes personal identity on the view I am urging (call it the "self-understanding view"), one must not just know about some collection of past experiences and think of them as hers, she must see her life as unfolding according to an intelligible trajectory, where present states follow meaningfully from past ones, and the future is anticipated to bear certain predictable relations to the present. This does not mean that a person's life course is entirely under her control, only that she can see connections between how things were, how they are, and how they are likely to be. Having a self-conception does not just amount to knowing that one has a past and will have a future, but also involves seeing these as inherently interconnected and rich with implications for one another.

This understanding changes the fundamental nature of the self-awareness that constitutes us as persons. It is no longer a passive knowing that we have had experiences, but a more active attempt to make sense of those experiences and understand where they are leading us. Fully understood, Locke's fundamental insight is that as self-conscious entities we are interested in the character of our experience, and also in what we should do and what kind of person we should be. What this means, however, is that we are constantly self-monitoring, keeping track of how we are feeling, what we are doing, and what we are like. This self-monitoring is mostly implicit. There are many occasions where we introspect and consciously consider the trajectory of our lives and how its episodes fit together, but usually we are caught up in the activity of living, and this work goes on in the background. On the self-understanding view, it is this self-monitoring that gives us our sense of continuation and coherence as a self, and so provides the kind of self-conception and relation to a particular past that constitutes personal identity.

The basic picture of this self-monitoring is nicely developed by Raymond Martin in his book *Self-Concern*. There Martin develops the notion of a "perceiver self." We experience the world, Martin says, as if one part of the self were split off from the flux of events as an observer, watching and recording the stream of our experience. Martin argues that the perceiver-self is an illusion, and of course in some sense it must be; there is no homuncular entity within people who is the observer of their experience. Nevertheless, as Martin indicates, the sense that there is such a self is a robust and pervasive element of experience, and a central feature of human psychological organization. He also suggests that in thinking about personal survival it is the continuation of this self in which people are interested; they think they have survived if the perceiver-self continues, and that they will die if it does not.

Obviously, there are many issues to be settled about the nature and function of the perceiver-self before any forceful claims can be made about its role in personal identity. Martin says a great deal on this subject, and there will doubtless be much more discussion to come.[5] For present purposes, however, it is not necessary to put too much metaphysical weight on the concept; it can simply be used to represent a widespread and familiar picture of psychological continuation and personal survival. A somewhat more whimsical version of this picture is found in Michael Frayn's novel *Headlong,* where the protagonist undertakes a common sort of internal dialogue to convince himself to do what he knows to be wrong:

> Odd, though, all these dealings of mine with myself. First I've agreed to a principle with myself, now I'm making out a case to myself and debating my own feelings and intentions with myself. Who is this *self*, this phantom internal partner, with whom I'm entering into all of these arrangements? (I ask myself.)
>
> Well, who am I talking to now? Who is the ghostly audience for the long tale I tell through every minute of the day? This silent judge sitting, face shrouded, in perpetual closed session? (Frayn 1999, 126–127)

The "perceiver-self" then should be thought of as a stable observer who views and records the passing flux of experience, and recognizes it as part of a single life; it need not be an actually persisting agent, or even a truly continuous psychological process, but it is a process that gives rise to the background sense of a stable self of the sort whose existence seems crucial to personal identity on the view we have been exploring. My suggestion is that it is this sense of a stable perceiver-self, rather than a simple knowledge that one has had experiences in the past, that constitutes the continuation of consciousness that constitutes personal identity over time.

One way to make this rather abstract conception more concrete is to connect this self-monitoring to certain capacities. One quite simple implication of having such a self-conception is that a person can generally answer questions such as, "Why do I feel this way?" or "Why am I doing this?" should they arise. If she cannot answer them, she should be motivated to look for an answer. Answers to questions of this sort usually involve a number of factors. If one cannot easily make sense of the way one is feeling or choosing to act, however, it is natural to look for external explanations, considering the environment carefully to see if there is some hitherto undetected factor that is exerting an influence. In this way one might notice that it is the gathering clouds outside that are making one gloomy or anxious, even if one had not noticed them before; or that one's mother is constantly sending off subtle signals of disapproval and that this can explain one's guilt.

Sometimes, however, scrutiny of our environment and of our conscious internal states still leaves us baffled about why we feel or act as we do. This unintelligibility threatens our integrity as self-conscious subjects—in the subject, as in the world more generally, there should be no events that are simply uncaused. This does not mean that we must fully understand all of our feelings or motives, but only that we should not be at a loss as to where to start in such self-understanding. This really would undermine the difference between punishment and being created miserable. If we are at a loss, and no overlooked external factors can be found, it is natural to look for occult internal causes—nonconscious memories or impulses. Descartes offers an early example of this strategy with respect to his perceptions in the course of his *Meditations on First Philosophy*. He recognizes that he had previously taken his perceptual images to come from external objects because he was not aware of bringing them about himself. In the context of the meditations, however, he is supposing that there are no external objects, and so wonders if the images might come instead from some unknown part of himself. Although he ultimately decides that they come from an external world via God, his reflections demonstrate nicely the kind of dynamic I have in mind—first, the basic idea that it is our responsibility not only to know the contents of our consciousness but to understand their origins, and second the willingness to consider that we could, unknowingly, be the cause of our conscious experience. In a context more directly related to the current discussion, Freud's "discovery" of the unconscious follows just this logic, and it is, of course, this insight which is the inspiration of the self-understanding view with its emphasis on the importance of being intelligible to ourselves.

In postulating inner sources for our experiences and actions we recognize that there are parts of ourselves that we are not conscious of, but that are yet part of our psychological lives in an importantly intimate way. These experiences impact the nature of our conscious experience, and hence should be part of the purview of our self-interested concern. They also influence what we do, and lead to experiences of guilt, shame, or pride, and so are connected to our moral agency. To have an identity-constituting self-conception, then, a person must demand (at least implicitly) a kind of coherence and intelligibility to the course of her life. The past should not only be remembered; it should help to explain the present, which in turn should help predict the future. To achieve this intelligibility, we often need to allow for the impact of psychological features and experiences of which we are not directly conscious. The suggestion is thus that the attribution of individual states should be on this basis. Those memories or desires or motivations whose existence as part of the psychological economy must be postulated to make sense of a person's experience or the course of her life will be considered her experiences. In this way, we can make room for the attributions of experiences that are nonconscious without violating the fundamental Lockean insight. These experiences still affect us along the dimension of pleasure and pain, and are still connected to our capacities for moral agency. They are part of what determines how our lives will unfold, and what our experience will be like.[6]

The proposed alternative to the psychological continuity theory is thus a view that develops Locke's idea that to be a person is to understand oneself as a persisting being in terms of the demands we make that our lives be intelligible. To be a person on this view is implicitly to keep track of the unfolding of one's life. The particular type of self-concern that Locke takes to be definitive of personhood, as well as the capacity for moral agency, depends on our not just knowing ourselves to persist, but actively seeking to understand how our lives come to be pleasant or unpleasant, learning lessons from the past and applying them to the future. The stream of consciousness that we count as personal continuation involves understanding how the connections between past, present, and future work for us—not just seeing the present as connected to the past, but as flowing from it. This sometimes depends on the recognition of psychological states that play a role in determining our conscious experience, although they are not themselves conscious. It is important to understand that for such states to be attributed to a person, she need not consciously reflect on her history and accept their existence. This is worthy work and may be well worth undertaking for many reasons. For us to say of a person that a nonconscious experience is hers, however, all that is required is that it in fact be necessary to make her psychological life intelligible, whether she recognizes this fact or not.

There is a longstanding idea that memory plays a crucial role in the constitution of personal identity over time. This idea is tied to the Lockean insight about the importance of continuity of consciousness for personal identity. There is also a sense that a person can obviously have experiences she does not remember. This conflict of intuitions seems to be more than simply a conflict over whether persons are to be viewed as psychological subjects or substances. It is also internal to the view of persons as subjects. Psychological continuity theorists attempt to reconcile this conflict by developing a view where a sufficient number of memory connections between one moment and the next defines the basic continuity of the person, and attribution of forgotten experiences takes place through the relation of personal identity over time. Although this is a move in the right direction, it fails to capture the Lockean insight in many respects, and also fails to capture the way in which unconscious states can be part of who we are. An alternative account—the self-understanding view—recognizes the original conflict as between intuitions that identify the psychological subject with conscious states and intuitions that see psychological life and the subject itself as involving much that is unconscious as well. We can accommodate this latter understanding of the person and still retain Locke's insight if we simply recognize the fact that unconscious states have a powerful effect on consciousness and self-consciousness. The self-consciousness that Locke is after requires more than memory, it requires a certain level of self-understanding, and this, in turn, leads us to the attribution of psychological elements, which help explain how our conscious experience comes to be as it is. The memory theory on its own is obviously too simple to explain what is distinctive about being a person, but the idea that we are what we are—and who we are—because we understand ourselves in a certain way is not. On at least one important conception, to be a person is, as Locke says, to recognize oneself as a person, and here identity is indeed determined by self-understanding. Given that we are ultimately trying to define beings as complex as ourselves, however, it should be no surprise that this self-understanding involves more than a simple act of recollection.

## NOTES

1. I do not mean to imply that these are the only difficulties with a memory theory of identity. There are many other famous objections raised in the literature. These are, however, the objections that are important in what follows.

2. In a slightly different context, I have called these, respectively, the "reidentifcation question" and the "characterization question" (Schechtman, 1996, 1–2).

3. These theorists all differ from one another in a variety of details of course. Parfit, in particular, differs from the others in one of the details I have discussed here. He does not require any particular causal connection between recollections and the experiences they recollect to make them identity constituting. This is a significant deviation from the standard view, but because it only makes it harder for Parfit to speak to the difficulties I raise in the next section, I ignore it in what follows.

4. I have no technical sense of "unconscious" in mind here. For now when I talk about "unconscious" and "nonconscious" psychological states, I mean only states that are not consciously entertained, but are nonetheless part of the overall psychological economy. I will say a bit more about this in a few pages.

5. Martin believes that this assessment of the conditions of survival is ultimately a mistake because the perceiver-self never actually persists (and people do sometimes survive). An alternative way of reading these facts would be to say that, to capture what is accurate in this intuitive sense of survival, it is essential to think of the continuation of the perceiver-self as a phenomenological rather than metaphysical fact. That is, if a person can experience the perceiver-self as continuous and persistent she will have the kind of psychological continuation that, in at least some moods, is taken to constitute personal survival. Resolving these issues is, of course, a matter for a different series of papers.

6. It is worth noting that it may be absence of this kind of intelligibility as much as the unity of body that stands behind our hesitations to say that there is more than one person present in cases of Multiple Personality Disorder. In most such cases, there are periods of blackout and a variety of other puzzling events that keep any of the streams of consciousness from providing a really intelligible life narrative. From the outside, moreover, it often seems clear that if the streams of consciousness could have access to each other, the intelligibility of each would be greatly increased. In this respect, this is more like a case of a person having experiences of which he is not conscious than a case where they are not his at all. This account can thus capture both our inclination to say these cases involve more than one person sharing a single body and our inclination to say that this is not so.

## ACKNOWLEDGMENT

I am grateful to Grant Gillett for helpful comments throughout the process of writing this paper.

## REFERENCES

Descartes, R. 1992. *Meditations on first philosophy: In which the existence of God and the distinction of the human soul from the body are demonstrat-*

*ed*, ed. and trans. G. Heffernan. Notre Dame: Notre Dame University Press.
Frayn, M. 1999. *Headlong*. New York: Picador.
Grice, H. P. 1976. Personal identity. In *Personal identity*, ed. J. Perry, 73–95. Berkeley and Los Angeles: University of California Press.
James, W. 1950. *The Principles of psychology*, Vol. 1. New York: Dover.
Lewis, D. 1983. *Philosophical papers*, Vol. 1. Oxford, UK: Oxford University Press.
Locke, J. 1979. *An essay concerning human understanding*, ed. P. Nidditch. Oxford, UK: Clarendon Press.
Martin, R. 1998. *Self-Concern: An experiential approach to what matters in survival.* Cambridge/New York: Cambridge University Press.
Parfit, D. 1984. *Reasons and persons*. Oxford, UK: Clarendon Press.
Perry, J. 1976. The importance of being identical. In *The identities of persons*, ed. A. Rorty, 67–90. Berkeley and Los Angeles: University of California Press.
Reid, T. 1976. Of Mr. Locke's account of our personal identity. In *Personal identity*, ed. J. Perry, 113–118. Berkeley and Los Angeles: University of California Press.
Schechtman, M. 1996. *The constitution of selves.* Ithaca, NY: Cornell University Press.
Shoemaker, S. 1984. A materialist's account. In *Personal identity*, ed. S. Shoemaker and R. Swinburne, 67–132. Oxford, UK: Blackwell.

# Part Four:

# Free Will

# FREEDOM AND DETERMINISM

## Baron d'Holbach

French Enlightenment philosopher Paul-Henri Thiry, Baron d'Holbach (1723–89) lived in Paris, famously hosting dinner parties attended by leading intellectuals of his day, such as philosophers David Hume and Jean-Jacques Rousseau. *The System of Nature*, which was published under the pseudonym M. Mirabaud in 1770, was condemned by the Paris parliament and publicly burned because Holbach's materialist metaphysics denied the existence of god, the soul, and free will.—TR

## Of the System of Man's Free Agency

From *The System of Nature*

### 1. Materialism

Those who have pretended that the *soul* is distinguished from the body, is immaterial, draws its ideas from its own peculiar source, acts by its own energies, without the aid of any exterior object, have, by a consequence of their own system, enfranchised it from those physical laws according to which all beings of which we have a knowledge are obliged to act. They have believed that the soul is mistress of its own conduct, is able to regulate its own peculiar operations, has the faculty to determine its will by its own natural energy; in a word, they have pretended that man is a *free agent*.

It has been already sufficiently proved that the soul is nothing more than the body considered relatively to some of its functions more concealed than others: it has been shown that this soul, even when it shall be supposed immaterial, is continually modified conjointly with the body, is submitted to all its motion, and that without this it would remain inert and dead: that, consequently, it is subjected to the influence of those material and physical causes which give impulse to the body; of which the mode of existence, whether habitual or transitory, depends upon the material elements by which it is surrounded, that form its texture, constitute its temperament, enter into it by means of the aliments, and penetrate it by their subtility. The faculties which are called *intellectual*, and those qualities which are styled *moral*, have been explained in a manner purely physical and natural. In the last place it has been demonstrated that all the ideas, all the systems, all the affections, all the opinions, whether true or false, which man forms to himself, are to be attributed to his physical and material senses. Thus man is a being purely physical; in whatever manner he is considered, he is connected to universal nature, and submitted to the necessary and immutable laws that she imposes on all the beings she contains, according to their peculiar essences or conformable to the respective properties with which, without consulting them, she endows each particular species. Man's life is a line that nature commands him to describe upon the surface of the earth, without his ever being able to swerve from it, even for an instant. He is born without his own consent; his organization does in nowise depend upon himself; his ideas come to him involuntarily; his habits are in the power of those who cause him to contract them; he is unceasingly modified by causes, whether visible or concealed, over which he has no control, which necessarily regulate his mode of existence, give the hue to his way of thinking, and determine his manner of acting. He is good or bad, happy or miserable, wise or foolish, reasonable or irrational, without his will being for anything in these various states. Nevertheless, despite the shackles by which he is bound, it is pretended he is a free agent, or that independent of the causes by which he is moved, he determines his own will and regulates his own condition.

However slender the foundation of this opinion, of which everything ought to point out to him the error, it is current at this day and passes for an incontestable truth with a great number of people, otherwise extremely enlightened; it is the basis for religion, which, supposing relations between man and the unknown being she has placed above nature, has been incapable of imagining how man could either merit reward or deserve punishment from this being, if he was not a free agent. Society has been believed interested in this system because an idea has gone abroad that if all the actions of man were to be contemplated as necessary, the right of punishing those who injure their associates would no longer exist. At length human vanity accommodated itself to a hypothesis which, unquestionably, appears to distinguish man from all other physical beings, by assigning to him the special privilege of a total independence of all other causes, but of which a very little reflection would have shown him the impossibility.

## 2. Will as a Modification of the Brain

The will, as we have elsewhere said, is a modification of the brain, by which it is disposed to action, or prepared to give play to the organs. This will is necessarily determined by the qualities, good or bad, agreeable or painful, of the object or the motive that acts upon his senses, or of which the idea remains with him, and is resuscitated by his memory. In consequence, he acts necessarily, his action is the result of the impulse he receives either from the motive, from the object, or from the idea which has modified his brain, or disposed his will. When he does not act according to this impulse, it is because there comes some new cause, some new motive, some new idea, which modifies his brain in a different manner, gives him a new impulse, determines his will in another way, by which the action of the former impulse is suspended: thus, the sight of an agreeable object, or its idea, determines his will to set him in action to procure it; but if a new object or a new idea more powerfully attracts him, it gives a new direction to his will, annihilates the effect of the former, and prevents the action by which it was to be procured. This is the mode in which reflection, experience, reason, necessarily arrests or suspends the action of man's will: without this he would of necessity have followed the anterior impulse which carried him towards a then desirable object. In all this he always acts according to necessary laws, from which he has no means of emancipating himself.

If when tormented with violent thirst, he figures to himself in idea, or really perceives a fountain, whose limpid streams might cool his feverish want, is he sufficient master of himself to desire or not to desire the object competent to satisfy so lively a want? It will no doubt be conceded that it is impossible he should not be desirous to satisfy it; but it will be said—if at this moment it is announced to him that the water he so ardently desires is poisoned, he will, notwithstanding his vehement thirst, abstain from drinking it: and it has, therefore, been falsely concluded that he is a free agent. The fact, however, is that the motive in either case is exactly the same: his own conservation. The same necessity that determined him to drink before he knew the water was deleterious, upon this new discovery equally determines him not to drink; the desire of conserving himself either annihilates or suspends the former impulse; the second motive becomes stronger than the preceding, that is, the fear of death, or the desire of preserving himself, necessarily prevails over the painful sensation caused by his eagerness to drink: but, it will be said, if the thirst is very parching, an inconsiderate man without regarding the danger will risk swallowing the water. Nothing is gained by this remark: in this case, the anterior impulse only regains the ascendency; he is persuaded that life may possibly be longer preserved, or that he shall derive a greater good by drinking the poisoned water than by enduring the torment, which, to his mind, threatens instant dissolution: thus, the first becomes the strongest and necessarily urges him on to action. Nevertheless, in either case, whether he partakes of the water, or whether he does not, the two actions will be equally necessary; they will be the effect of that motive which finds itself most powerful, which consequently acts in the most coercive manner upon his will.

This example will serve to explain the whole phenomenon of the human will. This will, or rather the brain, finds itself in the same situation as a bowl, which, although it has received an impulse that drives it forward in a straight line, is deranged in its course whenever a force superior to the first obliges it to change its direction. The man who drinks the poisoned water appears a madman; but the actions of fools are as necessary as those of the most prudent individuals.

## 3. Choice Does Not Prove Freedom

Choice by no means proves the free agency of man: he only deliberates when he does not yet know which to choose of the many objects that move him, he is then in an embarrassment, which does not terminate until his will is decided by the greater advantage he believes he shall find in the object he chooses, or the action he undertakes. From whence it may be seen that choice is necessary, because he would not determine for an object, or for an action, if he did not believe that he should find in it some direct advantage. That man should have free agency it were needful that he should be able to will or choose without motive, or that he could prevent motives coercing his will. Action always being the effect of his will once determined, and as his will cannot be determined but by a motive which is not in his own power, it follows that he is never the master of the determination of his own peculiar will; that consequently he never acts as a free agent. It has been believed that man was a free agent because he had a will with the power of choosing; but attention has not been paid to the fact that even his will is moved by causes independent of himself; is owing to that which is inherent in his own organization, or which belongs to the nature of the beings acting on him. Is he the master of willing not to withdraw his hand from the fire when he fears it will be burnt? Or has he the power to take away from fire the property which makes him fear it? Is he the master of not choosing a dish of meat, which he knows to be agreeable, or analogous to his palate; of not preferring it to that which he knows to be disagreeable or dangerous? It is always according to his sensations, to his own peculiar experience, or to his suppositions, that he judges of things, either well or ill; but whatever may be his judgment, it depends necessarily on his mode of feeling, whether habitual or accidental, and the qualities he finds in the causes that move him, which exist in spite of himself. [. . .]

Despite these proofs of the want of free agency in man, so clear to unprejudiced minds, it will, perhaps, be insisted upon with no small feeling of triumph that if it be proposed to anyone to move or not to move his hand, an action in the number of those called *indifferent*, he evidently appears to be the master of choosing; from which it is concluded that evidence has been offered of his free agency. The reply is, this example is perfectly simple; man in performing some action which he is resolved on doing does not by any means prove his free agency: the very desire of displaying this quality, excited by the dispute, becomes a necessary motive, which decides his will either for the one or the other of these actions: what deludes him in this instance, or that which persuades him he is a free agent at this moment, is that he does not discern the true motive which sets him in action, namely, the desire of convincing his opponent: if in the heat of the dispute he insists and asks, "Am I not the master of throwing myself out of the window?" I shall answer him, no; that whilst he preserves his reason there is no probability that the desire of proving his free agency will become a motive sufficiently powerful to make him sacrifice his life to the attempt; if, notwithstanding this, to prove he is a free agent, he should actually precipitate himself from the window, it would not be a sufficient warranty to conclude he acted freely, but rather that it was the violence of his temperament which spurred him on to this folly. Madness is a state that depends upon the heat of the blood, not upon the will. A fanatic or a hero braves death as necessarily as a more phlegmatic man or a coward flies from it.[1]

## 4. Freedom Is Not Absence of Constraint

It is said that free agency is the absence of those obstacles competent to oppose themselves to the actions of man, or to the exercise of his faculties: it is pretended that he is a free agent whenever, making use of these faculties, he produces the effect he has proposed to himself. In reply to this reasoning, it is sufficient to consider that it in nowise depends upon himself to place or remove the obstacles that either determine or resist him; the motive that causes his action is no more in his own power than the obstacle that impedes him, whether this obstacle or motive be within his own machine or exterior of his person: he is not master of the thought presented to his mind, which determines his will; this thought is excited by some cause independent of himself.

To be undeceived on the system of his free agency, man has simply to recur to the motive by which his will is determined; he will always find this motive is out of his own control. It is said that in consequence of an idea to which the mind gives birth, man acts freely if he encounters no obstacle. But the question is, what gives birth to this idea in his brain? Was he the master either to prevent it from presenting itself, or from renewing itself in his brain? Does not this idea depend either upon objects that strike him exteriorly despite himself, or upon causes that without his knowledge act within himself and modify his brain? Can he prevent his eyes, cast without design upon any object whatever, from giving him an idea of this object, and from moving his brain? He is not more master of the obstacles; they are the necessary effects of either interior or exterior causes, which always act according to their given properties. A man insults a coward, this necessarily irritates him against his insulter, but his will cannot vanquish the obstacle that cowardice places to the object of his desire because his natural conformation, which does not depend upon himself, prevents his having courage. [. . .]

The partisans of the system of free agency appear ever to have confounded constraint with necessity. Man believes he acts as a free agent every time he does not see anything that places obstacles to his actions; he does not perceive that the motive which causes him to will is always necessary and independent of himself. A prisoner loaded with chains is compelled to remain in prison; but he is not a free agent in the desire to emancipate himself; his chains prevent him from acting, but they do not prevent him from willing; he would save himself if they would loose his fetters; but he would not save himself as a free agent; fear or the idea of punishment would be sufficient motives for his action.

Man may, therefore, cease to be restrained, without, for that reason, becoming a free agent: in whatever manner he acts, he will act necessarily, according to motives by which he shall be determined. He may be compared to a heavy body that finds itself arrested in its descent by any obstacle whatever: take away this obstacle, it will gravitate or continue to fall; but who shall say this dense body is free to fall or not? Is not its descent the necessary effect of its own specific gravity? The virtuous Socrates submitted to the laws of his country, although they were unjust; and though the doors of his jail were left open to him, he would not save himself; but in this he did not act as a free agent: the invisible chains of opinion, the secret love of decorum, the inward respect for the laws, even when they were iniquitous, the fear of tarnishing his glory, kept him in his prison; they were motives sufficiently powerful with this enthusiast for virtue to induce him to wait death with tranquillity; it was not in his power to save himself because he could find no potential motive to bring him to depart, even for an instant, from those principles to which his mind was accustomed.

## 5. Multiplicity of Causes Mistaken for Freedom

When it is said that man is not a free agent, it is not pretended to compare him to a body moved by a simple impulsive cause: he contains within himself causes inherent to his existence; he is moved by an interior organ, which has its own peculiar laws, and is itself necessarily determined in consequence of ideas formed from perceptions resulting from sensations which it receives from exterior objects. As the mechanism of these sensations, of these perceptions, and the manner they engrave ideas on the brain of man are not known to him; because he is unable to unravel all these motions; because he cannot perceive the chain of operations in his soul, or the motive principle that acts within him, he supposes himself a free agent; which, literally translated, signifies that he moves himself by himself; that he determines himself without cause: when he rather ought to say that he is ignorant how or for why he acts in the manner he does. It is true the soul enjoys an activity peculiar to itself: but it is equally certain that this activity would never be displayed, if some motive or some cause did not put it in a condition to exercise itself: at least it will not be pretended that the soul is able either to love or to hate without being moved, without knowing the objects, without having some idea of their qualities. Gunpowder has unquestionably a particular activity, but this activity will never display itself, unless fire be applied to it; this, however, immediately sets it in motion.

It is the great complication of motion in man, it is the variety of his action, it is the multiplicity of causes that move him, whether simultaneously or in continual succession, that persuades him he is a free agent: if all his motions were simple, if the causes that move him did not confound themselves with each other, if they were distinct, if his machine were less complicated, he would perceive that all his actions were necessary because he would be enabled to recur instantly to the cause that made him act. [. . .]

It is, then, for want of recurring to the causes that move him; for want of being able to analyze, from not being competent to decompose the complicated motion of his machine, that man believes himself a free agent: it is only upon his own ignorance that he founds the profound yet deceitful notion he has of his free agency; that he builds those opinions which he brings forward as a striking proof of his pretended freedom of action. If, for a short time, each man was willing to examine his own peculiar actions, search out their true motives to discover their concatenation, he would remain convinced that the sentiment he has of his natural free agency is a chimera that must speedily be destroyed by experience.

## 6. Morals

However this may be, man either sees or believes he sees much more distinctly the necessary relation of effects with their causes in natural philosophy than in the human heart: at least he sees in the former that sensible causes constantly produce sensible effects, ever the same, when the circumstances are alike. After this he hesitates not to look upon physical effects as necessary; whilst he refuses to acknowledge necessity in the acts of the human will: these he has, without any just foundation, attributed to a motive-power that acts independently by its own peculiar energy, which is capable of modifying itself without the concurrence of exterior causes, and which is distinguished from all material or physical beings. Agriculture is founded upon the assurance, afforded by experience, that the earth, cultivated and sown in a certain manner, when it has otherwise the requisite qualities, will furnish grain, fruit, and flowers, either necessary for subsistence or pleasing to the senses. If things were considered without prejudice, it would be perceived that in morals, education is nothing more than *the agriculture of the mind*; that, like the earth, by reason of its natural disposition, of the culture bestowed upon it, of the seeds with which it is sown, of the seasons, more or less favourable that conduct it to maturity, we may be assured that the soul will produce either virtue or vice—*moral fruit*, that will be either salubrious for man or baneful to society. *Morals* is the science of the relations that subsist between the minds, the wills, and the actions of men, in the same manner that geometry is the science of the relations that are found between bodies. Morals would be a chimera and would have no certain principles, if it was not founded upon the knowledge of the motives which must necessarily have an influence upon the human will, and which must necessarily determine the actions of human beings.

If, in the moral as well as in the physical world, a cause, of which the action is not interrupted, be necessarily followed by a given effect, it flows consecutively that a reasonable education, grafted upon truth, and founded upon wise laws; that honest principles instilled during youth; virtuous examples continually held forth; esteem attached solely to merit and good actions; contempt and shame and chastisements regularly visiting vice and falsehood and crime, are causes that would necessarily act on the will of man, and would determine the greater number of his species to exhibit virtue. But if, on the contrary, religion, politics, example, public opinion, all labour to countenance wickedness and to train man viciously; if, instead of fanning his virtues, they stifle good principles; if, instead of directing his studies to his advantage, they render his education either useless or unprofitable; if this education itself, instead of grounding him in virtue, only inoculates him with vice; if, instead of inculcating reason, it imbues him with prejudice; if, instead of making him enamoured of truth, it furnishes him with false notions and with dangerous opinions; if, instead of fostering mildness and forbearance, it kindles in his breast only those passions which are incommodious to himself and hurtful to others; it must be of necessity that the will of the greater number shall determine them to evil. [. . .]

In spite of the gratuitous ideas which man has formed to himself on his pretended free agency; in defiance of the illusions of this supposed intimate sense, which, notwithstanding his experience, persuades him that he is master of his will; all his institutions are really founded upon necessity: on this, as on a variety of other occasions, practice throws aside speculation. Indeed, if it was not believed that certain motives embraced the power requisite to determine the will of man, to arrest the progress of his passions; to direct them towards an end, to modify him, of what use would be the faculty of speech? What benefit could arise from education, from legislation, from morals, even from religion itself? What does education achieve, save give the first impulse to the human will; make man contract habits; oblige him to persist in them; furnish him with motives, whether true or false, to act after a given manner? When the father either menaces his son with punishment, or promises him a reward, is he not convinced these things will act upon his will? What does legislation attempt except it be to present to the citizens of a state those motives which are supposed necessary to determine them to perform some actions that are considered worthy; to abstain from committing others that are looked upon as unworthy? What is the object of morals, if it be not to show man that his interest exacts he should suppress the momentary ebullition of his passions, with a view to promote a more certain happiness, a more lasting well being, than can possibly result from the gratification of his transitory desires? Does not the religion of all countries suppose the human race, together with the entire of nature, submitted to the irresistible will of a necessary being who regulates their condition after the eternal laws of immutable wisdom?

## 7. Necessity

From all that has been advanced in this chapter, it results that in no one moment of his existence man is a free agent. He is not the architect of his own conformation, which he holds from nature; he has no control over his own ideas, or over the modification of his brain; these are due to causes that, in spite of him, and without his own knowledge, unceasingly act upon him; he is not the master of not loving or coveting that which he finds amiable or desirable; he is not capable of refusing to deliberate when he is uncertain of the effects certain objects will produce upon him; he cannot avoid choosing that which he believes will be most advantageous to him; in the moment when his will is determined by his choice, he is not competent to act otherwise than he does. In what instance, then, is he the master of his own actions? In what moment is he a free agent?

That which a man is about to do, is always a consequence of that which he has been—of that which he is—of that which he has done up to the moment of the action: his total and actual existence, considered under all its possible circumstances, contains the sum of all the motives to the action he is about to commit; this is a principle, the truth of which no thinking being will be able to refuse accrediting: his life is a series of necessary moments; his conduct, whether good or bad, virtuous or vicious, useful or prejudicial, either to himself or to others, is a concatenation of action, as necessary as all the moments of his existence. *To live*, is to exist in a necessary mode during the points of that duration which succeed each other necessarily: *to will*, is to acquiesce or not in remaining such as he is: *to be free*, is to yield to the necessary motives he carries within himself.

If he understood the play of his organs, if he was able to recall to himself all the impulsions they have received, all the modifications they have undergone, all the effects they have produced, he would perceive that all his actions are submitted to that *fatality*, which regulates his own particular system, as it does the entire system of the universe: no one effect in him, any more than in nature, produces itself by *chance*; this, as has been before proved, is a word void of sense. All that passes in him; all that is done by him; as well as all that happens in nature, or that is attributed to her, is derived from necessary causes, which act according to necessary laws, and which produce necessary effects from whence necessarily flow others.

*Fatality*, is the eternal, the immutable, the necessary order, established in nature; or the indispensable connection of causes that act, with the effects they operate. Conforming to this order, heavy bodies fall; light bodies rise; that which is analogous in matter reciprocally attracts; that which is heterogeneous mutually repels; man congregates himself in society, modifies each his fellow; becomes either virtuous or wicked; either contributes to his mutual happiness, or reciprocates his misery; either loves his neighbour, or hates his companion necessarily, according to the manner in which the one acts upon the other. From whence it may be seen that the same necessity which regulates the physical, also regulates the moral world, in which everything is in consequence submitted to fatality. Man, in running over, frequently without his own knowledge, often in spite of himself, the route which nature has marked out for him, resembles a swimmer who is obliged to follow the current that carries him along: he believes himself a free agent because he sometimes consents, sometimes does not consent, to glide with the stream, which, notwithstanding, always hurries him forward; he believes himself the master of his condition because he is obliged to use his arms under the fear of sinking.

The false ideas he has formed to himself upon free agency, are in general thus founded: there are certain events which he judges *necessary*; either because he sees that they are effects constantly and invariably linked to certain causes, which nothing seems to prevent; or because he believes he has discovered the chain of causes and effects that is put in play to produce those events: whilst he contemplates as *contingent* other events of whose causes he is ignorant, and with whose mode of acting he is unacquainted: but in nature, where everything is connected by one common bond, there exists no effect without a cause. In the moral as well as in the physical world, everything that happens is a necessary consequence of causes, either visible or concealed, which are of necessity obliged to act after their peculiar essences. *In man, free agency is nothing more than necessity contained within himself.* [. . .]

## Note

1. There is, in point of fact, no difference between the man that is cast out of the window by another, and the man who throws himself out of it, except that the impulse in the first instance comes immediately from without, whilst that which determines the fall in the second case, springs from within his own peculiar machine, having its more remote cause also exterior.

# COMPATIBILISM: THE CASE FOR DETERMINISM AND ITS COMPATIBILITY WITH THE MOST IMPORTANT SENSE OF FREE WILL

## Freedom and Necessity

A. J. AYER

A. J. Ayer (1910–1991), a distinguished British philosopher, was a leading spokesman for the school of philosophers known as Logical Positivists.

When I am said to have done something of my own free will it is implied that I could have acted otherwise; and it is only when it is believed that I could have acted otherwise that I am held to be morally responsible for what I have done. For a man is not thought to be morally responsible for an action that it was not in his power to avoid. But if human behaviour is entirely governed by causal laws, it is not clear how any action that is done could ever have been avoided. It may be said of the agent that he would have acted otherwise if the causes of his action had been different, but they being what they were, it seems to follow that he was bound to act as he did. Now it is commonly assumed both that men are capable of acting freely, in the sense that is required to make them morally responsible, and that human behaviour is entirely governed by causal laws: and it is the apparent conflict between these two assumptions that gives rise to the philosophical problem of the freedom of the will.

Confronted with this problem, many people will be inclined to agree with Dr. Johnson: 'Sir, we *know* our will is free, and *there's* an end on't.' But, while this does very well for those who accept Dr. Johnson's premiss, it would hardly convince anyone who denied the freedom of the will. Certainly, if we do know that our wills are free, it follows that they are so. But the logical reply to this might be that since our wills are not free, it follows that no one can know that they are: so that if anyone claims, like Dr. Johnson, to know that they are, he must be mistaken. What is evident, indeed, is that people often believe themselves to be acting freely; and it is to this 'feeling' of freedom that some philosophers appeal when they wish, in the supposed interests of morality, to prove that not all human action is causally determined. But if these philosophers are right in their assumption that a man cannot be acting freely if his action is causally determined, then the fact that someone feels free to do, or not to do, a certain action does not prove that he really is so. It may prove that the agent does not himself know what it is that makes him act in one way rather than another: but from the fact that a man is unaware of the causes of his action, it does not follow that no such causes exist.

So much may be allowed to the determinist; but his belief that all human actions are subservient to causal laws still remains to be justified. If, indeed, it is necessary that every event should have a cause, then the rule must apply to human behaviour as much as to anything else. But why should it be supposed that every event must have a cause? The contrary is not unthinkable. Nor is the law of universal causation a necessary presupposition of scientific thought. The scientist may try to discover causal laws, and in many cases he succeeds; but sometimes he has to be content with statistical laws, and sometimes he comes upon events which, in the present state of his knowledge, he is not able to subsume under any law at all. In the case of these events he assumes that if he knew more he would be able to discover some law, whether causal or statistical, which would enable him to account for them. And this assumption cannot be disproved. For however far he may have carried his investigation, it is always open to him to carry it further; and it is always conceivable that if he carried it further he would discover the connection which had hitherto escaped him. Nevertheless, it is also conceivable that the events with which he is concerned are not systematically connected with any others: so that the reason why he does not discover the sort of laws that he requires is simply that they do not obtain.

Now in the case of human conduct the search for explanations has not in fact been altogether fruitless. Certain scientific laws have been established; and with the help of these laws we do make a number of successful predictions about the ways in which different people will behave. But these predictions do not always cover every detail. We may be able to predict that in certain circumstances a particular man will be angry, without being able to prescribe the precise form that the expression of his anger will take. We may be reasonably sure that he will shout, but not sure how loud his shout will be, or exactly what words he will use. And it is only a small proportion of human actions that we are able to forecast even so precisely as this. But that, it may be said, is because we have not carried our investigations very far. The science of psychology is still in its infancy and, as it is developed, not only will more human actions be explained, but the explanations will go into greater detail. The ideal of complete explanation may never in fact be attained: but it is theoretically attainable. Well, this may be so: and certainly it is impossible to show *a priori* that it is not so: but equally it cannot be shown that it is. This will not, however, discourage the scientist who, in the field of human behaviour, as elsewhere, will continue to formulate theories and test them by the facts. And in this he is justified. For since he has no reason *a priori* to admit that there is a limit to what he can discover, the fact that he also cannot be sure that there is no limit does not make it unreasonable for him to devise theories, nor, having devised them, to try constantly to improve them.

But now suppose it to be claimed that, so far as men's actions are concerned, there is a limit: and that this limit is set by the fact of human freedom. An obvious objection is that in many cases in which a person feels himself to be free to do, or not to do, a certain action, we are even now able to explain, in causal terms, why it is that he acts as he does. But it might be argued that even if men are sometimes mistaken in believing that they act freely, it does not follow that they are always so mistaken. For it is not always the case that when a man believes that he has acted freely we are in fact able to account for his action in causal terms. A determinist would say that we should be able to account for it if we had more knowledge of the circumstances, and had been able to discover the appropriate natural laws. But until those discoveries have been made, this remains only a pious hope. And may it not be true that, in some cases at least, the reason why we can give no causal explanation is that no causal explanation is available; and that this is because the agent's choice was literally free, as he himself felt it to be?

The answer is that this may indeed be true, inasmuch as it is open to anyone to hold that no explanation is possible until some explanation is actually found. But even so it does not give the moralist what he wants. For he is anxious to show that men are capable of acting freely in order to infer that they can be morally responsible for what they do. But if it is a matter of pure chance that a man should act in one way rather than another, he may be free but can hardly be responsible. And indeed when a man's actions seem to us quite unpredictable, when, as we say, there is no knowing what he will do, we do not look upon him as a moral agent. We look upon him as a lunatic.

To this it may be objected that we are not dealing fairly with the moralist. For when he makes it a condition of my being morally responsible that I should act freely, he does not wish to imply that it is purely a matter of chance that I act as I do. What he wishes to imply is that my actions are the result of my own free choice: and it is because they are the result of my own free choice that I am held to be morally responsible for them.

But now we must ask how it is that I come to make my choice. Either it is an accident that I choose to act as I do or it is not. If it is an accident, then it is merely a matter of chance that I did not choose otherwise; and if it is merely a matter of chance that I did not choose otherwise, it is surely irrational to hold me morally responsible for choosing as I did. But if it is not an accident that I choose to do one thing rather than another, then presumably there is some causal explanation of my choice: and in that case we are led back to determinism.

Again, the objection may be raised that we are not doing justice to the moralist's case. His view is not that it is a matter of chance that I choose to act as I do, but rather that my choice depends upon my character. Nevertheless he holds that I can still be free in the sense that he requires; for it is I who am responsible for my character. But in what way am I responsible for my character? Only, surely, in the sense that there is a causal connection between what I do now and what I have done in the past. It is only this that justifies the statement that I have made myself what I am: and even so this is an over-simplification, since it takes no account of the external influences to which I have been subjected. But, ignoring the external influences, let us assume that it is in fact the case that I have made myself what I am. Then it is still legitimate to ask how it is that I have come to make myself one sort of person rather than another. And if it be answered that it is a matter of my strength of will, we can put the same question in another form by asking how it is that my will has the strength that it has and not some other degree of strength. Once more, either it is an accident or it is not. If it is an accident, then by the same argument as before, I am not morally responsible, and if it is not an accident we are led back to determinism.

Furthermore, to say that my actions proceed from my character or, more colloquially, that I act in character, is to say that my behaviour is consistent and to that extent predictable: and since it is, above all, for the actions that I perform in character that I am held to be morally responsible, it looks as if the admission of moral responsibility,. so far from being incompatible with determinism, tends rather to presuppose it. But how can this be so if it is a necessary condition of moral responsibility that the person who is held responsible should have acted freely? It seems that if we are to retain this idea of moral responsibility, we must either show that men can be held responsible for actions which they do not do freely, or else find some way of reconciling determinism with the freedom of the will.

It is no doubt with the object of effecting this reconciliation that some philosophers have defined freedom as the consciousness of necessity. And by so doing they are able to say not only that a man can be acting freely when his action is causally determined, but even that his action must be causally determined for it to be possible for him to be acting freely. Nevertheless this definition has the serious disadvantage that it gives to the word 'freedom' a meaning quite different from any that it ordinarily bears. It is indeed obvious that if we are allowed to give the word 'freedom' any meaning that we please, we can find a meaning that will reconcile it with determinism: but this is no more a solution of our present problem than the fact that the word 'horse' could be arbitrarily used to mean what is ordinarily meant by 'sparrow' is a proof that horses have wings. For suppose that I am compelled by another person to do something 'against my will.' In that case, as the word 'freedom' is ordinarily used, I should not be said to be acting freely: and the fact that I am fully aware of the constraint to which I am subjected makes no difference to the matter. I do not become free by becoming conscious that I am not. It may, indeed, be possible to show that my being aware that my action is causally determined is not incompatible with my acting freely: but it by no means follows that it is in this that my freedom consists. Moreover, I suspect that one of the reasons why people are inclined to define freedom as the consciousness of necessity is that they think that if one is conscious of necessity one may somehow be able to master it. But this is a fallacy. It is like someone's saying that he wishes he could see into the future, because if he did he would know what calamities lay in wait for him and so would be able to avoid them. But if he avoids the calamities then they don't lie in the future and it is not true that he foresees them. And similarly if I am able to master necessity, in the sense of escaping the operation of a necessary law, then the law in question is not necessary. And if the law is not necessary, then neither my freedom nor anything else can consist in my knowing that it is.

Let it be granted, then, when we speak of reconciling freedom with determination we are using the word 'freedom' in an ordinary sense. It still remains for us to make this usage clear: and perhaps the best way to make it clear is to show what it is that freedom, in this sense, is contrasted with. Now we began with the assumption that freedom is contrasted with causality: so that a man cannot be said to be acting freely if his action is causally determined. But this assumption has led us into difficulties and I now wish to suggest that it is mistaken. For it is not, I think, causality that freedom is to be contrasted with, but constraint. And while it is true that being constrained to do an action entails being caused to do it, I shall try to show that the converse does not hold. I shall try to show that from the fact that my action is causally determined it does not necessarily follow that I am constrained to do it: and this is equivalent to saying that it does not necessarily follow that I am not free.

*If I am constrained, I do not act freely.* But in what circumstances can I legitimately be said to be constrained? An obvious instance is the case in which I am compelled by another person to do what he wants. In a case of this sort the compulsion need not be such as to deprive one of the power of choice. It is not required that the other person should have hypnotized me, or that he should make it physically impossible for me to go against his will. It is enough that he should induce me to do what he wants by making it clear to me that, if I do not, he will bring about some situation that I regard as even more undesirable than the consequences of the action that he wishes me to do. Thus, if the man points a pistol at my head I may still choose to disobey him: but this does not prevent its being true that if I do fall in with his wishes he can legitimately be said to have compelled me. And if the circumstances are such that no reasonable person would be expected to choose the other alternative, then the action that I am made to do is not one for which I am held to be morally responsible.

A similar, but still somewhat different, case is that in which another person has obtained an habitual ascendancy over me. Where this is so, there may be no question of my being induced to act as the other person wishes by being confronted with a still more disagreeable alternative: for if I am sufficiently under his influence this special stimulus will not be necessary. Nevertheless I do not act freely, for the reason that I have been deprived of the power of choice. And this means that I have acquired so strong a habit of obedience that I no longer go through any process of deciding whether or not to do what the other person wants. About other matters I may still deliberate: but as regards the fulfilment of this other person's wishes, my own deliberations have ceased to be a causal factor in my behaviour. And it is in this sense that I may be said to be constrained. It is not, however, necessary that such constraint should take the form of subservience to another person. A kleptomaniac is not a free agent, in respect of his stealing, because he does not go through any process of deciding whether or not to steal. Or rather, if he does go through such a process, it is irrelevant to his behaviour. Whatever he resolved to do, he would steal all the same. And it is this that distinguishes him from the ordinary thief.

But now it may be asked whether there is any essential difference between these cases and those in which the agent is commonly thought to be free. No doubt the ordinary thief does go through a process of deciding whether or not to steal, and no doubt it does affect his behaviour. If he resolved to refrain from stealing, he could carry his resolution out. But if it be allowed that his making or not making this resolution is causally determined, then how can he be any more free than the kleptomaniac? It may be true that unlike the kleptomaniac he could refrain from stealing if he chose: but if there is a cause, or set of causes, which necessitate his choosing as he does, how can he be said to have the power of choice? Again, it may be true that no one now compels me to get up and walk across the room: but if my doing so can be causally explained in terms of my history or my environment, or whatever it may be, then how am I any more free than if some other person had compelled me? I do not have the feeling of constraint that I have when a pistol is manifestly pointed at my head: but the chains of causation by which I am bound are no less effective for being invisible.

The answer to this is that the cases I have mentioned as examples of constraint do differ from the others: and they differ just in the ways that I have tried to bring out. If I suffered from a compulsion neurosis, so that I got up and walked across the room, whether I wanted to or not, or if I did so because somebody else compelled me, then I should not be acting freely. But if I do it now, I shall be acting freely, just because these conditions do not obtain; and the fact that my action may nevertheless have a cause is, from this point of view, irrelevant. For it is not when my action has any cause at all, but only when it has a special sort of cause, that it is reckoned not to be free.

But here it may be objected that, even if this distinction corresponds to ordinary usage, it is still very irrational. For why should we distinguish, with regard to a person's freedom, between the operations of one sort of cause and those of another? Do not all causes equally necessitate? And is it not therefore arbitrary to say that a person is free when he is necessitated in one fashion but not when he is necessitated in another?

That all causes equally necessitate is indeed a tautology, if the word 'necessitate' is taken merely as equivalent to 'cause': but if, as the objection requires, it is taken as equivalent to 'constrain' or 'compel,' then I do not think that this proposition is true. For all that is needed for one event to be the cause of another is that, in the given circumstances, the event which is said to be the effect would not have occurred if it had not been for the occurrence of the event which is said to be the cause, or vice versa, according as causes are interpreted as necessary, or sufficient, conditions: and this fact is usually deducible from some causal law which states that whenever an event of the one kind occurs then, given suitable conditions, an event of the other kind will occur in a certain temporal or spatio-temporal relationship to it. In short, there is an invariable concomitance between the two classes of events; but there is no compulsion, in any but a metaphorical sense. Suppose, for example, that a psycho-analyst is able to account for some aspect of my behaviour by referring it to some lesion that I suffered in my childhood. In that case, it may be said that my childhood experience, together with certain other events, necessitates my behaving as I do. But all that this involves is that it is found to be true in general that when people have had certain experiences as children, they subsequently behave in certain specifiable ways; and my case is just another instance of this general law. It is in this way indeed that my behaviour is explained. But from the fact that my behaviour is capable of being explained, in the sense that it can be subsumed under some natural law, it does not follow that I am acting under constraint.

If this is correct, to say that I could have acted otherwise is to say, first, that I should have acted otherwise if I had so chosen; secondly, that my action was voluntary in the sense in which the actions, say, of the kleptomaniac are not; and thirdly, that nobody compelled me to choose as I did: and these three conditions may very well be fulfilled. When they are fulfilled, I may be said to have acted freely. But this is not to say that it was a matter of chance that I acted as I did, or, in other words, that my action could not be explained. And that my actions should be capable of being explained is all that is required by the postulate of determinism.

If more than this seems to be required it is, I think, because the use of the very word 'determinism' is in some degree misleading. For it tends to suggest that one event is somehow in the power of another, whereas the truth is merely that they are factually correlated. And the same applies to the use, in this context, of the word 'necessity' and even of the word 'cause' itself.

Moreover, there are various reasons for this. One is the tendency to confuse causal with logical necessitation, and so to infer mistakenly that the effect is contained in the cause. Another is the uncritical use of a concept of force which is derived from primitive experiences of pushing and striking. A third is the survival of an animistic conception of causality, in which all causal relationships are modelled on the example of one person's exercising authority over another. As a result we tend to form an imaginative picture of an unhappy effect trying vainly to escape from the clutches of an over-mastering cause. But, I repeat, the fact is simply that when an event of one type occurs, an event of another type occurs also, in a certain temporal or spatio-temporal relation to the first. The rest is only metaphor. And it is because of the metaphor, and not because of the fact, that we come to think that there is an antithesis between causality and freedom.

Nevertheless, it may be said, if the postulate of determinism is valid, then the future can be explained in terms of the past: and this means that if one knew enough about the past one would be able to predict the future. But in that case what will happen in the future is already decided. And how then can I be said to be free? What is going to happen is going to happen and nothing that I do can prevent it. If the determinist is right, I am the helpless prisoner of fate.

But what is meant by saying that the future course of events is already decided? If the implication is that some person has arranged it, then the proposition is false. But if all that is meant is that it is possible, in principle, to deduce it from a set of particular facts about the past, together with the appropriate general laws, then, even if this is true, it does not in the least entail that I am the helpless prisoner of fate. It does not even entail that my actions make no difference to the future: for they are causes as well as effects; so that if they were different their consequences would be different also. What it does entail is that my behaviour can be predicted: but to say that my behaviour can be predicted is not to say that I am acting under constraint. It is indeed true that I cannot escape my destiny if this is taken to mean no more than that I shall do what I shall do. But this is a tautology, just as it is a tautology that what is going to happen is going to happen. And such tautologies as these prove nothing whatsoever about the freedom of the will.

# E. FREEDOM, DETERMINISM, AND RESPONSIBILITY

## *Human Freedom and the Self*

RODERICK M. CHISHOLM

Roderick M. Chisholm (1916–1999) was an influential American philosopher who worked mainly in metaphysics and epistemology. His major work was *Person and Object,* but his other works include *A Theory of Knowledge, The Problem of the Criterion,* and *Perception.*

"A staff moves a stone, and is moved by a hand, which is moved by a man."

*Aristotle,* Physics, *256a.*

1. The **metaphysical** problem of human **freedom** might be summarized in the following way: Human beings are responsible agents; but this fact appears to conflict with a **deterministic** view of human action (the view that every event that is involved in an act is caused by some other event); and it *also* appears to conflict with an indeterministic view of human action (the view that the act, or some event that is essential to the act, is not caused at all). To solve the problem, I believe, we must make somewhat far-reaching assumptions about the self or the agent—about the man who performs the act.

Perhaps it is needless to remark that, in all likelihood, it is impossible to say anything significant about this ancient problem that has not been said before.[1]

2. Let us consider some deed, or misdeed, that may be attributed to a responsible agent: one man, say, shot another. If the man *was* responsible for what he did, then, I would urge, what was to happen at the time of the shooting was something that was entirely up to the man himself. There was a moment at which it was true, both that he could have fired the shot and also that he could have refrained from firing it. And if this is so, then, even though he did fire it, he could have done something else instead. (He didn't find himself firing the shot "against his will," as we say.) I think we can say, more generally, then, that if a man is responsible for a certain event or a certain state of affairs (in our example, the shooting of another man), then that event or state of affairs was brought about by some act of his, and the act was something that was in his power either to perform or not to perform.

But now if the act which he *did* perform was an act that was also in his power *not* to perform, then it could not have been caused or determined by any event that was not itself within his power either to bring about or not to bring about. For example, if what we say he did was really something that was brought about by a second man, one who forced his hand upon the trigger, say, or who, by means of hypnosis, compelled him to perform the act, then since the act was caused by the *second* man it was nothing that was within the power of the *first* man to

From *The Lindley Lectures,* 1964, pp. 3–15, Copyright © 1964 by the Department of Philosophy, University of Kansas. Reprinted by permission.

prevent. And precisely the same thing is true, I think, if instead of referring to a second man who compelled the first one, we speak instead of the *desires* and *beliefs* which the first man happens to have had. For if what we say he did was really something that was brought about by his own beliefs and desires, if these beliefs and desires in the particular situation in which he happened to have found himself caused him to do just what it was that we say he did do, then, since *they* caused it, *he* was unable to do anything other than just what it was that he did do. It makes no difference whether the cause of the deed was internal or external; if the cause was some state or event for which the man himself was not responsible, then he was not responsible for what we have been mistakenly calling his act. If a flood caused the poorly constructed dam to break, then, given the flood and the constitution of the dam, the break, we may say, *had* to occur and nothing could have happened in its place. And if the flood of desire caused the weak-willed man to give in, then he, too, had to do just what it was that he did do and he was no more responsible than was the dam for the results that followed. (It is true, of course, that if the man is responsible for the beliefs and desires that he happens to have, then he may also be responsible for the things they lead him to do. But the question now becomes: *is* he responsible for the beliefs and desires he happens to have? If he is, then there was a time when they were within his power either to acquire or not to acquire, and we are left, therefore, with our general point.)

One may object: But surely if there were such a thing as a man who is really *good,* then he would be responsible for things that he would do; yet, he would be unable to do anything other than just what it is that he does do, since, being good, he will always choose to do what is best. The answer, I think, is suggested by a comment that Thomas Reid makes upon an ancient author. The author had said of Cato, "He was good because he could not be otherwise," and Reid observes: "This saying, if understood literally and strictly, is not the praise of Cato, but of his constitution, which was no more the work of Cato than his existence."[2] If Cato was himself responsible for the good things that he did, then Cato, as Reid suggests, was such that, although he had the power to do what was not good, he exercised his power only for that which was good.

All of this, if it is true, may give a certain amount of comfort to those who are tender-minded. But we should remind them that it also conflicts with a familiar view about the nature of God—with the view that St. Thomas Aquinas expresses by saying that "every movement both of the will and of nature proceeds from God as the Prime Mover."[3] If the act of the sinner *did* proceed from God as the Prime Mover, then God was in the position of the second agent we just discussed—the man who forced the trigger finger, or the hypnotist—and the sinner, so-called, was *not* responsible for what he did. (This may be a bold assertion, in view of the history of western theology, but I must say that I have never encountered a single good reason for denying it.)

There is one standard objection to all of this and we should consider it briefly.

3. The objection takes the form of a stratagem—one designed to show that determinism (and divine providence) is consistent with human responsibility. The stratagem is one that was used by Jonathan Edwards and by many philosophers in the present century, most notably, G. E. Moore.[4]

One proceeds as follows: The expression

(a) He could have done otherwise, it is argued, means no more nor less than
(b) If he had chosen to do otherwise, then he would have done otherwise.

(In place of "chosen," one might say "tried," "set out," "decided," "undertaken," or "willed.") The truth of statement (b), it is then pointed out, is consistent with determinism (and with divine providence); for even if all of the man's actions were causally determined, the man could still be such that, *if* he had chosen otherwise, then he would have done otherwise. What the murderer saw, let us suppose, along with his beliefs and desires, *caused* him to fire the shot; yet he was such that *if,* just then, he had chosen or decided *not* to fire the shot, then he would not have fired it. All of this is certainly possible. Similarly, we could say, of the dam, that the flood caused it to break and also that the dam was such that, *if* there had been no flood or any similar pressure, then the dam would have remained intact. And therefore, the argument proceeds, if (b) is consistent with determinism, and if (a) and (b) say the same thing, then (a) is also consistent with determinism; hence we can say that the agent *could* have done otherwise even though he was caused to do what he did do; and therefore determinism and moral responsibility are compatible.

Is the argument sound? The conclusion follows from the premises, but the catch, I think, lies in the first premise—the one saying that statement (a) tells us no more nor less than what statement (b) tells us. For (b), it would seem, could be true while (a) is false. That is to say, our man might be such that, if he had chosen to do otherwise, then he would have done otherwise, and yet *also* such that he could not have done otherwise. Suppose, after all, that our murderer could not have *chosen,* or could not have *decided,* to do otherwise. Then the fact that he happens also to be a man such that, if he had chosen not to shoot he would not have shot, would make no difference. For if he could *not* have chosen *not* to shoot, then he could not have done anything other than just what it was that he did do. In a word: from our statement (b) above ("If he had chosen to do otherwise, then he would have done otherwise"), we cannot make an inference to (a) above ("He could have done otherwise") unless we can *also* assert:

(c) He could have chosen to do otherwise.

And therefore, if we must reject this third statement (c), then, even though we may be justified in asserting (b), we are not justified in asserting (a). If the man could not have chosen to do otherwise, then he would not have done otherwise—*even if* he was such that, if he *had* chosen to do otherwise, then he would have done otherwise.

The stratagem in question, then, seems to me not to work, and I would say, therefore, that the ascription of responsibility conflicts with a deterministic view of action.

4. Perhaps there is less need to argue that the ascription of responsibility also conflicts with an indeterministic view of action—with the view that the act, or some event that is essential to the act, is not caused at all. If the act—the firing of the shot—was not caused at all, if it was fortuitous or capricious, happening so to speak out of the blue, then, presumably, no one—and nothing—was responsible for the act. Our conception of action, therefore, should be neither deterministic nor indeterministic. Is there any other possibility?

5. We must not say that every event involved in the act is caused by some other event; and we must not say that the act is something that is not caused at all. The possibility that remains, therefore, is this: We should say that at least one of the events that are involved in the act is caused, not by any other events, but by something else instead. And this something else can only be the agent—the man. If there is an event that is caused, not by other events, but by the man, then there are some events involved in the act that are not caused by other events. But if the event in question is caused by the man then it *is* caused and we are not committed to saying that there is something involved in the act that is not caused at all.

But this, of course, is a large consequence, implying something of considerable importance about the nature of the agent or the man.

6. If we consider only inanimate natural objects, we may say that causation, if it occurs, is a relation between *events* or *states of affairs.* The dam's breaking was an event that was caused by a set of other events—the dam being weak, the flood being strong, and so on. But if a man is responsible for a particular deed, then, if what I have said is true, there is some event, or set of events, that is caused, *not* by other events or states of affairs, but by the agent, whatever he may be.

I shall borrow a pair of medieval terms, using them, perhaps, in a way that is slightly different from that for which they were originally intended. I shall say that when one event or state of affairs (or set of events or states of affairs) causes some other event or state of affairs, then we have an instance of ***transeunt* causation**. And I shall say that when an *agent,* as distinguished from an event, causes an event or state of affairs, then we have an instance of ***immanent* causation**.

The nature of what is intended by the expression "immanent causation" may be illustrated by this sentence from Aristotle's *Physics:* "Thus, a staff moves a stone, and is moved by a hand, which is moved by a man." (VII, 5, 256a, 6–8) If the man was responsible, then we have in this illustration a number of instances of causation—most of them transeunt but at least one of them immanent. What the staff did to the stone was an instance of transeunt causation, and thus we may describe it as a relation between events: "the motion of the staff caused the motion of the stone." And similarly for what the hand did to the staff: "the motion of the hand caused the motion of the staff." And, as we know from physiology, there are still other events which caused the motion of the hand. Hence we need not introduce the agent at this particular point, as Aristotle does—we *need* not, though we *may*. We *may* say that the hand was moved by the man, but we may also say that the motion of the hand was caused by the motion of certain muscles; and we may say that the motion of the muscles was caused by certain events that took place within the brain. But some event, and presumably one of those that took place within the brain, was caused by the agent and not by any other events.

There are, of course, objections to this way of putting the matter; I shall consider the two that seem to me to be most important.

7. One may object, firstly: "If the *man* does anything, then, as Aristotle's remark suggests, what he does is to move the *hand*. But he certainly does not *do* anything to his brain—he may not even know that he *has* a brain. And if he doesn't do anything to the brain, and if the motion of the hand was caused by something that happened within the brain, then there is no point in appealing to 'immanent causation' as being something incompatible with 'transeunt causation'—for the whole thing, after all, is a matter of causal relations among events or states of affairs."

The answer to this objection, I think, is this: It is true that the agent does not *do* anything with his brain, or to his brain, in the sense in which he *does* something with his hand and does something to the staff. But from this it does not follow that the agent was not the immanent cause of something that happened within his brain.

We should note a useful distinction that has been proposed by Professor A. I. Melden—namely, the distinction between "making something A happen" and "doing A."[5] If I reach for the staff and pick it up, then one of the things that I *do* is just that—reach for the staff and pick it up. And if it is something that I do, then there is a very clear sense in which it may be said to be something that I know that I do. If you ask me, "Are you doing something, or trying to do something, with the staff?", I will have no difficulty in finding an answer. But in doing something with the staff, I also make various things happen which are not in this same sense things that I do: I will make various air-particles move; I will free a number of blades of grass from the pressure that had been upon them; and I may cause a shadow to move from one place to another. If these are merely things that I make happen, as distinguished from things that I do, then I may know nothing whatever about them; I may not have the slightest idea that, in moving the staff, I am bringing about any such thing as the motion of air-particles, shadows, and blades of grass.

We may say, in answer to the first objection, therefore, that it is true that our agent does nothing to his brain or with his brain; but from this it does not follow that the agent is not the immanent cause of some event within his brain; for the brain event may be something which, like the motion of the air-particles, he made happen in picking up the staff. The only difference between the two cases is this: in each case, he made something happen when he picked up the staff; but in the one case—the motion of the air-particles or of the shadows—it was the motion of the staff that caused the event to happen; and in the other case—the event that took place in the brain—it was this event that caused the motion of the staff.

The point is, in a word, that whenever a man does something A, then (by "immanent causation") he makes a certain cerebral event happen, and this cerebral event (by "transeunt causation") makes A happen.

8. The second objection is more difficult and concerns the very concept of "immanent causation," or causation by an agent, as this concept is to be interpreted here. The concept is subject to a difficulty which has long been associated with that of the prime mover unmoved. We have said that there must be some event A, presumably some cerebral event, which is caused not by any other event, but by the agent. Since A was not caused by any other event, then the agent himself cannot be said to have

undergone any change or produced any other event (such as "an act of will" or the like) which brought A about. But if, when the agent made A happen, there was no event involved other than A itself, no event which could be described as *making* A happen, what did the agent's causation consist of? What, for example, is the difference between A's just happening, and the agent's *causing* A to happen? We cannot attribute the difference to any event that took place within the agent. And so far as the event A itself is concerned, there would seem to be no discernible difference. Thus Aristotle said that the activity of the prime mover is nothing in addition to the motion that it produces, and Suarez said that "the action is in reality nothing but the effect as it flows from the agent."[6] Must we conclude, then, that there is no more to the man's action in causing event A than there is to the event A's happening by itself? Here we would seem to have a distinction without a difference—in which case we have failed to find a *via media* between a deterministic and an indeterministic view of action.

The only answer, I think, can be this: that the difference between the man's causing A, on the one hand, and the event A just happening, on the other, lies in the fact that, in the first case but not the second, the event A *was* caused and was caused by the man. There was a brain event A; the agent did, in fact, cause the brain event; but there was nothing that he did to cause it.

This answer may not entirely satisfy and it will be likely to provoke the following question: "But what are you really *adding* to the assertion that A happened when you utter the words 'The agent *caused* A to happen'?" As soon as we have put the question this way, we see, I think, that whatever difficulty we may have encountered is one that may be traced to the concept of causation generally—whether "immanent" or "transeunt." The problem, in other words, is not a problem that is peculiar to our conception of human action. It is a problem that must be faced by anyone who makes use of the concept of causation at all; and therefore, I would say, it is a problem for everyone but the complete indeterminist.

For the problem, as we put it, referring just to "immanent causation," or causation by an agent, was this: "What is the difference between saying, of an event A, that A just happened and saying that someone caused A to happen?" The analogous problem, which holds for "transeunt causation," or causation by an event, is this: "What is the difference between saying, of two events A and B, that B happened and then A happened, and saying that B's happening was the *cause* of A's happening?" And the only answer that one can give is this—that in the one case the agent was the cause of A's happening and in the other case event B was the cause of A's happening. The nature of transeunt causation is no more clear than is that of immanent causation.

9. But we may plausibly say—and there is a respectable philosophical tradition to which we may appeal—that the notion of immanent causation, or causation by an agent, is in fact more clear than that of transeunt causation, or causation by an event, and that it is only by understanding our own causal efficacy, as agents, that we can grasp the concept of *cause* at all. Hume may be said to have shown that we do not derive the concept of *cause* from what we perceive of external things. How, then, do we derive it? The most plausible suggestion, it seems to me, is that of Reid, once again: namely that "the conception of an **efficient cause** may very probably be derived from the experience we have had . . . of our own power to produce certain effects."[7] If we did not understand the concept of immanent causation, we would not understand that of transeunt causation.

10. It may have been noted that I have avoided the term "**free will**" in all of this. For even if there is such a faculty as "the will," which somehow sets our acts agoing, the question of freedom, as John Locke said, is not the question "*whether the will be free*"; it is the question "*whether a man be free.*"[8] For if there is a "will," as a moving faculty, the question is whether the man is free to will to do those things that he does will to do—and also whether he is free *not* to will any of those things that he does will to do, and, again, whether he is free to will any of those things that he does not will to do. Jonathan Edwards tried to restrict himself to the question—"Is the man free to do what it is that he wills?"—but the answer to this question will not tell us whether the man is responsible for what it is that he *does* will to do. Using still another pair of medieval terms, we may say that the metaphysical problem of freedom does not concern

the *actus imperatus;* it does not concern the question whether we are free to accomplish whatever it is that we will or set out to do; it concerns the *actus elicitus,* the question whether we are free to will or to set out to do those things that we do will or set out to do.

11. If we are responsible, and if what I have been trying to say is true, then we have a prerogative which some would attribute only to God: each of us, when we act, is a prime mover unmoved. In doing what we do, we cause certain events to happen, and nothing—or no one—causes us to cause those events to happen.

12. If we are thus prime movers unmoved and if our actions, or those for which we are responsible, are not causally determined, then they are not causally determined by our *desires.* And this means that the relation between what we want or what we desire, on the one hand, and what it is that we do, on the other, is not as simple as most philosophers would have it.

We may distinguish between what we might call the "Hobbist approach" and what we might call the "Kantian approach" to this question. The Hobbist approach is the one that is generally accepted at the present time, but the Kantian approach, I believe, is the one that is true. According to Hobbism, if we *know,* of some man, what his beliefs and desires happen to be and how strong they are, if we know what he feels certain of, what he desires more than anything else, and if we know the state of his body and what stimuli he is being subjected to, then we may *deduce,* logically, just what it is that he will do—or, more accurately, just what it is that he will try, set out, or undertake to do. Thus Professor Melden has said that "the connection between wanting and doing is logical."[9] But according to the Kantian approach to our problem, and this is the one that I would take, there is no such logical connection between wanting and doing, nor need there even be a causal connection. No set of statements about a man's desires, beliefs, and stimulus situation at any time implies any statement telling us what the man will try, set out, or undertake to do at that time. As Reid put it, though we may "reason from men's motives to their actions and, in many cases, with great probability," we can never do so "with absolute certainty."[10]

This means that, in one very strict sense of the terms, there can be no science of man. If we think of science as a matter of finding out what laws happen to hold, and if the statement of a law tells us what kinds of events are caused by what other kinds of events, then there will be human actions which we cannot explain by subsuming them under any laws. We cannot say, "It is causally necessary that, given such and such desires and beliefs, and being subject to such and such stimuli, the agent will do so and so." For at times the agent, if he chooses, may rise above his desires and do something else instead.

But all of this is consistent with saying that, perhaps more often than not, our desires do exist under conditions such that those conditions necessitate us to act. And we may also say, with Leibniz, that at other times our desires may "incline without necessitating."

13. Leibniz's phrase presents us with our final philosophical problem. What does it mean to say that a desire, or a motive, might "incline without necessitating"? There is a temptation, certainly, to say that "to incline" means to cause and that "not to necessitate" means not to cause, but obviously we cannot have it both ways.

Nor will Leibniz's own solution do. In his letter to Coste, he puts the problem as follows: "When a choice is proposed, for example to go out or not to go out, it is a question whether, with all the circumstances, internal and external, motives, perceptions, dispositions, impressions, passions, inclinations taken together, I am still in a contingent state, or whether I am necessitated to make the choice, for example, to go out; that is to say, whether this proposition true and determined in fact, *In all these circumstances taken together I shall choose to go out,* is contingent or necessary."[11] Leibniz's answer might be put as follows: in one sense of the terms "necessary" and "contingent," the proposition "In all these circumstances taken together I shall choose to go out," may be said to be contingent and not necessary, and in another sense of these terms, it may be said to be necessary and not contingent. But the sense in which the proposition may be said to be contingent, according to Leibniz, is only this: there is no logical contradiction involved in denying the proposition. And the sense in which it may be said to be necessary is this: since "nothing ever occurs without cause or determining reason," the proposition is causally necessary. "Whenever all the circumstances taken together are such that the balance of deliberation is heavier on one side than on the other, it is certain and infallible that that is the side that is going to win out." But if what we have been saying is true, the proposition "In all these circumstances taken together I shall choose to go out," may be causally as well as logically contingent. Hence we must find another interpretation for Leibniz's statement that our motives and desires may incline us, or influence us, to choose without thereby necessitating us to choose.

Let us consider a public official who has some moral scruples but who also, as one says, could be had. Because of the scruples that he does have, he would never take any positive steps to receive a bribe—he would not actively solicit one. But his morality has its limits and he is also such that, if we were to confront him with a *fait accompli* or to let him see what is about to happen ($10,000 in cash is being deposited behind the garage), then he would succumb and be unable to resist. The general situation is a familiar one and this is one reason that people pray to be delivered from temptation. (It also justifies Kant's remark: "And how many there are who may have led a long blameless life, who are only *fortunate* in having escaped so many temptations."[12] Our relation to the misdeed that we contemplate may not be a matter simply of being able to bring it about or not to bring it about. As St. Anselm noted, there are at least four possibilities. We may illustrate them by reference to our public official and the event which is his receiving the bribe, in the following way: (i) he may be able to bring the event about himself (*facere esse*), in which case he would actively cause himself to receive the bribe; (ii) he may be able to refrain from bringing it about himself (*non facere esse*), in which case he would not himself do anything to insure that he receive the bribe; (iii) he may be able to do something to prevent the event from occurring (*facere non esse*), in which case he would make sure that the $10,000 was *not* left behind the garage; or (iv) he may be unable to do anything to prevent the event from occurring (*non facere non esse*), in which case, though he may not solicit the bribe, he would allow himself to keep it.[13] We have envisaged our official as a man who can resist the temptation to (i) but cannot resist the temptation to (iv): he can refrain from bringing the event about himself, but he cannot bring himself to do anything to prevent it.

Let us think of "inclination without necessitation," then, in such terms as these. First we may contrast the two propositions:

1. He can resist the temptation to do something in order to make A happen;
2. He can resist the temptation to allow A to happen (i.e., to do nothing to prevent A from happening).

We may suppose that the man has some desire to have A happen and thus has a motive for making A happen. His motive for making A happen, I suggest, is one that *necessitates* provided that, because of the motive, (1) is false; he cannot resist the temptation to do something in order to make A happen. His motive for making A happen is one that *inclines* provided that, because of the motive, (2) is false; like our public official, he cannot bring himself to do anything to prevent A from happening. And therefore we can say that his motive for making A happen is one that *inclines but does not necessitate* provided that, because of the motive, (1) is true and (2) is false; he can resist the temptation to make it happen but he cannot resist the temptation to allow it to happen.

## NOTES

1. The general position to be presented here is suggested in the following writings, among others: Aristotle, *Eudemian Ethics,* Book II, Ch. 6; *Nicomachean Ethics,* Book III, Ch. 1–5; Thomas Reid, *Essays on the Active Powers of Man;* C. A. Campbell, "Is 'Free Will' a Pseudo-Problem?" *Mind,* N.S. Vol. LX (1951), pp. 441–465; Roderick M. Chisholm, "Responsibility and Avoidability," and Richard Taylor, "Determination and the Theory of Agency," in Sidney Hook, ed., *Determinism and Freedom in the Age of Modern Science* (New York 1958).

2. Thomas Reid, *Essays on the Active Powers of Man,* Essay IV, Chapter 4 (*Works,* p. 600).
3. *Summa Theologica,* First Part of the Second Part, Question VI ("On the Voluntary and Involuntary").
4. Jonathan Edwards, *Freedom of the Will* (New Haven 1957); G. E. Moore, *Ethics* (Home University Library 1912), Chapter Six.
5. A. I. Melden, *Free Action* (London 1961), especially Chapter Three. Mr. Melden's own views, however, are quite the contrary of those that are proposed here.
6. Aristotle, *Physics,* Book III, Chapter 3; Suarez, *Disputations Metaphysicae,* Disputation, 18, Section 10.
7. Reid, *Works,* p. 524.
8. *Essay Concerning Human Understanding,* Book II, Chapter XXI.
9. *Op. cit.,* p. 166.
10. Reid, *Works,* pp. 608, 612.
11. "Lettre a Mr. Coste de la Nécessité et de la Contingence" (1707) in *Opera Philosophica,* ed. Erdmann, pp. 447–449.
12. In the Preface to the *Metaphysical Elements of Ethics,* in T. K. Abbott, ed., *Kant's Critique of Practical Reason and Other Works on the Theory of Ethics* (London 1959), p. 303.
13. Cf. D. P. Henry, "Saint Anselm's *De 'Grammatico',*" *Philosophical Quarterly,* Vol. X (1960), pp. 115–126. St. Anselm noted that (i) and (iii), respectively, may be thought of as forming the upper left and the upper right corners of a square of opposition, and (ii) and (iv) the lower left and the lower right.

## KEY TERMS

Metaphysical
Freedom
Deterministic
Transeunt causation
Immanent causation
Efficient cause
Free will

## STUDY QUESTIONS

1. According to Chisholm, what is the problem of human freedom?
2. Why doesn't Chisholm like the suggestion that "he could have done otherwise" means nothing more nor less than "if he had chosen to do otherwise, then he would have done otherwise"?
3. Chisholm's solution to the problem relies on the idea that a *human* can cause an event. Does this idea even make sense? How would you explain it to someone who wasn't familiar with the idea?
4. How is immanent causation a *via media* between deterministic and indeterministic accounts of human action?
5. How does Chisholm propose that we understand the phrase "inclination without necessitation"?

Journal of Philosophy, Inc.

Alternate Possibilities and Moral Responsibility
Author(s): Harry G. Frankfurt
Source: *The Journal of Philosophy*, Vol. 66, No. 23 (Dec. 4, 1969), pp. 829-839
Published by: Journal of Philosophy, Inc.
Stable URL: http://www.jstor.org/stable/2023833

approached this subject with medieval language and modern skill. We would, of course, consistent with the position taken on war, grant to Aryans the right to wage the war of extermination of the Jews, provided of course that the pogrom be declared by the duly constituted authority, be carried out with due decorum proportional to the threat, and with a just end in view. With this much granted, citizens would then see that they must kill Jews if their prince commanded it in the name of national defense (not unlike the Aryan concern with racial defense). Citizens would then implement the State department plan of containment of Judaism (not unlike containment of Communism) and seek by every means to rid the world of the threat of creeping Judaism. With no more effort than our war leaders now exert, we would carry out essentially what the Nazis did carry out, and do it according to the laws of pogroms (not unlike the much advertised "laws of wars"). Our means would naturally be humane gas chambers and sanitary ovens. If we put it this way, then the doctrine of the "just war"—like that of the "just pogrom"—would justify too much.

DONALD A. WELLS

University of Illinois, Chicago Circle

## ALTERNATE POSSIBILITIES AND MORAL RESPONSIBILITY

A DOMINANT role in nearly all recent inquiries into the free-will problem has been played by a principle which I shall call "the principle of alternate possibilities." This principle states that a person is morally responsible for what he has done only if he could have done otherwise. Its exact meaning is a subject of controversy, particularly concerning whether someone who accepts it is thereby committed to believing that moral responsibility and determinism are incompatible. Practically no one, however, seems inclined to deny or even to question that the principle of alternate possibilities (construed in some way or other) is true. It has generally seemed so overwhelmingly plausible that some philosophers have even characterized it as an *a priori* truth. People whose accounts of free will or of moral responsibility are radically at odds evidently find in it a firm and convenient common ground upon which they can profitably take their opposing stands.

But the principle of alternate possibilities is false. A person may well be morally responsible for what he has done even though he could not have done otherwise. The principle's plausibility is an illusion, which can be made to vanish by bringing the relevant moral phenomena into sharper focus.

I

In seeking illustrations of the principle of alternate possibilities, it is most natural to think of situations in which the same circumstances both bring it about that a person does something and make it impossible for him to avoid doing it. These include, for example, situations in which a person is coerced into doing something, or in which he is impelled to act by a hypnotic suggestion, or in which some inner compulsion drives him to do what he does. In situations of these kinds there are circumstances that make it impossible for the person to do otherwise, and these very circumstances also serve to bring it about that he does whatever it is that he does.

However, there may be circumstances that constitute sufficient conditions for a certain action to be performed by someone and that therefore make it impossible for the person to do otherwise, but that do not actually impel the person to act or in any way produce his action. A person may do something in circumstances that leave him no alternative to doing it, without these circumstances actually moving him or leading him to do it—without them playing any role, indeed, in bringing it about that he does what he does.

An examination of situations characterized by circumstances of this sort casts doubt, I believe, on the relevance to questions of moral responsibility of the fact that a person who has done something could not have done otherwise. I propose to develop some examples of this kind in the context of a discussion of coercion and to suggest that our moral intuitions concerning these examples tend to disconfirm the principle of alternate possibilities. Then I will discuss the principle in more general terms, explain what I think is wrong with it, and describe briefly and without argument how it might appropriately be revised.

II

It is generally agreed that a person who has been coerced to do something did not do it freely and is not morally responsible for having done it. Now the doctrine that coercion and moral responsibility are mutually exclusive may appear to be no more than a somewhat particularized version of the principle of alternate possibilities. It is natural enough to say of a person who has been coerced to do something that he could not have done otherwise. And it may easily seem that being coerced deprives a person of freedom and of moral responsibility simply because it is a special case of being unable to do otherwise. The principle of alternate possibilities may in this way derive some credibility from its association with the very plausible proposition that moral responsibility is excluded by coercion.

It is not right, however, that it should do so. The fact that a person was coerced to act as he did may entail both that he could not have done otherwise and that he bears no moral responsibility for his action. But his lack of moral responsibility is not entailed by his having been unable to do otherwise. The doctrine that coercion excludes moral responsibility is not correctly understood, in other words, as a particularized version of the principle of alternate possibilities.

Let us suppose that someone is threatened convincingly with a penalty he finds unacceptable and that he then does what is required of him by the issuer of the threat. We can imagine details that would make it reasonable for us to think that the person was coerced to perform the action in question, that he could not have done otherwise, and that he bears no moral responsibility for having done what he did. But just what is it about situations of this kind that warrants the judgment that the threatened person is not morally responsible for his act?

This question may be approached by considering situations of the following kind. Jones decides for reasons of his own to do something, then someone threatens him with a very harsh penalty (so harsh that any reasonable person would submit to the threat) unless he does precisely that, and Jones does it. Will we hold Jones morally responsible for what he has done? I think this will depend on the roles we think were played, in leading him to act, by his original decision and by the threat.

One possibility is that $Jones_1$ is not a reasonable man: he is, rather, a man who does what he has once decided to do no matter what happens next and no matter what the cost. In that case, the threat actually exerted no effective force upon him. He acted without any regard to it, very much as if he were not aware that it had been made. If this is indeed the way it was, the situation did not involve coercion at all. The threat did not lead $Jones_1$ to do what he did. Nor was it in fact sufficient to have prevented him from doing otherwise: if his earlier decision had been to do something else, the threat would not have deterred him in the slightest. It seems evident that in these circumstances the fact that $Jones_1$ was threatened in no way reduces the moral responsibility he would otherwise bear for his act. This example, however, is not a counterexample either to the doctrine that coercion excuses or to the principle of alternate possibilities. For we have supposed that $Jones_1$ is a man upon whom the threat had no coercive effect and, hence, that it did not actually deprive him of alternatives to doing what he did.

Another possibility is that $Jones_2$ was stampeded by the threat. Given that threat, he would have performed that action regardless of what decision he had already made. The threat upset him so profoundly, moreover, that he completely forgot his own earlier decision and did what was demanded of him entirely because he was terrified of the penalty with which he was threatened. In this case, it is not relevant to his having performed the action that he had already decided on his own to perform it. When the chips were down he thought of nothing but the threat, and fear alone led him to act. The fact that at an earlier time $Jones_2$ had decided for his own reasons to act in just that way may be relevant to an evaluation of his character; he may bear full moral responsibility for having made *that* decision. But he can hardly be said to be morally responsible for his action. For he performed the action simply as a result of the coercion to which he was subjected. His earlier decision played no role in bringing it about that he did what he did, and it would therefore be gratuitous to assign it a role in the moral evaluation of his action.

Now consider a third possibility. $Jones_3$ was neither stampeded by the threat nor indifferent to it. The threat impressed him, as it would impress any reasonable man, and he would have submitted to it wholeheartedly if he had not already made a decision that coincided with the one demanded of him. In fact, however, he performed the action in question on the basis of the decision he had made before the threat was issued. When he acted, he was not actually motivated by the threat but solely by the considerations that had originally commended the action to him. It was not the threat that led him to act, though it would have done so if he had not already provided himself with a sufficient motive for performing the action in question.

No doubt it will be very difficult for anyone to know, in a case like this one, exactly what happened. Did $Jones_3$ perform the action because of the threat, or were his reasons for acting simply those which had already persuaded him to do so? Or did he act on the basis of two motives, each of which was sufficient for his action? It is not impossible, however, that the situation should be clearer than situations of this kind usually are. And suppose it is apparent to us that $Jones_3$ acted on the basis of his own decision and not because of the threat. Then I think we would be justified in regarding his moral responsibility for what he did as unaffected by the threat even though, since he would in any case have submitted to the threat, he could not have avoided doing what he did. It would be entirely reasonable for us to make the same judgment concerning his moral responsibility that we would have made if we had not known of the threat. For the threat did not in fact influence his performance of the action. He did what he did just as if the threat had not been made at all.

III

The case of $Jones_3$ may appear at first glance to combine coercion and moral responsibility, and thus to provide a counterexample to the doctrine that coercion excuses. It is not really so certain that it does so, however, because it is unclear whether the example constitutes a genuine instance of coercion. Can we say of $Jones_3$ that he was coerced to do something, when he had already decided on his own to do it and when he did it entirely on the basis of that decision? Or would it be more correct to say that $Jones_3$ was not coerced to do what he did, even though he himself recognized that there was an irresistible force at work in virtue of which he had to do it? My own linguistic intuitions lead me toward the second alternative, but they are somewhat equivocal. Perhaps we can say either of these things, or perhaps we must add a qualifying explanation to whichever of them we say.

This murkiness, however, does not interfere with our drawing an important moral from an examination of the example. Suppose we decide to say that $Jones_3$ was *not* coerced. Our basis for saying this will clearly be that it is incorrect to regard a man as being coerced to do something unless he does it *because of* the coercive force exerted against him. The fact that an irresistible threat is made will not, then, entail that the person who receives it is coerced to do what he does. It will also be necessary that the threat is what actually accounts for his doing it. On the other hand, suppose we decide to say that $Jones_3$ *was* coerced. Then we will be bound to admit that being coerced does not exclude being morally responsible. And we will also surely be led to the view that coercion affects the judgment of a person's moral responsibility only when the person acts as he does because he is coerced to do so—i.e., when the fact that he is coerced is what accounts for his action.

Whichever we decide to say, then, we will recognize that the doctrine that coercion excludes moral responsibility is not a particularized version of the principle of alternate possibilities. Situations in which a person who does something cannot do otherwise because he is subject to coercive power are either not instances of coercion at all, or they are situations in which the person may still be morally responsible for what he does if it is not because of the coercion that he does it. When we excuse a person who has been coerced, we do not excuse him because he was unable to do otherwise. Even though a person is subject to a coercive force that precludes his performing any action but one, he may nonetheless bear full moral responsibility for performing that action.

## IV

To the extent that the principle of alternate possibilities derives its plausibility from association with the doctrine that coercion excludes moral responsibility, a clear understanding of the latter diminishes the appeal of the former. Indeed the case of $Jones_3$ may appear to do more than illuminate the relationship between the two doctrines. It may well seem to provide a decisive counterexample to the principle of alternate possibilities and thus to show that this principle is false. For the irresistibility of the threat to which $Jones_3$ is subjected might well be taken to mean that he cannot but perform the action he performs. And yet the threat, since $Jones_3$ performs the action without regard to it, does not reduce his moral responsibility for what he does.

The following objection will doubtless be raised against the suggestion that the case of $Jones_3$ is a counterexample to the principle of alternate possibilities. There is perhaps a sense in which $Jones_3$ cannot do otherwise than perform the action he performs, since he is a reasonable man and the threat he encounters is sufficient to move any reasonable man. But it is not this sense that is germane to the principle of alternate possibilities. His knowledge that he stands to suffer an intolerably harsh penalty does not mean that $Jones_3$, strictly speaking, *cannot* perform any action but the one he does perform. After all it is still open to him, and this is crucial, to defy the threat if he wishes to do so and to accept the penalty his action would bring down upon him. In the sense in which the principle of alternate possibilities employs the concept of "could have done otherwise," $Jones_3$'s inability to resist the threat does not mean that he cannot do otherwise than perform the action he performs. Hence the case of $Jones_3$ does not constitute an instance contrary to the principle.

I do not propose to consider in what sense the concept of "could have done otherwise" figures in the principle of alternate possibilities, nor will I attempt to measure the force of the objection I have just described.[1] For I believe that whatever force this objection may be thought to have can be deflected by altering the example in the following way.[2] Suppose someone—Black, let us say—wants $Jones_4$ to perform a certain action. Black is prepared to go to considerable lengths to get his way, but he prefers to avoid showing his hand unnecessarily. So he waits until $Jones_4$ is about to make up his mind what to do, and he does nothing unless it is clear to him (Black is an excellent judge of such things) that $Jones_4$ is going to decide to do something *other* than what he wants him to do. If it does become clear that $Jones_4$ is going to decide to do something else, Black takes effective steps to ensure that $Jones_4$ decides to do, and that he does do, what he wants him to do.[3] Whatever $Jones_4$'s initial preferences and inclinations, then, Black will have his way.

What steps will Black take, if he believes he must take steps, in order to ensure that $Jones_4$ decides and acts as he wishes? Anyone with a theory concerning what "could have done otherwise" means may answer this question for himself by describing whatever measures he would regard as sufficient to guarantee that, in the relevant sense, $Jones_4$ cannot do otherwise. Let Black pronounce a terrible threat, and in this way both force $Jones_4$ to perform the desired action and prevent him from performing a forbidden one. Let Black give $Jones_4$ a potion, or put him under hypnosis, and in some such way as these generate in $Jones_4$ an irresistible inner compulsion to perform the act Black wants performed and to avoid others. Or let Black manipulate the minute processes of $Jones_4$'s brain and nervous system in some more direct way, so that causal forces running

[1] The two main concepts employed in the principle of alternate possibilities are "morally responsible" and "could have done otherwise." To discuss the principle without analyzing either of these concepts may well seem like an attempt at piracy. The reader should take notice that my Jolly Roger is now unfurled.

[2] After thinking up the example that I am about to develop I learned that Robert Nozick, in lectures given several years ago, had formulated an example of the same general type and had proposed it as a counterexample to the principle of alternate possibilities.

[3] The assumption that Black can predict what $Jones_4$ will decide to do does not beg the question of determinism. We can imagine that $Jones_4$ has often confronted the alternatives—*A* and *B*—that he now confronts, and that his face has invariably twitched when he was about to decide to do *A* and never when he was about to decide to do *B*. Knowing this, and observing the twitch, Black would have a basis for prediction. This does, to be sure, suppose that there is some sort of causal relation between $Jones_4$'s state at the time of the twitch and his subsequent states. But any plausible view of decision or of action will allow that reaching a decision and performing an action both involve earlier and later phases, with causal relations between them, and such that the earlier phases are not themselves part of the decision or of the action. The example does not require that these earlier phases be deterministically related to still earlier events.

in and out of his synapses and along the poor man's nerves determine that he chooses to act and that he does act in the one way and not in any other. Given any conditions under which it will be maintained that $Jones_4$ cannot do otherwise, in other words, let Black bring it about that those conditions prevail. The structure of the example is flexible enough, I think, to find a way around any charge of irrelevance by accommodating the doctrine on which the charge is based.[4]

Now suppose that Black never has to show his hand because $Jones_4$, for reasons of his own, decides to perform and does perform the very action Black wants him to perform. In that case, it seems clear, $Jones_4$ will bear precisely the same moral responsibility for what he does as he would have borne if Black had not been ready to take steps to ensure that he do it. It would be quite unreasonable to excuse $Jones_4$ for his action, or to withhold the praise to which it would normally entitle him, on the basis of the fact that he could not have done otherwise. This fact played no role at all in leading him to act as he did. He would have acted the same even if it had not been a fact. Indeed, everything happened just as it would have happened without Black's presence in the situation and without his readiness to intrude into it.

In this example there are sufficient conditions for $Jones_4$'s performing the action in question. What action he performs is not up to him. Of course it is in a way up to him whether he acts on his own or as a result of Black's intervention. That depends upon what action he himself is inclined to perform. But whether he finally acts on his own or as a result of Black's intervention, he performs the same action. He has no alternative but to do what Black wants him to do. If he does it on his own, however, his moral responsibility for doing it is not affected by the fact that Black was lurking in the background with sinister intent, since this intent never comes into play.

## V

The fact that a person could not have avoided doing something is a sufficient condition of his having done it. But, as some of my examples show, this fact may play no role whatever in the explanation of why he did it. It may not figure at all among the circumstances

[4] The example is also flexible enough to allow for the elimination of Black altogether. Anyone who thinks that the effectiveness of the example is undermined by its reliance on a human manipulator, who imposes his will on $Jones_4$, can substitute for Black a machine programmed to do what Black does. If this is still not good enough, forget both Black and the machine and suppose that their role is played by natural forces involving no will or design at all.

that actually brought it about that he did what he did, so that his action is to be accounted for on another basis entirely. Even though the person was unable to do otherwise, that is to say, it may not be the case that he acted as he did *because* he could not have done otherwise. Now if someone had no alternative to performing a certain action but did not perform it because he was unable to do otherwise, then he would have performed exactly the same action even if he *could* have done otherwise. The circumstances that made it impossible for him to do otherwise could have been subtracted from the situation without affecting what happened or why it happened in any way. Whatever it was that actually led the person to do what he did, or that made him do it, would have led him to do it or made him do it even if it had been possible for him to do something else instead.

Thus it would have made no difference, so far as concerns his action or how he came to perform it, if the circumstances that made it impossible for him to avoid performing it had not prevailed. The fact that he could not have done otherwise clearly provides no basis for supposing that he *might* have done otherwise if he had been able to do so. When a fact is in this way irrelevant to the problem of accounting for a person's action it seems quite gratuitous to assign it any weight in the assessment of his moral responsibility. Why should the fact be considered in reaching a moral judgment concerning the person when it does not help in any way to understand either what made him act as he did or what, in other circumstances, he might have done?

This, then, is why the principle of alternate possibilities is mistaken. It asserts that a person bears no moral responsibility—that is, he is to be excused—for having performed an action if there were circumstances that made it impossible for him to avoid performing it. But there may be circumstances that make it impossible for a person to avoid performing some action without those circumstances in any way bringing it about that he performs that action. It would surely be no good for the person to refer to circumstances of this sort in an effort to absolve himself of moral responsibility for performing the action in question. For those circumstances, by hypothesis, actually had nothing to do with his having done what he did. He would have done precisely the same thing, and he would have been led or made in precisely the same way to do it, even if they had not prevailed.

We often do, to be sure, excuse people for what they have done when they tell us (and we believe them) that they could not have done otherwise. But this is because we assume that what they tell us serves to explain why they did what they did. We take it for granted that they are not being disingenuous, as a person would be who cited as an excuse the fact that he could not have avoided doing what he did but who knew full well that it was not at all because of this that he did it.

What I have said may suggest that the principle of alternate possibilities should be revised so as to assert that a person is not morally responsible for what he has done if he did it because he could not have done otherwise. It may be noted that this revision of the principle does not seriously affect the arguments of those who have relied on the original principle in their efforts to maintain that moral responsibility and determinism are incompatible. For if it was causally determined that a person perform a certain action, then it will be true that the person performed it because of those causal determinants. And if the fact that it was causally determined that a person perform a certain action means that the person could not have done otherwise, as philosophers who argue for the incompatibility thesis characteristically suppose, then the fact that it was causally determined that a person perform a certain action will mean that the person performed it because he could not have done otherwise. The revised principle of alternate possibilities will entail, on this assumption concerning the meaning of 'could have done otherwise', that a person is not morally responsible for what he has done if it was causally determined that he do it. I do not believe, however, that this revision of the principle is acceptable.

Suppose a person tells us that he did what he did because he was unable to do otherwise; or suppose he makes the similar statement that he did what he did because he had to do it. We do often accept statements like these (if we believe them) as valid excuses, and such statements may well seem at first glance to invoke the revised principle of alternate possibilities. But I think that when we accept such statements as valid excuses it is because we assume that we are being told more than the statements strictly and literally convey. We understand the person who offers the excuse to mean that he did what he did *only because* he was unable to do otherwise, or *only because* he had to do it. And we understand him to mean, more particularly, that when he did what he did it was not because that was what he really wanted to do. The principle of alternate possibilities should thus be replaced, in my opinion, by the following principle: a person is not morally responsible for what he has done if he did it only because he could not have done otherwise. This principle does not appear to conflict with the view that moral responsibility is compatible with determinism.

The following may all be true: there were circumstances that made it impossible for a person to avoid doing something; these circumstances actually played a role in bringing it about that he did it, so that it is correct to say that he did it because he could not have done otherwise; the person really wanted to do what he did; he did it because it was what he really wanted to do, so that it is not correct to say that he did what he did only because he could not have done otherwise. Under these conditions, the person may well be morally responsible for what he has done. On the other hand, he will not be morally responsible for what he has done if he did it only because he could not have done otherwise, even if what he did was something he really wanted to do.

HARRY G. FRANKFURT

The Rockefeller University

## BOOK REVIEWS

*Selected Letters of Friedrich Nietzsche.* Edited and translated by CHRISTOPHER MIDDLETON. Chicago: University Press. xvii, 370 p. $10.

Nietzsche is one of the small company of important philosophers who were also great writers. But not even his most ardent admirers need claim that he was a great letter writer. There are fascinating passages in many of his letters, and there is evidence in his correspondence of the power of his literary style, his wisdom, and his wit, but the place to find these most fully and at their best is in the works he himself designed for publication.

Though Christopher Middleton, professor of Germanic languages and literatures at the University of Texas, apparently recognizes this, he makes what seem to me somewhat excessive claims for the book under review. In his Introduction to the 206 letters he selected for translation, approximately one-tenth of the total number available, the editor expresses the hope that these "letters would reveal the man behind the immoralist, behind the visionary, behind the terrorist of metaphysical revolt." Middleton himself states the principal difficulty in realizing this hope: Nietzsche, he writes, "was a reticent man, in his conversation as in his letters." Though Nietzsche "seldom takes us down the darker galleries of his labyrinth . . . nevertheless I believe that the selection (here provided) presents a ground plan of the labyrinth."

THE JOURNAL OF PHILOSOPHY

VOLUME LXVIII, NO. 1, JANUARY 14, 1971

## FREEDOM OF THE WILL AND THE CONCEPT OF A PERSON

WHAT philosophers have lately come to accept as analysis of the concept of a person is not actually analysis of *that* concept at all. Strawson, whose usage represents the current standard, identifies the concept of a person as "the concept of a type of entity such that *both* predicates ascribing states of consciousness *and* predicates ascribing corporeal characteristics . . . are equally applicable to a single individual of that single type." [1] But there are many entities besides persons that have both mental and physical properties. As it happens—though it seems extraordinary that this should be so—there is no common English word for the type of entity Strawson has in mind, a type that includes not only human beings but animals of various lesser species as well. Still, this hardly justifies the misappropriation of a valuable philosophical term.

Whether the members of some animal species are persons is surely not to be settled merely by determining whether it is correct to apply to them, in addition to predicates ascribing corporeal characteristics, predicates that ascribe states of consciousness. It does violence to our language to endorse the application of the term 'person' to those numerous creatures which do have both psychological and material properties but which are manifestly not persons in any normal sense of the word. This misuse of language is doubtless innocent of any theoretical error. But although the offense is "merely

[1] P. F. Strawson, *Individuals* (London: Methuen, 1959), pp. 101–102. Ayer's usage of 'person' is similar: "it is characteristic of persons in this sense that besides having various physical properties . . . they are also credited with various forms of consciousness" [A. J. Ayer, *The Concept of a Person* (New York: St. Martin's, 1963), p. 82]. What concerns Strawson and Ayer is the problem of understanding the relation between mind and body, rather than the quite different problem of understanding what it is to be a creature that not only has a mind and a body but is also a person.

verbal," it does significant harm. For it gratuitously diminishes our philosophical vocabulary, and it increases the likelihood that we will overlook the important area of inquiry with which the term 'person' is most naturally associated. It might have been expected that no problem would be of more central and persistent concern to philosophers than that of understanding what we ourselves essentially are. Yet this problem is so generally neglected that it has been possible to make off with its very name almost without being noticed and, evidently, without evoking any widespread feeling of loss.

There is a sense in which the word 'person' is merely the singular form of 'people' and in which both terms connote no more than membership in a certain biological species. In those senses of the word which are of greater philosophical interest, however, the criteria for being a person do not serve primarily to distinguish the members of our own species from the members of other species. Rather, they are designed to capture those attributes which are the subject of our most humane concern with ourselves and the source of what we regard as most important and most problematical in our lives. Now these attributes would be of equal significance to us even if they were not in fact peculiar and common to the members of our own species. What interests us most in the human condition would not interest us less if it were also a feature of the condition of other creatures as well.

Our concept of ourselves as persons is not to be understood, therefore, as a concept of attributes that are necessarily species-specific. It is conceptually possible that members of novel or even of familiar nonhuman species should be persons; and it is also conceptually possible that some members of the human species are not persons. We do in fact assume, on the other hand, that no member of another species is a person. Accordingly, there is a presumption that what is essential to persons is a set of characteristics that we generally suppose—whether rightly or wrongly—to be uniquely human.

It is my view that one essential difference between persons and other creatures is to be found in the structure of a person's will. Human beings are not alone in having desires and motives, or in making choices. They share these things with the members of certain other species, some of whom even appear to engage in deliberation and to make decisions based upon prior thought. It seems to be peculiarly characteristic of humans, however, that they are able to form what I shall call "second-order desires" or "desires of the second order."

Besides wanting and choosing and being moved *to do* this or that, men may also want to have (or not to have) certain desires and motives. They are capable of wanting to be different, in their preferences and purposes, from what they are. Many animals appear to have the capacity for what I shall call "first-order desires" or "desires of the first order," which are simply desires to do or not to do one thing or another. No animal other than man, however, appears to have the capacity for reflective self-evaluation that is manifested in the formation of second-order desires.[2]

## I

The concept designated by the verb 'to want' is extraordinarily elusive. A statement of the form "*A* wants to *X*"—taken by itself, apart from a context that serves to amplify or to specify its meaning—conveys remarkably little information. Such a statement may be consistent, for example, with each of the following statements: (a) the prospect of doing *X* elicits no sensation or introspectible emotional response in *A*; (b) *A* is unaware that he wants to *X*; (c) *A* believes that he does not want to *X*; (d) *A* wants to refrain from *X*-ing; (e) *A* wants to *Y* and believes that it is impossible for him both to *Y* and to *X*; (f) *A* does not "really" want to *X*; (g) *A* would rather die than *X*; and so on. It is therefore hardly sufficient to formulate the distinction between first-order and second-order desires, as I have done, by suggesting merely that someone has a first-order desire when he wants to do or not to do such-and-such, and that he has a second-order desire when he wants to have or not to have a certain desire of the first order.

As I shall understand them, statements of the form "*A* wants to *X*" cover a rather broad range of possibilities.[3] They may be true even when statements like (a) through (g) are true: when *A* is unaware of any feelings concerning *X*-ing, when he is unaware that he wants to *X*, when he deceives himself about what he wants and

[2] For the sake of simplicity, I shall deal only with what someone wants or desires, neglecting related phenomena such as choices and decisions. I propose to use the verbs 'to want' and 'to desire' interchangeably, although they are by no means perfect synonyms. My motive in forsaking the established nuances of these words arises from the fact that the verb 'to want', which suits my purposes better so far as its meaning is concerned, does not lend itself so readily to the formation of nouns as does the verb 'to desire'. It is perhaps acceptable, albeit graceless, to speak in the plural of someone's "wants." But to speak in the singular of someone's "want" would be an abomination.

[3] What I say in this paragraph applies not only to cases in which 'to *X*' refers to a possible action or inaction. It also applies to cases in which 'to *X*' refers to a first-order desire and in which the statement that '*A* wants to *X*' is therefore a shortened version of a statement—"*A* wants to want to *X*"—that identifies a desire of the second order.

believes falsely that he does not want to *X*, when he also has other desires that conflict with his desire to *X*, or when he is ambivalent. The desires in question may be conscious or unconscious, they need not be univocal, and *A* may be mistaken about them. There is a further source of uncertainty with regard to statements that identify someone's desires, however, and here it is important for my purposes to be less permissive.

Consider first those statements of the form "*A* wants to *X*" which identify first-order desires—that is, statements in which the term 'to *X*' refers to an action. A statement of this kind does not, by itself, indicate the relative strength of *A*'s desire to *X*. It does not make it clear whether this desire is at all likely to play a decisive role in what *A* actually does or tries to do. For it may correctly be said that *A* wants to *X* even when his desire to *X* is only one among his desires and when it is far from being paramount among them. Thus, it may be true that *A* wants to *X* when he strongly prefers to do something else instead; and it may be true that he wants to *X* despite the fact that, when he acts, it is not the desire to *X* that motivates him to do what he does. On the other hand, someone who states that *A* wants to *X* may mean to convey that it is this desire that is motivating or moving *A* to do what he is actually doing or that *A* will in fact be moved by this desire (unless he changes his mind) when he acts.

It is only when it is used in the second of these ways that, given the special usage of 'will' that I propose to adopt, the statement identifies *A*'s will. To identify an agent's will is either to identify the desire (or desires) by which he is motivated in some action he performs or to identify the desire (or desires) by which he will or would be motivated when or if he acts. An agent's will, then, is identical with one or more of his first-order desires. But the notion of the will, as I am employing it, is not coextensive with the notion of first-order desires. It is not the notion of something that merely inclines an agent in some degree to act in a certain way. Rather, it is the notion of an *effective* desire—one that moves (or will or would move) a person all the way to action. Thus the notion of the will is not coextensive with the notion of what an agent intends to do. For even though someone may have a settled intention to do *X*, he may nonetheless do something else instead of doing *X* because, despite his intention, his desire to do *X* proves to be weaker or less effective than some conflicting desire.

Now consider those statements of the form "*A* wants to *X*" which identify second-order desires—that is, statements in which the term 'to *X*' refers to a desire of the first order. There are also two kinds of situation in which it may be true that *A* wants to want to *X*. In the first place, it might be true of *A* that he wants to have a desire to *X* despite the fact that he has a univocal desire, altogether free of conflict and ambivalence, to refrain from *X*-ing. Someone might want to have a certain desire, in other words, but univocally want that desire to be unsatisfied.

Suppose that a physician engaged in psychotherapy with narcotics addicts believes that his ability to help his patients would be enhanced if he understood better what it is like for them to desire the drug to which they are addicted. Suppose that he is led in this way to want to have a desire for the drug. If it is a genuine desire that he wants, then what he wants is not merely to feel the sensations that addicts characteristically feel when they are gripped by their desires for the drug. What the physician wants, insofar as he wants to have a desire, is to be inclined or moved to some extent to take the drug.

It is entirely possible, however, that, although he wants to be moved by a desire to take the drug, he does not want this desire to be effective. He may not want it to move him all the way to action. He need not be interested in finding out what it is like to take the drug. And insofar as he now wants only to *want* to take it, and not to *take* it, there is nothing in what he now wants that would be satisfied by the drug itself. He may now have, in fact, an altogether univocal desire *not* to take the drug; and he may prudently arrange to make it impossible for him to satisfy the desire he would have if his desire to want the drug should in time be satisfied.

It would thus be incorrect to infer, from the fact that the physician now wants to desire to take the drug, that he already does desire to take it. His second-order desire to be moved to take the drug does not entail that he has a first-order desire to take it. If the drug were now to be administered to him, this might satisfy no desire that is implicit in his desire to want to take it. While he wants to want to take the drug, he may have *no* desire to take it; it may be that *all* he wants is to taste the desire for it. That is, his desire to have a certain desire that he does not have may not be a desire that his will should be at all different than it is.

Someone who wants only in this truncated way to want to *X* stands at the margin of preciosity, and the fact that he wants to want to *X* is not pertinent to the identification of his will. There is, however, a second kind of situation that may be described by '*A* wants to want to *X*'; and when the statement is used to describe a situation of this second kind, then it does pertain to what *A* wants his will to be. In such cases the statement means that A wants the desire to *X* to be the desire that moves him effectively to act. It is not merely that he wants the desire to *X* to be among the desires by which, to one degree or another, he is moved or inclined to act. He wants this desire to be effective—that is, to provide the motive in what he actually does. Now when the statement that *A* wants to want to *X* is used in this way, it does entail that *A* already has a desire to *X*. It could not be true both that *A* wants the desire to *X* to move him into action and that he does not want to *X*. It is only if he does want to *X* that he can coherently want the desire to *X* not merely to be one of his desires but, more decisively, to be his will.[4]

Suppose a man wants to be motivated in what he does by the desire to concentrate on his work. It is necessarily true, if this supposition is correct, that he already wants to concentrate on his work. This desire is now among his desires. But the question of whether or not his second-order desire is fulfilled does not turn merely on whether the desire he wants is one of his desires. It turns on whether this desire is, as he wants it to be, his effective desire or will. If, when the chips are down, it is his desire to concentrate on his work that moves him to do what he does, then what he wants at that time is indeed (in the relevant sense) what he wants to want. If it is some other desire that actually moves him when he acts, on the other hand, then what he wants at that time is not (in the relevant sense) what he wants to want. This will be so despite the fact that the desire to concentrate on his work continues to be among his desires.

## II

Someone has a desire of the second order either when he wants simply to have a certain desire or when he wants a certain desire to be his will. In situations of the latter kind, I shall call his second-order desires "second-order volitions" or "volitions of the second order." Now it is having second-order volitions, and not having second-order desires generally, that I regard as essential to being a person. It is

[4] It is not so clear that the entailment relation described here holds in certain kinds of cases, which I think may fairly be regarded as nonstandard, where the essential difference between the standard and the nonstandard cases lies in the kind of description by which the first-order desire in question is identified. Thus, suppose that *A* admires *B* so fulsomely that, even though he does not know what *B* wants to do, he wants to be effectively moved by whatever desire effectively moves *B*; without knowing what *B*'s will is, in other words, *A* wants his own will to be the same. It certainly does not follow that *A* already has, among his desires, a desire like the one that constitutes *B*'s will. I shall not pursue here the questions of whether there are genuine counterexamples to the claim made in the text or of how, if there are, that claim should be altered.

logically possible, however unlikely, that there should be an agent with second-order desires but with no volitions of the second order. Such a creature, in my view, would not be a person. I shall use the term 'wanton' to refer to agents who have first-order desires but who are not persons because, whether or not they have desires of the second order, they have no second-order volitions.[5]

The essential characteristic of a wanton is that he does not care about his will. His desires move him to do certain things, without its being true of him either that he wants to be moved by those desires or that he prefers to be moved by other desires. The class of wantons includes all nonhuman animals that have desires and all very young children. Perhaps it also includes some adult human beings as well. In any case, adult humans may be more or less wanton; they may act wantonly, in response to first-order desires concerning which they have no volitions of the second order, more or less frequently.

The fact that a wanton has no second-order volitions does not mean that each of his first-order desires is translated heedlessly and at once into action. He may have no opportunity to act in accordance with some of his desires. Moreover, the translation of his desires into action may be delayed or precluded either by conflicting desires of the first order or by the intervention of deliberation. For a wanton may possess and employ rational faculties of a high order. Nothing in the concept of a wanton implies that he cannot reason or that he cannot deliberate concerning how to do what he wants to do. What distinguishes the rational wanton from other rational agents is that he is not concerned with the desirability of his desires themselves. He ignores the question of what his will is to be. Not only does he pursue whatever course of action he is most strongly inclined to pursue, but he does not care which of his inclinations is the strongest.

Thus a rational creature, who reflects upon the suitability to his desires of one course of action or another, may nonetheless be a wanton. In maintaining that the essence of being a person lies not in reason but in will, I am far from suggesting that a creature without reason may be a person. For it is only in virtue of his rational

[5] Creatures with second-order desires but no second-order volitions differ significantly from brute animals, and, for some purposes, it would be desirable to regard them as persons. My usage, which withholds the designation 'person' from them, is thus somewhat arbitrary. I adopt it largely because it facilitates the formulation of some of the points I wish to make. Hereafter, whenever I consider statements of the form "*A* wants to want to *X*," I shall have in mind statements identifying second-order volitions and not statements identifying second-order desires that are not second-order volitions.

capacities that a person is capable of becoming critically aware of his own will and of forming volitions of the second order. The structure of a person's will presupposes, accordingly, that he is a rational being.

The distinction between a person and a wanton may be illustrated by the difference between two narcotics addicts. Let us suppose that the physiological condition accounting for the addiction is the same in both men, and that both succumb inevitably to their periodic desires for the drug to which they are addicted. One of the addicts hates his addiction and always struggles desperately, although to no avail, against its thrust. He tries everything that he thinks might enable him to overcome his desires for the drug. But these desires are too powerful for him to withstand, and invariably, in the end, they conquer him. He is an unwilling addict, helplessly violated by his own desires.

The unwilling addict has conflicting first-order desires: he wants to take the drug, and he also wants to refrain from taking it. In addition to these first-order desires, however, he has a volition of the second order. He is not a neutral with regard to the conflict between his desire to take the drug and his desire to refrain from taking it. It is the latter desire, and not the former, that he wants to constitute his will; it is the latter desire, rather than the former, that he wants to be effective and to provide the purpose that he will seek to realize in what he actually does.

The other addict is a wanton. His actions reflect the economy of his first-order desires, without his being concerned whether the desires that move him to act are desires by which he wants to be moved to act. If he encounters problems in obtaining the drug or in administering it to himself, his responses to his urges to take it may involve deliberation. But it never occurs to him to consider whether he wants the relations among his desires to result in his having the will he has. The wanton addict may be an animal, and thus incapable of being concerned about his will. In any event he is, in respect of his wanton lack of concern, no different from an animal.

The second of these addicts may suffer a first-order conflict similar to the first-order conflict suffered by the first. Whether he is human or not, the wanton may (perhaps due to conditioning) both want to take the drug and want to refrain from taking it. Unlike the unwilling addict, however, he does not prefer that one of his conflicting desires should be paramount over the other; he does not prefer that one first-order desire rather than the other should constitute his will. It would be misleading to say that he is neutral as to the conflict between his desires, since this would suggest that he regards them as equally acceptable. Since he has no identity apart from his first-order desires, it is true neither that he prefers one to the other nor that he prefers not to take sides.

It makes a difference to the unwilling addict, who is a person, which of his conflicting first-order desires wins out. Both desires are his, to be sure; and whether he finally takes the drug or finally succeeds in refraining from taking it, he acts to satisfy what is in a literal sense his own desire. In either case he does something he himself wants to do, and he does it not because of some external influence whose aim happens to coincide with his own but because of his desire to do it. The unwilling addict identifies himself, however, through the formation of a second-order volition, with one rather than with the other of his conflicting first-order desires. He makes one of them more truly his own and, in so doing, he withdraws himself from the other. It is in virtue of this identification and withdrawal, accomplished through the formation of a second-order volition, that the unwilling addict may meaningfully make the analytically puzzling statements that the force moving him to take the drug is a force other than his own, and that it is not of his own free will but rather against his will that this force moves him to take it.

The wanton addict cannot or does not care which of his conflicting first-order desires wins out. His lack of concern is not due to his inability to find a convincing basis for preference. It is due either to his lack of the capacity for reflection or to his mindless indifference to the enterprise of evaluating his own desires and motives.[6] There is only one issue in the struggle to which his first-order conflict may lead: whether the one or the other of his conflicting desires is the stronger. Since he is moved by both desires, he will not be altogether satisfied by what he does no matter which of them is effective. But it makes no difference *to him* whether his craving or his aversion gets the upper hand. He has no stake in the conflict between them and so, unlike the unwilling addict, he can neither

[6] In speaking of the evaluation of his own desires and motives as being characteristic of a person, I do not mean to suggest that a person's second-order volitions necessarily manifest a *moral* stance on his part toward his first-order desires. It may not be from the point of view of morality that the person evaluates his first-order desires. Moreover, a person may be capricious and irresponsible in forming his second-order volitions and give no serious consideration to what is at stake. Second-order volitions express evaluations only in the sense that they are preferences. There is no essential restriction on the kind of basis, if any, upon which they are formed.

win nor lose the struggle in which he is engaged. When a *person* acts, the desire by which he is moved is either the will he wants or a will he wants to be without. When a *wanton* acts, it is neither.

III

There is a very close relationship between the capacity for forming second-order volitions and another capacity that is essential to persons—one that has often been considered a distinguishing mark of the human condition. It is only because a person has volitions of the second order that he is capable both of enjoying and of lacking freedom of the will. The concept of a person is not only, then, the concept of a type of entity that has both first-order desires and volitions of the second order. It can also be construed as the concept of a type of entity for whom the freedom of its will may be a problem. This concept excludes all wantons, both infrahuman and human, since they fail to satisfy an essential condition for the enjoyment of freedom of the will. And it excludes those suprahuman beings, if any, whose wills are necessarily free.

Just what kind of freedom is the freedom of the will? This question calls for an identification of the special area of human experience to which the concept of freedom of the will, as distinct from the concepts of other sorts of freedom, is particularly germane. In dealing with it, my aim will be primarily to locate the problem with which a person is most immediately concerned when he is concerned with the freedom of his will.

According to one familiar philosophical tradition, being free is fundamentally a matter of doing what one wants to do. Now the notion of an agent who does what he wants to do is by no means an altogether clear one: both the doing and the wanting, and the appropriate relation between them as well, require elucidation. But although its focus needs to be sharpened and its formulation refined, I believe that this notion does capture at least part of what is implicit in the idea of an agent who *acts* freely. It misses entirely, however, the peculiar content of the quite different idea of an agent whose *will* is free.

We do not suppose that animals enjoy freedom of the will, although we recognize that an animal may be free to run in whatever direction it wants. Thus, having the freedom to do what one wants to do is not a sufficient condition of having a free will. It is not a necessary condition either. For to deprive someone of his freedom of action is not necessarily to undermine the freedom of his will. When an agent is aware that there are certain things he is not free to do, this doubtless affects his desires and limits the range of choices he can make. But suppose that someone, without being aware of it, has in fact lost or been deprived of his freedom of action. Even though he is no longer free to do what he wants to do, his will may remain as free as it was before. Despite the fact that he is not free to translate his desires into actions or to act according to the determinations of his will, he may still form those desires and make those determinations as freely as if his freedom of action had not been impaired.

When we ask whether a person's will is free we are not asking whether he is in a position to translate his first-order desires into actions. That is the question of whether he is free to do as he pleases. The question of the freedom of his will does not concern the relation between what he does and what he wants to do. Rather, it concerns his desires themselves. But what question about them is it?

It seems to me both natural and useful to construe the question of whether a person's will is free in close analogy to the question of whether an agent enjoys freedom of action. Now freedom of action is (roughly, at least) the freedom to do what one wants to do. Analogously, then, the statement that a person enjoys freedom of the will means (also roughly) that he is free to want what he wants to want. More precisely, it means that he is free to will what he wants to will, or to have the will he wants. Just as the question about the freedom of an agent's action has to do with whether it is the action he wants to perform, so the question about the freedom of his will has to do with whether it is the will he wants to have.

It is in securing the conformity of his will to his second-order volitions, then, that a person exercises freedom of the will. And it is in the discrepancy between his will and his second-order volitions, or in his awareness that their coincidence is not his own doing but only a happy chance, that a person who does not have this freedom feels its lack. The unwilling addict's will is not free. This is shown by the fact that it is not the will he wants. It is also true, though in a different way, that the will of the wanton addict is not free. The wanton addict neither has the will he wants nor has a will that differs from the will he wants. Since he has no volitions of the second order, the freedom of his will cannot be a problem for him. He lacks it, so to speak, by default.

People are generally far more complicated than my sketchy account of the structure of a person's will may suggest. There is as much opportunity for ambivalence, conflict, and self-deception with regard to desires of the second order, for example, as there is with regard to first-order desires. If there is an unresolved conflict among someone's second-order desires, then he is in danger of having no second-order volition; for unless this conflict is resolved, he has no preference concerning which of his first-order desires is to be his will. This condition, if it is so severe that it prevents him from identifying himself in a sufficiently decisive way with *any* of his conflicting first-order desires, destroys him as a person. For it either tends to paralyze his will and to keep him from acting at all, or it tends to remove him from his will so that his will operates without his participation. In both cases he becomes, like the unwilling addict though in a different way, a helpless bystander to the forces that move him.

Another complexity is that a person may have, especially if his second-order desires are in conflict, desires and volitions of a higher order than the second. There is no theoretical limit to the length of the series of desires of higher and higher orders; nothing except common sense and, perhaps, a saving fatigue prevents an individual from obsessively refusing to identify himself with any of his desires until he forms a desire of the next higher order. The tendency to generate such a series of acts of forming desires, which would be a case of humanization run wild, also leads toward the destruction of a person.

It is possible, however, to terminate such a series of acts without cutting it off arbitrarily. When a person identifies himself *decisively* with one of his first-order desires, this commitment "resounds" throughout the potentially endless array of higher orders. Consider a person who, without reservation or conflict, wants to be motivated by the desire to concentrate on his work. The fact that his second-order volition to be moved by this desire is a decisive one means that there is no room for questions concerning the pertinence of desires or volitions of higher orders. Suppose the person is asked whether he wants to want to want to concentrate on his work. He can properly insist that this question concerning a third-order desire does not arise. It would be a mistake to claim that, because he has not considered whether he wants the second-order volition he has formed, he is indifferent to the question of whether it is with this volition or with some other that he wants his will to accord. The decisiveness of the commitment he has made means that he has decided that no further question about his second-order volition, at any higher order, remains to be asked. It is relatively unimportant whether we explain this by saying that this commitment implicitly generates an endless series of confirming desires of higher orders, or by saying that the commitment is tantamount to a dissolution of the pointedness of all questions concerning higher orders of desire.

Examples such as the one concerning the unwilling addict may suggest that volitions of the second order, or of higher orders, must be formed deliberately and that a person characteristically struggles to ensure that they are satisfied. But the conformity of a person's will to his higher-order volitions may be far more thoughtless and spontaneous than this. Some people are naturally moved by kindness when they want to be kind, and by nastiness when they want to be nasty, without any explicit forethought and without any need for energetic self-control. Others are moved by nastiness when they want to be kind and by kindness when they intend to be nasty, equally without forethought and without active resistance to these violations of their higher-order desires. The enjoyment of freedom comes easily to some. Others must struggle to achieve it.

## IV

My theory concerning the freedom of the will accounts easily for our disinclination to allow that this freedom is enjoyed by the members of any species inferior to our own. It also satisfies another condition that must be met by any such theory, by making it apparent why the freedom of the will should be regarded as desirable. The enjoyment of a free will means the satisfaction of certain desires—desires of the second or of higher orders—whereas its absence means their frustration. The satisfactions at stake are those which accrue to a person of whom it may be said that his will is his own. The corresponding frustrations are those suffered by a person of whom it may be said that he is estranged from himself, or that he finds himself a helpless or a passive bystander to the forces that move him.

A person who is free to do what he wants to do may yet not be in a position to have the will he wants. Suppose, however, that he enjoys both freedom of action and freedom of the will. Then he is not only free to do what he wants to do; he is also free to want what he wants to want. It seems to me that he has, in that case, all the freedom it is possible to desire or to conceive. There are other good things in life, and he may not possess some of them. But there is nothing in the way of freedom that he lacks.

It is far from clear that certain other theories of the freedom of the will meet these elementary but essential conditions: that it be understandable why we desire this freedom and why we refuse to ascribe it to animals. Consider, for example, Roderick Chisholm's quaint version of the doctrine that human freedom entails an absence of causal determination.[7] Whenever a person performs a free action, according to Chisholm, it's a miracle. The motion of a person's hand, when the person moves it, is the outcome of a series of physical causes; but some event in this series, "and presumably one of those that took place within the brain, was caused by the agent and not by any other events" (18). A free agent has, therefore, "a prerogative which some would attribute only to God: each of us, when we act, is a prime mover unmoved" (23).

This account fails to provide any basis for doubting that animals of subhuman species enjoy the freedom it defines. Chisholm says nothing that makes it seem less likely that a rabbit performs a miracle when it moves its leg than that a man does so when he moves his hand. But why, in any case, should anyone *care* whether he can interrupt the natural order of causes in the way Chisholm describes? Chisholm offers no reason for believing that there is a discernible difference between the experience of a man who miraculously initiates a series of causes when he moves his hand and a man who moves his hand without any such breach of the normal causal sequence. There appears to be no concrete basis for preferring to be involved in the one state of affairs rather than in the other.[8]

It is generally supposed that, in addition to satisfying the two conditions I have mentioned, a satisfactory theory of the freedom of the will necessarily provides an analysis of one of the conditions of moral responsibility. The most common recent approach to the problem of understanding the freedom of the will has been, indeed, to inquire what is entailed by the assumption that someone is morally responsible for what he has done. In my view, however, the relation between moral responsibility and the freedom of the will has been very widely misunderstood. It is not true that a person is morally responsible for what he has done only if his will was free when he did it. He may be morally responsible for having done it even though his will was not free at all.

A person's will is free only if he is free to have the will he wants. This means that, with regard to any of his first-order desires, he is free either to make that desire his will or to make some other first-

[7] "Freedom and Action," in K. Lehrer, ed., *Freedom and Determinism* (New York: Random House, 1966), pp. 11–44.

[8] I am not suggesting that the alleged difference between these two states of affairs is unverifiable. On the contrary, physiologists might well be able to show that Chisholm's conditions for a free action are not satisfied, by establishing that there is no relevant brain event for which a sufficient physical cause cannot be found.

order desire his will instead. Whatever his will, then, the will of the person whose will is free could have been otherwise; he could have done otherwise than to constitute his will as he did. It is a vexed question just how 'he could have done otherwise' is to be understood in contexts such as this one. But although this question is important to the theory of freedom, it has no bearing on the theory of moral responsibility. For the assumption that a person is morally responsible for what he has done does not entail that the person was in a position to have whatever will he wanted.

This assumption *does* entail that the person did what he did freely, or that he did it of his own free will. It is a mistake, however, to believe that someone acts freely only when he is free to do whatever he wants or that he acts of his own free will only if his will is free. Suppose that a person has done what he wanted to do, that he did it because he wanted to do it, and that the will by which he was moved when he did it was his will because it was the will he wanted. Then he did it freely and of his own free will. Even supposing that he could have done otherwise, he would not have done otherwise; and even supposing that he could have had a different will, he would not have wanted his will to differ from what it was. Moreover, since the will that moved him when he acted was his will because he wanted it to be, he cannot claim that his will was forced upon him or that he was a passive bystander to its constitution. Under these conditions, it is quite irrelevant to the evaluation of his moral responsibility to inquire whether the alternatives that he opted against were actually available to him.[9]

In illustration, consider a third kind of addict. Suppose that his addiction has the same physiological basis and the same irresistible thrust as the addictions of the unwilling and wanton addicts, but that he is altogether delighted with his condition. He is a willing addict, who would not have things any other way. If the grip of his addiction should somehow weaken, he would do whatever he could to reinstate it; if his desire for the drug should begin to fade, he would take steps to renew its intensity.

The willing addict's will is not free, for his desire to take the drug will be effective regardless of whether or not he wants this desire to constitute his will. But when he takes the drug, he takes it freely and of his own free will. I am inclined to understand his situation as involving the overdetermination of his first-order de-

[9] For another discussion of the considerations that cast doubt on the principle that a person is morally responsible for what he has done only if he could have done otherwise, see my "Alternate Possibilities and Moral Responsibility," this JOURNAL, LXVI, 23 (Dec. 4, 1969): 829–839.

sire to take the drug. This desire is his effective desire because he is physiologically addicted. But it is his effective desire also because he wants it to be. His will is outside his control, but, by his second-order desire that his desire for the drug should be effective, he has made this will his own. Given that it is therefore not only because of his addiction that his desire for the drug is effective, he may be morally responsible for taking the drug.

My conception of the freedom of the will appears to be neutral with regard to the problem of determinism. It seems conceivable that it should be causally determined that a person is free to want what he wants to want. If this is conceivable, then it might be causally determined that a person enjoys a free will. There is no more than an innocuous appearance of paradox in the proposition that it is determined, ineluctably and by forces beyond their control, that certain people have free wills and that others do not. There is no incoherence in the proposition that some agency other than a person's own is responsible (even *morally* responsible) for the fact that he enjoys or fails to enjoy freedom of the will. It is possible that a person should be morally responsible for what he does of his own free will and that some other person should also be morally responsible for his having done it.[10]

On the other hand, it seems conceivable that it should come about by chance that a person is free to have the will he wants. If this is conceivable, then it might be a matter of chance that certain people enjoy freedom of the will and that certain others do not. Perhaps it is also conceivable, as a number of philosophers believe, for states of affairs to come about in a way other than by chance or as the outcome of a sequence of natural causes. If it is indeed conceivable for the relevant states of affairs to come about in some third way, then it is also possible that a person should in that third way come to enjoy the freedom of the will.

HARRY G. FRANKFURT

The Rockefeller University

[10] There is a difference between being *fully* responsible and being *solely* responsible. Suppose that the willing addict has been made an addict by the deliberate and calculated work of another. Then it may be that both the addict and this other person are fully responsible for the addict's taking the drug, while neither of them is solely responsible for it. That there is a distinction between full moral responsibility and sole moral responsibility is apparent in the following example. A certain light can be turned on or off by flicking either of two switches, and each of these switches is simultaneously flicked to the "on" position by a different person, neither of whom is aware of the other. Neither person is solely responsible for the light's going on, nor do they share the responsibility in the sense that each is partially responsible; rather, each of them is fully responsible.

# Sanity and the Metaphysics of Responsibility

SUSAN WOLF

Susan Wolf teaches philosophy at the University of North Carolina, Chapel Hill.

Philosophers who study the problems of free will and responsibility have an easier time than most in meeting challenges about the relevance of their work to ordinary, practical concerns. Indeed, philosophers who study these problems are rarely faced with such challenges at all, since questions concerning the conditions of responsibility come up so obviously and so frequently in everyday life. Under scrutiny, however, one might question whether the connections between philosophical and nonphilosophical concerns in this area are real.

In everyday contexts, when lawyers, judges, parents, and others are concerned with issues of responsibility, they know, or think they know, what in general the conditions of responsibility are. Their questions are questions of application: Does this or that particular person meet this or that particular condition? Is this person mature enough, or informed enough, or sane enough to be responsible? Was he or she acting under posthypnotic suggestion or under the influence of a mind-impairing drug? It is assumed, in these contexts, that normal, fully developed adult human beings are responsible beings. The questions have to do with whether a given individual falls within the normal range.

By contrast, philosophers tend to be uncertain about the general conditions of responsibility, and they care less about dividing the responsible from the nonresponsible agents than about determining whether, and if so why, any of us are ever responsible for anything at all.

In the classroom, we might argue that the philosophical concerns grow out of the nonphilosophical ones, that they take off where the nonphilosophical questions stop. In this way, we might convince our students that even if they are not plagued by the philosophical worries, they ought to be. If they worry about whether a person is mature enough, informed enough, and sane enough to be responsible, then they should worry about whether that person is metaphysically free enough, too.

The argument I make here, however, goes in the opposite direction. My aim is not to convince people who are interested in the apparently nonphilosophical conditions of responsibility that they should go on to worry about the philosophical conditions as well, but rather to urge those who already worry about the philosophical problems not to leave the more mundane, prephilosophical problems behind. In particular, I suggest that the mundane recognition that *sanity* is a condition of responsibility has more to do with the murky and apparently metaphysical problems which surround the issue of responsibility than at first meets the eye. Once the significance of the condition of sanity is fully appreciated, at least some of the apparently insuperable metaphysical aspects of the problem of responsibility will dissolve.

My strategy is to examine a recent trend in philosophical discussions of responsibility, a trend that tries, but I think ultimately fails, to give an acceptable analysis of the conditions of responsibility. It fails due to what at first appear to be deep and irresolvable metaphysical problems. It is here that I suggest that the condition of sanity comes to the rescue. What at first

From Ferdinand David Schoeman (ed.). *Responsibility, Character, and the Emotions: New Essays in Moral Psychology* (New York: Cambridge University Press, 1988), pp. 46–62. Reprinted with the permission of Cambridge University Press.

appears to be an impossible requirement for responsibility—the requirement that the responsible agent have created her- or himself—turns out to be the vastly more mundane and non controversial requirement that the responsible agent must, *in a fairly standard sense, be sane.*

## FRANKFURT, WATSON, AND TAYLOR

The trend I have in mind is exemplified by the writings of Harry Frankfurt, Gary Watson, and Charles Taylor. I will briefly discuss each of their separate proposals, and then offer a composite view that, while lacking the subtlety of any of the separate accounts, will highlight some important insights and some important blind spots they share.

In his seminal article "Freedom of the Will and the Concept of a Person,"[1] Harry Frankfurt notes a distinction between freedom of action and freedom of the will. A person has freedom of action, he points out, if she (or he) has the freedom to do whatever she wills to do—the freedom to walk or sit, to vote liberal or conservative, to publish a book or open a store, in accordance with her strongest desires. Even a person who has freedom of action may fail to be responsible for her actions, however, if the wants or desires she has the freedom to convert into action are themselves not subject to her control. Thus, the person who acts under posthypnotic suggestion, the victim of brainwashing, and the kleptomaniac might all possess freedom of action. In the standard contexts in which these examples are raised, it is assumed that none of the individuals is locked up or bound. Rather, these individuals are understood to act on what, at one level at least, must be called *their own desires.* Their exemption from responsibility stems from the fact that their own desires (or at least the ones governing their actions) are not up to them. These cases may be described in Frankfurt's terms as cases of people who possess freedom of action, but who fail to be responsible agents because they lack freedom of the will.

Philosophical problems about the conditions of responsibility naturally focus on an analysis of this latter kind of freedom: What *is* freedom of the will, and under what conditions can we reasonably be thought to possess it? Frankfurt's proposal is to understand freedom of the will by analogy to freedom of action. As freedom of action is the freedom to do whatever one wills *to do, freedom of the will is the freedom to* will whatever one wants to will. To make this point clearer, Frankfurt introduces a distinction between first-order and second-order desires. First-order desires are desires to do or to have various things; second-order desires are desires about what desires to have or what desires to make effective in action. In order for an agent to have both freedom of action and freedom of the will, that agent must be capable of governing his or her actions by first-order desires *and* capable of governing his or her first-order desires by second-order desires.

Gary Watson's view of free agency[2]—free and responsible agency, that is—is similar to Frankfurt's in holding that an agent is responsible for an action only if the desires expressed by that action are of a particular kind. While Frankfurt identifies the right kind of desires as desires that are supported by second-order desires, however, Watson draws a distinction between "mere" desires, so to speak, and desires that are *values.* According to Watson, the difference between free action and unfree action cannot be analyzed by reference to the logical form of the desires from which these various actions arise, but rather must relate to a difference in the quality of their source. Whereas some of my desires are just appetites or conditioned responses I find myself "stuck with," others are expressions of judgments on my part that the objects I desire are good. Insofar as my actions can be governed by the latter type of desire—governed, that is, by my values or valuational system—they are actions that I perform freely and for which I am responsible.

Frankfurt's and Watson's accounts may be under stood as alternate developments of the intuition that in order to be responsible for one's actions, one must be responsible for the self that performs these actions. Charles Taylor, in an article entitled "Responsibility for Self,"[3] is concerned with the same intuition. Although Taylor does not describe his view in terms of *different levels or types of desire, his view is related,* for he claims that our freedom and responsibility depend on our ability to reflect on, criticize, and revise our selves. Like Frankfurt and Watson, Taylor seems to believe that if the characters from which our actions flowed were simply and permanently *given* to us, implanted by heredity, environment, or God, then we would be mere vehicles through which the causal forces of the world traveled, no more responsible than dumb animals or young children or machines. But like the others, he points out that, for most of us, our characters and desires are not so brutely implanted—or, at any rate, if they are, they are subject to revision by our own reflecting, valuing, or second-order desiring selves. We human beings—and as far as we know, only we human beings—have the ability to step back from ourselves and decide whether we are the selves we want to be. Because of this, these philosophers think, we are responsible for our selves and for the actions that we produce.

Although there are subtle and interesting differences among the accounts of Frankfurt, Watson, and Taylor, my concern is with features of their views that are common to them all. All share the idea that responsible agency involves something more than intentional agency. All agree that if we are responsible agents, it is not just because our actions are within the control of our wills, but because, in addition, our wills are not just psychological states *in* us, but expressions of characters that come *from* us, or that at any rate are acknowledged and affirmed *by* us. For Frankfurt, this means that our wills must be ruled by our second-order desires; for Watson, that our wills must be governable by our system of values: for Taylor, that our wills must issue from selves that are subject to self-assessment and redefinition in terms of a vocabulary of worth. In one way or another, all these philosophers seem to be saying that the key to responsibility lies in the fact that responsible agents are those for whom it is not just the case that their actions are within the control of their wills, but also the case that their wills are within the control of their *selves* in some deeper sense. Because, at one level, the differences among Frankfurt, Watson, and Taylor may be understood as differences *in the analysis or interpretation of what it is for an* action to be under the control of this deeper self, we may speak of their separate positions as variations of one basic view about responsibility: the *deep-self view.*

## THE DEEP-SELF VIEW

Much more must be said about the notion of a deep self before a fully satisfactory account of this view can be given. Providing a careful, detailed analysis of that notion poses an interesting, important, and difficult task in its own right. The degree of understanding achieved by abstraction from the views of Frankfurt, Watson, and Taylor, however, should be sufficient to allow us to recognize some important virtues as well as some important drawbacks of the deep-self view.

One virtue is that this view explains a good portion of our pretheoretical intuitions about responsibility. It explains why kleptomaniacs, victims of brainwashing, and people acting under posthypnotic suggestion may not be responsible for their actions, although most of us typically are. In the cases of people in these special categories, the connection between the agents' deep selves and their wills is dramatically severed—their wills are governed not by their deep selves, but by forces external to and independent from them. A different intuition is that we adult human beings can be responsible for our actions in a way that dumb animals, infants, and machines cannot. Here the explanation is not in terms of a split between these beings' deep selves and their wills; rather, the point is that these beings *lack* deep selves altogether. Kleptomaniacs and victims of hypnosis exemplify individuals whose selves are *alienated* from their actions; lower animals and machines, on the other hand, do not have the sorts of selves from which actions *can* be alienated, and so they do not have the sort of selves from which, in the happier cases, actions can responsibly flow.

At a more theoretical level, the deep-self view has another virtue: It responds to at least one way in which the fear of determinism presents itself.

A naive reaction to the idea that everything we do is completely determined by a causal chain that extends backward beyond the times of our births involves thinking that in that case we would have no control over our behavior whatsoever. If everything is determined, it is thought, then what happens happens, whether we want it to or not. A common, and proper, response to this concern points out that determinism does not deny the causal efficacy an agent's desires might have on his or her behavior. On the contrary, determinism in its more plausible forms tends to affirm this connection, merely adding that as one's behavior is determined by one's desires, so one's desires are determined by something else.[4]

Those who were initially worried that determinism implied fatalism, however, are apt to find their fears merely transformed rather than erased. If our desires are governed by something else, they might say, they are not *really* ours after all—or, at any rate, they are ours in only a superficial sense.

The deep-self view offers an answer to this transformed fear of determinism, for it allows us to distinguish cases in which desires are determined by forces foreign to oneself from desires which are determined *by* one's self—by one's "real," or second-order desiring, or valuing, or deep self, that is. Admittedly, there are cases, like that of the kleptomaniac or the victim of hypnosis, in which the agent acts on desires that "belong to" him or her in only a superficial sense. But the proponent of the deep-self view will point out that even if determinism is true, ordinary adult human action can be distinguished from this. Determinism implies that the desires which govern our actions are in turn governed by something else, but that something else will, in the fortunate cases, be our own deeper selves.

This account of responsibility thus offers a response to our fear of determinism; but it is a response with which many will remain unsatisfied. Even if my actions are governed by my desires and my desires are governed by my own deeper self, there remains the question: Who, or what, is responsible for this deeper self? The response above seems only to have pushed the problem further back.

Admittedly, some versions of the deep-self view, including Frankfurt's and Taylor's seem to anticipate this question by providing a place for the ideal that an agent's deep self may be governed by a still deeper self. Thus, for Frankfurt, second-order desires may themselves be governed by third-order desires, third-order desires by fourth-order desires, and so on. Also, Taylor points out that, as we can reflect on and evaluate our prereflective selves, so we can reflect on and evaluate the selves who are doing the first reflecting and evaluating, and so on. However, this capacity to recursively create endless levels of depth ultimately misses the criticism's point.

First of all, even if there is no *logical* limit to the number of levels of reflection or depth a person may have, there is certainly a psychological limit—it is virtually impossible imaginatively to conceive a fourth-, much less an eighth-order, desire. More important, no matter how many levels of self we posit, there will still, in any individual case, be a last level—a deepest self about whom the question "What governs it?" will arise, as problematic as ever. If determinism is true, it implies that even if my actions are governed by my desires, and my desires are governed by my deepest self, my deepest self will still be governed by something that must, logically, be external to myself altogether. Though I can step back from the values my parents and teachers have given me and ask whether these are the values I really want, the "I" that steps back will itself be a product of the parents and teachers I am questioning.

The problem seems even worse when one sees that one fares no better if determinism is false. For if my deepest self is not determined by something external to myself, it will still not be determined by *me*. Whether I am a product of carefully controlled forces or a result of random mutations, whether there is a complete explanation of my origin or no explanation at all, *I* am not, in any case, responsible for my existence; I am not in control of my deepest self.

Thus, though the claim that an agent is responsible for only those actions that are within the control of his or her deep self correctly identifies a necessary condition for responsibility—a condition that separates the hypnotized and the brainwashed, the immature and the lower animals from ourselves, for example—it fails to provide a sufficient condition of responsibility that puts all fears of determinism to rest. For one of the fears invoked by the thought of determinism seems to be connected to its implication that we are but intermediate links in a causal chain, rather than ultimate, self-initiating sources of movement and change. From the point of view of one who has this fear, the deep-self view seems merely to add loops to the chain, complicating the picture but not really improving it. From the point of view of one who has this fear, responsibility seems to require being a prime mover unmoved, whose deepest self is itself neither random *nor* externally determined, but is rather determined *by* itself—who is, in other words, self-created.

At this point, however, proponents of the deep-self view may wonder whether this fear is legitimate. For although people evidently can be brought to the point where they feel that responsible agency requires them to be ultimate sources of power, to the point where it seems that nothing short of self-creation will do, a return to the internal standpoint of the agent whose responsibility is in question makes it hard to see what good this metaphysical status is supposed to provide or what evil its absence is supposed to impose.

From the external standpoint, which discussions of determinism and indeterminism encourage us to take up, it may appear that a special metaphysical status is required to distinguish us significantly from other members of the natural world. But proponents of the deep-self view will suggest this is an illusion that a return to the internal standpoint should dispel. The possession of a deep self that is effective in governing one's actions is a sufficient distinction, they will say. For while other members of the natural world are not in control of the selves that they are, we, possessors of effective deep selves, are in control. We can reflect on what sorts of beings we are, and on what sorts of marks we make on the world. We can change what we don't like about ourselves, and keep what we do. Admittedly, we do not create ourselves from nothing. But as long as we can revise ourselves, they will suggest, it is hard to find reason to complain. Harry Frankfurt writes that a person who is free to do what he wants to do and also free to want what he wants to want has "all the freedom it is possible to desire or to conceive."[5] This suggests a rhetorical question: If you are free to control your actions by your desires, and free to control your desires by your deeper desires, and free to control those desires by still deeper desires, what further kind of freedom can you want?

## THE CONDITION OF SANITY

Unfortunately, there is a further kind of freedom we can want, which it is reasonable to think necessary for responsible agency. The deep-self view fails to be convincing when it is offered as a complete account of the conditions of responsibility. To see why, it will be helpful to consider another example of an agent whose responsibility is in question.

JoJo is the favorite son of Jo the First, an evil and sadistic dictator of a small, undeveloped country. Because of his father's special feelings for the boy, JoJo is given a special education and is allowed to accompany his father and observe his daily routine. In light of this treatment, it is not surprising that little JoJo takes his father as a role model and develops values very much like Dad's. As an adult, he does many of the same sorts of things his father did, including sending people to prison or to death or to torture chambers on the basis of whim. He is not *coerced* to do these things, he acts according to his own desires. Moreover, these are desires he wholly *wants* to have. When he steps back and asks, "Do I really want to be this sort of person?" his answer is resoundingly "Yes," for this way of life expresses a crazy sort of power that forms part of his deepest ideal.

In light of JoJo's heritage and upbringing—both of which he was powerless to control—it is dubious at best that he should be regarded as responsible for what he does. It is unclear whether anyone with a childhood such as his could have developed into anything but the twisted and perverse sort of person that he has become. However, note that JoJo is someone whose actions are controlled by his desires and whose desires are the desires he wants to have: That is, his actions are governed by desires that are governed by and expressive of his deepest self.

The Frankfurt–Watson–Taylor strategy that allowed us to differentiate our normal selves from the victims of hypnosis and brainwashing will not allow us to differentiate ourselves from the son of Jo the First. In the case of these earlier victims, we were able to say that although the actions of these individuals were, at one level, in control of the individuals themselves, these individuals themselves, qua agents, were not the selves they more deeply wanted to be. In this respect, these people were unlike our happily more integrated selves. However, we cannot say of JoJo that his self, qua agent, is not the self he wants it to be. It *is* the self he wants it to be. From the inside, he feels as integrated, free, and responsible as we do.

Our judgment that JoJo is not a responsible agent is one that we can make only from the outside—from reflecting on the fact, it seems, that his deepest self is not up to him. Looked at from the outside, however, our situation seems no different from his—for in the last analysis, it is not up to any of us to have the deepest selves we do. Once more, the problem seems metaphysical—and not just metaphysical, but insuperable. For, as I mentioned before, the problem is independent of the truth of determinism. Whether we are determined or undetermined, we cannot have created our deepest selves. Literal self-creation is not just empirically, but logically impossible.

If JoJo is not responsible because his deepest self is not up to him, then we are not responsible either. Indeed, in that case responsibility would be impossible for anyone to achieve. But I believe the appearance that literal self-creation is required for freedom and responsibility is itself mistaken.

The deep-self view was right in pointing out that freedom and responsibility require us to have certain distinctive types of control over our behavior and our selves. Specifically, our actions need to be under the control of our selves, and our (superficial) selves need to be under the control of our deep selves. Having seen that these types of control are not enough to guarantee us the status of responsible agents, we are tempted to go on to suppose that we must have yet another kind of control to assure us that even our deepest selves are somehow up to us. But not all the things necessary for freedom and responsibility must be types of power and control. We may need simply to *be* a certain way, even though it is not within our power to determine whether we are that way or not.

Indeed, it becomes obvious that at least one condition of responsibility is of this form as soon as we remember what, in everyday contexts, we have known all along—namely, that in order to be responsible, an agent must be *sane.* It is not ordinarily in our power to determine whether we are or are not sane. Most of us, it would seem, are lucky, but some of us are not. Moreover, being sane does not necessarily mean that one has any type of power or control an insane person lacks. Some insane people, like JoJo and some actual political leaders who resemble him, may have complete control of their actions, and even complete control of their acting selves. The desire to be sane is thus not a desire for another form of control; it is rather a desire that one's self be connected to the world in a certain way—we could even say it is a desire that one's self be *controlled by* the world in certain ways and not in others.

This becomes clear if we attend to the criteria for sanity that have historically been dominant in legal questions about responsibility. According to the M'Naughten Rule, a person is sane if (1) he knows what he is doing and (2) he knows that what he is doing is, as the case may be, right or wrong. Insofar as one's desire to be sane involves a desire to know what one is doing—or more generally, a desire to live in the real world—it is a desire to be a controlled (to have, in this case, one's *beliefs* controlled) by perceptions and sound reasoning that produce an accurate conception of the world, rather than by blind or distorted forms of response. The same goes for the second constituent of sanity—only, in this case, one's hope is that one's *values* be controlled by processes that afford an accurate conception of the world.[6] Putting these two conditions together, we may understand sanity, then, as the minimally sufficient ability cognitively and normatively to recognize and appreciate the world for what it is.

There are problems with this definition of sanity, at least some of which will become obvious in what follows, that make it ultimately unacceptable either as a gloss on or an improvement of the meaning of the term in many of the contexts in which it is used. The definition offered does seem to bring out the interest sanity has for us in connection with issues of responsibility, however, and some pedagogical as well as stylistic purposes will be served if we use sanity hereafter in this admittedly specialized sense.

## THE SANE DEEP-SELF VIEW

So far I have argued that the conditions of responsible agency offered by the deep-self view are necessary but not sufficient. Moreover, the gap left open by the deep-self view seems to be one that can be filled only by a metaphysical, and, as it happens, metaphysically impossible addition. I now wish to argue, however, that the condition of sanity, as characterized above, is sufficient to fill the gap. In other words, the deep-self view, supplemented by the condition of sanity, provides a satisfying conception of responsibility. The conception of responsibility I am proposing, then, agrees with the deep-self view in requiring that a responsible agent be able to govern her (or his) actions by her desires and to govern her desires by her deep self. In addition, my conception insists that the agent's deep self be sane, and claims that this is *all* that is needed for responsible agency. By contrast to the plain deep-self view, let us call this new proposal the *sane deep-self view.*

It is worth noting, to begin with, that this new proposal deals with the case of JoJo and related cases of deprived childhood victims in ways that better match our pretheoretical intuitions. Unlike the plain deep-self view, the sane deep-self view offers a way of explaining why JoJo is not responsible for his actions without throwing our own responsibility into doubt. For, although like us, JoJo's actions flow from desires that flow from his deep self, unlike us, JoJo's deep self is itself insane. Sanity, remember, involves the ability to know the difference between right and wrong, and a person who, even on reflection, cannot see that having someone tortured because he failed to salute you is wrong plainly lacks the requisite ability.

Less obviously, but quite analogously, this new proposal explains why we give less than full responsibility to persons who, though acting badly, act in ways that are strongly encouraged by their societies—the slaveowners of the 1850s, the Nazis of the 1930s, and many male chauvinists of our fathers' generation, for example. These are people, we imagine, who falsely believe that the ways in which they are acting are morally acceptable, and so, we may assume, their behavior is expressive of or at least in accordance with these agents' deep selves. But their false beliefs in the moral permissibility of their actions and the false values from which these beliefs derived may have been inevitable, given the social circumstances in which they developed. If we think that the agents could not help but be mistaken about their values, we do not blame them for the actions those values inspired?[7]

It would unduly distort ordinary linguistic practice to call the slaveowner, the Nazi, or the male chauvinist even partially or locally insane. Nonetheless, the reason for withholding blame from them is at bottom the same as the reason for withholding it from JoJo. Like JoJo, they are, at the deepest level, unable cognitively and normatively to recognize and appreciate the world for what it is. In our sense of the term, their deepest selves are not fully *sane.*

The sane deep-self view thus offers an account of why victims of deprived childhoods as well as victims of misguided societies may not be responsible for their actions, without implying that we are not responsible for ours. The actions of these others are governed by mistaken conceptions of value that the agents in question cannot help but have. Since, as far as we know, our values are not, like theirs, unavoidably mistaken, the fact that these others are not responsible for their actions need not force us to conclude that we are not responsible for ours.

But it may not yet be clear why sanity, in this special sense, should make such a difference—why, in particular, the question of whether someone's values are unavoidably *mistaken* should have any bearing on their status as responsible agents. The fact that the sane deep-self view implies judgments that match our intuitions about the difference in status between characters like JoJo and ourselves provides little support for it if it cannot also defend these intuitions. So we must consider an objection that comes from the point of view we considered earlier which rejects the intuition that a relevant difference can be found.

Earlier, it seemed that the reason JoJo was not responsible for his actions was that although his actions were governed by his deep self, his deep self was not up to him. But this had nothing to do with his deep self's being mistaken or not mistaken, evil or good, insane or sane. If JoJo's values are unavoidably mistaken, our values, even if not mistaken, appear to be just as unavoidable. When it comes to freedom and responsibility, isn't it the unavoidability, rather than the mistakenness, that matters?

Before answering this question, it is useful to point out a way in which it is ambiguous: The concepts of avoidability and mistakenness are not unequivocally distinct. One may, to be sure, construe the notion of avoidability in a purely metaphysical way. Whether an event or state of affairs is unavoidable under this construal depends, as it were, on the tightness of the causal connections that bear on the event's or state of affairs' coming about. In this sense, our deep selves do seem as unavoidable for us as JoJo's and the others' are for them. For presumably we are just as influenced by our parents, our cultures, and our schooling as they are influenced by theirs. In another sense, however, our characters are not similarly unavoidable.

In particular, in the cases of JoJo and the others, there are certain features of their characters that they cannot avoid *even though these features are seriously mistaken, misguided, or bad.* This is so because, in our special sense of the term, these characters are less than fully sane. Since these characters lack the ability to know right from wrong, they are unable to revise their characters on the basis of right and wrong, and so their deep selves lack the resources and the reasons that might have served as a basis for self-correction. Since the deep selves *we* unavoidably have, however, are sane deep selves—deep selves, that is, that unavoidably *contain* the ability to know right from wrong—we unavoidably do have the resources and reasons on which to base self-correction. What this means is that though in one sense we are no more in control of our deepest selves than JoJo et al., it does not follow in our case, as it does in theirs, that we would be the way we are, even if it is a bad or wrong way to be. However, if this does not follow, it seems to me, our absence of control at the deepest level should not upset us.

Consider what the absence of control at the deepest level amounts to for us: Whereas JoJo is unable to control the fact that, at the deepest level, he is not fully sane, we are not responsible for the fact that, at the deepest level, we are. It is not up to us to *have* minimally sufficient abilities cognitively and normatively to recognize and appreciate the world for what it is. Also, presumably, it is not up to us to have lots of other properties, at least to begin with—a fondness for purple, perhaps, or an antipathy for beets. As the proponents of the plain deep-self view have been at pains to point out, however, we do, if we are lucky, have the ability to revise our selves in terms of the values that are held by or constitutive of our deep selves. If we are lucky enough both to have this ability and to have our deep selves be sane, it follows that although there is much in our characters that we did not choose to have, there is nothing irrational or objectionable in our characters that we are compelled to keep.

Being sane, we are able to understand and evaluate our characters in a reasonable way, to notice what there is reason to hold on to, what there is reason to eliminate, and what, from a rational and reasonable standpoint, we may retain or get rid of as we please. Being able as well to govern our superficial selves by our deep selves, then, we are able to change the things we find there is reason to change. This being so, it seems that although we may not be *metaphysically* responsible for ourselves—for, after all, we did not create ourselves from nothing—we are *morally* responsible for ourselves, for we are able to understand and appreciate right and wrong, and to change our characters and our actions accordingly.

## SELF-CREATION, SELF-REVISION, AND SELF-CORRECTION

At the beginning of this chapter, I claimed that recalling that sanity was a condition of responsibility would dissolve at least some of the appearance that responsibility was metaphysically impossible. To see how this is so, and to get a fuller sense of the sane deep-self view, it may be helpful to put that view into perspective by comparing it to the other views we have discussed along the way.

As Frankfurt, Watson, and Taylor showed us, in order to be free and responsible we need not only to be able to control our actions in accordance with our desires, we need to be able to control our desires in accordance with our deepest selves. We need, in other words, to be able to *revise* ourselves—to get rid of some desires and traits, and perhaps replace them with others on the basis of our deeper desires or values or reflections. However, consideration of the fact that the selves who are doing the revising might themselves be either brute products of external forces or arbitrary outputs of random generation made us wonder whether the capacity for self-revision was enough to assure us of responsibility—and the example of JoJo added force to the suspicion that it was not. Still, if the ability to revise ourselves is not enough, the ability to create ourselves does not seem necessary either. Indeed, when you think of it, it is unclear why anyone should want self-creation. Why should anyone be disappointed at having to accept the idea that one has to get one's start somewhere? It is an idea that most of us have lived with quite contentedly all along. What we do have reason to want, then, is something more than the ability to revise ourselves, but less than the ability to create ourselves. Implicit in the sane deep-self view is the idea that what is needed is the ability to *correct* (or improve) ourselves.

Recognizing that in order to be responsible for our actions, we have to be responsible for our selves, the sane deep-self view analyzes what is necessary in order to be responsible for our selves as (1) the ability to evaluate ourselves sensibly and accurately, and (2) the ability to transform ourselves insofar as our evaluation tells us to do so. We may understand the exercise of these abilities as a process whereby we *take* responsibility for the selves that we are but did not ultimately create. The condition of sanity is intrinsically connected to the first ability; the condition that we able to control our superficial selves by our deep selves is intrinsically connected to the second.

The difference between the plain deep-self view and the sane deep-self view, then, is the difference between the requirement of the capacity for self-revision and the requirement of the capacity for self-correction. Anyone with the first capacity can *try* to take responsibility for himself or herself. However, only someone with a sane deep self—a deep self that can see and appreciate the world for what it is—can self-evaluate sensibly and accurately. Therefore, although insane selves can try to take responsibility for themselves, only sane selves will properly be accorded responsibility.

## TWO OBJECTIONS CONSIDERED

At least two problems with the sane deep-self view are so glaring as to have certainly struck many readers. In closing, I shall briefly address them. First, some will be wondering how, in light of my specialized use of the term "sanity," I can be so sure that "we" are any saner than the nonresponsible individuals I have discussed. What justifies my confidence that, unlike the slaveowners, Nazis, and male chauvinists, not to mention JoJo himself, we are able to understand and appreciate the world for what it is? The answer to this is that nothing justifies this except widespread intersubjective agreement and the considerable success we have in getting around in the world and satisfying our needs. These are not sufficient grounds for the smug assumption that we are in a position to see the truth about *all* aspects of ethical and social life. Indeed, it seems more reasonable to expect that time will reveal blind spots in our cognitive and normative outlook, just as it has revealed errors in the outlooks of those who have lived before. But our judgments of responsibility can only be made from here, on the basis of the understandings and values that we can develop by exercising the abilities we do possess as well and as fully as possible.

If some have been worried that my view implicitly expresses an overconfidence in the assumption that we are sane and therefore right about the world, others will be worried that my view too closely connects sanity with being right about the world, and fear that my view implies that anyone who acts wrongly or has false beliefs about the world is therefore insane and so not responsible for his or her actions. This seems to me to be a more serious worry, which I am sure I cannot answer to everyone's satisfaction.

First, it must be admitted that the sane deep-self view embraces a conception of sanity that is explicitly normative. But this seems to me a strength of that view, rather than a defect. Sanity *is* a normative concept, in its ordinary as well as in its specialized sense, and severely deviant behavior, such as that of a serial murderer of a sadistic dictator, does constitute evidence of a psychological defect in the agent. The suggestion that the most horrendous, stomach-turning crimes could be committed only by an insane person—an inverse of Catch-22, as it were—must be regarded as a serious possibility, despite the practical problems that would accompany general acceptance of that conclusion.

But, it will be objected, there is no justification, in the sane deep-self view, for regarding only horrendous and stomach-turning crimes as evidence of insanity in its specialized sense. If sanity is the ability cognitively and normatively to understand and appreciate the world for what it is, then *any* wrong action or false belief will count as evidence of the absence of that ability. This point may also be granted, but we must be careful about what conclusion to draw. To be sure, when someone acts in a way that is not in accordance with acceptable standards of rationality and reasonableness, it is always appropriate to look for an explanation of why he or she acted that way. The hypothesis that the person was unable to understand and appreciate that an action fell outside acceptable bound will always be a possible explanation. Bad performance on a math test always suggests the possibility that the testee is stupid. Typically, however, other explanations will be possible, too—for example, that the agent was too lazy to consider whether his or her action was acceptable, or too greedy to care, or, in the case of the math testee, that he or she was too occupied with other interests to attend class or study. Other facts about the agent's history will help us decide among these hypotheses.

This brings out the need to emphasize that sanity, in the specialized sense, is defined as the *ability* cognitively and normatively to understand and appreciate the world for what it is. According to our commonsense understandings, having this ability is one thing and exercising it is another—at least some wrong-acting, responsible agents presumably fall within the gap. The notion of "ability" is notoriously problematic, however, and there is a long history of controversy about whether the truth of determinism would show our ordinary ways of thinking to be simply confused on this matter. At this point, then, metaphysical concerns may voice themselves again—but at least they will have been pushed into a narrower, and perhaps a more manageable, corner.

The sane deep-self view does not, then, solve all the philosophical problems connected to the topics of free will and responsibility. If anything, it highlights some of the practical and empirical problems, rather than solves them. It may, however, resolve some of the philosophical, and particularly, some of the metaphysical problems, and reveal how intimate are the connections between the remaining philosophical problems and the practical ones.

## NOTES

1. Harry Frankfurt, "Freedom of the Will and the Concept of a Person," *Journal of Philosophy* LXVIII (1971), pp. 5–20.
2. Gary Watson, "Free Agency," *Journal of Philosophy* LXXII (1975), pp. 205–20.
3. Charles Taylor, "Responsibility for Self," in A. E. Rorty, ed., *The Identities of Persons* (Berkeley: University of California Press, 1976 pp. 381–99.
4. See, e.g., David Hume. *A Treatise of Human Nature* (Oxford: Oxford University Press, 1967), pp. 399–406, and R. E. Hobart, "Free Will as Involving Determination and Inconceivable Without It," *Mind* 43 (1934).

5. Frankfurt, p. 16.
6. Strictly speaking, perception and sound reasoning may not be enough to ensure the ability to achieve an accurate conception of what one is doing and especially to achieve a reasonable normative assessment of one's situation. Sensitivity and exposure to certain realms of experience may also be necessary for these goals. For the purpose of this essay, I understand 'sanity' to include whatever it takes to enable one to develop an adequate conception of one's world. In other contexts, however, this would be an implausibly broad construction of the term.
7. Admittedly, it is open to question whether these individuals were in fact unable to help having mistaken values, and indeed, whether recognizing the errors of their society would even have required exceptional independence or strength of mind. This is presumably an empirical question, the answer to which is extraordinarily hard to determine. My point here is simply that *if* we believe they are unable to recognize that their values are mistaken, we do not hold them responsible for the actions that flow from these values, and *if* we believe their ability to recognize their normative errors is impaired, we hold them less than fully responsible for relevant actions.

# Part Five:
# Morality

EUTHYPHRO: I would certainly say that the pious is what all the gods love, and the opposite, what all the gods hate, is the impious. e

SOCRATES: Then let us again examine whether that is a sound statement, or do we let it pass, and if one of us, or someone else, merely says that something is so, do we accept that it is so? Or should we examine what the speaker means?

EUTHYPHRO: We must examine it, but I certainly think that this is now a fine statement.

10 SOCRATES: We shall soon know better whether it is. Consider this: Is the pious being loved by the gods because it is pious, or is it pious because it is being loved by the gods?

EUTHYPHRO: I don't know what you mean, Socrates.

SOCRATES: I shall try to explain more clearly: we speak of something carried and something carrying, of something led and something leading, of something seen and something seeing, and you understand that these things are all different from one another and how they differ?

EUTHYPHRO: I think I do.

SOCRATES: So there is also something loved and—a different thing—something loving.

EUTHYPHRO: Of course.

b SOCRATES: Tell me then whether the thing carried is a carried thing because it is being carried, or for some other reason?

EUTHYPHRO: No, that is the reason.

SOCRATES: And the thing led is so because it is being led, and the thing seen because it is being seen?

EUTHYPHRO: Certainly.

SOCRATES: It is not being seen because it is a thing seen but on the contrary it is a thing seen because it is being seen; nor is it because it is something led that it is being led but because it is being led that it is something led; nor is something being carried because it is something carried, but it is something carried because it is being carried. Is what
c I want to say clear, Euthyphro? I want to say this, namely, that if anything is being changed or is being affected in any way, it is not being changed because it is something changed, but rather it is something changed because it is being changed; nor is it being affected because it is something affected, but it is something affected because it is being affected.[10] Or do you not agree?



EUTHYPHRO: I do.

SOCRATES: Is something loved either something changed or something affected by something?

EUTHYPHRO: Certainly.

SOCRATES: So it is in the same case as the things just mentioned; it is not being loved by those who love it because it is something loved, but it is something loved because it is being loved by them?

EUTHYPHRO: Necessarily.

SOCRATES: What then do we say about the pious, Euthyphro? Surely that it is being loved by all the gods, according to what you say?

EUTHYPHRO: Yes.

SOCRATES: Is it being loved because it is pious, or for some other reason?

EUTHYPHRO: For no other reason.

SOCRATES: It is being loved then because it is pious, but it is not pious because it is being loved?

EUTHYPHRO: Apparently.

SOCRATES: And yet it is something loved and god-loved because it is being loved by the gods?

EUTHYPHRO: Of course.

SOCRATES: Then the god-loved is not the same as the pious, Euthyphro, nor the pious the same as the god-loved, as you say it is, but one differs from the other.

EUTHYPHRO: How so, Socrates?

SOCRATES: Because we agree that the pious is being loved for this reason, that it is pious, but it is not pious because it is being loved. Is that not so?

EUTHYPHRO: Yes.

SOCRATES: And that the god-loved, on the other hand, is so because it is being loved by the gods, by the very fact of being loved, but it is not being loved because it is god-loved.

EUTHYPHRO: True.

---

10. Here Socrates gives the general principle under which, he says, the specific cases already examined—those of leading, carrying, and seeing—all fall. It is by being changed by something that changes *it* (e.g., by carrying it somewhere) that anything is a changed thing—not vice versa: it is not by something's being a changed thing that something *else* then changes it so that it comes to be being changed (e.g., by carrying it somewhere). Likewise for "affections" such as being seen by someone: it is by being "affected" by something that "affects" it that anything is an "affected" thing, not vice versa. It is not by being an "affected" thing (e.g., a thing seen) that something else then "affects" it.

Socrates: But if the god-loved and the pious were the same, my dear Euthyphro, then if the pious was being loved because it was pious, the god-loved would also be being loved because it was god-loved; and if the god-loved was god-loved because it was being loved by the gods, then the pious would also be pious because it was being loved by the gods. But now you see that they are in opposite cases as being altogether different from each other: the one is such as to be loved because it is being loved, the other is being loved because it is such as to be loved. I'm afraid, Euthyphro, that when you were asked what piety is, you did not wish to make its nature clear to me, but you told me an affect or a quality of it, that the pious has the quality of being loved by all the gods, but you have not yet told me what the pious is. Now, if you will, do not hide things from me but tell me again from the beginning what piety is, whether being loved by the gods or having some other quality—we shall not quarrel about that—but be keen to tell me what the pious and the impious are.

Euthyphro: But Socrates, I have no way of telling you what I have in mind, for whatever proposition we put forward goes around and refuses to stay put where we establish it.

# Ethical Relativism

RUSS SHAFER-LANDAU

## TWO KINDS OF ETHICAL RELATIVISM

As you may already have noticed, ethical relativism isn't just a single doctrine. It actually comes in two varieties: cultural relativism and individual relativism (usually referred to as ethical subjectivism, a name I'll use from now on). *Cultural relativism claims that the correct moral standards* are relative to cultures, or societies; ethical subjectivism claims that the correct moral standards are those endorsed by each individual. The difference amounts to whether society, or each person, has the final say about what is right and wrong. This is undoubtedly an important difference, but as we'll see, both the advantages and the drawbacks of cultural relativism and ethical subjectivism are remarkably similar.

Consider subjectivism first. It says that *an act is morally acceptable just because (a) I approve of it, or (b) my commitments allow it. An action is wrong just because (a) I disapprove of it, or (b) my commitments forbid it.* My commitments are the principles I support, the values I stand for. In this line of thinking, personal conviction is the ultimate measure of morality. Right and wrong are wholly in the eyes of the beholder.

Subjectivists think that there are right answers in ethics, but that these are always relative to each person's moral standards. There is no superior moral code that can measure the accuracy of each person's moral outlook. If subjectivism is correct, each person's moral standards are equally plausible.

Cultural relativism instead locates the ultimate standard of morality within each culture's commitments. It says that *an act is morally acceptable just because it is allowed by the guiding ideals of the society in which it is performed, and immoral just because it is forbidden by those ideals.*

Both subjectivists and relativists regard people as the authors of morality. In both of these views, morality is made by and for human beings. Before we were around, nothing was right and wrong. If our species ever becomes extinct, morality will cease to exist. The fundamental difference between these two views is whether each person, or each society, gets to have the final say in ethics.

Despite their disagreement about whose views are morally authoritative, both ethical subjectivism and cultural relativism share a number of similar elements that make it easy to evaluate them in tandem. Let's now have a look at some of the most important features of these views.

## SOME IMPLICATIONS OF ETHICAL SUBJECTIVISM AND CULTURAL RELATIVISM

### Moral Infallibility

Subjectivism and relativism occupy a middle ground between moral nihilism and ethical objectivism. There are legitimate moral standards (contrary to nihilism), but their legitimacy depends crucially on our support (contrary to objectivism).

But subjectivists and relativists do not always see eye to eye. Subjectivists are suspicious of cultural relativism because of their belief that societies can be deeply mistaken about what is right and wrong. If a social code can contain some serious moral errors, then cultural relativism is in trouble, since it says that whatever society holds most dear is morally right.

Relativists admit that some social beliefs can be morally mistaken. These are the ones that clash with society's most cherished ideals. But if relativists are right, those ideals can never be mistaken, since they just are the ultimate moral standards for each society.

---

*Fundamentals of Ethics* by Russ Shafer-Landau (2010), pp. 278–288. By permission of Oxford University Press.

And yet societies are sometimes based on principles of slavery, of war-like aggression, or of sexual, religious, or ethnic oppression. Cultural relativism would turn these founding ideals into iron-clad moral duties, making slavery, sexism, and racism the moral duty of all citizens of those societies. The iconoclast—the person deeply opposed to conventional wisdom—would, by definition, always be morally mistaken. This has struck many people as seriously implausible.

But subjectivism is not in the clear here. It faces a similar problem. The cultural relativist makes societies morally infallible—incapable of error—at least with regard to their foundational principles. Yet subjectivists make *each person's basic commitments* morally infallible. True, subjectivism allows that people can make moral mistakes, but only if they fail to realize the implications of their own commitments. When it comes to the basic commitments themselves, subjectivism denies that these can ever be false or immoral.

If morality is in the eye of the beholder, then everyone is seeing things equally well. Millions of people have very sincerely endorsed programs of ethnic cleansing, male domination, and chattel slavery. Subjectivism turns these prejudices into moral truths.

### Moral Equivalence

Subjectivists grant that your moral values, which very likely oppose the ones just mentioned, are also correct. The biased and the bigoted have no monopoly on the truth. Ethical subjectivism is a doctrine of moral equivalence; everyone's basic moral views are as plausible as everyone else's. This can sound liberating and tolerant, and can be put to good use in cutting arrogant people down to size. Such people usually claim to have found the Truth, and often think that they have a special license to force this Truth on others. If subjectivism is correct, the views of such zealots are no better than those of their intended victims.

But they are no worse, either. If ethical subjectivism is correct, then the moral outlooks of Hitler or Stalin are just as plausible as those of a Nobel Peace laureate. [I]f all moral views are on a par with one another, then this is a threat to tolerance, rather than support for it, since those with intolerant outlooks would have a moral view as good as that of their opponents.

Cultural relativists fare a bit better here. They will deny that everyone's moral views are equally plausible. Some people are much wiser in moral matters than others, since some people are better attuned to what their society really stands for. But when it comes to evaluating the basic codes of each society, relativists must allow that every code is equally good. Since the ultimate moral standards are those endorsed by each society, none is better than any other. That may sound egalitarian and open-minded, but what it means in practice is that social codes that treat women or ethnic minorities as property are just as morally attractive as those that don't. That's not an easy thing to accept.

### No Intrinsic Value

Here is an ancient moral question: Is something good because we like it, or do we like things because they are good? Ethical subjectivism goes for the first option. There is nothing intrinsically good about promise-keeping, generosity, kindness, or caring. Subjectivists think that these things are valuable, if they are, only because people approve of them. Were our tastes to change, the morality of such actions and character traits would change with them.

That might strike you as suspicious. If it does, then cultural relativism might seem a good alternative. For in that view, moral standards do not depend on the possibly fickle choices of any single person.

Yet cultural relativism faces the same worry. For the relativist, the value of something depends entirely on whether a society's guiding ideals approve of it. When these ideals change, the moral code changes with them. If societies place no value on tolerance, or sexual equality, then in those societies such things have no moral value at all. An open, tolerant society that eventually became a fascist tyranny would not be falling into moral error. If relativism is true, then a society's basic moral ideals (no matter what they stand for) are correct. They are not correct because they measure up to some independent standard. They are correct because a society embraces them.

The problem with such a view is that the ultimate moral principles—whether fixed by each individual or by each society—can be based on prejudice, ignorance, superficial thinking, or brainwashing, *and still be correct.* According to both kinds of relativism, the origins of our basic moral beliefs are irrelevant. No matter how we came by them, the relativist claims that our ultimate moral beliefs cannot be mistaken.

### Questioning Our Own Commitments

If subjectivism is correct, then I know what is right so long as I know what I approve of. That's because my approvals (according to subjectivism) are the ultimate test of morality. But what about the situations where I want to know whether my commitments are worthwhile? In these cases, I know what I like, but am still up in the air about its value. This sort of puzzlement *seems* to make sense. I have been in such situations before, where I am unsure of whether I am right to like someone so much, or wrong to be so critical of some action. But if subjectivism is true, this *cannot* make sense, since my approvals and disapprovals are the ultimate test of right and wrong.

The same sort of problem faces cultural relativism. There is no room in this theory to second-guess the guiding ideals of one's own society, since (by definition) they are the correct moral standards of that society. And yet it sometimes does seem to make sense to ask whether the basic principles of one's society are also morally acceptable. If relativism is correct, however, such questioning reveals a confusion about what morality is all about.

### Moral Progress

It seems that both individuals and societies can make moral progress. We can do this when our actions become morally better than they used to be. But I am thinking here of progress in our moral beliefs. This occurs when more of them are true and, in particular, when our most fundamental beliefs change for the better.

The gradual reduction in racist and sexist attitudes in the United States seems to represent this sort of moral progress. The kind of repentant self-examination that German society undertook (and continues to undertake) after World War II also seems a clear improvement over Nazi ideology. When I examine my own life, I see several moral views that I held when I was younger that I now regard as seriously mistaken. I am probably not alone in this.

The problem for relativism and subjectivism is that it does not seem to be able to make sense of the most basic kind of moral progress. If a person's or a society's deepest beliefs are true by definition, then they *cannot* change for the better. They can change, of course. But if subjectivism or relativism is true, then this change cannot represent moral progress.

To measure moral progress, you need a standard. In ethics, that standard is the ultimate moral rule (or rules, if we are pluralists). If subjectivism is correct, that ultimate rule is personal opinion. If relativism is correct, that ultimate rule is given by a society's basic ideals. These cannot be mistaken. If a society gradually eases out of its deeply sexist attitudes, for instance, that cannot be moral progress. That can only be a change to a different moral code. And if relativism is correct, different moral codes are not better or worse than one another. They are morally equivalent.

According to these views, moral improvement is possible only if our more specific moral beliefs line up better with our deepest moral convictions. But these deepest convictions can never improve. No change in them can ever represent moral progress, since they are the ultimate standard by which any such progress could be measured.

If subjectivism is correct, then inmates who experience a deep change of heart while in prison, who adopt new aims of charity and repentance, cannot be showing moral progress. If relativism is correct, then a society that rejects its earlier ideals of racial purity and genocide cannot be making moral progress. That is difficult to believe.

In sum, both forms of relativism encounter some serious difficulties. They make the deepest commitments of each person or society morally infallible, no matter whether such commitments reflect ignorance, bias, sloppy thinking, etc. They are doctrines of moral equivalence, and so deny that compassion, kindness, and benevolence are morally superior to treachery, betrayal, and violence.

In rejecting the idea that any actions or character traits are intrinsically good, they make morality subject to the whims of individuals or societies, as changeable as personal or social opinions. When we search for guidance in examining our most basic commitments, both forms of relativism have nothing to offer. Indeed, they think that such questioning is confused, since (by their lights) things are good only because we value them, and not the other way around. Finally, neither form of relativism can make sense of fundamental moral progress, understood as an improvement in our deepest moral beliefs.

### Contradiction and Disagreement

A final problem for both theories is one that you've probably already thought of. It is the problem of contradiction. A contradiction occurs when a statement is said to be both true and false at the same time. It's a contradiction, for instance, to both assert and deny that the Empire State Building is in New York. Theories that generate contradictions are incoherent. They can't be true; they are muddled and inconsistent.

It looks like subjectivism leads to contradiction. For consider its test of truth and falsity:

> (S) A moral judgment is true if it accurately reports one's feelings or commitments, and is false otherwise.

If S is correct, then people on opposite sides of a moral debate are both saying something true. The pro-choicer is speaking the truth when saying that abortion is morally right. And the abortion opponent is also speaking the truth when saying that it is immoral. But abortion can't be both right and wrong. That is a contradiction. Since subjectivism generates contradictions, it must be false.

There is a solution to this problem, but it has its costs. The solution implies that we usually don't mean what we say in our moral debates. What we say are things such as:

- The death penalty is immoral.
- Abortion is wrong.
- Eating animals is okay.

But what we *mean* is:

- The death penalty is wrong, according to me.
- I disapprove of abortion.
- As I see it, eating animals is okay.

And just like that, the contradictions disappear! Suppose that you and your friend disagree about whether eating animals is wrong. You say it is; she says it isn't. As the subjectivist sees things, you are saying that you disapprove of meat-eating; she says that she approves of it. These claims don't contradict each other. This sort of strategy will work across the board, for all moral claims, and so we can save subjectivism from contradiction.

Here are the costs. First, subjectivists have to accuse nearly everyone of misunderstanding their own moral claims. And second, such a view eliminates the possibility of moral disagreement.

To illustrate the first problem, consider this conversation:

> Me: Genocide is immoral.
> Subjectivist: What I'm hearing is—you disapprove of genocide.
> Me: Yes, I disapprove of genocide. But that's not what I'm saying. I'm not talking about my attitudes, I'm talking about genocide. You're changing the subject.

Subjectivists can't make sense of my reply here. It's not that my reply might be false. Rather, my reply is unintelligible, since it assumes that moral talk is about something other than my own commitments. Most of us assume precisely that. If subjectivism is right, we are badly mistaken.

In order to avoid the problem of contradiction, subjectivists have to say that our moral assertions report facts only about our own commitments. When I say that genocide is wrong, I am not saying that it has a certain feature—wrongness. I am saying that I disapprove of it or that my principles forbid it. I am talking about myself. That's not what most people think they are doing when they make their moral judgments.

The second problem is even more serious. Subjectivism is unable to explain the existence of moral disagreement. In order to avoid generating contradictions, subjectivists have to understand all moral judgments as reports of whether I approve of something or not. The claim that meat-eating is wrong becomes the claim that I disapprove of meat-eating. The judgment that bravery is a virtue becomes the claim that bravery is something I admire. And so on. But on this line, moral debates that seem to involve intense disagreement become something completely different. In fact, it now becomes *impossible* for people to morally disagree with one another.

To see this, imagine an earlier dispute.

YOU SAY: It's wrong to eat meat.

AND YOUR FRIEND SAYS: It's okay to eat meat.

The subjectivist translates this as follows:

YOU: I disapprove of eating meat.

YOUR FRIEND: I approve of eating meat.

The contradiction has indeed disappeared. But so has the disagreement. If you are both taking this seriously, you'll agree with your friend's claim, and she with yours. If all that moral judgments do is report people's outlooks, then there is no way to morally disagree with anyone—except to charge them with insincerity. But that seems plainly wrong.

Subjectivism reduces all moral talk to autobiographical reports. Disagreement is impossible, because there is no common subject matter to disagree about. Those who debate the merits of abortion may think that they are discussing abortion, and whether it is has a certain feature—namely, that of being morally acceptable. Not so. They are instead talking about their attitudes of approval and disapproval. If that were true, there would be no point in debating morality at all.

But there certainly seems to be a point (or rather, many points) to engaging in moral discussion. And the appearance of moral disagreement is very vivid. Perhaps such appearances are all illusions. And perhaps moral debate really is pointless. It would indeed be pointless if all we could possibly talk about were our own thoughts about things, rather than about the moral features of the things themselves.

In short, subjectivism faces a dilemma. If we take moral claims at face value, then subjectivism generates contradictions, and so it must be false. If we reinterpret all moral claims to be focused on our attitudes, then the contradictions disappear, but so, too, does moral disagreement.

Cultural relativism faces the same dilemma. It says that *a moral judgment is true just because it correctly describes what a society really stands for.* For instance, if different societies disagree about the appropriate political status of women, then each is speaking the truth when it asserts (or denies) female moral equality. But that is impossible. The statement that women are deserving of full political equality cannot be simultaneously true and false.

Relativists can escape this problem in familiar ways. They will claim that moral judgments are true only relative to social agreements. In this line of thinking, moral judgments are just like legal ones. It isn't contradictory to say that smoking marijuana, for instance, is both legal and illegal, so long as we qualify things to note that it is legal in some areas and illegal in others.

Relativists will say that all of our moral claims have to be understood by reference to social agreements. When you say that meat-eating is right, and your Hindu friend from Calcutta says that it is wrong, what is really being said is:

YOU: Meat-eating is accepted by my social customs.

YOUR FRIEND: Meat-eating is forbidden by my social customs.

And again, both of these claims can be true: The contradiction disappears. There is no single judgment that is both true and false.

But then the existence of cross-cultural moral disagreement also disappears. If the ultimate moral standard is each society's ethical code, and our moral judgments are attempts to describe what our society believes, then the only way to criticize someone is to say that he has mistaken what his society really stands for. It doesn't seem as if that is what serious, engaged moral debate is all about. For instance, it appears possible to note that a society approves of making wives domestic slaves and yet to disagree with the morality of that policy. But that's not so if relativism is to escape the contradiction problem.

So the cultural relativist faces the same dilemma as the subjectivist. Indeed, the relativist is in one way more vulnerable than the subjectivist here. For the cultural relativist may be unable to escape contradiction after all.

People who are members of subcultures—smaller cultural groups located within larger ones—often face a familiar problem: They are forced to choose between allegiance to the larger society and to their particular subculture. They are members of at least two societies, and when their ethical codes conflict, these unfortunate people are faced with contradictory moral advice.

This isn't some philosopher's fiction. Such cases happen all the time. We could easily multiply examples, but this famous one from my home state should be enough to make the point.

Consider the facts of *Wisconsin v. Yoder,* a case resolved by the U.S. Supreme Court in 1972. Wisconsin then required regular school attendance of all children up to the age of sixteen. The sons of three Old Order Amish families had stopped going to school after the eighth grade, in obedience to their parents' beliefs that continued schooling would conflict with their religious values. The students were found guilty of violating the state law, but the verdict was overturned by the State's Supreme Court. Wisconsin then appealed to the U.S. Supreme Court, which sided with the Amish families.

In its decision, the Court's majority announced that:

> They [the Amish families] object to the high school, and higher education generally, because the values they teach are in marked variance with Amish values and the Amish way of life; they view secondary school education as an impermissible exposure of their children to a "worldly" influence in conflict with their beliefs. The high school tends to emphasize intellectual and scientific accomplishments, self-distinction, competitiveness, worldly success, and social life with other students. Amish society emphasizes informal learning-through-doing; a life of "goodness," rather than a life of intellect; wisdom, rather than technical knowledge; community welfare, rather than competition; and separation from, rather than integration with, contemporary worldly society.

The schoolchildren lived in (at least) two societies at once: their Amish community and the larger state of Wisconsin. If relativism is correct, than the morality of your actions depends entirely on whether they are allowed by the standards of the society they are performed in. But if you live in different societies, and their ethical codes clash, then your actions will be both moral and immoral. That is a contradiction.

We could solve this problem if we could figure out which society's code is more important. But relativism doesn't allow us to do that. By its lights no society's moral code is any better than another's. We might be tempted to let the children decide, and say that the social code that takes priority is the one that the children prefer. But this would undermine cultural relativism, since such a move would make the morality of their actions depend on personal choice. They would get to pick the code that is to govern their lives. That is subjectivism, not relativism.

Indeed, critics of cultural relativism often say that the doctrine eventually collapses into subjectivism. When your views and society's views clash, why think that society is always right? If morality is created by humans, then it is hard to justify the claim that moral wisdom always lies with the masses rather than with individuals. The majority may have the power to force the minority to do as it says. But might doesn't make right.

Subjectivists claim that in conflicts between personal and social commitments, the individual is always morally wiser. Cultural relativists take the opposite line. But perhaps things are not so cut and dried. Sometimes individuals have the upper hand; sometimes societies do. And sometimes perhaps, both individuals and societies are mistaken, even in their deepest commitments. If that is ever so, then we must look elsewhere for an account of morality's true nature.

# Psychological Egoism

JOEL FEINBERG

## A. THE THEORY

1. "Psychological egoism" is the name given to a theory widely held by ordinary people, and at one time almost universally accepted by political economists, philosophers, and psychologists, according to which all human actions when properly understood can be seen to be motivated by selfish desires. More precisely, psychological egoism is the doctrine that the only thing anyone is capable of desiring or pursuing ultimately (as an end in itself) is his own self-interest. No psychological egoist denies that people sometimes do desire things other than their own welfare—the happiness of other people, for example; but all psychological egoists insist that people are capable of desiring the happiness of others only when they take it to be a *means* to their own happiness. In short, purely altruistic and benevolent actions and desires do not exist: but people sometimes appear to be acting unselfishly and disinterestedly when they take the interests of others to be means to the promotion of their own self-interest.

2. This theory is called *psychological* egoism to indicate that it is not a theory about what *ought* to be the case, but rather about what, as a matter of fact, *is* the case. That is, the theory claims to be a description of psychological facts, not a prescription of ethical ideals. It asserts, however, not merely that all men do as a contingent matter of fact "put their own interests first," but also that they are capable of nothing else, human nature being what it is. Universal selfishness is not just an accident or a coincidence on this view; rather, it is an unavoidable consequence of psychological laws.

The theory is to be distinguished from another doctrine, so-called "ethical egoism," according to which all people *ought* to pursue their own well-being. This doctrine, being a prescription of what *ought* to be the case, makes no claim to be a psychological theory of human motives; hence the word "ethical" appears in its name to distinguish it from *psychological* egoism.

3. There are a number of types of motives and desires which might reasonably be called "egoistic" or "selfish," and corresponding to each of them is a possible version of psychological egoism. Perhaps the most common version of the theory is that apparently held by Jeremy Bentham.[1] According to this version, all persons have only one ultimate motive in all their voluntary behavior and that motive is a selfish one; more specifically, it is one particular kind of selfish motive—namely, a desire for one's own *pleasure*. According to this version of the theory, "the only kind of ultimate desire is the desire to get or to prolong pleasant experiences, and to avoid or to cut short unpleasant experiences for oneself."[2] This form

of psychological egoism is often given the cumbersome name—*psychological egoistic hedonism.*

### B. PRIMA FACIE REASONS IN SUPPORT OF THE THEORY

4. Psychological egoism has seemed plausible to many people for a variety of reasons, of which the following are typical:

a. "Every action of mine is prompted by motives or desires or impulses which are *my* motives and not somebody else's. This fact might be expressed by saying that whenever I act I am always pursuing my own ends or trying to satisfy my own desires. And from this we might pass on to—'I am always pursuing something for myself or seeking my own satisfaction.' Here is what seems like a proper description of a man acting selfishly, and if the description applies to all actions of all men, then it follows that all men in all their actions are selfish."[3]

b. It is a truism that when a person gets what he wants he characteristically feels pleasure. This has suggested to many people that what we really want in every case is our own pleasure, and that we pursue other things only as a means.

c. *Self-Deception.* Often we deceive ourselves into thinking that we desire something fine or noble when what we really want is to be thought well of by others or to be able to congratulate ourselves, or to be able to enjoy the pleasures of a good conscience. It is a well-known fact that people tend to conceal their true motives from themselves by camouflaging them with words like "virtue," "duty," etc. Since we are so often misled concerning both our own real motives and the real motives of others, is it not reasonable to suspect that we might *always* be deceived when we think motives disinterested and altruistic? Indeed, it is a simple matter to explain away all allegedly unselfish motives: "Once the conviction that selfishness is universal finds root in a person's mind, it is very likely to burgeon out in a thousand corroborating generalizations. It will be discovered that a friendly smile is really only an attempt to win an approving nod from a more or less gullible recording angel; that a charitable deed is, for its performer, only an opportunity to congratulate himself on the good fortune or the cleverness that enables him to be charitable; that a public benefaction is just plain good business advertising. It will emerge that gods are worshipped only because they indulge men's selfish fears, or tastes, or hopes; that the 'golden rule' is no more than an eminently sound success formula; that social and political codes are created and subscribed to only because they serve to restrain other men's egoism as much as one's own, morality being only a special sort of 'racket' or intrigue using weapons of persuasion in place of bombs and machine guns. Under this interpretation of human nature, the categories of commercialism replace those of disinterested service and the spirit of the horse trader broods over the face of the earth."[4]

d. *Moral Education.* Morality, good manners, decency, and other virtues must be teachable. Psychological egoists often notice that moral education and the inculcation of manners usually utilize what Bentham calls the "sanctions of pleasure and pain."[5] Children are made to acquire the civilizing virtues only by the method of enticing rewards and painful punishments. Much the same is true of the history of the race. People in general have been inclined to behave well only when it is made plain to them that there is "something in it for them." Is it not then highly probable that just such a mechanism of human motivation as Bentham describes must be presupposed by our methods of moral education?

### C. CRITIQUE OF PSYCHOLOGICAL EGOISM: CONFUSIONS IN THE ARGUMENTS

5. *Non-Empirical Character of the Arguments.* If the arguments of the psychological egoist consisted for the most part of carefully acquired empirical evidence (well-documented reports of controlled experiments, surveys, interviews, laboratory data, and so on), then the critical philosopher would have no business carping at them. After all, since

psychological egoism purports to be a scientific theory of human motives, it is the concern of the experimental psychologist, not the philosopher, to accept or reject it. But as a matter of fact, empirical evidence of the required sort is seldom presented in support of psychological egoism. Psychologists, on the whole, shy away from generalizations about human motives which are so sweeping and so vaguely formulated that they are virtually incapable of scientific testing. It is usually the "armchair scientist" who holds the theory of universal selfishness, and his usual arguments are either based simply on his "impressions" or else are largely of a non-empirical sort. The latter are often shot full of a very subtle kind of logical confusion, and this makes their criticism a matter of special interest to the analytic philosopher.

6. The psychological egoist's first argument (4a, above) is a good example of logical confusion. It begins with a truism—namely, that all of my motives and desires are *my* motives and desires and not someone else's. (Who would deny this?) But from this simple tautology nothing whatever concerning the nature of my motives or the objective of my desires can possibly follow. The fallacy of this argument consists in its violation of the general logical rule that analytic statements (tautologies) cannot entail synthetic (factual) ones.[6] That every voluntary act is prompted by the agent's own motives is a tautology; hence, it cannot be equivalent to "A person is always seeking something for himself" or "All of a person's motives are selfish," which are synthetic. What the egoist must prove is not merely:

> (i) Every voluntary action is prompted by a motive of the agent's own.

but rather:

> (ii) Every voluntary action is prompted by a motive of a quite particular kind, viz. a selfish one.

Statement (i) is obviously true, but it cannot all by itself give any logical support to statement (ii).

The source of the confusion in this argument is readily apparent. It is not the genesis of an action or the *origin* of its motives which makes it a "selfish" one, but rather the "purpose" of the act or the *objective* of its motives; *not where the motive comes from* (in voluntary actions it always comes from the agent) but *what it aims at* determines whether or not it is selfish. There is surely a valid distinction between voluntary behavior, in which the agent's action is motivated by purposes of his own, and *selfish* behavior in which the agent's motives are of one exclusive sort. The egoist's argument assimilates all voluntary action into the class of selfish action, by requiring, in effect, that an unselfish action be one which is not really motivated at all. In the words of Lucius Garvin, "to say that an act proceeds from our own. . . . desire is only to say that the act is our own. To demand that we should act on motives that are not our own is to ask us to make ourselves living contradictions in terms."[7]

7. But if argument 4a fails to prove its point, argument 4b does no better. From the fact that all our successful actions (those in which we get what we were after) are accompanied or followed by pleasure it does not follow, as the egoist claims, that the *objective* of every action is to get pleasure for oneself. To begin with, the premise of the argument is not, strictly speaking, even true. Fulfillment of desire (simply getting what one was after) is no guarantee of satisfaction (pleasant feelings of gratification in the mind of the agent). Sometimes when we get what we want we *also* get, as a kind of extra dividend, a warm, glowing feeling of contentment; but often, far too often, we get no dividend at all, or, even worse, the bitter taste of ashes. Indeed, it has been said that the characteristic psychological problem of our time is the *dissatisfaction* that attends the fulfillment of our very most powerful desires.

Even if we grant, however, for the sake of argument, that getting what one wants *usually* yields satisfaction, the egoist's conclusion does not follow. We can concede that we normally get pleasure (in the sense of satisfaction) when our desires are satisfied, *no matter what our desires are for*; but it does not follow from this roughly accurate generalization that the only thing we ever desire is our own satisfaction. Pleasure may well be the usual accompaniment of all actions in which the agent gets what he wants; but to infer from this that what the agent always wants is his own pleasure is like arguing, in William James's example,[8] that because an ocean liner constantly consumes coal on its trans-Atlantic passage that therefore the *purpose* of its voyage is to consume coal. The immediate inference from even constant accompaniment to purpose (or motive) is always a *non sequitur.*

Perhaps there is a sense of "satisfaction" (desire fulfillment) such that it is certainly and universally true that we get satisfaction whenever we get what we want. But satisfaction in this sense is simply the "coming into existence of that which is desired." Hence, to say that desire fulfillment always yields "satisfaction" in this sense is to say no more than that we always get what we want when we get what we want, which is to utter a tautology like "a rose is a rose." It can no more entail a synthetic truth in psychology (like the egoistic thesis) than "a rose is a rose" can entail significant information in botany.

8. *Disinterested Benevolence.* The fallacy in argument 4b then consists, as Garvin puts it, "in the supposition that the apparently unselfish desire to benefit others is transformed into a selfish one by the fact that we derive pleasure from carrying it out."[9] Not only is this argument fallacious; it also provides us with a suggestion of a counterargument to show that its conclusion (psychological egoistic hedonism) is false. Not only is the presence of pleasure (satisfaction) as a by-product of an action no proof that the action was selfish; in some special cases it provides rather conclusive proof that the action was *unselfish.* For in those special cases the fact that we get pleasure from a particular action *presupposes that we desired something else*—something other than our own pleasure—as an end in itself and not merely as a means to our own pleasant state of mind.

This way of turning the egoistic hedonist's argument back on him can be illustrated by taking a typical egoist argument, one attributed (perhaps apocryphally) to Abraham Lincoln, and then examining it closely:

> Mr. Lincoln once remarked to a fellow-passenger on an old-time mud-coach that all men were prompted by selfishness in doing good. His fellow-passenger was antagonizing this position when they were passing over a corduroy bridge that spanned a slough. As they crossed this bridge they espied an old razor-backed sow on the bank making a terrible noise because her pigs had got into the slough and were in danger of drowning. As the old coach began to climb the hill, Mr. Lincoln called out, "Driver, can't you stop just a moment?" Then Mr. Lincoln jumped out, ran back and lifted the little pigs out of the mud and water and placed them on the bank. When he returned, his companion remarked: "Now Abe, where does selfishness come in on this little episode?" "Why, bless your soul Ed, that was the very essence of selfishness. I should have had no peace of mind all day had I gone on and left that suffering old sow worrying over those pigs. I did it to get peace of mind, don't you see?"[10]

If Lincoln had cared not a whit for the welfare of the little pigs and their "suffering" mother, but only for his own "peace of mind," it would be difficult to explain how he could have derived pleasure from helping them. The very fact that he did feel satisfaction as a result of helping the pigs presupposes that he had a preexisting desire for something other than his own happiness. Then when *that* desire was satisfied, Lincoln of course derived pleasure. The *object* of Lincoln's desire was not pleasure; rather pleasure was the *consequence* of his preexisting desire for something else. If Lincoln had been wholly indifferent to the plight of the little pigs as he claimed, how could he possibly have derived any pleasure from helping them? He could not have achieved peace of mind from rescuing the pigs, had he not a prior concern—on which his peace of mind depended—for the welfare of the pigs for its own sake.

In general, the psychological hedonist analyzes apparent benevolence into a desire for "benevolent pleasure." No doubt the benevolent person does get pleasure from his benevolence, but in most cases, this is only because he has previously desired the good of some person, or animal, or mankind at large. Where there is no such desire, benevolent conduct is not generally found to give pleasure to the agent.

9. *Malevolence.* Difficult cases for the psychological egoist include not only instances of disinterested benevolence, but also cases of "disinterested malevolence." Indeed, malice and hatred are generally no more "selfish" than benevolence. Both are motives likely to cause an agent to sacrifice

his own interests—in the case of benevolence, in order to help someone else, in the case of malevolence in order to harm someone else. The selfish person is concerned ultimately only with his own pleasure, happiness, or power; the benevolent person is often equally concerned with the happiness of others; to the malevolent person, the *injury* of another is often an end in itself—an end to be pursued sometimes with no thought for his own interests. There is reason to think that people have as often sacrificed themselves to injure or kill others as to help or to save others, and with as much "heroism" in the one case as in the other. The unselfish nature of malevolence was first noticed by the Anglican Bishop and moral philosopher Joseph Butler (1692–1752), who regretted that people are no more selfish than they are.[11]

10. *Lack of Evidence for Universal Self-Deception.* The more cynical sort of psychological egoist who is impressed by the widespread phenomenon of self-deception (see 4c above) cannot be so quickly disposed of, for he has committed no *logical* mistakes. We can only argue that the acknowledged frequency of self-deception is insufficient evidence for his universal generalization. His argument is not fallacious, but inconclusive.

No one but the agent himself can ever be certain what conscious motives really prompted his action, and where motives are disreputable, even the agent may not admit to himself the true nature of his desires. Thus, for every apparent case of altruistic behavior, the psychological egoist can argue, with some plausibility, that the true motivation *might* be selfish, appearance to the contrary. Philanthropic acts are really motivated by the desire to receive gratitude; acts of self-sacrifice, when truly understood, are seen to be motivated by the desire to feel self-esteem; and so on. We must concede to the egoist that all apparent altruism might be deceptive in this way; but such a sweeping generalization requires considerable empirical evidence, and such evidence is not presently available.

11. *The "Paradox of Hedonism" and Its Consequences for Education.* The psychological egoistic Hedonist (e.g., Jeremy Bentham) has the simplest possible theory of human motivation. According to this variety of egoistic theory, all human motives without exception can be reduced to one—namely, the desire for one's own pleasure. But this theory, despite its attractive simplicity, or perhaps because of it, involves one immediately in a paradox. Astute observers of human affairs from the time of the ancient Greeks have often noticed that pleasure, happiness, and satisfaction are states of mind which stand in a very peculiar relation to desire. An exclusive desire for happiness is the surest way to prevent happiness from coming into being. Happiness has a way of "sneaking up" on persons when they are preoccupied with other things; but when persons deliberately and single-mindedly set off in pursuit of happiness, it vanishes utterly from sight and cannot be captured. This is the famous "paradox of hedonism": the single-minded pursuit of happiness is necessarily self-defeating, for *the way to get happiness is to forget it;* then perhaps it will come to you. If you aim exclusively at pleasure itself, with no concern for the things that bring pleasure, then pleasure will never come. To derive satisfaction, one must ordinarily first desire something other than satisfaction, and then find the means to get what one desires.

To feel the full force of the paradox of hedonism the reader should conduct an experiment in his imagination. Imagine a person (let's call him "Jones") who is, first of all, devoid of intellectual curiosity. He has no desire to acquire any kind of knowledge for its own sake, and thus is utterly indifferent to questions of science, mathematics, and philosophy. Imagine further that the beauties of nature leave Jones cold: he is unimpressed by the autumn foliage, the snow-capped mountains, and the rolling oceans. Long walks in the country on spring mornings and skiing forays in the winter are to him equally a bore. Moreover, let us suppose that Jones can find no appeal in art. Novels are dull, poetry a pain, paintings nonsense and music just noise. Suppose further that Jones has neither the participant's nor the spectator's passion for baseball, football, tennis, or any other sport. Swimming to him is a cruel aquatic form of calisthenics, the sun only a cause of sunburn. Dancing is coeducational idiocy, conversation a waste of time, the other sex an unappealing mystery. Politics is a fraud, religion mere superstition; and the misery of millions of underprivileged human beings is nothing to be concerned with or excited about. Suppose finally that Jones has no talent for any kind of handicraft, industry, or commerce, and that he does not regret that fact.

What then is Jones interested in? He must desire something. To be sure, he does. Jones has an overwhelming passion for, a complete preoccupation with, his own happiness. The one exclusive desire of his life is *to be happy.* It takes little imagination at this point to see that Jones's one desire is bound to be frustrated. People who—like Jones—most hotly pursue their own happiness are the least likely to find it. Happy people are those who successfully pursue such things as aesthetic or religious experience, self-expression, service to others, victory in competitions, knowledge, power, and so on. If none of these things in themselves and for their own sakes mean anything to a person, if they are valued at all then only as a means to one's own pleasant states of mind—then that pleasure can never come. The way to achieve happiness is to pursue something else.

Almost all people at one time or another in their lives feel pleasure. Some people (though perhaps not many) really do live lives which are on the whole happy. But if pleasure and happiness presuppose desires for something other than pleasure and happiness, then the existence of pleasure and happiness in the experience of some people proves that those people have strong desires for something other than their own happiness—egoistic hedonism to the contrary.

The implications of the "paradox of hedonism" for educational theory should be obvious. The parents least likely to raise a happy child are those who, even with the best intentions, train their child to seek happiness directly. How often have we heard parents say:

> I don't care if my child does not become an intellectual, or a sports star, or a great artist. I just want her to be a plain average sort of person. Happiness does not require great ambitions and great frustrations; it's not worth it to suffer and become neurotic for the sake of science, art, or do-goodism. I just want my child to be happy.

This can be a dangerous mistake, for it is the child (and the adult for that matter) without "outer-directed" interests who is the most likely to be unhappy. The pure egoist would be the most wretched of persons.

The educator might well beware of "life adjustment" as the conscious goal of the educational process for similar reasons. "Life adjustment" can be achieved only as a by-product of other pursuits. A whole curriculum of "life adjustment courses" unsupplemented by courses designed to incite an interest in things other than life adjustment would be tragically self-defeating.

As for moral education, it is probably true that punishment and reward are indispensable means of inculcation. But if the child comes to believe that the *sole* reasons for being moral are that he will escape the pain of punishment thereby and/or that he will gain the pleasure of a good reputation, then what is to prevent him from doing the immoral thing whenever he is sure that he will not be found out? While punishment and reward then are important tools for the moral educator, they obviously have their limitations. Beware of the man who does the moral thing only out of fear of pain or love of pleasure. He is not likely to be wholly trustworthy. Moral education is truly successful when it produces persons who are willing to do the right thing *simply because it is right,* and not merely because it is popular or safe.

12. *Pleasure as Sensation.* One final argument against psychological hedonism should suffice to put that form of the egoistic psychology to rest once and for all. The egoistic hedonist claims that all desires can be reduced to the single desire for one's own *pleasure.* Now the word "pleasure" is ambiguous. On the one hand, it can stand for a certain indefinable, but very familiar and specific kind of sensation, or more accurately, a property of sensations; and it is generally, if not exclusively, associated with the senses. For example, certain taste sensations such as sweetness, thermal sensations of the sort derived from a hot bath or the feel of the August sun while one lies on a sandy beach, erotic sensations, olfactory sensations (say) of the fragrance of flowers or perfume, and tactual and kinesthetic sensations from a good massage, are

all pleasant in this sense. Let us call this sense of "pleasure," which is the converse of "physical pain," $pleasure_1$.

On the other hand, the word "pleasure" is often used simply as a synonym for "satisfaction" (in the sense of gratification, not mere desire fulfillment.) In this sense, the existence of pleasure presupposes the prior existence of desire. Knowledge, religious experience, aesthetic expression, and other so-called "spiritual activities" often give pleasure in this sense. In fact, as we have seen, we tend to get pleasure in this sense whenever we get what we desire, no matter what we desire. The masochist even derives pleasure (in the sense of "satisfaction") from his own physically painful sensations. Let us call the sense of "pleasure" which means "satisfaction"—$pleasure_2$.

Now we can evaluate the psychological hedonist's claim that the sole human motive is a desire for one's own pleasure, bearing in mind (as he often does not) the ambiguity of the word "pleasure." First, let us take the hedonist to be saying that it is the desire for $pleasure_1$ (pleasant sensation) which is the sole ultimate desire of all people and the sole desire capable of providing a motive for action. Now I have little doubt that all (or most) people desire their own pleasure, *sometimes*. But even this familiar kind of desire occurs, I think, rather rarely. When I am very hungry, I often desire to eat, or, more specifically, to eat this piece of steak and these potatoes. Much less often do I desire to eat certain morsels simply for the sake of the pleasant gustatory sensations they might cause. I have, on the other hand, been motivated in the latter way when I have gone to especially exotic (and expensive) French or Chinese restaurants; but normally, pleasant gastronomic sensations are simply a happy consequence or by-product of my eating not the antecedently desired objective of my eating. There are, of course, others who take gustatory sensations far more seriously: the *gourmet* who eats only to savor the textures and flavors of fine foods, and the wine fancier who "collects" the exquisitely subtle and very pleasant tastes of rare old wines. Such people are truly absorbed in their taste sensations when they eat and drink, and there may even be some (rich) persons whose desire for such sensations is the sole motive for eating and drinking. It should take little argument, however, to convince the reader that such persons are extremely rare.

Similarly, I usually derive pleasure from taking a hot bath, and on occasion (though not very often) I even decide to bathe simply for the sake of such sensations. Even if this is equally true of everyone, however, it hardly provides grounds for inferring that *no one ever* bathes from *any* other motive. It should be empirically obvious that we sometimes bathe simply in order to get clean, or to please others, or simply from habit.

The view then that we are never after anything in our actions but our own pleasure—that all people are complete "gourmets" of one sort or another—is not only morally cynical; it is also contrary to common sense and everyday experience. In fact, the view that pleasant sensations play such an enormous role in human affairs is so patently false, on the available evidence, that we must conclude that the psychological hedonist has the other sense of "pleasure"—satisfaction—in mind when he states his thesis. If, on the other hand, he really does try to reduce the apparent multitude of human motives to the one desire for pleasant sensations, then the abundance of historical counterexamples justifies our rejection out of hand of his thesis. It surely seems incredible that the Christian martyrs were ardently pursuing their own pleasure when they marched off to face the lions, or that what the Russian soldiers at Stalingrad "really" wanted when they doused themselves with gasoline, ignited themselves, and then threw the flaming torches of their own bodies on German tanks, was simply the experience of pleasant physical sensations.

13. *Pleasure as Satisfaction.* Let us consider now the other interpretation of the hedonist's thesis, that according to which it is one's own $pleasure_2$ (satisfaction) and not merely $pleasure_1$ (pleasant sensation) which is the sole ultimate objective of all voluntary behavior. In one respect, the "satisfaction thesis" is even less plausible than the "physical sensation thesis"; for the latter at least is a genuine empirical hypothesis, testable in experience, though contrary to the facts which experience discloses. The former, however, is so confused that it cannot even be completely stated without paradox.

It is, so to speak, defeated in its own formulation. Any attempted explication of the theory that all men at all times desire only their own satisfaction leads to an *infinite regress* in the following way:

> "All men desire only satisfaction."
> "Satisfaction of what?"
> "Satisfaction of their desires."
> "Their desires for what?"
> "Their desires for satisfaction."
> "Satisfaction of what?"
> "Their desires."
> "For what?"
> "For satisfaction"—etc., *ad infinitum.*

In short, psychological hedonism interpreted in this way attributes to all people as their sole motive a wholly vacuous and infinitely self-defeating desire. The source of this absurdity is in the notion that satisfaction can, so to speak, feed on itself, and perform the miracle of perpetual self-regeneration in the absence of desires for anything other than itself.

To summarize the argument of sections 12 and 13: The word "pleasure" is ambiguous. $\text{Pleasure}_1$ means a certain indefinable characteristic of physical sensation. $\text{Pleasure}_2$ refers to the feeling of satisfaction that often comes when one gets what one desires whatever be the nature of that which one desires. Now, if the hedonist means $\text{pleasure}_1$ when he says that one's own pleasure is the ultimate objective of all of one's behavior, then his view is not supported by the facts. On the other hand, if he means $\text{pleasure}_2$, then his theory cannot even be clearly formulated, since it leads to the following infinite regress: "I desire only satisfaction of my desire for satisfaction of my desire for satisfaction . . . etc., *ad infinitum.*" I conclude then that psychological hedonism (the most common form of psychological egoism), however interpreted, is untenable.

## D. CRITIQUE OF PSYCHOLOGICAL EGOISM: UNCLEAR LOGICAL STATUS OF THE THEORY

14. There remain, however, other possible forms of the egoistic psychology. The egoist might admit that not all human motives can be reduced to the one ultimate desire for one's own pleasure, or happiness, and yet still maintain that our ultimate motives, whether they be desire for happiness (J. S. Mill), self-fulfillment (Aristotle), power (Hobbes), or whatever, are always *self-regarding* motives. He might still maintain that, given our common human nature, wholly disinterested action impelled by exclusively other-regarding motives is psychologically impossible, and that therefore there is a profoundly important sense in which it is true that, whether they be hedonists or not, *all people are selfish.*

Now it seems to me that this highly paradoxical claim cannot be finally evaluated until it is properly understood, and that it cannot be properly understood until one knows what the psychological egoist is willing to accept as evidence either for or against it. In short, there are two things that must be decided: (a) whether the theory is true or false and (b) whether its truth or falsity (its truth value) depends entirely on the *meanings* of the words in which it is expressed or whether it is made true or false by certain *facts,* in this case the facts of psychology.

15. *Analytic Statements.* Statements whose truth is determined solely by the meanings of the words in which they are expressed, and thus can be held immune from empirical evidence, are often called analytic statements or tautologies. The following are examples of tautologies:

(1) All bachelors are unmarried.
(2) All effects have causes.
(3) Either Providence is the capital of Rhode Island or it is not.

The truth of (1) is derived solely from the meaning of the word "bachelor," which is defined (in part) as "unmarried man." To find out whether (1) is true or false we need not conduct interviews, compile statistics, or perform experiments. All empirical evidence is superfluous and irrelevant; for if we know the meanings of "bachelor" and "unmarried," then we know not only that (1) is true, but that it is *necessarily* true—i.e., that it cannot possibly be false, that no future experiences or observations could possibly upset it, that to deny it would be to assert a logical contradiction. But notice that what a tautology gains in certainty ("necessary truth") it loses in descriptive content. Statement (1) imparts no information whatever about any matter of fact; it simply records our determination to use certain words in a certain way. As we say, "It is true by definition."

Similarly, (2) is (necessarily) true solely in virtue of the meanings of the words "cause" and "effect" and thus requires no further observations to confirm it. And of course, no possible observations could falsify it, since it asserts no matter of fact. And finally, statement (3) is (necessarily) true solely in virtue of the meaning of the English expression "either . . . or." Such terms as "either . . . or," "If . . . then," "and," and "not" are called by logicians "logical constants." The *definitions* of logical constants are made explicit in the so-called "laws of thought"—the law of contradiction, the law of the excluded middle, and the law of identity. These "laws" are not laws in the same sense as are (say) the laws of physics. Rather, they are merely consequences of the *definitions* of logical constants, and as such, though they are necessarily true, they impart no information about the world. "Either Providence is the capital of Rhode Island or it is not" tells us nothing about geography; and "Either it is now raining or else it is not" tells us nothing about the weather. You don't have to look at a map or look out the window to know that they are true. Rather, they are known to be true *a priori* (independently of experience); and, like all (or many)[12] *a priori* statements, they are *vacuous*. i.e., devoid of informative content.

The denial of an analytic statement is called a contradiction. The following are typical examples of contradictions: "Some bachelors are married." "Some causes have no effects," "Providence both is and is not the capital of Rhode Island." As in the case of tautologies, the truth value of contradictions (their falsehood) is logically necessary, not contingent on any facts of experience, and uninformative. Their falsity is derived from the meanings (definitions) of the words in which they are expressed.

16. *Synthetic Statements.* On the other hand, statements whose truth or falsity is derived not from the meanings of words but rather from the facts of experience (observations) are called *synthetic.*[13] Prior to experience, there can be no good reason to think either that they are true or that they are false. That is to say, their truth value is *contingent;* and they can be confirmed or disconfirmed only by *empirical* evidence,[14] i.e., controlled observations of the world. Unlike analytic statements, they do impart information about matters of fact. Obviously, "It is raining in Newport now," if true, is more informative than "Either it is raining in Newport now or it is not," even though the former *could* be false, while the latter is necessarily true. I take the following to be examples of synthetic (contingent) statements:

(1') All bachelors are neurotic.

(2') All events have causes.

(3') Providence is the capital of Rhode Island.

(3") Newport is the capital of Rhode Island.

Statement (3') is true; (3") is false; and (1') is a matter for a psychologist (not for a philosopher) to decide; and the psychologist himself can only decide *empirically,* i.e., by making many observations. The status of (2') is very difficult and its truth value is a matter of great controversy. That is because its truth or falsity depends on *all* the facts ("all events"); and, needless to say, not all of the evidence is in.

17. *Empirical Hypotheses.* Perhaps the most interesting subclass of synthetic statements are those generalizations of experience of the sort characteristically made by scientists; e.g., "All released objects heavier than air fall," "All swans are white," "All men have Oedipus complexes." I shall call such statements "empirical hypotheses" to indicate that their function is to sum up past experience and enable us successfully to predict or anticipate future experience.[15] They are never logically certain, since it is always at least conceivable that future experience will disconfirm them. For example, zoologists once believed that all swans are white, until black swans were discovered in Australia. The most important characteristic of empirical hypotheses for our present purposes is their relation to evidence. A person can be said to understand an empirical hypothesis only if he knows how to recognize evidence against it. *If a person asserts or believes*

*a general statement in such a way that he cannot conceive of any possible experience which he would count as evidence against it, them he cannot be said to be asserting or believing an empirical hypothesis.* We can refer to this important characteristic of empirical hypotheses as *falsifiability in principle.*

Some statements only appear to be empirical hypotheses but are in fact disguised tautologies reflecting the speaker's determination to use words in certain (often eccentric) ways. For example, a zoologist might refuse to allow the existence of "Australian swans" to count as evidence against the generalization that all swans are white, on the grounds that the black Australian swans are not "really" swans at all. This would indicate that he is holding *whiteness* to be part of the definition of "swan," and that therefore, the statement "All swans are white" is, for him, "true by definition"—and thus just as immune from counterevidence as the statement "All spinsters are unmarried." Similarly, most of us would refuse to allow any possible experience to count as evidence against "2 + 2 = 4." or "Either unicorns exist or they do not," indicating that the propositions of arithmetic and logic are not empirical hypotheses.

18. *Ordinary Language and Equivocation.* Philosophers, even more than ordinary people, are prone to make startling and paradoxical claims that take the form of universal generalizations and hence resemble empirical hypotheses. For example, "All things are mental (there are no physical objects)," "All things are good (there is no evil)," "All voluntary behavior is selfish," etc. Let us confine our attention for the moment to the latter which is a rough statement of psychological egoism. At first sight, the statement "All voluntary behavior is selfish" seems obviously false. One might reply to the psychological egoist in some such manner as this:

> I *know* some behavior, at least, is unselfish, because I saw my Aunt Emma yesterday give her last cent to a beggar. Now she will have to go a whole week with nothing to eat. Surely, *that* was not selfish of her.

Nevertheless, the psychological egoist is likely not to be convinced, and insist that, in this case, if we knew enough about Aunt Emma, we would learn that her primary motive in helping the beggar was to promote her own happiness or assuage her own conscience, or increase her own selfesteem, etc. We might then present the egoist with even more difficult cases for his theory—saints, martyrs, military heroes, patriots, and others who have sacrificed themselves for a cause. If psychological egoists nevertheless refuse to accept any of these as examples of unselfish behavior, then we have a right to be puzzled about what they are saying. Until we know what they would count as *unselfish* behavior, we can't very well know what they mean when they say that all voluntary behavior is *selfish.* And at this point we may suspect that they are holding their theory in a "privileged position"—that of immunity to evidence, that they would allow no *conceivable* behavior to count as evidence against it. What they say then, if true, must be true in virtue of the way they define—or redefine—the word "selfish." And in that case, it cannot be an empirical hypothesis.

If what the psychological egoist says is "true by redefinition," then I can "agree" with him and say "It is true that in *your* sense of the word 'selfish' my Aunt Emma's behavior was selfish; but in the ordinary sense of 'selfish,' which implies blameworthiness, she surely was not selfish." There is no point of course in arguing about a mere word. The important thing is not what particular words a person uses, but rather whether what he wishes to say in those words is true. Departures from ordinary language can often be justified by their utility for certain purposes; but they are dangerous when they invite equivocation. The psychological egoist may be saying something which is true when he says that Emma is selfish in *his* sense, but if he doesn't realize that his sense of "selfish" differs from the ordinary one, he may be tempted to infer that Emma is selfish in the ordinary sense which implies blameworthiness; and this of course would be unfair and illegitimate. It is indeed an extraordinary extension of the meaning of the word "self-indulgent" (as C. G. Chesterton remarks somewhere) which allows a philosopher to say that a man is self-indulgent when he wants to be burned at the stake.

19. *The Fallacy of the Suppressed Correlative.* Certain words in the English language operate in pairs—e.g., "selfish-unselfish," "good-bad," "large-small," "mental-physical." To assert that a thing has one of

the above characteristics is to *contrast* it with the opposite in the pair. To know the meaning of one term in the pair, we must know the meaning of the correlative term with which it is contrasted. If we could not conceive of what it would be like for a thing to be bad, for example, then we could not possibly understand what is being said of a thing when it is called "good." Similarly, unless we had a notion of what it would be like for action to be *unselfish.* we could hardly understand the sentence "So-and-so acted selfishly"; for we would have nothing to contrast "selfishly" with. The so-called "fallacy of the suppressed correlative"[16] is committed by a person who consciously or unconsciously redefines one of the terms in a contrasting pair in such a way that its new meaning incorporates the sense of its correlative.

*Webster's Collegiate Dictionary* defines "selfish" (in part) as "regarding one's own comfort, advantage, etc. in disregard of, or at the expense of that of others." In this ordinary and proper sense of "selfish," Aunt Emma's action in giving her last cent to the beggar certainly was *not* selfish. Emma *disregarded* her *own* comfort (it is not "comfortable" to go a week without eating) and advantage (there is no "advantage" in malnutrition) *for the sake of* (not "at the expense of") another. Similarly, the martyr marching off to the stake is foregoing (not indulging) his "comfort" and indeed his very life for the sake of (not at the expense of) a cause. If Emma and the martyr then are "selfish," they must be so in a strange new sense of the word.

A careful examination of the egoist's arguments (see especially 4a above) reveals what new sense he gives to the word "selfish." He redefines the word so that it means (roughly) "motivated," or perhaps "intentional." "After all," says the egoist, "Aunt Emma had some *purpose* in giving the beggar all her money, and this purpose (desire, intention, motive, aim) was *her* purpose and no one else's. She was out to further some aim of her own, wasn't she? Therefore, she was pursuing her own ends (acting from her own motives); she was after something *for herself* in so acting, and that's what I mean by calling her action selfish. Moreover, all intentional action—action done 'on purpose,' deliberately from the agent's own motives—is selfish in the same sense." We can see now, from this reply, that since the egoist apparently means by "selfish" simply "motivated," when he says that all motivated action is selfish *he is not asserting a synthetic empirical hypothesis about human motives; rather, his statement is a tautology roughly equivalent to "all motivated actions are motivated."* And if that is the case, then what he says is true enough; but, like all tautologies, it is empty, uninteresting, and trivial.

Moreover, in redefining "selfish" in this way, the psychological egoist has committed the fallacy of the suppressed correlative. For what can we now contrast "selfish voluntary action" with? Not only are there no *actual* cases of unselfish voluntary actions on the new definition; there are not even any *theoretically possible* or *conceivable* cases of unselfish voluntary actions. And if we cannot even conceive of what an unselfish voluntary action would be like, how can we give any sense to the expression "selfish voluntary action"? The egoist, so to speak, has so blown up the sense of "selfish" that, like inflated currency, it will no longer buy anything.

20. *Psychological Egoism as a Linguistic Proposal.* There is still one way out for the egoist. He might admit that his theory is not really a psychological hypothesis about human nature designed to account for the facts and enable us to predict or anticipate future events. He may even willingly concede that his theory is really a disguised redefinition of a word. Still, he might argue, he has made no claim to be giving an accurate description of actual linguistic usage. Rather, he is making a proposal to *revise* our usage in the interest of economy and convenience, just as the biologists once proposed that we change the ordinary meaning of "insect" in such a way that spiders are no longer called insects, and the ordinary meaning of "fish" so that whales and seals are no longer called fish.

What are we to say to this suggestion? First of all, stipulative definitions (proposals to revise usage) are never true or false. They are simply useful or not useful. Would it be useful to redefine "selfish" in the way the egoist recommends? It is difficult to see what would be gained thereby. The egoist has noticed some respects in which actions normally called "selfish" and actions normally called "unselfish" are alike, namely they are both motivated and they both can give satisfaction—either in prospect or in retrospect—to the agent. Because of these likenesses, the egoist feels justified in attaching the label "selfish" to *all* actions. Thus one word—"selfish"—must for him do the work of two words ("selfish" and "unselfish" in their old meanings); and, as a result, a very real distinction, that between actions for the sake of others and actions at the expense of others, can no longer be expressed in the language. Because the egoist has noticed some respects in which two types of actions are alike, he wishes to make it impossible to describe the respects in which they differ. It is difficult to see any utility in this state of affairs.

But suppose we adopt the egoist's "proposal" nevertheless. Now we would have to say that all actions are selfish; but, in addition, we would want to say that there are two different kinds of selfish actions, those which regard the interests of others and those which disregard the interests of others, and, furthermore, that only the latter are blameworthy. After a time our ear would adjust to the new uses of the word "selfish," and we would find nothing at all strange in such statements as "Some selfish actions are morally praiseworthy." After a while, we might even invent two new words, perhaps "selfitic" and "unselfitic," to distinguish the two important classes of "selfish" actions. Then we would be right back where we started, with new linguistic tools ("selfish" for "motivated," "selfitic" for "selfish," and "unselfitic" for "unselfish") to do the same old necessary jobs. That is, until some new egoistic philosopher arose to announce with an air of discovery that "All selfish behavior is really selfitic—there are no truly unselfitic selfish actions." Then, God help us!

## NOTES

1. See his *Introduction to the Principles of Morals and Legislation* (1789), Chap. I, first paragraph: "Nature has placed mankind under the governance of two sovereign masters, *pain* and *pleasure*. It is for them alone to point out what we ought to do, as well as to determine what we shall do. . . . They govern us in all we do, in all we say, in all we think: every effort we can make to throw off our subjection will serve but to demonstrate and confirm it."
2. C. D. Broad, *Ethics and the History of Philosophy* (New York: The Humanities Press, 1952), Essay 10—"Egoism as a Theory of Human Motives," p. 218. This essay is highly recommended.
3. Austin Duncan-Jones, *Butler's Moral Philosophy* (London; Penguin Books, 1952), p. 96. Duncan-Jones goes on to reject this argument. See p. 512f.
4. Lucius Garvin, *A Modem Introduction to Ethics* (Boston: Houghton Mifflin, 1953), p. 37. Quoted here by permission of the author and publisher.
5. Ibid., Chap. III.
6. See Part D, 15 and 16, below.
7. Garvin, *A Modern Introduction*, p. 39.
8. *The Principles of Psychology* (New York: Henry Holt, 1890), Vol. II, p. 558.
9. Ibid., p. 39.
10. Quoted from the *Springfield* (Illinois) *Monitor*, by F. C. Sharp in his *Ethics* (New York: Appleton-Century, 1928), p. 75.
11. See his *Fifteen Sermons on Human Nature Preached at the Rolls Chapel* (1726), especially the first and eleventh.
12. Whether or not there are some *a priori* statements that are not merely analytic, and hence *not* vacuous, is still a highly controversial question among philosophers.
13. Some philosophers (those called "rationalists" believe that there are some synthetic statements whose truth can be known *a priori* (see footnote 12). If they are right, then the statement above is not entirely accurate.
14. Again, subject to the qualification in footnotes 12 and 13.
15. The three examples given above all have the generic character there indicated, but they also differ from one another in various other ways, some of which are quite important. For our present purposes however, we can ignore the ways in which, they differ from one another and concentrate on their common character as generalizations of experience ("inductive generalizations"). As such they are sharply contrasted with such a generalization as "All puppies are young dogs," which is analytic.
16. The phrase was coined by J. Lowenberg. See his article "What Is Empirical?" in the *Journal of Philosophy*, May 1940.

CHAPTER 5

# Ethical Egoism

The achievement of his own happiness is man's highest moral purpose.

AYN RAND, *THE VIRTUE OF SELFISHNESS* (1961)

## 5.1. Is There a Duty to Help Starving People?

Each year millions of people die of malnutrition and related health problems. A common pattern among children in poor countries is death from dehydration caused by diarrhea brought on by malnutrition. Researchers estimate that nearly 5000 children die in this way every day. That comes to 1.8 million children every year. If we add in those children who die from other preventable causes, the number goes over 10 million. Even if this estimate is too high, the number who die is staggering.

For those of us in the affluent countries, this poses an acute problem. We spend money on ourselves, not only for the necessities of life but for countless luxuries—for nice cars, expensive clothes, CD players, movie tickets, and so on. In America, even people with modest incomes enjoy such things. The problem is that we could forgo our luxuries and give the money for famine relief instead. The fact that we don't suggests that we regard our luxuries as more important than their lives.

Why do we allow people to starve when we could save them? Few of us actually believe our luxuries are that important. Most of us, if asked the question directly, would probably be a bit embarrassed, and we would say that we probably should do more to help. The explanation of why we do not is, at least in part, that we hardly ever think about the problem. Living our own comfortable lives, we are insulated from it. The starving people are dying at some distance from us; we do not see them





and we can avoid even thinking of them. When we do think of them, it is only abstractly, as statistics. Unfortunately for the hungry, statistics do not have much power to move us.

We respond differently when there is a "crisis," as when a tsunami devastated Indonesia in 2004 or when Hurricane Katrina flooded New Orleans in 2005. Then it is front-page news and relief efforts are mobilized. But when the needy are scattered, the situation does not seem so pressing. The 1.8 million children are unfortunate that they are not all gathered in, say, Chicago.

But leaving aside the question of why we behave as we do, what is our duty? What *should* we do? We might think of this as the "commonsense" view of the matter: Morality requires that we balance our own interests against the interests of others. It is understandable, of course, that we look out for ourselves, and no one can be faulted for attending to their own basic needs. But at the same time, the needs of others are important, and when we can help others—especially at little cost to ourselves—we should do so. So, if you have an extra 10 dollars, and giving it to a famine relief agency would help to save the life of a child, then commonsense morality would say that you should do so.

This way of thinking involves a general assumption about our moral duties: that we have moral duties to other people, and not merely duties that we create, such as by making a promise or incurring a debt. We have "natural" duties to others simply because *they are people who could be helped or harmed by what we do.* If a certain action would benefit (or harm) other people, then that is a reason why we should (or should not) perform that action. The commonsense assumption is that other people's interests *count,* for their own sakes, from a moral point of view.

But one person's common sense is another person's naïve platitude. Some thinkers have maintained that, in fact, we have no duties to other people. Ethical Egoism is the idea that each person ought to pursue his or her own self-interest exclusively. On this theory, our only duty is to do what is best for ourselves.

Ethical Egoism is a challenging theory. It contradicts some of our deepest moral beliefs—beliefs held by most of us, at any rate—and it is not easy to refute. We will examine the most important arguments for and against it. If it turns out to be true, then that is immensely important. But even if it turns out to be false, we can still learn from it, for we may gain some insight into the reasons why we *do* have obligations to other people.

## 5.2. Psychological Egoism

Ethical Egoism must be carefully distinguished from a different theory known as Psychological Egoism. Ethical Egoism claims that each person *ought* to pursue his or her own self-interest exclusively. Psychological Egoism, by contrast, asserts that each person *does in fact* pursue his or her own self-interest alone. Thus, these two theories are very different. It is one thing to say that people are self-interested and that our neighbors therefore will not give to charity. It is quite another to say that people *ought* to be self-interested and so our neighbors *ought* not to give to charity. Psychological Egoism makes a claim about human nature, or about the way things are; Ethical Egoism makes a claim about morality, or about the way things should be.

Psychological Egoism is not a theory of ethics; rather, it is a theory of human psychology. Nevertheless, moral philosophers have always been worried about it. If Psychological Egoism were true, it would seem to have devastating consequences for morality. If people are moved only by their own welfare, isn't it pointless to talk about what we "ought" to do? If we are just self-interested beings, then aren't we going to behave selfishly no matter what our well-meaning but naïve moral theories tell us to do? Before returning to the topic of Ethical Egoism, let us first assess Psychological Egoism and see if morality has anything to worry about.

**Is Altruism Possible?** Raoul Wallenberg, a Swedish businessman who could have stayed safely at home, spent the closing months of World War II in Budapest, Hungary. Wallenberg had volunteered to be sent there as part of Sweden's diplomatic mission after he heard reports about Hitler's "final solution to the Jewish problem." Once there, he successfully pressured the Hungarian government to stop the deportations to the concentration camps. When the Hungarian government was replaced by a Nazi puppet regime, and the deportations resumed, Wallenberg issued "Swedish Protective Passes" to thousands of Jews, insisting that they all had connections with Sweden and were under the protection of his government. He helped many people find places to hide. When they were rounded up, Wallenberg would stand between them and the Nazis, telling the Germans that they would have to shoot him first. At the very end of the war,



when everything was chaos and other diplomats were fleeing, Wallenberg stayed behind. He is credited with saving as many as 100,000 lives. When the war was over, he disappeared, and for a long time no one knew what had happened to him. Now it is believed that he was killed, not by the Germans, but by Soviet occupation forces.

Wallenberg's story is more dramatic than most, but it is not unique. The Israeli government recognizes over 20,000 Gentiles who risked their lives trying to save Jews from being murdered in the Holocaust. And though few of us have saved lives, acts of altruism appear to be common. People do favors for one another. They build homeless shelters. They volunteer in hospitals. They read to the blind. They give blood. Many people donate money to worthy causes when they could keep that money for themselves. In some cases, the amount given is extraordinary. David Allsop, an Australian civil servant, donates half of his income to environmental causes. Zell Kravinsky, an American real estate investor, gave his entire $45-million fortune to charity. And then, for good measure, Kravinsky donated one of his kidneys to a complete stranger.

These are remarkable deeds, but should they be taken at face value? According to Psychological Egoism, we may believe ourselves to be noble and self-sacrificing, but that is only an illusion. In reality, we care only for ourselves. Could this theory possibly be true? Why have people believed it, in the face of so much evidence to the contrary? Two arguments have often been advanced in favor of Psychological Egoism.

**The Argument That We Always Do What We Most Want to Do.** If we describe one person's action as altruistic and another person's action as self-interested, we are overlooking the fact that in both cases *the person is merely doing what he or she most wants to do.* If Raoul Wallenberg chose to go to Hungary, and no one was coercing him, that only shows that he wanted to go there more than he wanted to remain in Sweden—and why should he be praised for altruism when he was only doing what he wanted to do? His action was dictated by his own desires, his own sense of what he wanted. Thus, he was moved by his own self-interest. And since exactly the same may be said about any alleged act of kindness, we can conclude that Psychological Egoism must be true.

This argument, however, is flawed. There are things that we do, not because we want to, but because we feel that we *ought* to. For example, someone may do something because she has promised to do it, and thus feels obligated, even though she does not want to do it. It is sometimes suggested that in such cases we carry out the action because, after all, we most want to keep our promises. But that is not true. In such cases, it is simply false to say that what I most want is to keep my promise. My strongest desire is to break my promise, but I keep it anyway. For all we know, Wallenberg was in this position: Perhaps he wanted to stay in Sweden, but he felt that he had to go to Budapest. In any case, the fact that he chose to go does not imply that he most wanted to do so.

The argument has a second flaw. Suppose we concede that we always act on our strongest desires. Even if this were granted, it would not follow that Wallenberg was acting out of self-interest. For if he wanted to help other people, even at great risk to himself, that is precisely what makes his action a refutation of Psychological Egoism. The mere fact that you act on your own desires does not mean that you are looking out for yourself; rather, it depends on *what it is* that you desire. If you care only about your own welfare and give no thought to others, then you are acting out of self-interest; but if you want other people to be happy, and you act on that desire, then you are not. To put the point another way: In assessing whether an action is self-interested, the issue is not *whether* the action is based on a desire; the issue is *what kind of desire it is based on.* If what you want is to help someone else, then your motive is altruistic, not self-interested.

Therefore, this argument goes wrong in just about every way that an argument can go wrong: The premise is not true, and even if it were, the conclusion would not follow from it.

**The Argument That We Do What Makes Us Feel Good.** The second argument for Psychological Egoism appeals to the fact that so-called altruistic actions produce a sense of self-satisfaction in the person who performs them. Acting "unselfishly" makes people feel good about themselves, and that is the real point of it.

According to a 19th-century newspaper, this argument was advanced by Abraham Lincoln. The Springfield, Illinois, *Monitor* reported:



> Mr. Lincoln once remarked to a fellow-passenger on an old-time mud coach that all men were prompted by selfishness in doing good. His fellow-passenger was antagonizing this position when they were passing over a corduroy bridge that spanned a slough. As they crossed this bridge they espied an old razor-backed sow on the bank making a terrible noise because her pigs had got into the slough and were in danger of drowning. As the old coach began to climb the hill, Mr. Lincoln called out, "Driver, can't you stop just a moment?" Then Mr. Lincoln jumped out, ran back, and lifted the little pigs out of the mud and water and placed them on the bank. When he returned, his companion remarked: "Now, Abe, where does selfishness come in on this little episode?" "Why, bless your soul, Ed, that was the very essence of selfishness. I should have had no peace of mind all day had I gone on and left that suffering old sow worrying over those pigs. I did it to get peace of mind, don't you see?"

In this story, Honest Abe employs a time-honored tactic of Psychological Egoism: *the strategy of reinterpreting motives.* Everyone knows that people sometimes seem to act altruistically; but if we look deeper, we may find that something else is going on. And usually it is not hard to discover that the "unselfish" behavior is actually connected with some benefit for the person who does it. Thus, Lincoln talks about the peace of mind he got from rescuing the pigs.

Other examples of alleged altruism can also be reinterpreted. According to some of Raoul Wallenberg's friends, before traveling to Hungary, he was depressed and unhappy that his life didn't seem to be amounting to much. So he undertook deeds that would make him a heroic figure. His quest for a more significant life was spectacularly successful—here we are, more than a half-century after his death, talking about him. Mother Teresa, the nun who spent her life working among the poor in Calcutta, is often cited as a perfect example of altruism—but, of course, she believed that she would be handsomely rewarded in heaven. David Allsop, who gives half of his income to environmental causes, "had previously worked as a campaigner himself, and said he found it deeply satisfying now to be able to provide the financial support for others to campaign." And as for Zell Kravinsky, who gave away both his fortune and a kidney, his parents never gave him much praise, so he was always trying to do things that even they couldn't deny were admirable. Kravinsky himself said that, as he began to give away his money, he came to think of a donation as "a treat to myself. I really thought of it as something pleasurable."

Despite all this, Lincoln's argument is badly flawed. It may be true that one of Lincoln's motives in saving the pigs was to preserve his own peace of mind. *But the fact that Lincoln had a self-interested motive doesn't mean that he didn't have benevolent motives as well.* In fact, Lincoln's desire to help the pigs may have been even greater than his desire to preserve his own peace of mind. And if this isn't true in Lincoln's case, it will be true in other cases: If I see a child drowning, my desire to help that child will usually be greater than my desire to avoid a guilty conscience. Cases like these are counterexamples to Psychological Egoism.

In many instances of altruism, we don't even have self-interested motives. If I quickly decide to jump into the water to save the child, I may not have time to think about myself at all—I may be thinking only of the child. There is a general lesson to be learned here, one having to do with the nature of desire and its objects. We desire all sorts of things—money, a new car, video games, a spouse, and so on—and because we desire these things, we may derive satisfaction from getting them. But the object of our desire is not the feeling of satisfaction—that is not what we are after. What we are after is simply the money, the car, the game, or the marriage. It is the same with helping others. Our desire to help others often comes first; the good feelings we may get are merely a by-product.

**Conclusion about Psychological Egoism.** If Psychological Egoism is so implausible, why have many intelligent people been attracted to it? Part of the attraction is the theory's hardheaded, deflationary attitude toward human pretensions. Psychological Egoism provides a theoretical rebuttal to human vanity. Also, people are drawn to it because it is beautifully simple. It would be pleasing to find a single formula that explains all human behavior. And since self-regard is a tremendously important factor in motivation, it is natural to try to use it to account for all human action. However, every attempt to do so seems strained and implausible; Psychological Egoism is not a credible theory.



Thus, we may conclude that morality has nothing to fear from Psychological Egoism. Since we *can* be moved by regard for others, it is not pointless to talk about whether we *should* care about our neighbors. Moral theorizing need not be a naïve endeavor, based on an unrealistic view of human nature.

## 5.3. Three Arguments for Ethical Egoism

Ethical Egoism, again, is the idea that each person ought to pursue his or her own self-interest exclusively. Before we talk about the arguments that have been made in its favor, we should understand exactly what this theory says and what it does not say. In the first place, Ethical Egoism does not say that one should promote one's own interests *in addition to* the interests of others. That would be an ordinary, commonsense view. Ethical Egoism is the radical idea that one's *only* duty is to promote one's own interests. According to Ethical Egoism, there is only one ultimate principle of conduct, that of self-interest, and this principle sums up all of one's obligations.

However, Ethical Egoism does not say that you should *avoid* actions that help others. It may happen in many instances that your interests coincide with the interests of others, so that in helping yourself you will be helping them. Or it may happen that aiding others is an effective means for creating some benefit for yourself. Ethical Egoism does not forbid such actions; in fact, it may recommend them. The theory insists only that in such cases the benefit to others is not what makes the act right. Rather, what makes the act right is the fact that it is to one's own advantage.

Finally, Ethical Egoism does not imply that in pursuing one's interests one ought always to do what one wants to do, or what gives one the most pleasure in the short run. Someone may want to smoke cigarettes, or bet all his money at the racetrack, or set up a meth lab in his basement. Ethical Egoism would frown on all this, regardless of the momentary pleasure it brings. Ethical Egoism says that a person ought to do what really is in his or her own best interests, over the long run. It endorses selfishness, not foolishness.

What arguments can be advanced to support this doctrine? Unfortunately, the theory is asserted more often than it is argued for—many of its supporters apparently think its truth is self-evident, so that arguments are not needed. When it is argued for, three lines of reasoning are most commonly used.

**The Argument That Altruism Is Self-Defeating.** The first argument has several variations, each suggesting the same general point:

- Each of us is intimately familiar with our own individual wants and needs. Moreover, each of us is uniquely placed to pursue those wants and needs effectively. At the same time, we know the desires and needs of other people only imperfectly, and we are not well situated to pursue them. Therefore, it is reasonable to believe that if we set out to be "our brother's keeper," we will often bungle the job and end up doing more harm than good.
- At the same time, the policy of "looking out for others" is an offensive intrusion into other people's privacy; it is essentially a policy of minding other people's business.
- Making other people the object of one's "charity" is degrading to them; it robs them of their dignity and self-respect. The offer of charity says, in effect, that they are not competent to care for themselves; and the statement is self-fulfilling. They cease to be self-reliant and become passively dependent on others. That is why the recipients of "charity" are so often resentful rather than appreciative.

Thus, the policy of "looking out for others" is said to be self-defeating. If we want to do what is best for people, we should not adopt so-called altruistic policies. On the contrary, if each person looks after his or her own interests, it is more likely that everyone will be better off. As Alexander Pope put it:

> Thus God and nature link'd the general frame
> And bade self-love and social be the same.

It is possible to object to this argument on a number of grounds. Of course, no one favors bungling, butting in, or depriving people of their self-respect. But is that really what we are doing when we feed hungry children? Is the starving child in Niger really harmed when we "intrude" into "her business" by supplying food? It hardly seems likely. Yet we can set this point aside, for considered as an argument for Ethical Egoism, this way of thinking has an even more serious defect.

The trouble is that it isn't really an argument for Ethical Egoism at all. The argument concludes that we should adopt certain policies of behavior, and on the surface, they appear to be egoistic policies. However, the *reason* we should adopt those policies is decidedly unegoistic. It is said that we should adopt those policies because doing so will promote the betterment of society—but according to Ethical Egoism, that is not something we should be concerned about. Spelled out fully, with everything laid on the table, the argument says:

**(1)** We ought to do whatever will best promote everyone's interests.

**(2)** The best way to promote everyone's interests is for each of us to adopt the policy of pursuing our own interests exclusively.

**(3)** Therefore, each of us should adopt the policy of pursuing our own interests exclusively.

If we accept this reasoning, then we are not ethical egoists. Even though we might end up behaving like egoists, our ultimate principle is one of beneficence—we are doing what we think will help everyone, not merely what we think will benefit ourselves. Rather than being egoists, we turn out to be altruists with a peculiar view of what in fact promotes the general welfare.

**Ayn Rand's Argument.** Ayn Rand is not much read by philosophers, largely because the leading ideas associated with her name—that capitalism is a morally superior economic system and that morality demands absolute respect for the rights of individuals—are developed more rigorously by other writers. Nevertheless, she was a charismatic figure who attracted a devoted following during her lifetime, and today, more than 20 years after her death, the Ayn Rand industry is still going strong. Among 20th-century writers, the idea of Ethical Egoism is probably more closely associated with her than with anyone else.

Ayn Rand regarded the "ethics of altruism" as a totally destructive idea, both in society as a whole and in the lives of individuals taken in by it. Altruism, to her way of thinking, leads to a denial of the value of the individual. It says to a person: Your life is merely something that may be sacrificed. "If a man accepts the ethics of altruism," she writes, "his first concern is not how to live his life, but how to sacrifice it." Those who promote the ethics of altruism are beneath contempt—they are parasites who, rather than working to build and sustain their own lives, leech off those who do. Rand continues:

> Parasites, moochers, looters, brutes and thugs can be of no value to a human being—nor can he gain any benefit from living in a society geared to *their* needs, demands and protections, a society that treats him as a sacrificial animal and penalizes him for his virtues in order to reward *them* for their vices, which means: a society based on the ethics of altruism.

By "sacrificing one's life" Rand does not mean anything so dramatic as dying. A person's life consists, in part, of projects undertaken and goods earned and created. Thus, to demand that a person abandon his projects or give up his goods is an effort to "sacrifice his life."

Rand also suggests that there is a metaphysical basis for egoistic ethics. Somehow, it is the only ethic that takes seriously the *reality* of the individual person. She bemoans "the enormity of the extent to which altruism erodes men's capacity to grasp . . . the value of an individual life; it reveals a mind from which the reality of a human being has been wiped out."

What, then, of the hungry children? It might be argued that Ethical Egoism itself "reveals a mind from which the reality of a human being has been wiped out," namely, the human being who is starving. But Rand quotes with approval the answer given by one of her followers: "Once, when Barbara Brandon was asked by a student: 'What will happen to the poor . . . ?' she answered: 'If *you* want to help them, you will not be stopped.'"

All these remarks are, I think, part of one continuous argument that can be summarized like this:

**(1)** Each person has only one life to live. If we value the individual—that is, if the individual has moral worth—then we must agree that this life is of supreme importance. After all, it is all one has, and all one is.

**(2)** The ethics of altruism regards the life of the individual as something one must be ready to sacrifice for the good of others. Therefore, the ethics of altruism does not take seriously the value of the individual.

**(3)** Ethical Egoism, which allows each person to view his or her own life as being of ultimate value, does take the individual seriously—it is, in fact, the only philosophy that does so.

**(4)** Thus, Ethical Egoism is the philosophy that we ought to accept.



One problem with this argument, as you may have noticed, is that it assumes we have only two choices: Either we accept the ethics of altruism, or we accept Ethical Egoism. The choice is then made to look obvious by depicting the ethics of altruism as an insane doctrine that only an idiot would accept. The ethics of altruism is said to be the view that one's own interests have *no* value and that one must be ready to sacrifice oneself *totally* any time *anybody* asks it. If this is the alternative, then any other view, including Ethical Egoism, will look good by comparison.

But that is hardly a fair picture of the choices. What we called the commonsense view stands between the two extremes. It says that one's own interests and the interests of others are *both* important, and must be balanced against each other. Sometimes, when the balancing is done, it will turn out that one should act in the interests of others; other times, it will turn out that one should take care of oneself. So, even if we should reject the extreme ethics of altruism, it does not follow that we must accept the other extreme of Ethical Egoism. There is a middle ground.

**Ethical Egoism as Compatible with Commonsense Morality.** The third line of reasoning takes a different approach. Ethical Egoism is usually presented as a *revisionist* moral philosophy, that is, as a philosophy that says our commonsense moral views are mistaken and need to be changed. It is possible, however, to interpret Ethical Egoism in a much less radical way, as a theory that accepts commonsense morality and offers a surprising account of its basis.

The less radical interpretation goes as follows: Ordinary morality consists in obeying certain rules. We must speak the truth, keep our promises, avoid harming others, and so on. At first glance, these duties appear to have little in common—they are just a bunch of discrete rules. Yet, from a theoretical point of view, we may wonder whether there is not some hidden unity underlying the hodgepodge of separate duties. Perhaps a few fundamental principles explain all the rest, just as in physics certain basic principles bring together and explain diverse phenomena. From a theoretical point of view, the smaller the number of basic principles, the better. Best of all would be one fundamental principle, from which all the rest could be derived. Ethical egoists would say that all these duties are ultimately derived from the one fundamental principle of self-interest.

Understood in this way, Ethical Egoism is not such a radical doctrine. It does not challenge commonsense morality; it only tries to explain and systematize it. And it does a surprisingly successful job. It can provide plausible explanations of the duties mentioned above, and more:

- *The duty not to harm others:* If we make a habit of doing things that harm other people, other people will not mind doing things that harm us. We will be shunned and despised; others will not have us as friends and will not do us favors when we need them. If our offenses against others are serious enough, we may even end up in jail. Thus, it is to our own advantage to avoid harming others.
- *The duty not to lie:* If we lie to other people, we will suffer all the ill effects of a bad reputation. People will distrust us and avoid doing business with us. We need people to be honest with us, but we can hardly expect them to do so if we have not been honest with them. Thus, it is to our own advantage to be truthful.
- *The duty to keep our promises:* It is to our own advantage to enter into mutually beneficial arrangements with other people. To benefit from those arrangements, we need to be able to rely on others to keep their word—we need them to keep their promises. But we can hardly expect them to do so if we do not keep our promises to them. Therefore, from the point of view of self-interest, we should keep our promises.

Pursuing this line of reasoning, Thomas Hobbes suggested that the principle of Ethical Egoism leads to nothing less than the



Golden Rule: We should "do unto others" because if we do, others will be more likely to "do unto us."

Does this argument succeed in establishing Ethical Egoism as a viable theory of morality? It is, in my opinion at least, the best try. But there are two serious problems with it. First, the argument does not prove quite as much as it needs to prove. At best, it shows only that it is *mostly* to one's advantage to avoid harming others. It does not show that this is *always* to one's advantage. And it cannot show that. Sometimes one can benefit from treating another person badly. In that case, the obligation not to harm the other person could not be derived from the principle of Ethical Egoism. Thus, it appears that not all our moral obligations can be derived from self-interest.

But set that point aside. There is a still more fundamental problem. Suppose it is true that, say, contributing money for famine relief is somehow to one's own advantage. It does not follow that this is the only reason, or even the most basic reason, why doing so is a good thing. For example, the most basic reason might be *to help the starving people.* The fact that doing so is also to one's own advantage might be only a secondary, less important consideration. Thus, although Ethical Egoism says that self-interest is the *only* reason why we should help others, nothing in the present argument really supports that.

## 5.4. Three Arguments against Ethical Egoism

Ethical Egoism haunts moral philosophy. It is not a popular doctrine; the most important philosophers have rejected it outright. But it has never been very far from their minds. Almost every ethicist has felt it necessary to explain what's wrong with the theory, as though the very possibility that it might be correct was hanging in the air, threatening to smother their other ideas. As the merits of the various "refutations" have been debated, philosophers have returned to it again and again.

Curiously, philosophers have not paid much attention to the most obvious argument against Ethical Egoism, namely that it endorses wicked actions—provided, of course, that those actions benefit the person who does them. Here are some examples, taken from various newspapers: To increase his profits, a pharmacist filled prescriptions for cancer patients using watered-down drugs. A nurse raped two patients while they were unconscious. A paramedic gave emergency patients injections of sterile water rather than morphine, so he could sell the morphine. Parents fed a baby acid so that they could fake a lawsuit, claiming the baby's formula was tainted. A 13-year-old girl was kidnapped by a neighbor and kept shackled in an underground bomb shelter for 181 days, where she was sexually abused. A 60-year-old man shot his letter carrier seven times because he was $90,000 in debt and thought that being in federal prison would be better than being homeless.

Suppose that, by doing such things, someone could actually gain some benefit for himself. Of course, this means that he would have to avoid being caught. But if he could get away with it, wouldn't Ethical Egoism have to say that such actions are permissible? This seems enough by itself to discredit the doctrine. I believe this is a valid complaint. Nonetheless, one might think that it begs the question against Ethical Egoism, because in saying that these actions are wicked, we are appealing to a non-egoistic conception of wickedness. So, we might ask if there isn't some further problem with Ethical Egoism, one that doesn't beg the question.

Thus, some philosophers have tried to show that there are deeper logical problems with Ethical Egoism. The following arguments are typical of the refutations they have proposed.

**The Argument That Ethical Egoism Cannot Handle Conflicts of Interest.** In his book *The Moral Point of View,* Kurt Baier argues that Ethical Egoism cannot be correct because it cannot provide solutions for conflicts of interest. We need moral rules, he says, only because our interests sometimes conflict—if they never conflicted, then there would be no problems to solve, and hence no need for the kind of guidance that morality provides. But Ethical Egoism does not help to resolve conflicts of interest; it only makes them worse.

To illustrate his point, Baier asks us to suppose that there are two individuals, B and K, running for president. (Given that Baier wrote this in the 1950s, he can't have meant Bush and Kerry!) Since it would be in B's interest to win, it would also be in B's interest to murder K. From this it follows that B ought to murder K, that it would be wrong for B not to murder K,



and that B has not "done his duty" until he has murdered K. But it is also true that it is in K's interest not to be murdered. From this it follows that K ought to stop B from murdering him, that it would be wrong for K not to stop B, and that K has not "done his duty" until he has made sure of stopping B. Baier concludes:

> This is obviously absurd. For morality is designed to apply in just such cases, namely, those where interests conflict. But if the point of view of morality were that of self-interest, then there could never be moral solutions of conflicts of interest.

Does this argument prove that Ethical Egoism is unacceptable? It does, *if* the conception of morality to which it appeals is accepted. The argument assumes that an adequate morality must provide solutions for conflicts of interest in such a way that everyone concerned can live together harmoniously. The conflict between B and K, for example, should be resolved so that they would no longer be at odds with one another. (One would not then have a duty to do something that the other has a duty to prevent.) Ethical Egoism does not do that, and if you think an ethical theory should, then you will not find Ethical Egoism acceptable.

But a defender of Ethical Egoism might reply that he does not accept this conception of morality. For him, life is essentially a long series of conflicts in which each person is struggling to come out on top; and the principle he accepts—the principle of Ethical Egoism—grants to each person the right to do his or her best to win. On this view, the moralist is not like a courtroom judge, who resolves disputes. Instead, he is like the referee in an Ultimate Fighting competition, who urges each fighter to do his best. (The difference is that in Ultimate Fighting, there are some things you *can't* do, such as biting and eye gouging. These things are allowed by Ethical Egoism.) So, the conflict between B and K will be "resolved" not by the application of an ethical principle but by one of them winning the struggle. The egoist will not be embarrassed by this. On the contrary, he will think it is no more than a realistic view of the nature of things.

**The Argument That Ethical Egoism Is Logically Inconsistent.** Some philosophers, including Baier, have leveled an even more serious charge against Ethical Egoism. They have argued that it leads to logical contradictions. If this is true, then Ethical Egoism is indeed a mistaken theory, for no theory can be true if it is self-contradictory.

Consider B and K again. As Baier explains their predicament, it is in B's interest to kill K, and it is in K's interest to prevent this. But, Baier says:

> If K prevents B from liquidating him, his act must be said to be both wrong and not wrong—wrong because it is the prevention of what B ought to do, his duty, and wrong for B not to do it; not wrong because it is what K ought to do, his duty, and wrong for K not to do it. But one and the same act (logically) cannot be both morally wrong and not morally wrong.

Now, does *this* argument prove that Ethical Egoism is unacceptable? At first glance, it seems persuasive. However, it is complicated, so we need to set it out with each step individually identified. Then we will be in a better position to evaluate it. Spelled out fully, it looks like this:

**(1)** Suppose it is each person's duty to do what is in his own best interests.

**(2)** It is in B's best interest to murder K.

**(3)** It is in K's best interest to prevent B from murdering him.

**(4)** Therefore, B's duty is to murder K, and K's duty is to prevent B from doing it.

**(5)** But it is wrong to prevent someone from doing his duty.

**(6)** Therefore, it is wrong for K to prevent B from murdering him.

**(7)** Therefore, it is both wrong and not wrong for K to prevent B from murdering him.

**(8)** But no act can be both wrong and not wrong; that is a self-contradiction.

**(9)** Therefore, the assumption with which we started—that it is each person's duty to do what is in his own best interests—cannot be true.

When the argument is set out in this way, we can see its hidden flaw. The logical contradiction—that it is both wrong and not wrong for K to prevent B from murdering him—does not follow simply from the principle of Ethical Egoism. It follows from that principle *together with* the additional premise expressed in step (5), namely, that "it is wrong to prevent someone from doing his duty." Thus, we are not compelled by the logic of the argument to reject Ethical Egoism. Instead, we could simply reject this additional premise and thereby avoid the contradiction. That is surely what the ethical egoist would do, for the ethical egoist would never say, without qualification, that it is always wrong to prevent someone from doing his duty. He would say, instead, that whether one ought to prevent someone from doing his duty depends entirely on whether it would be to one's own advantage to do so. Regardless of whether we think this is a correct view, it is, at the very least, a consistent view, and so this attempt to convict the ethical egoist of self-contradiction fails.



**The Argument That Ethical Egoism Is Unacceptably Arbitrary.** Finally, we come to the argument that I think comes closest to an outright refutation of Ethical Egoism. It is also the most interesting of the arguments, because it provides some insight into why the interests of other people *should* matter to us. But before presenting this argument, we need to look at a general point about moral values. So let us set Ethical Egoism aside for now and consider a related matter.

There is a whole family of moral views that have this in common: They all involve dividing people into groups and saying that the interests of some groups count more than the interests of other groups. Racism is the most conspicuous example; racism divides people into groups according to race and assigns greater importance to the interests of one race than to others. The practical result is that members of one race are treated better than the others. All forms of discrimination work this way: anti-Semitism, nationalism, sexism, ageism, and so on. People in the grip of such views will think, in effect, "*My* race counts for more," or "Those who believe in *my* religion count for more," or "*My* country counts for more," and so on.

Can such views be defended? The people who accept such views are usually not much interested in argument—racists, for example, rarely try to offer rational grounds for their beliefs. But suppose they did. What could they say?

There is a general principle that stands in the way of any such defense. Let's call this the Principle of Equal Treatment: *We should treat people in the same way unless there is a relevant difference between them.* For example, suppose we're considering whether to admit two students to law school. If both students graduated from college with honors and aced the entrance exam—if both are equally well qualified—then it is merely arbitrary to admit one but not the other. However, if one graduated with honors and scored well on the admissions test while the other dropped out of college and never took the test, then it is acceptable to admit the first student but not the second.

Two points should be made about this principle. The first is that treating people in the same way does not always mean giving them the same outcome. During the Vietnam War, young American men desperately wanted to avoid the draft, and the government had to decide the order in which draft boards would call people up. In 1969, the first "draft lottery" was televised to a national audience. Here is how it worked: The days of the year were written on 366 slips of paper (one slip for February 29) and inserted into blue plastic capsules. Those capsules were placed in a glass jar and mixed up. Then, one by one, the capsules were drawn. The first was for September 14—young men with that birthday, age 18–26, would be drafted first. The winners of the lottery, drawn last, were born on June 8. In college dormitories, groups of students watched the drawings live, and it was easy to tell whose birthday had just come up—whoever just cursed or groaned. Obviously, the outcomes were different: In the end, some people got drafted and others didn't. However, the process was fair. By giving everyone an equal chance in the lottery, the government treated everyone in the same way.

A second point concerns the scope of the principle, or its range of application. Suppose you're not going to use your ticket to the big game, so you give it to a friend. In doing so, you are treating your friend better than everyone else you could have given the ticket to. Does your action violate the Principle of Equal Treatment? Does it need justification? Moral philosophers disagree on this question. Some think that the principle does not apply to cases like this. The principle applies only in "moral contexts," and what you should do with your ticket is not important enough to count as a moral question. Others think that your action does require justification, and various justifications might be offered. Your action might be justified by the nature of friendship, or by the fact that the ticket belongs to you, or by the fact that it would be impossible for you to hold a lottery at the last minute for all the ticketless fans. It doesn't matter, from our point of view, who is right about the scope of the principle. Suffice it to say that everyone accepts the Principle of Equal Treatment, in one form or another.



Let's now apply that principle to racism. Can a racist point to any differences between, say, white people and black people that would justify treating them differently? In the past, racists have sometimes tried to do this by portraying blacks as lazy, stupid, threatening, and hypersexual. If these accusations were true, then they might justify treating blacks differently, in at least some circumstances. (This is the deep purpose of racist stereotypes: to provide the "relevant differences" needed to justify differences in treatment.) But, of course, they are not true; there are no such general differences between the races. Thus, racism is an arbitrary doctrine, in that it advocates treating people differently even though there are no differences between them to justify it.

Ethical Egoism is a moral theory of the same type. It advocates that each of us divide the world into two categories of people—ourselves and all the rest—and that we regard the interests of those in the first group as more important than the interests of those in the second group. But each of us can ask, What is the difference between me and everyone else that justifies placing myself in this special category? Am I more intelligent? Do I enjoy my life more? Are my accomplishments greater? Do I have needs or abilities that are so different from the needs or abilities of others? In short, *what makes me so special?* Failing an answer, it turns out that Ethical Egoism is an arbitrary doctrine, in the same way that racism is arbitrary. Both doctrines violate the Principle of Equal Treatment. And this, in addition to explaining why Ethical Egoism is unacceptable, also sheds light on the question of why we should care about others.

We should care about the interests of other people for the same reason we care about our own interests, for their needs and desires are comparable to our own. Consider, one last time, the starving children we could feed by giving up some of our luxuries. Why should we care about them? We care about ourselves, of course—if we were starving, we would go to almost any lengths to get food. But what is the difference between us and them? Does hunger affect them any less? Are they somehow less deserving than we are? If we can find no relevant difference between us and them, then we must admit that, if our needs should be met, so should theirs. It is this realization—that we are on a par with one another—that is the deepest reason why our morality must include some recognition of the needs of others, and why, ultimately, Ethical Egoism fails as a moral theory.

Famine, Affluence, and Morality
Peter Singer
Philosophy and Public Affairs, vol. 1, no. 1 (Spring 1972), pp. 229-243 [revised edition]

---

As I write this, in November 1971, people are dying in East Bengal from lack of food, shelter, and medical care. The suffering and death that are occurring there now are not inevitable, not unavoidable in any fatalistic sense of the term. Constant poverty, a cyclone, and a civil war have turned at least nine million people into destitute refugees; nevertheless, it is not beyond the capacity of the richer nations to give enough assistance to reduce any further suffering to very small proportions. The decisions and actions of human beings can prevent this kind of suffering. Unfortunately, human beings have not made the necessary decisions. At the individual level, people have, with very few exceptions, not responded to the situation in any significant way. Generally speaking, people have not given large sums to relief funds; they have not written to their parliamentary representatives demanding increased government assistance; they have not demonstrated in the streets, held symbolic fasts, or done anything else directed toward providing the refugees with the means to satisfy their essential needs. At the government level, no government has given the sort of massive aid that would enable the refugees to survive for more than a few days. Britain, for instance, has given rather more than most countries. It has, to date, given £14,750,000. For comparative purposes, Britain's share of the nonrecoverable development costs of the Anglo-French Concorde project is already in excess of £275,000,000, and on present estimates will reach £440,000,000. The implication is that the British government values a supersonic transport more than thirty times as highly as it values the lives of the nine million refugees. Australia is another country which, on a per capita basis, is well up in the "aid to Bengal" table. Australia's aid, however, amounts to less than one-twelfth of the cost of Sydney's new opera house. The total amount given, from all sources, now stands at about £65,000,000. The estimated cost of keeping the refugees alive for one year is £464,000,000. Most of the refugees have now been in the camps for more than six months. The World Bank has said that India needs a minimum of £300,000,000 in assistance from other countries before the end of the year. It seems obvious that assistance on this scale will not be forthcoming. India will be forced to choose between letting the refugees starve or diverting funds from her own development program, which will mean that more of her own people will starve in the future. [1]

These are the essential facts about the present situation in Bengal. So far as it concerns us here, there is nothing unique about this situation except its magnitude. The Bengal emergency is just the latest and most acute of a series of major emergencies in various parts of the world, arising both from natural and from manmade causes. There are also many parts of the world in which people die from malnutrition and lack of food independent of any special emergency. I take Bengal as my example only because it is the present concern, and because the size of the problem has ensured that it has been given adequate publicity. Neither individuals nor governments can claim to be unaware of what is happening there.

What are the moral implications of a situation like this? In what follows, I shall argue that the way people in relatively affluent countries react to a situation like that in Bengal cannot be justified; indeed, the whole way we look at moral issues - our moral conceptual scheme - needs to be altered, and with it, the way of life that has come to be taken for granted in our society.

In arguing for this conclusion I will not, of course, claim to be morally neutral. I shall, however, try to argue for the moral position that I take, so that anyone who accepts certain assumptions, to be made explicit, will, I hope, accept my conclusion.

I begin with the assumption that suffering and death from lack of food, shelter, and medical care are bad. I think most people will agree about this, although one may reach the same view by different routes. I shall not argue for this view. People can hold all sorts of eccentric positions, and perhaps from some of them it would not follow that death by starvation is in itself bad. It is difficult, perhaps impossible, to refute such positions, and so for brevity I will henceforth take this assumption as accepted. Those who disagree need read no further.

My next point is this: if it is in our power to prevent something bad from happening, without thereby sacrificing anything of comparable moral importance, we ought, morally, to do it. By "without sacrificing anything of comparable moral importance" I mean without causing anything else comparably bad to happen, or doing something that is wrong in itself, or failing to promote some moral good, comparable in significance to the bad thing that we can prevent. This principle seems almost as uncontroversial as the last one. It requires us only to prevent what is bad, and to promote what is good, and it requires this of us only when we can do it without sacrificing anything that is, from the moral point of view, comparably important. I could even, as far as the application of my argument to the Bengal emergency is concerned, qualify the point so as to make it: if it is in our power to prevent something very bad from happening, without thereby sacrificing anything morally significant, we ought, morally, to do it. An application of this principle would be as follows: if I am walking past a shallow pond and see a child drowning in it, I ought to wade in and pull the child out. This will mean getting my clothes muddy, but this is insignificant, while the death of the child would presumably be a very bad thing.

The uncontroversial appearance of the principle just stated is deceptive. If it were acted upon, even in its qualified form, our lives, our society, and our world would be fundamentally changed. For the principle takes, firstly, no account of proximity or distance. It makes no moral difference whether the person I can help is a neighbor's child ten yards from me or a Bengali whose name I shall never know, ten thousand miles away. Secondly, the principle makes no distinction between cases in which I am the only person who could possibly do anything and cases in which I am just one among millions in the same position.

I do not think I need to say much in defense of the refusal to take proximity and distance into account. The fact that a person is physically near to us, so that we have personal contact with him, may make it more likely that we *shall* assist him, but this does not show that we *ought* to help him rather than another who happens to be further away. If we accept any principle of impartiality, universalizability, equality, or whatever, we cannot discriminate against someone merely because he is far away from us (or we are far away from him). Admittedly, it is possible that we are in a better position to judge what needs to be done to help a person near to us than one far away, and perhaps also to provide the assistance we judge to be necessary. If this were the case, it would be a reason for helping those near to us first. This may once have been a justification for being more concerned with the poor in one's town than with famine victims in India. Unfortunately for those who like to keep their moral responsibilities limited, instant communication and swift transportation have changed the situation. From the moral point of view, the development of the world into a "global village" has made an important, though still unrecognized, difference to our moral situation. Expert observers and supervisors, sent out by famine relief organizations or permanently stationed in famine-prone areas, can direct our aid to a refugee in Bengal almost as effectively as we could get it to someone in our own block. There would seem, therefore, to be no possible justification for discriminating on geographical grounds.

There may be a greater need to defend the second implication of my principle - that the fact that there are millions of other people in the same position, in respect to the Bengali refugees, as I am, does not make the situation significantly different from a situation in which I am the only person who can prevent something very bad from occurring. Again, of course, I admit that there is a psychological difference between the cases; one feels less guilty about doing nothing if one can point to others, similarly placed, who have also done nothing. Yet this can make no real difference to our moral obligations. [2] Should I consider that I am less obliged to pull the drowning child out of the pond if on looking around I see other people, no further away than I am, who have also noticed the child but are doing nothing? One has only to ask this question to see the absurdity of the view that numbers lessen obligation. It is a view that is an ideal excuse for inactivity; unfortunately most of the major evils - poverty, overpopulation, pollution - are problems in which everyone is almost equally involved.

The view that numbers do make a difference can be made plausible if stated in this way: if everyone in circumstances like mine gave £5 to the Bengal Relief Fund, there would be enough to provide food, shelter, and medical care for the refugees; there is no reason why I should give more than anyone else in the same circumstances as I am; therefore I have no obligation to give more than £5. Each premise in this argument is true, and the argument looks sound. It may convince us, unless we notice that it is based on a hypothetical premise, although the conclusion is not stated hypothetically. The argument would be sound if the conclusion were: if everyone in circumstances like mine were to give £5, I would have no obligation to give more than £5. If the conclusion were so stated, however, it would be obvious that the argument has no bearing on a situation in which it is not the case that everyone else gives £5. This, of course, is the actual situation. It is more or less certain that not everyone in circumstances like mine will give £5. So there will not be enough to provide the needed food, shelter, and medical care. Therefore by giving more than £5 I will prevent more suffering than I would if I gave just £5.

It might be thought that this argument has an absurd consequence. Since the situation appears to be that very few people are likely to give substantial amounts, it follows that I and everyone else in similar circumstances ought to give as much as possible, that is, at least up to the point at which by giving more one would begin to cause serious suffering for oneself and one's dependents - perhaps even beyond this point to the point of marginal utility, at which by giving more one would cause oneself and one's dependents as much suffering as one would prevent in Bengal. If everyone does this, however, there will be more than can be used for the benefit of the refugees, and some of the sacrifice will have been unnecessary. Thus, if everyone does what he ought to do, the result will not be as good as it would be if everyone did a little less than he ought to do, or if only some do all that they ought to do.

The paradox here arises only if we assume that the actions in question - sending money to the relief funds - are performed more or less simultaneously, and are also unexpected. For if it is to be expected that everyone is going to contribute something, then clearly each is not obliged to give as much as he would have been obliged to had others not been giving too. And if everyone is not acting more or less simultaneously, then those giving later will know how much more is needed, and will have no obligation to give more than is necessary to reach this amount. To say this is not to deny the principle that people in the same circumstances have the same obligations, but to point out that the fact that others have given, or may be expected to give, is a relevant circumstance: those giving after it has become known that many others are giving and those giving before are not in the same circumstances. So the seemingly absurd consequence of the principle I have put forward can occur only if people are in error about the actual circumstances - that is, if they think they are giving when others are not, but in fact they are giving when others are. The result of everyone doing what he really ought to do cannot be worse than the result of everyone doing less than he ought to do, although the result of everyone doing what he reasonably believes he ought to do could be.

If my argument so far has been sound, neither our distance from a preventable evil nor the number of other people who, in respect to that evil, are in the same situation as we are, lessens our obligation to mitigate or prevent that evil. I shall therefore take as established the principle I asserted earlier. As I have already said, I need to assert it only in its qualified form: if it is in our power to prevent something very bad from happening, without thereby sacrificing anything else morally significant, we ought, morally, to do it.

The outcome of this argument is that our traditional moral categories are upset. The traditional distinction between duty and charity cannot be drawn, or at least, not in the place we normally draw it. Giving money to the Bengal Relief Fund is regarded as an act of charity in our society. The bodies which collect money are known as "charities." These organizations see themselves in this way - if you send them a check, you will be thanked for your "generosity." Because giving money is regarded as an act of charity, it is not thought that there is anything wrong with not giving. The charitable man may be praised, but the man who is not charitable is not condemned. People do not feel in any way ashamed or guilty about spending money on new clothes or a new car instead of giving it to famine relief. (Indeed, the alternative does not occur to them.) This way of looking at the matter cannot be justified. When we buy new clothes not to keep ourselves warm but to look "well-dressed" we are not providing for any important need. We would not be sacrificing anything significant if we were to continue to wear our old clothes, and give the money to famine relief. By doing so, we would be preventing another person from starving. It follows from what I have said earlier that we ought to give money away, rather than spend it on clothes which we do not need to keep us warm. To do so is not charitable, or generous. Nor is it the kind of act which philosophers and theologians have called "supererogatory" - an act which it would be good to do, but not wrong not to do. On the contrary, we ought to give the money away, and it is wrong not to do so.

I am not maintaining that there are no acts which are charitable, or that there are no acts which it would be good to do but not wrong not to do. It may be possible to redraw the distinction between duty and charity in some other place. All I am arguing here is that the present way of drawing the distinction, which makes it an act of charity for a man living at the level of affluence which most people in the "developed nations" enjoy to give money to save someone else from starvation, cannot be supported. It is beyond the scope of my argument to consider whether the distinction should be redrawn or abolished altogether. There would be many other possible ways of drawing the distinction - for instance, one might decide that it is good to make other people as happy as possible, but not wrong not to do so.

Despite the limited nature of the revision in our moral conceptual scheme which I am proposing, the revision would, given the extent of both affluence and famine in the world today, have radical implications. These implications may lead to further objections, distinct from those I have already considered. I shall discuss two of these.

One objection to the position I have taken might be simply that it is too drastic a revision of our moral scheme. People do not ordinarily judge in the way I have suggested they should. Most people reserve their moral condemnation for those who violate some moral norm, such as the norm against taking another person's property. They do not condemn those who indulge in luxury instead of giving to famine relief. But given that I did not set out to present a morally neutral description of the way people make moral judgments, the way people do in fact judge has nothing to do with the validity of my conclusion. My conclusion follows from the principle which I advanced earlier, and unless that principle is rejected, or the arguments are shown to be unsound, I think the conclusion must stand, however strange it appears. It might, nevertheless, be interesting to consider why our society, and most other societies, do judge differently from the way I have suggested they should. In a wellknown article, J. O. Urmson suggests that the imperatives of duty, which tell us what we must do, as distinct from what it would be good to do but not wrong not to do, function so as to prohibit behavior that is intolerable if men are to live together in society. [3] This may explain the origin and continued existence of the present division between acts of duty and acts of charity. Moral attitudes are shaped by the needs of society, and no doubt society needs people who will observe the rules that make social existence tolerable. From the point of view of a particular society, it is essential to prevent violations of norms against killing, stealing, and so on. It is quite inessential, however, to help people outside one's own society.

If this is an explanation of our common distinction between duty and supererogation, however, it is not a justification of it. The moral point of view requires us to look beyond the interests of our own society. Previously, as I have already mentioned, this may hardly have been feasible, but it is quite feasible now. From the moral point of view, the prevention of the starvation of millions of people outside our society must be considered at least as pressing as the upholding of property norms within our society.

It has been argued by some writers, among them Sidgwick and Urmson, that we need to have a basic moral code which is not too far beyond the capacities of the ordinary man, for otherwise there will be a general breakdown of compliance with the moral code. Crudely stated, this argument suggests that if we tell people that they ought to refrain from murder and give everything they do not really need to famine relief, they will do neither, whereas if we tell them that they ought to refrain from murder and that it is good to give to famine relief but not wrong not to do so, they will at least refrain from murder. The issue here is: Where should we draw the line between conduct that is required and conduct that is good although not required, so as to get the best possible result? This would seem to be an empirical question, although a very difficult one. One objection to the Sidgwick-Urmson line of argument is that it takes insufficient account of the effect that moral standards can have on the decisions we make. Given a society in which a wealthy man who gives 5 percent of his income to famine relief is regarded as most generous, it is not surprising that a proposal that we all ought to give away half our incomes will be thought to be absurdly unrealistic. In a society which held that no man should have more than enough while others have less than they need, such a proposal might seem narrow-minded. What it is possible for a man to do and what he is likely to do are both, I think, very greatly influenced by what people around him are doing and expecting him to do. In any case, the possibility that by spreading the idea that we ought to be doing very much more than we are to relieve famine we shall bring about a general breakdown of moral behavior seems remote. If the stakes are an end to widespread starvation, it is worth the risk. Finally, it should be emphasized that these considerations are relevant only to the issue of what we should require from others, and not to what we ourselves ought to do.

The second objection to my attack on the present distinction between duty and charity is one which has from time to time been made against utilitarianism. It follows from some forms of utilitarian theory that we all ought, morally, to be working full time to increase the balance of happiness over misery. The position I have taken here would not lead to this conclusion in all circumstances, for if there were no bad occurrences that we could prevent without sacrificing something of comparable moral importance, my argument would have no application. Given the present conditions in many parts of the world, however, it does follow from my argument that we ought, morally, to be working full time to relieve great suffering of the sort that occurs as a result of famine or other disasters. Of course, mitigating circumstances can be adduced - for instance, that if we wear ourselves out through overwork, we shall be less effective than we would otherwise have been. Nevertheless, when all considerations of this sort have been taken into account, the conclusion remains: we ought to be preventing as much suffering as we can without sacrificing something else of comparable moral importance. This conclusion is one which we may be reluctant to face. I cannot see, though, why it should be regarded as a criticism of the position for which I have argued, rather than a criticism of our ordinary standards of behavior. Since most people are self-interested to some degree, very few of us are likely to do everything that we ought to do. It would, however, hardly be honest to take this as evidence that it is not the case that we ought to do it.

It may still be thought that my conclusions are so wildly out of line with what everyone else thinks and has always thought that there must be something wrong with the argument somewhere. In order to show that my conclusions, while certainly contrary to contemporary Western moral standards, would not have seemed so extraordinary at other times and in other places, I would like to quote a passage from a writer not normally thought of as a way-out radical, Thomas Aquinas.

Now, according to the natural order instituted by divine providence, material goods are provided for the satisfaction of human needs. Therefore the division and appropriation of property, which proceeds from human law, must not hinder the satisfaction of man's necessity from such goods. Equally, whatever a man has in superabundance is owed, of natural right, to the poor for their sustenance. So Ambrosius says, and it is also to be found in the *Decretum Gratiani*: "The bread which you withhold belongs to the hungry; the clothing you shut away, to the naked; and the money you bury in the earth is the redemption and freedom of the penniless." [4]

I now want to consider a number of points, more practical than philosophical, which are relevant to the application of the moral conclusion we have reached. These points challenge not the idea that we ought to be doing all we can to prevent starvation, but the idea that giving away a great deal of money is the best means to this end.

It is sometimes said that overseas aid should be a government responsibility, and that therefore one ought not to give to privately run charities. Giving privately, it is said, allows the government and the noncontributing members of society to escape their responsibilities.

This argument seems to assume that the more people there are who give to privately organized famine relief funds, the less likely it is that the government will take over full responsibility for such aid. This assumption is unsupported, and does not strike me as at all plausible. The opposite view - that if no one gives voluntarily, a government will assume that its citizens are uninterested in famine relief and would not wish to be forced into giving aid - seems more plausible. In any case, unless there were a definite probability that by refusing to give one would be helping to bring about massive government assistance, people who do refuse to make voluntary contributions are refusing to prevent a certain amount of suffering without being able to point to any tangible beneficial consequence of their refusal. So the onus of showing how their refusal will bring about government action is on those who refuse to give.

I do not, of course, want to dispute the contention that governments of affluent nations should be giving many times the amount of genuine, no-strings-attached aid that they are giving now. I agree, too, that giving privately is not enough, and that we ought to be campaigning actively for entirely new standards for both public and private contributions to famine relief. Indeed, I would sympathize with someone who thought that campaigning was more important than giving oneself, although I doubt whether preaching what one does not practice would be very effective. Unfortunately, for many people the idea that "it's the government's responsibility" is a reason for not giving which does not appear to entail any political action either.

Another, more serious reason for not giving to famine relief funds is that until there is effective population control, relieving famine merely postpones starvation. If we save the Bengal refugees now, others, perhaps the children of these refugees, will face starvation in a few years' time. In support of this, one may cite the now well-known facts about the population explosion and the relatively limited scope for expanded production.

This point, like the previous one, is an argument against relieving suffering that is happening now, because of a belief about what might happen in the future; it is unlike the previous point in that very good evidence can be adduced in support of this belief about the future. I will not go into the evidence here. I accept that the earth cannot support indefinitely a population rising at the present rate. This certainly poses a problem for anyone who thinks it important to prevent famine. Again, however, one could accept the argument without drawing the conclusion that it absolves one from any obligation to do anything to prevent famine. The conclusion that should be drawn is that the best means of preventing famine, in the long run, is population control. It would then follow from the position reached earlier that one ought to be doing all one can to promote population control (unless one held that all forms of population control were wrong in themselves, or would have significantly bad consequences). Since there are organizations working specifically for population control, one would then support them rather than more orthodox methods of preventing famine.

A third point raised by the conclusion reached earlier relates to the question of just how much we all ought to be giving away. One possibility, which has already been mentioned, is that we ought to give until we reach the level of marginal utility - that is, the level at which, by giving more, I would cause as much suffering to myself or my dependents as I would relieve by my gift. This would mean, of course, that one would reduce oneself to very near the material circumstances of a Bengali refugee. It will be recalled that earlier I put forward both a strong and a moderate version of the principle of preventing bad occurrences. The strong version, which required us to prevent bad things from happening unless in doing so we would be sacrificing something of comparable moral significance, does seem to require reducing ourselves to the level of marginal utility. I should also say that the strong version seems to me to be the correct one. I proposed the more moderate version - that we should prevent bad occurrences unless, to do so, we had to sacrifice something morally significant - only in order to show that, even on this surely undeniable principle, a great change in our way of life is required. On the more moderate principle, it may not follow that we ought to reduce ourselves to the level of marginal utility, for one might hold that to reduce oneself and one's family to this level is to cause something significantly bad to happen. Whether this is so I shall not discuss, since, as I have said, I can see no good reason for holding the moderate version of the principle rather than the strong version. Even if we accepted the principle only in its moderate form, however, it should be clear that we would have to give away enough to ensure that the consumer society, dependent as it is on people spending on trivia rather than giving to famine relief, would slow down and perhaps disappear entirely. There are several reasons why this would be desirable in itself. The value and necessity of economic growth are now being questioned not only by conservationists, but by economists as well. [5] There is no doubt, too, that the consumer society has had a distorting effect on the goals and purposes of its members. Yet looking at the matter purely from the point of view of overseas aid, there must be a limit to the extent to which we should deliberately slow down our economy; for it might be the case that if we gave away, say, 40 percent of our Gross National Product, we would slow down the economy so much that in absolute terms we would be giving less than if we gave 25 percent of the much larger GNP that we would have if we limited our contribution to this smaller percentage.

I mention this only as an indication of the sort of factor that one would have to take into account in working out an ideal. Since Western societies generally consider 1 percent of the GNP an acceptable level for overseas aid, the matter is entirely academic. Nor does it affect the question of how much an individual should give in a society in which very few are giving substantial amounts.

It is sometimes said, though less often now than it used to be, that philosophers have no special role to play in public affairs, since most public issues depend primarily on an assessment of facts. On questions of fact, it is said, philosophers as such have no special expertise, and so it has been possible to engage in philosophy without committing oneself to any position on major public issues. No doubt there are some issues of social policy and foreign policy about which it can truly be said that a really expert assessment of the facts is required before taking sides or acting, but the issue of famine is surely not one of these. The facts about the existence of suffering are beyond dispute. Nor, I think, is it disputed that we can do something about it, either through orthodox methods of famine relief or through population control or both. This is therefore an issue on which philosophers are competent to take a position. The issue is one which faces everyone who has more money than he needs to support himself and his dependents, or who is in a position to take some sort of political action. These categories must include practically every teacher and student of philosophy in the universities of the Western world. If philosophy is to deal with matters that are relevant to both teachers and students, this is an issue that philosophers should discuss.

Discussion, though, is not enough. What is the point of relating philosophy to public (and personal) affairs if we do not take our conclusions seriously? In this instance, taking our conclusion seriously means acting upon it. The philosopher will not find it any easier than anyone else to alter his attitudes and way of life to the extent that, if I am right, is involved in doing everything that we ought to be doing. At the very least, though, one can make a start. The philosopher who does so will have to sacrifice some of the benefits of the consumer society, but he can find compensation in the satisfaction of a way of life in which theory and practice, if not yet in harmony, are at least coming together.

**Postscript**

The crisis in Bangladesh that spurred me to write the above article is now of historical interest only, but the world food crisis is, if anything, still more serious. The huge grain reserves that were then held by the United States have vanished. Increased oil prices have made both fertilizer and energy more expensive in developing countries, and have made it difficult for them to produce more food. At the same time, their population has continued to grow. Fortunately, as I write now, there is no major famine anywhere in the world; but poor people are still starving in several countries, and malnutrition remains very widespread. The need for assistance is, therefore, just as great as when I first wrote, and we can be sure that without it there will, again, be major famines.

The contrast between poverty and affluence that I wrote about is also as great as it was then. True, the affluent nations have experienced a recession, and are perhaps not as prosperous as they were in 1971. But the poorer nations have suffered as least as much from the recession, in reduced government aid (because if governments decide to reduce expenditure, they regard foreign aid as one of the expendable items, ahead of, for instance, defense or public construction projects) and in increased prices for goods and materials they need to buy. In any case, compared with the difference between the affluent nations and the poor nations, the whole recession was trifling; the poorest in the affluent nations remained incomparably better off than the poorest in the poor nations.

So the case for aid, on both a personal and a governmental level, remains as great now as it was in 1971, and I would not wish to change the basic argument that I put forward then.

There are, however, some matters of emphasis that I might put differently if I were to rewrite the article, and the most important of these concerns the population problem. I still think that, as I wrote then, the view that famine relief merely postpones starvation unless something is done to check population growth is not an argument against aid, it is only an argument against the *type* of aid that should be given. Those who hold this view have the same obligation to give to prevent starvation as those who do not; the difference is that they regard assisting population control schemes as a more effective way of preventing starvation in the long run. I would now, however, have given greater space to the discussion of the population problem; for I now think that there is a serious case for saying that if a country refuses to take any steps to slow the rate of its population growth, we should not give it aid. This is, of course, a very drastic step to take, and the choice it represents is a horrible choice to have to make; but if, after a dispassionate analysis of all the available information, we come to the conclusion that without population control we will not, in the long run, be able to prevent famine or other catastrophes, then it may be more humane in the long run to aid those countries that are prepared to take strong measures to reduce population growth, and to use our aid policy as a means of pressuring other countries to take similar steps.

It may be objected that such a policy involves an attempt to coerce a sovereign nation. But since we are not under an obligation to give aid unless that aid is likely to be effective in reducing starvation or malnutrition, we are not under an obligation to give aid to countries that make no effort to reduce a rate of population growth that will lead to catastrophe. Since we do not force any nation to accept our aid, simply making it clear that we will not give aid where it is not going to be effective cannot properly be regarded as a form of coercion.

I should also make it clear that the kind of aid that will slow population growth is not just assistance with the setting up of facilities for dispensing contraceptives and performing sterilizations. It is also necessary to create the conditions under which people do not wish to have so many children. This will involve, among other things, providing greater economic security for people, particularly in their old age, so that they do not need the security of a large family to provide for them. Thus, the requirements of aid designed to reduce population growth and aid designed to eliminate starvation are by no means separate; they overlap, and the latter will often be a means to the former. The obligation of the affluent is, I believe, to do both. Fortunately, there are now many people in the foreign aid field, including those in the private agencies, who are aware of this.

One other matter that I should now put forward slightly differently is that my argument does, of course, apply to assistance with development, particularly agricultural development, as well as to direct famine relief. Indeed, I think the former is usually the better long-term investment. Although this was my view when I wrote the article, the fact that I started from a famine situation, where the need was for immediate food, has led some readers to suppose that the argument is only about giving food and not about other types of aid. This is quite mistaken, and my view is that the aid should be of whatever type is most effective.

On a more philosophical level, there has been some discussion of the original article which has been helpful in clarifying the issues and pointing to the areas in which more work on the argument is needed. In particular, as John Arthur has shown in "Rights and the Duty to Bring Aid" (included in this volume), something more needs to be said about the notion of "moral significance." The problem is that to give an account of this notion involves nothing less than a full-fledged ethical theory; and while I am myself inclined toward a utilitarian view, it was my aim in writing "Famine, Affluence, and Morality" to produce an argument which would appeal not only to utilitarians, but also to anyone who accepted the initial premises of the argument, which seemed to me likely to have a very wide acceptance. So I tried to get around the need to produce a complete ethical theory by allowing my readers to fill in their own version - within limits - of what is morally significant, and then see what the moral consequences are. This tactic works reasonably well with those who are prepared to agree that such matters as being fashionably dressed are not really of moral significance; but Arthur is right to say that people could take the opposite view without being obviously irrational. Hence, I do not accept Arthur's claim that the weak principle implies little or no duty of benevolence, for it will imply a significant duty of benevolence for those who admit, as I think most nonphilosophers and even off-guard philosophers will admit, that they spend considerable sums on items that by their own standards are of no moral significance. But I do agree that the weak principle is nonetheless too weak, because it makes it too easy for the duty of benevolence to be avoided.

On the other hand, I think the strong principle will stand, whether the notion of moral significance is developed along utilitarian lines, or once again left to the individual reader's own sincere judgment. In either case, I would argue against Arthur's view that we are morally entitled to give greater weight to our own interests and purposes simply because they are our own. This view seems to me contrary to the idea, now widely shared by moral philosophers, that some element of impartiality or universalizability is inherent in the very notion of a moral judgment. (For a discussion of the different formulations of this idea, and an indication of the extent to which they are in agreement, see R. M. Hare, "Rules of War and Moral Reasoning," Philosophy & Public Affairs vol. 1, no. 2, 1972.) Granted, in normal circumstances, it may be better for everyone if we recognize that each of us will be primarily responsible for running our own lives and only secondarily responsible for others. This, however, is not a moral ultimate, but a secondary principle that derives from consideration of how a society may best order its affairs, given the limits of altruism in human beings. Such secondary principles are, I think, swept aside by the extreme evil of people starving to death.

Notes

1. There was also a third possibility: that India would go to war to enable the refugees to return to their lands. Since I wrote this paper, India has taken this way out. The situation is no longer that described above, but this does not affect my argument, as the next paragraph indicates.

2. In view of the special sense philosophers often give to the term, I should say that I

use "obligation" simply as the abstract noun derived from "ought," so that "I have an obligation to" means no more, and no less, than "I ought to." This usage is in accordance with the definition of "ought" given by the Shorter Oxford English Dictionary: "the general verb to express duty or obligation." I do not think any issue of substance hangs on the way the term is used; sentences in which I use "obligation" could all be rewritten, although somewhat clumsily, as sentences in which a clause containing "ought" replaces the term "obligation."

3. J. O. Urmson, "Saints and Heroes," in Essays in Moral Philosophy, ed. Abraham I. Melden (Seattle: University of Washington Press, 1958), p. 214. For a related but significantly different view see also Henry Sidgwick, The Methods of Ethics, 7th ed. (London: Dover Press, 1907), pp. 220-1, 492-3.

4. Summa Theologica, II-II, Question 66, Article 7, in Aquinas, Selected Political Writings, ed. A. P. d'Entrèves, trans. J. G. Dawson (Oxford: Basil Blackwell, 1948), p. 171.

5. See, for instance, John Kenneth Galbraith, The New Industrial State (Boston: Houghton Mifflin, 1967); and E. J. Mishan, The Costs of Economic Growth (New York: Praeger, 1967).

---

THE JOURNAL OF PHILOSOPHY

VOLUME LXXIX, NO. 8, AUGUST 1982

## MORAL SAINTS*

I DON'T know whether there are any moral saints. But if there are, I am glad that neither I nor those about whom I care most are among them. By *moral saint* I mean a person whose every action is as morally good as possible, a person, that is, who is as morally worthy as can be. Though I shall in a moment acknowledge the variety of types of person that might be thought to satisfy this description, it seems to me that none of these types serve as unequivocally compelling personal ideals. In other words, I believe that moral perfection, in the sense of moral saintliness, does not constitute a model of personal well-being toward which it would be particularly rational or good or desirable for a human being to strive.

Outside the context of moral discussion, this will strike many as an obvious point. But, within that context, the point, if it be granted, will be granted with some discomfort. For within that context it is generally assumed that one ought to be as morally good as possible and that what limits there are to morality's hold on us are set by features of human nature of which we ought not to be proud. If, as I believe, the ideals that are derivable from common sense and philosophically popular moral theories do not support these assumptions, then something has to change. Either we must change our moral theories in ways that will make them yield more palatable ideals, or, as I shall argue, we must change our conception of what is involved in affirming a moral theory.

In this paper, I wish to examine the notion of a moral saint, first, to understand what a moral saint would be like and why such a being would be unattractive, and, second, to raise some questions about the significance of this paradoxical figure for moral philo-

*I have benefited from the comments of many people who have heard or read an earlier draft of this paper. I wish particularly to thank Douglas MacLean, Robert Nozick, Martha Nussbaum, and the Society for Ethics and Legal Philosophy.

0022-362X/82/7908/0419$02.10 

sophy. I shall look first at the model(s) of moral sainthood that might be extrapolated from the morality or moralities of common sense. Then I shall consider what relations these have to conclusions that can be drawn from utilitarian and Kantian moral theories. Finally, I shall speculate on the implications of these considerations for moral philosophy.

## MORAL SAINTS AND COMMON SENSE

Consider first what, pretheoretically, would count for us—contemporary members of Western culture—as a moral saint. A necessary condition of moral sainthood would be that one's life be dominated by a commitment to improving the welfare of others or of society as a whole. As to what role this commitment must play in the individual's motivational system, two contrasting accounts suggest themselves to me which might equally be thought to qualify a person for moral sainthood.

First, a moral saint might be someone whose concern for others plays the role that is played in most of our lives by more selfish, or, at any rate, less morally worthy concerns. For the moral saint, the promotion of the welfare of others might play the role that is played for most of us by the enjoyment of material comforts, the opportunity to engage in the intellectual and physical activities of our choice, and the love, respect, and companionship of people whom we love, respect, and enjoy. The happiness of the moral saint, then, would truly lie in the happiness of others, and so he would devote himself to others gladly, and with a whole and open heart.

On the other hand, a moral saint might be someone for whom the basic ingredients of happiness are not unlike those of most of the rest of us. What makes him a moral saint is rather that he pays little or no attention to his own happiness in light of the overriding importance he gives to the wider concerns of morality. In other words, this person sacrifices his own interests to the interests of others, and feels the sacrifice as such.

Roughly, these two models may be distinguished according to whether one thinks of the moral saint as being a saint out of love or one thinks of the moral saint as being a saint out of duty (or some other intellectual appreciation and recognition of moral principles). We may refer to the first model as the model of the Loving Saint; to the second, as the model of the Rational Saint.

The two models differ considerably with respect to the qualities of the motives of the individuals who conform to them. But this difference would have limited effect on the saints' respective public personalities. The shared content of what these individuals are motivated to be—namely, as morally good as possible—would play the dominant role in the determination of their characters. Of course, just as a variety of large-scale projects, from tending the sick to political campaigning, may be equally and maximally morally worthy, so a variety of characters are compatible with the ideal of moral sainthood. One moral saint may be more or less jovial, more or less garrulous, more or less athletic than another. But, above all, a moral saint must have and cultivate those qualities which are apt to allow him to treat others as justly and kindly as possible. He will have the standard moral virtues to a nonstandard degree. He will be patient, considerate, even-tempered, hospitable, charitable in thought as well as in deed. He will be very reluctant to make negative judgments of other people. He will be careful not to favor some people over others on the basis of properties they could not help but have.

Perhaps what I have already said is enough to make some people begin to regard the absence of moral saints in their lives as a blessing. For there comes a point in the listing of virtues that a moral saint is likely to have where one might naturally begin to wonder whether the moral saint isn't, after all, too good—if not too good for his own good, at least too good for his own well-being. For the moral virtues, given that they are, by hypothesis, *all* present in the same individual, and to an extreme degree, are apt to crowd out the nonmoral virtues, as well as many of the interests and personal characteristics that we generally think contribute to a healthy, well-rounded, richly developed character.

In other words, if the moral saint is devoting all his time to feeding the hungry or healing the sick or raising money for Oxfam, then necessarily he is not reading Victorian novels, playing the oboe, or improving his backhand. Although no one of the interests or tastes in the category containing these latter activities could be claimed to be a necessary element in a life well lived, a life in which *none* of these possible aspects of character are developed may seem to be a life strangely barren.

The reasons why a moral saint cannot, in general, encourage the discovery and development of significant nonmoral interests and skills are not logical but practical reasons. There are, in addition, a class of nonmoral characteristics that a moral saint cannot encourage in himself for reasons that are not just practical. There is a more substantial tension between having any of these qualities unashamedly and being a moral saint. These qualities might be described as going against the moral grain. For example, a cynical or sarcastic wit, or a sense of humor that appreciates this kind of wit in others, requires that one take an attitude of resignation and pessimism toward the flaws and vices to be found in the world. A moral saint, on the other hand, has reason to take an attitude in opposition to this—he should try to look for the best in people, give them the benefit of the doubt as long as possible, try to improve regrettable situations as long as there is any hope of success. This suggests that, although a moral saint might well enjoy a good episode of *Father Knows Best,* he may not in good conscience be able to laugh at a Marx Brothers movie or enjoy a play by George Bernard Shaw.

An interest in something like gourmet cooking will be, for different reasons, difficult for a moral saint to rest easy with. For it seems to me that no plausible argument can justify the use of human resources involved in producing a *paté de canard en croute* against possible alternative beneficent ends to which these resources might be put. If there is a justification for the institution of haute cuisine, it is one which rests on the decision *not* to justify every activity against morally beneficial alternatives, and this is a decision a moral saint will never make. Presumably, an interest in high fashion or interior design will fare much the same, as will, very possibly, a cultivation of the finer arts as well.

A moral saint will have to be very, very nice. It is important that he not be offensive. The worry is that, as a result, he will have to be dull-witted or humorless or bland.

This worry is confirmed when we consider what sorts of characters, taken and refined both from life and from fiction, typically form our ideals. One would hope they would be figures who are morally good—and by this I mean more than just not morally bad—but one would hope, too, that they are not *just* morally good, but talented or accomplished or attractive in nonmoral ways as well. We may make ideals out of athletes, scholars, artists—more frivolously, out of cowboys, private eyes, and rock stars. We may strive for Katharine Hepburn's grace, Paul Newman's "cool"; we are attracted to the high-spirited passionate nature of Natasha Rostov; we admire the keen perceptiveness of Lambert Strether. Though there is certainly nothing immoral about the ideal characters or traits I have in mind, they cannot be superimposed upon the ideal of a moral saint. For although it is a part of many of these ideals that the characters set high, and not merely acceptable, moral standards for themselves, it is also essential to their power and attractiveness that the moral strengths go, so to speak, alongside of specific, independently admirable, nonmoral ground projects and dominant personal traits.

When one does finally turn one's eyes toward lives that are dominated by explicitly moral commitments, moreover, one finds oneself relieved at the discovery of idiosyncrasies or eccentricities not quite in line with the picture of moral perfection. One prefers the blunt, tactless, and opinionated Betsy Trotwood to the unfailingly kind and patient Agnes Copperfield; one prefers the mischievousness and the sense of irony in Chesterton's Father Brown to the innocence and undiscriminating love of St. Francis.

It seems that, as we look in our ideals for people who achieve nonmoral varieties of personal excellence in conjunction with or colored by some version of high moral tone, we look in our paragons of moral excellence for people whose moral achievements occur in conjunction with or colored by some interests or traits that have low moral tone. In other words, there seems to be a limit to how much morality we can stand.

One might suspect that the essence of the problem is simply that there is a limit to how much of *any* single value, or any single type of value, we can stand. Our objection then would not be specific to a life in which one's dominant concern is morality, but would apply to any life that can be so completely characterized by an extraordinarily dominant concern. The objection in that case would reduce to the recognition that such a life is incompatible with well-roundedness. If that were the objection, one could fairly reply that well-roundedness is no more supreme a virtue than the totality of moral virtues embodied by the ideal it is being used to criticize. But I think this misidentifies the objection. For the way in which a concern for morality may dominate a life, or, more to the point, the way in which it may dominate an ideal of life, is not easily imagined by analogy to the dominance an aspiration to become an Olympic swimmer or a concern pianist might have.

A person who is passionately committed to one of these latter concerns might decide that her attachment to it is strong enough to be worth the sacrifice of her ability to maintain and pursue a significant portion of what else life might offer which a proper devotion to her dominant passion would require. But a desire to be as morally good as possible is not likely to take the form of one desire among others which, because of its peculiar psychological strength, requires one to forego the pursuit of other weaker and separately less demanding desires. Rather, the desire to be as morally good as possible is apt to have the character not just of a stronger, but of a higher desire, which does not merely successfully compete with one's other desires but which rather subsumes or demotes them. The sacrifice of other interests for the interest in morality, then, will have the character, not of a choice, but of an imperative.

Moreover, there is something odd about the idea of morality itself, or moral goodness, serving as the object of a dominant passion in the way that a more concrete and specific vision of a goal (even a concrete *moral* goal) might be imagined to serve. Morality itself does not seem to be a suitable object of passion. Thus, when one reflects, for example, on the Loving Saint easily and gladly giving up his fishing trip or his stereo or his hot fudge sundae at the drop of the moral hat, one is apt to wonder not at how much he loves morality, but at how little he loves these other things. One thinks that, if he can give these up so easily, he does not know what it *is* to truly love them. There seems, in other words, to be a kind of joy which the Loving Saint, either by nature or by practice, is incapable of experiencing. The Rational Saint, on the other hand, might retain strong nonmoral and concrete desires—he simply denies himself the opportunity to act on them. But this is no less troubling. The Loving Saint one might suspect of missing a piece of perceptual machinery, of being blind to some of what the world has to offer. The Rational Saint, who sees it but foregoes it, one suspects of having a different problem—a pathological fear of damnation, perhaps, or an extreme form of self-hatred that interferes with his ability to enjoy the enjoyable in life.

In other words, the ideal of a life of moral sainthood disturbs not simply because it is an ideal of a life in which morality unduly dominates. The normal person's direct and specific desires for objects, activities, and events that conflict with the attainment of moral perfection are not simply sacrificed but removed, suppressed, or subsumed. The way in which morality, unlike other possible goals, is apt to dominate is particularly disturbing, for it seems to require either the lack or the denial of the existence of an identifiable, personal self.

This distinctively troubling feature is not, I think, absolutely unique to the ideal of the moral saint, as I have been using that phrase. It is shared by the conception of the pure aesthete, by a certain kind of religious ideal, and, somewhat paradoxically, by the model of the thorough-going, self-conscious egoist. It is not a coincidence that the ways of comprehending the world of which these ideals are the extreme embodiments are sometimes described as "moralities" themselves. At any rate, they compete with what we ordinarily mean by 'morality'. Nor is it a coincidence that these ideals are naturally described as fanatical. But it is easy to see that these other types of perfection cannot serve as satisfactory personal ideals; for the realization of these ideals would be straightforwardly immoral. It may come as a surprise to some that there may in addition be such a thing as a *moral* fanatic.

Some will object that I am being unfair to "common-sense morality"—that it does not really require a moral saint to be either a disgusting goody-goody or an obsessive ascetic. Admittedly, there is no logical inconsistency between having any of the personal characteristics I have mentioned and being a moral saint. It is not morally wrong to notice the faults and shortcomings of others or to recognize and appreciate nonmoral talents and skills. Nor is it immoral to be an avid Celtics fan or to have a passion for caviar or to be an excellent cellist. With enough imagination, we can always contrive a suitable history and set of circumstances that will embrace such characteristics in one or another specific fictional story of a perfect moral saint.

If one turned onto the path of moral sainthood relatively late in life, one may have already developed interests that can be turned to moral purposes. It may be that a good golf game is just what is needed to secure that big donation to Oxfam. Perhaps the cultivation of one's exceptional artistic talent will turn out to be the way one can make one's greatest contribution to society. Furthermore, one might stumble upon joys and skills in the very service of morality. If, because the children are short a ninth player for the team, one's generous offer to serve reveals a natural fielding arm or if one's part in the campaign against nuclear power requires accepting a lobbyist's invitation to lunch at Le Lion d'Or, there is no moral gain in denying the satisfaction one gets from these activities. The moral saint, then, may, by happy accident, find himself with nonmoral virtues on which he can capitalize morally or which make psychological demands to which he has no choice but to attend. The point is that, for a moral saint, the existence of these interests and skills can be given at best the status of happy accidents—they cannot be encouraged for their own sakes as distinct, independent aspects of the realization of human good.

It must be remembered that from the fact that there is a tension between having any of these qualities and being a moral saint it does not follow that having any of these qualities is immoral. For it is not part of common-sense morality that one ought to be a moral saint. Still, if someone just happened to want to be a moral saint, he or she would not have or encourage these qualities, and, on the basis of our common-sense values, this counts as a reason *not* to want to be a moral saint.

One might still wonder what kind of reason this is, and what kind of conclusion this properly allows us to draw. For the fact that the models of moral saints are unattractive does not necessarily mean that they are unsuitable ideals. Perhaps they are unattractive because they make us feel uncomfortable—they highlight our own weaknesses, vices, and flaws. If so, the fault lies not in the characters of the saints, but in those of our unsaintly selves.

To be sure, some of the reasons behind the disaffection we feel for the model of moral sainthood have to do with a reluctance to criticize ourselves and a reluctance to committing ourselves to trying to give up activities and interests that we heartily enjoy. These considerations might provide an *excuse* for the fact that we are not moral saints, but they do not provide a basis for criticizing sainthood as a possible ideal. Since these considerations rely on an appeal to the egoistic, hedonistic side of our natures, to use them as a basis for criticizing the ideal of the moral saint would be at best to beg the question and at worst to glorify features of ourselves that ought to be condemned.

The fact that the moral saint would be without qualities which we have and which, indeed, we like to have, does not in itself provide reason to condemn the ideal of the moral saint. The fact that some of these qualities are good qualities, however, and that they are qualities we *ought* to like, does provide reason to discourage this ideal and to offer other ideals in its place. In other words, some of the qualities the moral saint necessarily lacks are virtues, albeit nonmoral virtues, in the unsaintly characters who have them. The feats of Groucho Marx, Reggie Jackson, and the head chef at Lutèce are impressive accomplishments that it is not only permissible but positively appropriate to recognize as such. In general, the admiration of and striving toward achieving any of a great variety of forms of personal excellence are character traits it is valuable and desirable for people to have. In advocating the development of these varieties of excellence, we advocate nonmoral reasons for acting, and in thinking that it is good for a person to strive for an ideal that gives a substantial role to the interests and values that correspond to these virtues, we implicitly acknowledge the goodness of ideals incompatible with that of the moral saint. Finally, if we think that it is *as* good, or even better for a person to strive for one of these ideals than it is for him or her to strive for and realize the ideal of the moral saint, we express a conviction that it is good not to be a moral saint.

## MORAL SAINTS AND MORAL THEORIES

I have tried so far to paint a picture—or, rather, two pictures—of what a moral saint might be like, drawing on what I take to be the attitudes and beliefs about morality prevalent in contemporary, common-sense thought. To my suggestion that common-sense morality generates conceptions of moral saints that are unattractive or otherwise unacceptable, it is open to someone to reply, "so much the worse for common-sense morality." After all, it is often claimed that the goal of moral philosophy is to correct and improve upon common-sense morality, and I have as yet given no attention to the question of what conceptions of moral sainthood, if any, are generated from the leading moral theories of our time.

A quick, breezy reading of utilitarian and Kantian writings will suggest the images, respectively, of the Loving Saint and the Rational Saint. A utilitarian, with his emphasis on happiness, will certainly prefer the Loving Saint to the Rational one, since the Loving Saint will himself be a happier person than the Rational Saint. A Kantian, with his emphasis on reason, on the other hand, will find at least as much to praise in the latter as in the former. Still, both models, drawn as they are from common sense, appeal to an impure mixture of utilitarian and Kantian intuitions. A more careful examination of these moral theories raises questions about whether either model of moral sainthood would really be advocated by a believer in the explicit doctrines associated with either of these views.

Certainly, the utilitarian in no way denies the value of self-realization. He in no way disparages the development of interests, talents, and other personally attractive traits that I have claimed the moral saint would be without. Indeed, since just these features enhance the happiness both of the individuals who possess them and of those with whom they associate, the ability to promote these features both in oneself and in others will have considerable positive weight in utilitarian calculations.

This implies that the utilitarian would not support moral sainthood as a universal ideal. A world in which everyone, or even a large number of people, achieved moral sainthood—even a world in which they *strove* to achieve it—would probably contain less happiness than a world in which people realized a diversity of ideals involving a variety of personal and perfectionist values. More pragmatic considerations also suggest that, if the utilitarian wants to influence more people to achieve more good, then he would do better to encourage them to pursue happiness-producing goals that are more attractive and more within a normal person's reach.

These considerations still leave open, however, the question of what kind of an ideal the committed utilitarian should privately aspire to himself. Utilitarianism requires him to want to achieve the greatest general happiness, and this would seem to commit him to the ideal of the moral saint.

One might try to use the claims I made earlier as a basis for an argument that a utilitarian should choose to give up utilitarianism. If, as I have said, a moral saint would be a less happy person both to be and to be around than many other possible ideals, perhaps one could create more total happiness by not trying too hard to promote the total happiness. But this argument is simply unconvincing in light of the empirical circumstances of our world. The gain in happiness that would accrue to oneself and one's neighbors by a more well-rounded, richer life than that of the moral saint would be pathetically small in comparison to the amount by which one could increase the general happiness if one devoted oneself explicitly to the care of the sick, the downtrodden, the starving, and the homeless. Of course, there may be psychological limits to the extent to which a person can devote himself to such things without going crazy. But the utilitarian's individual limitations would not thereby become a positive feature of his personal ideals.

The unattractiveness of the moral saint, then, ought not rationally convince the utilitarian to abandon his utilitarianism. It may, however, convince him to take efforts not to wear his saintly moral aspirations on his sleeve. If it is not too difficult, the utilitarian will try not to make those around him uncomfortable. He will not want to appear "holier than thou"; he will not want to inhibit others' ability to enjoy themselves. In practice, this might make the perfect utilitarian a less nauseating companion than the moral saint I earlier portrayed. But insofar as this kind of reasoning produces a more bearable public personality, it is at the cost of giving him a personality that must be evaluated as hypocritical and condescending when his private thoughts and attitudes are taken into account.

Still, the criticisms I have raised against the saint of commonsense morality should make some difference to the utilitarian's conception of an ideal which neither requires him to abandon his utilitarian principles nor forces him to fake an interest he does not have or a judgment he does not make. For it may be that a limited and carefully monitored allotment of time and energy to be devoted to the pursuit of some nonmoral interests or to the development of some nonmoral talents would make a person a better contributor to the general welfare than he would be if he allowed himself no indulgences of this sort. The enjoyment of such activities in no way compromises a commitment to utilitarian principles as long as the involvement with these activities is conditioned by a willingness to give them up whenever it is recognized that they cease to be in the general interest.

This will go some way in mitigating the picture of the loving saint that an understanding of utilitarianism will on first impression suggest. But I think it will not go very far. For the limitations on time and energy will have to be rather severe, and the need to monitor will restrict not only the extent but also the quality of one's attachment to these interests and traits. They are only weak and somewhat peculiar sorts of passions to which one can consciously remain so conditionally committed. Moreover, the way in which the utilitarian can enjoy these "extra-curricular" aspects of his life is simply not the way in which these aspects are to be enjoyed insofar as they figure into our less saintly ideals.

The problem is not exactly that the utilitarian values these aspects of his life only as a means to an end, for the enjoyment he and others get from these aspects are not a means to, but a part of, the general happiness. Nonetheless, he values these things only because of and insofar as they *are* a part of the general happiness. He values them, as it were, under the description 'a contribution to the general happiness'. This is to be contrasted with the various ways in which these aspects of life may be valued by nonutilitarians. A person might love literature because of the insights into human nature literature affords. Another might love the cultivation of roses because roses are things of great beauty and delicacy. It may be true that these features of the respective activities also explain why these activities are happiness-producing. But, to the nonutilitarian, this may not be to the point. For if one values these activities in these more direct ways, one may not be willing to exchange them for others that produce an equal, or even a greater amount of happiness. From that point of view, it is not because they produce happiness that these activities are valuable; it is because these activities are valuable in more direct and specific ways that they produce happiness.

To adopt a phrase of Bernard Williams', the utilitarian's manner of valuing the not explicitly moral aspects of his life "provides (him) with one thought too many".[1] The requirement that the utilitarian have this thought—periodically, at least—is indicative of not only a weakness but a shallowness in his appreciation of the aspects in question. Thus, the ideals toward which a utilitarian could acceptably strive would remain too close to the model of the common-sense moral saint to escape the criticisms of that model which I earlier suggested. Whether a Kantian would be similarly committed to so restrictive and unattractive a range of possible ideals is a somewhat more difficult question.

The Kantian believes that being morally worthy consists in always acting from maxims that one could will to be universal law, and doing this not out of any pathological desire but out of reverence for the moral law as such. Or, to take a different formulation of the categorical imperative, the Kantian believes that moral action consists in treating other persons always as ends and never as means only. Presumably, and according to Kant himself, the Kantian thereby commits himself to some degree of benevolence as well as to the rules of fair play. But we surely would not will that *every* person become a moral saint, and treating others as ends hardly requires bending over backwards to protect and promote their interests. On one interpretation of Kantian doctrine, then, moral perfection would be achieved simply by unerring obedience to a limited set of side-constraints. On this interpretation, Kantian theory simply does not yield an ideal conception of a person of any fullness comparable to that of the moral saints I have so far been portraying.

On the other hand, Kant does say explicitly that we have a duty of benevolence, a duty not only to allow others to pursue their ends, but to take up their ends as our own. In addition, we have positive duties to ourselves, duties to increase our natural as well as our moral perfection. These duties are unlimited in the degree to which they *may* dominate a life. If action in accordance with and motivated by the thought of these duties is considered virtuous, it is natural to assume that the more one performs such actions, the more virtuous one is. Moreover, of virtue in general Kant says, "it is an ideal which is unattainable while yet our duty is constantly to approximate to it".[2] On this interpretation, then, the Kantian

[1] "Persons, Character and Morality" in Amelie Rorty, ed., *The Identities of Persons* (Berkeley: Univ. of California Press, 1976), p. 214.

[2] Immanuel Kant, *The Doctrine of Virtue*, Mary J. Gregor, trans. (New York: Harper & Row, 1964), p. 71.

moral saint, like the other moral saints I have been considering, is dominated by the motivation to be moral.

Which of these interpretations of Kant one prefers will depend on the interpretation and the importance one gives to the role of the imperfect duties in Kant's over-all system. Rather than choose between them here, I shall consider each briefly in turn.

On the second interpretation of Kant, the Kantian moral saint is, not surprisingly, subject to many of the same objections I have been raising against other versions of moral sainthood. Though the Kantian saint may differ from the utilitarian saint as to *which* actions he is bound to perform and which he is bound to refrain from performing, I suspect that the range of activities acceptable to the Kantian saint will remain objectionably restrictive. Moreover, the manner in which the Kantian saint must think about and justify the activities he pursues and the character traits he develops will strike us, as it did with the utilitarian saint, as containing "one thought too many." As the utilitarian could value his activities and character traits only insofar as they fell under the description of 'contributions to the general happiness', the Kantian would have to value his activities and character traits insofar as they were manifestations of respect for the moral law. If the development of our powers to achieve physical, intellectual, or artistic excellence, or the activities directed toward making others happy are to have any moral worth, they must arise from a reverence for the dignity that members of our species have as a result of being endowed with pure practical reason. This is a good and noble motivation, to be sure. But it is hardly what one expects to be dominantly behind a person's aspirations to dance as well as Fred Astaire, to paint as well as Picasso, or to solve some outstanding problem in abstract algebra, and it is hardly what one hopes to find lying dominantly behind a father's action on behalf of his son or a lover's on behalf of her beloved.

Since the basic problem with any of the models of moral sainthood we have been considering is that they are dominated by a single, all-important value under which all other possible values must be subsumed, it may seem that the alternative interpretation of Kant, as providing a stringent but finite set of obligations and constraints, might provide a more acceptable morality. According to this interpretation of Kant, one is as morally good as can be so long as one devotes some limited portion of one's energies toward altruism and the maintenance of one's physical and spiritual health, and otherwise pursues one's independently motivated interests and values in such a way as to avoid overstepping certain bounds. Certainly, if it be a requirement of an acceptable moral theory that perfect obedience to its laws and maximal devotion to its interests and concerns be something we can wholeheartedly strive for in ourselves and wish for in those around us, it will count in favor of this brand of Kantianism that its commands can be fulfilled without swallowing up the perfect moral agent's entire personality.

Even this more limited understanding of morality, if its connection to Kant's views is to be taken at all seriously, is not likely to give an unqualified seal of approval to the nonmorally directed ideals I have been advocating. For Kant is explicit about what he calls "duties of apathy and self-mastery" (69/70)—duties to ensure that our passions are never so strong as to interfere with calm, practical deliberation, or so deep as to wrest control from the more disinterested, rational part of ourselves. The tight and self-conscious rein we are thus obliged to keep on our commitments to specific individuals and causes will doubtless restrict our value in these things, assigning them a necessarily attenuated place.

A more interesting objection to this brand of Kantianism, however, comes when we consider the implications of placing the kind of upper bound on moral worthiness which seemed to count in favor of this conception of morality. For to put such a limit on one's capacity to be moral is effectively to deny, not just the moral necessity, but the moral goodness of a devotion to benevolence and the maintenance of justice that passes beyond a certain, required point. It is to deny the possibility of going morally above and beyond the call of a restricted set of duties. Despite my claim that all-consuming moral saintliness is not a particularly healthy and desirable ideal, it seems perverse to insist that, were moral saints to exist, they would not, in their way, be remarkably noble and admirable figures. Despite my conviction that it is as rational and as good for a person to take Katharine Hepburn or Jane Austen as her role model instead of Mother Theresa, it would be absurd to deny that Mother Theresa is a morally better person.

I can think of two ways of viewing morality as having an upper bound. First, we can think that altruism and impartiality are indeed positive moral interests, but that they are moral only if the degree to which these interests are actively pursued remains within certain fixed limits. Second, we can think that these positive interests are only incidentally related to morality and that the essence of morality lies elsewhere, in, say, an implicit social contract or in the recognition of our own dignified rationality. According to the first conception of morality, there is a cut-off line to the amount of altruism or to the extent of devotion to justice and fairness that is worthy of moral praise. But to draw this line earlier than the line that brings the altruist in question into a worse-off position than all those to whom he devotes himself seems unacceptably artificial and gratuitous. According to the second conception, these positive interests are not essentially related to morality at all. But then we are unable to regard a more affectionate and generous expression of good will toward others as a natural and reasonable extension of morality, and we encourage a cold and unduly self-centered approach to the development and evaluation of our motivations and concerns.

A moral theory that does not contain the seeds of an all-consuming ideal of moral sainthood thus seems to place false and unnatural limits on our opportunity to do moral good and our potential to deserve moral praise. Yet the main thrust of the arguments of this paper has been leading to the conclusion that, when such ideals are present, they are not ideals to which it is particularly reasonable or healthy or desirable for human beings to aspire. These claims, taken together, have the appearance of a dilemma from which there is no obvious escape. In a moment, I shall argue that, despite appearances, these claims should not be understood as constituting a dilemma. But, before I do, let me briefly describe another path which those who are convinced by my above remarks may feel inclined to take.

If the above remarks are understood to be implicitly critical of the views on the content of morality which seem most popular today, an alternative that naturally suggests itself is that we revise our views about the content of morality. More specifically, my remarks may be taken to support a more Aristotelian, or even a more Nietzschean, approach to moral philosophy. Such a change in approach involves substantially broadening or replacing our contemporary intuitions about which character traits constitute moral virtues and vices and which interests constitute moral interests. If, for example, we include personal bearing, or creativity, or sense of style, as features that contribute to one's *moral* personality, then we can create moral ideals which are incompatible with and probably more attractive than the Kantian and utilitarian ideals I have discussed. Given such an alteration of our conception of morality, the figures with which I have been concerned above might, far from being considered to be moral saints, be seen as morally inferior to other more appealing or more interesting models of individuals.

This approach seems unlikely to succeed, if for no other reason, because it is doubtful that any single, or even any reasonably small number of substantial personal ideals could capture the full range of possible ways of realizing human potential or achieving human good which deserve encouragement and praise. Even if we could provide a sufficiently broad characterization of the range of positive ways for human beings to live, however, I think there are strong reasons not to want to incorporate such a characterization more centrally into the framework of morality itself. For, in claiming that a character trait or activity is morally good, one claims that there is a certain kind of reason for developing that trait or engaging in that activity. Yet, lying behind our criticism of more conventional conceptions of moral sainthood, there seems to be a recognition that among the immensely valuable traits and activities that a human life might positively embrace are some of which we hope that, if a person does embrace them, he does so *not* for moral reasons. In other words, no matter how flexible we make the guide to conduct which we choose to label "morality," no matter how rich we make the life in which perfect obedience to this guide would result, we will have reason to hope that a person does not wholly rule and direct his life by the abstract and impersonal consideration that such a life would be morally good.

Once it is recognized that morality itself should not serve as a comprehensive guide to conduct, moreover, we can see reasons to retain the admittedly vague contemporary intuitions about what the classification of moral and nonmoral virtues, interests, and the like should be. That is, there seem to be important differences between the aspects of a person's life which are currently considered appropriate objects of moral evaluation and the aspects that might be included under the altered conception of morality we are now considering, which the latter approach would tend wrongly to blur or to neglect. Moral evaluation now is focused primarily on features of a person's life over which that person has control; it is largely restricted to aspects of his life which are likely to have considerable effect on other people. These restrictions seem as they should be. Even if responsible people could reach agreement as to what constituted good taste or a healthy degree of well-roundedness, for example, it seems wrong to insist that everyone try to achieve these things or to blame someone who fails or refuses to conform.

If we are not to respond to the unattractiveness of the moral ideals that contemporary theories yield either by offering alternative theories with more palatable ideals or by understanding these theories in such a way as to prevent them from yielding ideals at all, how, then, are we to respond? Simply, I think, by admitting that moral ideals do not, and need not, make the best personal ideals. Earlier, I mentioned one of the consequences of regarding as a test of an adequate moral theory that perfect obedience to its laws and maximal devotion to its interests be something we can wholeheartedly strive for in ourselves and wish for in those around us. Drawing out the consequences somewhat further should, I think, make us more doubtful of the proposed test than of the theories which, on this test, would fail. Given the empirical circumstances of our world, it seems to be an ethical fact that we have unlimited potential to be morally good, and endless opportunity to promote moral interests. But this is not incompatible with the not-so-ethical fact that we have sound, compelling, and not particularly selfish reasons to choose not to devote ourselves univocally to realizing this potential or to taking up this opportunity.

Thus, in one sense at least, I am not really criticizing either Kantianism or utilitarianism. Insofar as the point of view I am offering bears directly on recent work in moral philosophy, in fact, it bears on critics of these theories who, in a spirit not unlike the spirit of most of this paper, point out that the perfect utilitarian would be flawed in this way or the perfect Kantian flawed in that.[3] The assumption lying behind these claims, implicitly or explicitly, has been that the recognition of these flaws shows us something wrong with utilitarianism as opposed to Kantianism, or something wrong with Kantianism as opposed to utilitarianism, or something wrong with both of these theories as opposed to some nameless third alternative. The claims of this paper suggest, however, that this assumption is unwarranted. The flaws of a perfect master of a moral theory need not reflect flaws in the intramoral content of the theory itself.

## MORAL SAINTS AND MORAL PHILOSOPHY

In pointing out the regrettable features and the necessary absence of some desirable features in a moral saint, I have not meant to condemn the moral saint or the person who aspires to become one. Rather, I have meant to insist that the ideal of moral sainthood should not be held as a standard against which any other ideal must be judged or justified, and that the posture we take in response to the recognition that our lives are not as morally good as

[3] See, e.g., Williams, *op. cit.* and J. J. C. Smart and Bernard Williams, *Utilitarianism: For and Against* (New York: Cambridge, 1973). Also, Michael Stocker, "The Schizophrenia of Modern Ethical Theories," this JOURNAL, LXIII, 14 (Aug. 12, 1976): 453–466.

they might be need not be defensive.[4] It is misleading to insist that one is *permitted* to live a life in which the goals, relationships, activities, and interests that one pursues are not maximally morally good. For our lives are not so comprehensively subject to the requirement that we apply for permission, and our nonmoral reasons for the goals we set ourselves are not excuses, but may rather be positive, good reasons which do not exist *despite* any reasons that might threaten to outweigh them. In other words, a person may be *perfectly wonderful* without being *perfectly moral.*

Recognizing this requires a perspective which contemporary moral philosophy has generally ignored. This perspective yields judgments of a type that is neither moral nor egoistic. Like moral judgments, judgments about what it would be good for a person to be are made from a point of view outside the limits set by the values, interests, and desires that the person might actually have. And, like moral judgments, these judgments claim for themselves a kind of objectivity or a grounding in a perspective which any rational and perceptive being can take up. Unlike moral judgments, however, the good with which these judgments are concerned is not the good of anyone or any group other than the individual himself.

Nonetheless, it would be equally misleading to say that these judgments are made for the sake of the individual himself. For these judgments are not concerned with what kind of life it is in a person's interest to lead, but with what kind of interests it would be good for a person to have, and it need not be in a person's interest that he acquire or maintain objectively good interests. Indeed, the model of the Loving Saint, whose interests are identified with the interests of morality, is a model of a person for whom the dictates of rational self-interest and the dictates of morality coincide. Yet, I have urged that we have reason not to aspire to this ideal and that some of us would have reason to be sorry if our children aspired to and achieved it.

The moral point of view, we might say, is the point of view one takes up insofar as one takes the recognition of the fact that one is just one person among others equally real and deserving of the

[4] George Orwell makes a similar point in "Reflections on Gandhi," in *A Collection of Essays by George Orwell* (New York: Harcourt Brace Jovanovich, 1945), p. 176: "sainthood is . . . a thing that human beings must avoid . . . It is too readily assumed that . . . the ordinary man only rejects it because it is too difficult; in other words, that the average human being is a failed saint. It is doubtful whether this is true. Many people genuinely do not wish to be saints, and it is probable that some who achieve or aspire to sainthood have never felt much temptation to be human beings."

good things in life as a fact with practical consequences, a fact the recognition of which demands expression in one's actions and in the form of one's practical deliberations. Competing moral theories offer alternative answers to the question of what the most correct or the best way to express this fact is. In doing so, they offer alternative ways to evaluate and to compare the variety of actions, states of affairs, and so on that appear good and bad to agents from other, nonmoral points of view. But it seems that alternative interpretations of the moral point of view do not exhaust the ways in which our actions, characters, and their consequences can be comprehensively and objectively evaluated. Let us call the point of view from which we consider what kinds of lives are good lives, and what kinds of persons it would be good for ourselves and others to be, the *point of view of individual perfection.*

Since either point of view provides a way of comprehensively evaluating a person's life, each point of view takes account of, and, in a sense, subsumes the other. From the moral point of view, the perfection of an individual life will have some, but limited, value—for each individual remains, after all, just one person among others. From the perfectionist point of view, the moral worth of an individual's relation to his world will likewise have some, but limited, value—for, as I have argued, the (perfectionist) goodness of an individual's life does not vary proportionally with the degree to which it exemplifies moral goodness.

It may not be the case that the perfectionist point of view is like the moral point of view in being a point of view we are ever *obliged* to take up and express in our actions. Nonetheless, it provides us with reasons that are independent of moral reasons for wanting ourselves and others to develop our characters and live our lives in certain ways. When we take up this point of view and ask how much it would be good for an individual to act from the moral point of view, we do not find an obvious answer.[5]

The considerations of this paper suggest, at any rate, that the answer is not "as much as possible." This has implications both for the continued development of moral theories and for the development of metamoral views and for our conception of moral phil-

[5] A similar view, which has strongly influenced mine, is expressed by Thomas Nagel in "The Fragmentation of Value," in *Mortal Questions* (New York: Cambridge, 1979), pp. 128-141. Nagel focuses on the difficulties such apparently incommensurable points of view create for specific, isolable practical decisions that must be made both by individuals and by societies. In focusing on the way in which these points of view figure into the development of individual personal ideals, the questions with which I am concerned are more likely to lurk in the background of any individual's life.

osophy more generally. From the moral point of view, we have reasons to want people to live lives that seem good from outside that point of view. If, as I have argued, this means that we have reason to want people to live lives that are not morally perfect, then any plausible moral theory must make use of some conception of supererogation.[6]

If moral philosophers are to address themselves at the most basic level to the question of how people should live, however, they must do more than adjust the content of their moral theories in ways that leave room for the affirmation of nonmoral values. They must examine explicitly the range and nature of these nonmoral values, and, in light of this examination, they must ask how the acceptance of a moral theory is to be understood and acted upon. For the claims of this paper do not so much conflict with the content of any particular currently popular moral theory as they call into question a metamoral assumption that implicitly surrounds discussions of moral theory more generally. Specifically, they call into question the assumption that it is always better to be morally better.

The role morality plays in the development of our characters and the shape of our practical deliberations need be neither that of a universal medium into which all other values must be translated nor that of an ever-present filter through which all other values must pass. This is not to say that moral value should not be an important, even the most important, kind of value we attend to in evaluating and improving ourselves and our world. It is to say that our values cannot be fully comprehended on the model of a hierarchical system with morality at the top.

The philosophical temperament will naturally incline, at this point, toward asking, "What, then, *is* at the top—or, if there is no top, how *are* we to decide when and how much to be moral?" In other words, there is a temptation to seek a metamoral—though not, in the standard sense, metaethical—theory that will give us

[6] The variety of forms that a conception of supererogation might take, however, has not generally been noticed. Moral theories that make use of this notion typically do so by identifying some specific set of principles as universal moral requirements and supplement this list with a further set of directives which it is morally praiseworthy but not required for an agent to follow. [See, e.g., Charles Fried, *Right and Wrong* (Cambridge, Mass.: Harvard, 1979).] But it is possible that the ability to live a morally blameless life cannot be so easily or definitely secured as this type of theory would suggest. The fact that there are some situations in which an agent is morally required to do something and other situations in which it would be good but not required for an agent to do something does not imply that there are specific principles such that, in any situation, an agent is required to act in accordance with these principles and other specific principles such that, in any situation, it would be good but not required for an agent to act in accordance with those principles.

principles, or, at least, informal directives on the basis of which we can develop and evaluate more comprehensive personal ideals. Perhaps a theory that distinguishes among the various roles a person is expected to play within a life—as professional, as citizen, as friend, and so on—might give us some rules that would offer us, if nothing else, a better framework in which to think about and discuss these questions. I am pessimistic, however, about the chances of such a theory to yield substantial and satisfying results. For I do not see how a metamoral theory could be constructed which would not be subject to considerations parallel to those which seem inherently to limit the appropriateness of regarding moral theories as ultimate comprehensive guides for action.

This suggests that, at some point, both in our philosophizing and in our lives, we must be willing to raise normative questions from a perspective that is unattached to a commitment to any particular well-ordered system of values. It must be admitted that, in doing so, we run the risk of finding normative answers that diverge from the answers given by whatever moral theory one accepts. This, I take it, is the grain of truth in G. E. Moore's "open question" argument. In the background of this paper, then, there lurks a commitment to what seems to me to be a healthy form of intuitionism. It is a form of intuitionism which is not intended to take the place of more rigorous, systematically developed, moral theories—rather, it is intended to put these more rigorous and systematic moral theories in their place.

SUSAN WOLF

University of Maryland

## ON DOING GOOD: THE RIGHT AND THE WRONG WAY

IN this paper I am interested in the relations governing three fundamental moral injunctions: those bidding us to

(i) Do as much good as we can.
(ii) Save lives where we can.
(iii) Refrain from killing.

Recent ethicists have tended to focus on the relation between (ii) and (iii), on the question of whether there is any intrinsic moral difference between failing to save a life (letting someone die) and taking a life (killing someone). But though I shall often have occasion to refer to the literature on this subject, one of my main con-

0022-362X/82/7908/0439$01.60 